I highly recommend this book to Catholic educators and their students and also my fellow bishops, priests, religious men and women and everyone committed to the cause of Catholic education across the world.

Bishop Martin Mtumbuka, Catholic University of Malawi, Africa

Professor Gerald Grace has inspired many people i.e. Catholics, those of Other Faiths, Religious and lay faithful, scholars, researchers and students at various academic levels. He is very committed to his Faith and this is apparent in his many writings on Catholic education, research and developments. He is committed in his mission as a Professor and makes himself available to his students at all levels with the best supervising support possible (I write as his former student). He wants the Catholic Church internationally to enhance its own mission integrity by being true to its global promise that 'First and Foremost, the Church offers its educational services to the Poor' (1977)

Sister Dr Ugonna Igbo, DDL, Ph.D Regina Pacis College, Abuja, Nigeria

Without question, Grace's most significant legacy has been fostering a culture of disciplined innovation and systematic research in Catholic (and Other Faith) education. He has also revitalised the Spiritual mission of Catholic schooling with his ground-breaking writing on Spiritual Capital which has influenced other schools internationally. This Festschrift encourages educators and researchers to engage in new thinking, new scholarship and new research in order to strengthen the mission integrity of all forms of faith-based schooling which are attempting to realise the complete formation of the human person amidst a multitude of challenges in the 21st century.

Professor Magdalena Mo Ching Mok, Hong Kong Institute of Education, China

Prof. Gerald Grace's contribution through Catholic Education has been immense internationally. Therefore, I consider that he has the "Missionary Spirit" in him through research and educational scholarship. The impact of his endeavours have been greatly felt and acknowledged universally. He'll be remembered for promoting the values of Catholic Education in the years to come.

Dr Nicholas Tete, SJ, President, St Xavier's University College, Jharkhand, India

During this conflicted time in the Church when Catholic education seems to be endangered in so many ways, Gerald Grace's advocacy for systematic scholarship in the study of Catholic education has stirred powerful messages globally for more than two decades. As an author, editor, scholar and professor, his international leadership in advancing the field of Catholic education studies has no equal since the last quarter of the 20th century. Having collaborated with his edited publications of the International Handbook of Catholic Education (2007) and the journal

International Studies in Catholic Education (2009-2020) as author and editorial board member, Gerald Grace's outstanding works for Catholic schooling and their influence on his readers, students and colleagues remain enduring legacy. His strong support of Catholic Social Teaching in the curriculum, that highlights the 'preferential option for the poor' is an urgent agenda, particularly for those of us from the economically disadvantaged global south. While this festschrift celebrates his scholarly contributions, we are encouraged to continue his important theories about 'spiritual capital', faith-based school mission integrity vis-à-vis marketisation, and his vision that Catholic education studies be recognized as a significant discipline in the academia. This volume inspires us to face the questions he posed, to uphold the essential identity and nature of Catholic education, and to witness its 'diakonia' of truth today.

Dr Angelina Gutierrez, St Scholastica's College, Manila, Philippines

Gerald Grace brought a lifetime of scholarship, experience and global outlook to his pioneering and ground-breaking work on Catholic schools. He has dared to enquire into the most challenging questions around Catholic school mission and effectiveness, always addressing them with rigorous methodology and clear exposition.

Professor Brian Croke, KCSG Sydney University, Australia

Colleagues enter into dialogue with some of Grace's most innovative ideas and approaches. There is a special focus on the rich concept of Spiritual Capital in and of Catholic schools. The call for interdisciplinary research approaches into Catholic education serves as a unifying dimension of the collection, often setting the stage for future research agendas. This is indeed a valuable and worthy tribute to Professor Gerald Grace.

Professor Lieven Boeve, Catholic University of Leuven and Director-General of Catholic Education, Flanders, Belgium

Gerald Grace is the most well-known scholar researching Catholic education worldwide. His writings have helped to conceptualize the field and to develop an ambitious research agenda. This book, written in his honour, is an excellent example of the wide and interdisciplinary network of researchers who have been inspired by his vision.

Professor Maria del Mar Griera, Universitat Autònoma de Barcelona

Professor Gerald Grace has made significant contributions to Catholic education as it faces contemporary challenges of secularisation, marketisation, multi religious contexts and new emphases from the Second Vatican Council and later documents from the Congregation of Catholic Education. Jesuit Education, as part of Catholic Education, has been challenged by and benefited from, Grace's work and inspirations.

education can and should be. This book is a must read if you are interested in the nature and mission of Catholic education today—and is even more important for those who purport to care about church or world and think they are not interested in the topic!

Professor Mary Doak, Theology, University of San Diego, California, USA

Gerald Grace's wide-ranging research and scholarship could be considered intimidating, but his clarity of vision combines realism with hope. His reaffirmation that mission integrity is crucial as we confront mission drift in a world preoccupied by the market is a call that school and college leaders must hear.

Archbishop Michael Miller, CSB Vancouver, Canada, Former Secretary of the Congregation for Catholic Education, Rome

Gerald Grace's work has covered so many aspects of Catholic education. He has consistently maintained a firm grasp of the realities of the work of teachers. His research interviews with headteachers working in inner city areas have highlighted the 'spiritual capital' which sustains the vision and dedication of so many. He has also not hesitated to respond both to system failures and to new challenges.

Cardinal Vincent Nichols, Archbishop of Westminster, London, UK

This is no ordinary Festschrift, it is an overview of how Professor Gerald Grace has transformed Catholic education studies into a credible academic discipline both in the Catholic world and also among Other Faith communities. This book describes the impact of his leadership across the globe.

Abbot Christopher Jamison, OSB Abbot President of the English Benedictine Congregations

New Thinking, New Scholarship and New Research in Catholic Education is a worthy and appropriate title to celebrate the work of Professor Gerald Grace, who I am honoured to say, has been, and remains, closely associated with UCL Institute of Education as Visiting Professor, 1997-today. Of particular note is the originality of his research and conceptual tools which are theoretically informed but empirically derived, and which the international community have found to be profoundly meaningful, and incredibly influential. The book is a wonderful testament to his influence on the field of Catholic education but also on education more generally.

Professor Clare Brooks, Pro-Director, Education, UCL Institute of Education, London, UK

This is a powerful and important book, a testimony to how significant Gerald Grace's research and scholarship on Catholic education is in the modern world. He has almost single handedly established a new academic and professional field. The later chapters explore his very significant influence globally. These different contributions illuminate the continuing importance of the moral and spiritual dimensions of education. As such, the book has vitally important messages for all of us with an interest in education, whatever faith we profess.

John Furlong, OBE., Emeritus Professor of Education and former Director of the Department of Education, University of Oxford, UK

Over an academic lifetime, Gerald Grace has convincingly demonstrated how critical scholarship can illuminate and revitalise Catholic Education Studies. This edited collection provides an impressive genealogy of his intellectual journey in creating and validating a respected place for Catholic Education Studies in the academy. The chapters bring to life a remarkable journey enriched with strong theorising, intellectual creativity, but above all, a passionate commitment to social justice and the common good.

Professor Diane Reay, University of Cambridge, Faculty of Education, UK

New Thinking, New Scholarship and New Research in Catholic Education

New Thinking, New Scholarship and New Research in Catholic Education gives a forum to many established and leading scholars to review and critically appraise the research contribution of Gerald Grace to Catholic education. The book demonstrates the way in which the field of Catholic Education Studies has developed under the influence of Grace, to become internationally recognised.

This book demonstrates the ways in which Gerald Grace has shaped Catholic education since 1997. This begins with the primacy of empirical study and carefully conducted fieldwork when researching Catholic education. Many contributors focus on the way Grace champions the alignment between Catholic education and what we have come to know as the *option for the poor*. The collection also reflects Grace's intention to ensure the voices of women are properly represented in the field of Catholic education.

The book is based on an inclusive and open principle that seeks to establish dialogue with educators of different faiths and different religious backgrounds, as well as secular and humanist critics. It will be of great interest to academics, scholars and students of religious education, the history of education and all those interested in the developing field of Catholic Education Studies.

Sean Whittle is a Visiting Research Fellow at St Mary's University, London, and a Research Associate with the *Centre for Research and Development in Catholic Education*, with Professor Gerald Grace. Alongside these academic roles he works part-time as a secondary school RE teacher at Gumley House FCJ Catholic School. He serves as the secretary for the *Network for Researchers in Catholic Education* and is also vice-chair of the academic association AULRE.

Routledge Research in Education

This series aims to present the latest research from right across the field of education. It is not confined to any particular area or school of thought and seeks to provide coverage of a broad range of topics, theories and issues from around the world.

Recent titles in the series include:

Lessons from the Transition to Pandemic Education in the US
Analyses of Parent, Student and Educator Experiences
Edited by Marni E. Fisher, Kimiya Sohrab Maghzi, Charlotte Achieng-Evensen, Meredith A. Dorner, Holly Pearson and Mina Chun

International Perspectives on Drama and Citizenship Education
Acting Globally
Edited by Nicholas McGuinn, Norio Ikeno, Ian Davies and Edda Sant

Meeting the Challenges of Existential Threats through Educational Innovation
A Proposal for an Expanded Curriculum
Edited by Herner Saeverot

Lived Democracy in Education
Young Citizens' Democratic Lives in Kindergarten, School and Higher Education
Edited by Rune Herheim, Tobias Werler and Kjellrun Hiis Hauge

New Thinking, New Scholarship and New Research in Catholic Education
Responses to the Work of Professor Gerald Grace
Edited by Sean Whittle

For a complete list of titles in this series, please visit www.routledge.com/Routledge-Research-in-Education/book-series/SE0393

OUR·LADY·OF·ABINGDON

New Thinking, New Scholarship and New Research in Catholic Education

Responses to the Work of Professor Gerald Grace

Edited by Sean Whittle

Routledge
Taylor & Francis Group
LONDON AND NEW YORK

First published 2022
by Routledge
2 Park Square, Milton Park, Abingdon, Oxon OX14 4RN

and by Routledge
605 Third Avenue, New York, NY 10158

Routledge is an imprint of the Taylor & Francis Group, an informa business

British Library Cataloguing-in-Publication Data
A catalogue record for this book is available from the British Library

Library of Congress Cataloging-in-Publication Data
A catalog record has been requested for this book

ISBN: 978-0-367-72528-0 (hbk)
ISBN: 978-0-367-77472-1 (pbk)
ISBN: 978-1-003-17155-3 (ebk)

DOI: 10.4324/9781003171553

Typeset in Sabon
by Taylor & Francis Books

Contents

Illustrations

Figures

Tables

Contributors

Professor Jacinta Mary Adhiambo belongs to the Missionary Congregation of the Evangelizing Sisters (MCESM). Currently she is the Dean, Faculty of Education at the Catholic University of Eastern Africa. She is a seasoned educator and scholar who enjoys interacting with undergraduate and postgraduate students and mentoring them. A professional teacher with 19 years' experience in teaching at the university level, her research areas include management of education, leadership, Catholic education and higher education as evidenced in her many publications. Jacinta has a PhD from the Catholic University of Eastern Africa in the area of educational administration and planning. At the university, she sits in various committees including the Senate and has undertaken various roles as a leader in academics, quality assurance and community service projects. She has participated in various conferences locally and internationally.

Professor James Arthur OBE, University of Birmingham, is the Director of the Jubilee Centre for Character and Virtues. James is also Chair of the Society for Educational Studies, and was Head of the School of Education 2010–2015 and Deputy Pro-Vice Chancellor 2015–2019 at the University of Birmingham. He was previously Editor of the *British Journal of Educational Studies* for ten years and holds numerous honorary titles in the academe, including Honorary Professor of the University of Glasgow and Honorary Research Fellow at the University of Oxford. James was made an Officer of the British Empire by the Queen in 2018. He has written widely on the relationship between theory and practice in education, particularly the links between character, virtues, citizenship, religion and education. James established the Jubilee Centre in 2012, and the Centre has grown in size, scope and impact since its launch at the House of Lords in May 2012.

Dr Ann Casson is a Senior Research Fellow at the National Institute for Christian Education Research (NICER) at Canterbury Christ Church University. Her research interests include faith schools in a plural society and students' spiritual development in schools with a Christian foundation. Prior to becoming a full-time researcher, Ann taught religious education in Church of England, Catholic and community secondary schools across the north-east of England. Ann was the lead researcher on the *Lessons in Spiritual Development* project (2014–2017), which investigated the features that contribute to students' spiritual development in secondary schools with a Christian foundation. Her current research project, *Faith in the Nexus* (2017–2021), is investigating how church primary schools, working with the local church, facilitate opportunities for children to explore faith in the home. She is a member of the Editorial Board of *International Studies in Catholic Education*.

Professor Mary Darmanin studied at the Universities of Malta, Essex and Wales, College of Cardiff. She was the recipient of an Association of Commonwealth Universities Academic Staff Scholarship for three years. Her doctoral research was the first ethnographic study of Maltese schools. Mary has moved from research on state theory and ideologies of nationalism, teacher trade unionism and interest group formation in policy making, to research on the life-history of policy makers. She has also had a longstanding interest in gender issues in education and on women in the labour market. Recently she contributed a chapter on Catholic schooling and the changing role of women to the first *International Handbook of Catholic Education* (Grace and O'Keefe, eds. 2007). Other interests include the impact of transnational companies and supranational states on education policy. Her research has been published in a number of international journals as well as in edited collections. Mary has been on the editorial board of the journals, *International Journal of Inclusive Education* and *The Mediterranean Journal of Educational Studies* and is currently a member of the editorial board of *International Studies of Sociology of Education* and the online *Journal of Maltese Education Research*.

Dr Marie Griffin is a former CEO of the Catholic Education and Irish Schools' Trust (CEIST). Previously a principal in both a Catholic girls' second-level school and a state co-educational school in an area of designated disadvantage, Marie also worked as an Education Officer and acting CEO for a regional state educational organisation. She is now Chairperson of the Catholic Education Partnership. Marie has worked closely with Gerald Grace in encouraging schools in the CEIST trust to develop forms of self-evaluation of Catholic mission.

Dr Caroline Healy is a senior university lecturer for the MA in Catholic School Leadership and Doctor of Education (Ed.D.) programmes and a PhD supervisor at St Mary's University, London, and is also a Fellow of the Higher Education Academy. She has taught in higher education for over 25 years and has experience of teaching in the systems of the UK, United States and Ireland and carrying out research in collaboration with a number of European countries. Caroline is the General Secretary of the Catholic Association of Teachers, Schools and Colleges for England & Wales, which represents the majority of Catholic schools. She is an elected member of the Council of the

Catholic Union of Great Britain, which advances Catholic education in the wider public arena. She is a trustee of the St Mary's University charity, which promotes student and staff volunteering in schools and orphanages in Africa. Her current research interests concern how Catholic schools develop *spiritual capital*, which she most recently presented on at the NCEA Conference 2019, Chicago, and is working on an exciting Porticus-funded research project concerning the UK research capacity-building of post-doctoral researchers from Africa, a project facilitated by Gerald Grace.

Dr John Lydon KC*HS is an Associate Professor who holds degrees from the Universities of Durham, Liverpool and Surrey. His doctorate focused on teaching as a vocation in a contemporary context. He is a Senior Fellow of the Higher Education Academy. He is the Director of the MA in Catholic School Leadership Programme and Deputy Director of the Centre for Research and Development in Catholic Education, St Mary's University, London. He is also Associate Editor of the journal, *International Studies in Catholic Education*. He is an Adjunct Associate Professor and Co-Director of an undergraduate programme at the University of Notre Dame in London. He is a member of the Executives of the World Union of Catholic Teachers and the Catholic Association of Teachers, Schools and Colleges of England & Wales. John was recently appointed as Leader of the Thematic Group on Education of the Catholic-inspired NGO Forum for Education working in partnership with the Vatican Secretariat of State. He regularly gives lectures in the United States, especially at NCEA, but also in Europe, Africa, Asia and Australia. John's research interests focus on spiritual capital, Catholic school leadership and the maintenance of distinctive religious charisms. Some notable publications include *Transmission of a Charism* (2009); *The Contemporary Catholic Teacher: A Reappraisal of the Concept of Teaching as a Vocation* (2011) and *Contemporary Perspectives on Catholic Education* (2018).

Dr Cristóbal Madero S.J. is a Chilean Jesuit Priest. He is an Assistant Professor in the Department of Educational Policy and School Development at the Faculty of Education at Alberto Hurtado University, and Research Affiliate at the International Education Research Initiative at the University of Notre Dame. He is a sociologist and received his MA and PhD in educational policy from the University of California, Berkeley, and a Master's degree in Theology from Boston College. His research interests include teacher retention policies at primary and secondary levels, the evolution of Catholic educational subsystems, school inclusion policies, and the training of school leaders for new public education in Chile. He is part of the editorial board of the journal *International Studies in Catholic Education* and *The Boston College Jesuit Online Bibliography*.

Professor Meg Maguire, Kings College London, researches in the sociology of education, urban education and policy. She has a longstanding interest in the lives of teachers and has explored issues of class, race, gender and age in teachers' social and professional worlds. Meg has conducted ESRC-funded research into the experiences of minority ethnic trainee teachers, post-compulsory transitions and multi-agency policy in challenging school exclusion in urban primary schools.

Professor Stephen McKinney, School of Education, University of Glasgow, leads the research and teaching group, *Pedagogy, Praxis and Faith*. He is the past President of the Scottish Educational Research Association. He is on the Editorial Board of the *Journal of Beliefs and Values, Improving Schools*, and the *Scottish Educational Review*. He is a Visiting Professor in Catholic Education at Newman University, an Associate of the Irish Institute for Catholic Studies and on the steering group for the Network for Researchers in Catholic Education. He is a member of the European Educational Research Association Council. He is the Chair of the Board of Directors of the London School of Management Education. His research interests include Catholic schools and faith schools, and the impact of poverty on education and social justice; he has published widely on all of these topics. He has published more than 190 research articles, books, book chapters, research reports and briefings. His most recent major work is McKinney, S. and McCluskey, R. (2019) *A History of Catholic Education and Schooling in Scotland: New Perspectives*. Palgrave MacMillan.

Dr Helena Miller has a PhD in Jewish Education and has taught, researched and written widely. She is Co-Head of Teacher Training, Director of Degrees and a Senior Research Fellow at the London School of Jewish Studies. She heads the 'Jewish Lives' longitudinal study, following the cohort of young people who started in UK Jewish secondary schools in 2011. Helena is the senior editor of the two-volume *International Handbook of Jewish Education* (2011, Springer). She is the senior editor of the *Journal of Jewish Education*, and has both initiated, and been involved in, many innovative education, research and evaluation projects in the UK and overseas. Helena was co-chair of *Limmud International* 2009–2012, and received the Max Fisher Prize for outstanding contribution to Jewish Education in the Diaspora in 2012.

Professor François Moog holds a doctorate in theology from the Institut Catholique de Paris, France (STD) and the Université Laval de Québec, Canada (PhD). He is a Professor at the Theologicum, where he teaches ecclesiology and practical theology. After leading the Higher Institute of Catechetical Pastoral (ISPC) from 2007 to 2014, he was dean of the Faculty of Education from 2014 to 2019. He is attached to the Theology of Practices role within the research unit of *Religion, Culture and Society*. His current research focuses on Christian anthropology, from the angle of a fundamental theology of ecclesial practices, in particular from educational practices.

Joanna Marie S. Oliva has worked as Head of RE at Assumption College, San Lorenzo, which is a leading girls' school in the Philippines. Joanna gained an MA in Religious Studies from the Dom Bosco Centre of Studies (Philippines) and a second Masters (in Catholic School Leadership) from St Mary's University, London. She was awarded an All Hallows scholarship to begin her doctoral studies (starting in 2021) at St Mary's, London. Her research will focus on the extent to which Catholic education affects and influences the formation of women leaders of the Philippines.

Dr Kaetkaew Punnachet, SPC completed her PhD research under the supervision of Professor Gerald Grace at the Institute of Education, University of London. At present, she is the Deputy Director of the English programme at Saint Joseph's Convent, Bangkok, Thailand. Her co-authors are her Religious Sisters, firstly, Atchara Supavai, Ed.D., SPC, whose Ed.D. thesis was assisted by Professor Gerald Grace when she was studying for a doctoral degree at the University of Nottingham. At present, she is an active teacher, collaborator and Sister in Charge at Xavier Learning Community (Jesuit learning community in Thailand). The second co-author is Boonraksa Sritrakul, Ed.D., SPC. Professor Gerald Grace was her advisor when she was studying for a doctoral degree at the University of Nottingham. At present, she is the Provincial of Sisters of Saint Paul of Chartres in Thailand.

Professor Richard Pring is Emeritus Professor at the Department of Education, and Emeritus Fellow of Green Templeton College, University of Oxford, UK. He was Lead Director of the six-year Nuffield Review of 14–19 Education and Training for England and Wales, and until 2003, Professor of Educational Studies, University of Oxford, where he was Director of the department. Richard has a longstanding and deep interest in Catholic education. He is currently working on a book on faith schools. He is a member of the Editorial Board of International Studies in Catholic Education.

Professor Graham Rossiter is Professor of Religious and Moral Education at the Australian Institute of Theological Education and formerly at Australian Catholic University in Sydney. He has conducted professional development seminars throughout Australia and in a number of other countries and has published widely. Current interests are: young people's search for meaning, identity and spirituality; the spiritual and moral influence of culture – especially through media; values education; and religious education in Catholic schools.

Professor John Sullivan was Professor of Christian Education from 2002–2013 at Liverpool Hope University, where he is now Emeritus Professor. He taught in Catholic secondary schools (from classroom to headteacher) and then at St Mary's University, Twickenham. He is author and editor of eight books (most recently, The Christian Academic in Higher Education: The Consecration of Learning, Palgrave Macmillan, 2018) and almost 100 chapters and articles in the field of religion and education. He is currently working on two books: Lights for the Path and Christian Humanism and Education. John continues to be invited to provide professional development for university and school staff, for chaplains, heads and governors, as well as talks for parishes and church groups. His long-term interests include the mutual bearing on each other of theology and education, mission into practice, and vitality in the communication of Christian faith.

Dr **Paddy Walsh** was Deputy Director of the Centre for Research and Development in Catholic Education, at the Institute of Education, working closely with Professor Gerald Grace. His early career in Dublin and London was in philosophy, theology, secondary-school teaching and teacher education – all of which are abiding interests. This was followed by 30-plus years in the Department of Curriculum, Pedagogy and Assessment at the Institute of Education, doing the many things academics do. Now largely retired, he supervises research students, examines, contributes to 'Critical Realism' seminars and writes about Christian and Catholic education. A persistent theme in his writing is the primacy, rationally speaking, of 'love of the world' among educational aims. He has experienced and cared about Catholic schools in the roles of pupil, teacher, teacher-educator, parent, governor, researcher, thesis-supervisor, thinker, writer, consultant and – latterly – grandparent. He remains a governor of a Catholic secondary school in a depressed inner-city area, having recently retired (after ten years) from another in a leafy suburb.

Dr **Quentin Wodon** is a Lead Economist at the World Bank. Previous roles include managing the unit on values and development, serving as Lead Poverty Specialist for Africa, and working as Economist/Senior Economist for Latin America. Before joining the World Bank, he taught with tenure at the University of Namur. He has also taught at American University and Georgetown University. Quentin has more than 500 publications and his research has been covered by major news outlets. He has served as Associate Editor for journals and as President of two economics associations (the Society of Government Economists and the Association for Social Economics). A lifelong learner, he holds four PhDs in economics, environmental science, health sciences, and theology. Almost 30 years ago, he shifted careers and joined ATD Fourth World, a non-profit working with the extreme poor. He has tried to remain faithful to the cause of ending extreme poverty ever since. He also tries to remain (barely) fit with occasional marathons and triathlons, finishing at the end of the pack.

Dr **Sean Whittle** is a Visiting Research Fellow at St Mary's University, London, and a Research Associate with the Centre for Research and Development in Catholic Education, with Professor Gerald Grace. Alongside these academic roles he works part-time as a secondary-school RE teacher at Gumley House FCJ Catholic School in West London. His book, *A Theory of Catholic*

Education (Bloomsbury 2014), presents a robust philosophy of Catholic education that draws heavily on insights from Karl Rahner. He has edited four books on Catholic education (*Vatican II and New Thinking about Catholic Education*, 2016; *Researching Catholic Education*, 2018; *Religious Education in Catholic Schools in the UK and Ireland*, 2018; *Irish and British Reflections on Catholic Education*, 2021). In recent years he has been collaborating with other academics working in the field of Catholic education in order to create the Network for Researchers in Catholic Education (NfRCE). Over the past few years, he held a Post-Doctoral Research Fellowship at Brunel University on a Religious Literacy project, and prior to that was a visiting Research Fellow at Heythrop College. He is also a visiting lecturer at Newman University. He serves as the secretary for the NfRCE and is also vice-chair of the academic association AULRE. He is on the Editorial Board of *International Studies in Catholic Education*.

Foreword

The words 'Catholic' and 'Education' undoubtedly belong together. They belong together in the life of the Catholic Church across the centuries and in every part of the world. The presence of the Catholic Church always unfolds into the work of education. Wherever a community is formed, there education begins. It is sustained in the richness of the monastic tradition and in the wide variety of partnerships with governments and regimes in the provision of education available to the families and children which make up a society. These two words certainly belong together in the experience of the Catholic Church in England and Wales. Indeed, Catholic Education is one of our treasures and most important contributions to the life of these countries.

In every one of these circumstances, the motivation and inspiration for education provided by the Catholic Church has been elaborated, examined, revised and reinvigorated time and again. This has certainly been the case, in England and Wales, over the last 170 years, in constant dialogue and partnership with public authorities. Most consistently, the perspectives and convictions of faith have shaped the vision of education put forward by the Church. Its argumentation has proceeded from the desire and right of parents to have an effective choice in the kind of education offered to their children.

The work of Professor Gerald Grace has contributed very significantly to this process. I am therefore pleased to be able to offer these few words as a Foreword to this volume which celebrates that contribution in a timely and fulsome fashion.

His work has covered so many aspects of Catholic Education, often from refreshing perspectives. He has consistently maintained a firm grasp of the realities of the work of teachers. His interviews with head teachers working in inner-city areas have highlighted the 'spiritual capital' which sustains the vision and dedication of so many. This has also contributed so significantly to his research into the nature of school leadership in England, and the key role of Catholic head teachers as guardians of the 'mission integrity' of Catholic schools. At the same time, his serious academic scrutiny has helped to move the arguments supporting Catholic Education into a setting where it can be assessed in the light of scholarship and research as well as conviction. He has also not hesitated to highlight both failures and new challenges.

In a similar vein, his work has broadened to encompass the international aspects and features of Catholic Education, most notably in the journal he launched in 2009. The journal *International Studies in Catholic Education* has grown remarkably since then, such that it is now accessed in 112 countries. It monitors the challenges found and the responses to them by Catholic and other faith educators across the world. Contributions to this volume from around the world pay tribute to this achievement, as do the contributions from the Jewish and Muslim communities.

We are rightly accustomed to speaking of work in Catholic Education in the language of vocation. This highlights not only the effort so often made by those in Catholic Education, going beyond terms of contracts, but also the sense of service in the name of Jesus Christ which informs that admirable dedication. This language of vocation is most properly applied to Gerald Grace. This is the dedication of his life. He has known that his 'calling' has been to ensure that Catholic Education is respected on all levels. In order to serve that aim, his establishment of a prominent university-based Research Centre has been pivotal. It is, therefore, most appropriate that this tribute to his work is being published to mark the time when he finally relinquishes his position as Director of the *Centre for Research and Development in Catholic Education* at St Mary's University.

The work of Catholic Education is essentially and always a work of partnerships. This has never been truer than at the present moment when a combination of factors – social, political, financial and cultural – challenge the nature and even the very survival of Catholic Education in this country. New partnerships are needed in order to counter these challenges. Such partnerships require mutual trust and confidence and the common ground of the vision which informs this much-valued project. The contribution of Gerald Grace to this vision, and to its expression in so many different circumstances and cultures, has never been more relevant. So, I take this opportunity of thanking Professor Gerald Grace for his outstanding work, well appreciated not only in this volume but by so many around the world. In 2014, he was appointed by his Holiness, Pope Francis, as a Knight of the Order of St Gregory the Great (KSG) for 'his services to Catholic Education, nationally and internationally'.

Thank you, indeed.
Vincent Nichols MA, M.Ed., STL

Cardinal Archbishop of Westminster & Chancellor of
St Mary's University, London

Preface

It has been a pleasure to work on this volume. The origins lie in some informal conversations around the time that the *Centre for Research and Development in Catholic Education* (CRDCE) first moved to St. Mary's University, London. There was a sense that some sort of celebration or what used to be known as a *Festchrift* for Professor Gerald Grace would be a fitting tribute. The bustle of everyday life caused these tentative plans to be paused for a few years. Over the past five years, the CRDCE has settled in well to its new home, and the stage is set for its directorship to be gradually handed on from Professor Grace to others. This makes it an apt time to return to the project of recognising the outstanding contribution that Gerald Grace has made to the field of Catholic Education Studies.

Rather than simply being a flattering set of reflections, this volume has matured into a critical analysis of Grace's work in relation to his key concepts, in particular *Spiritual Capital*, and his role in editing the journal *International Studies in Catholic Education*. This is down to the high quality of the contributions in this volume. They have come from academics who have worked closely with Gerald Grace, many for over two decades. I am very grateful to each of the contributors, who have given generously of their time and considerable skill to compose chapters that deserve to be widely read and carefully scrutinised. I think that together, we have created a text that will be a major resource for teachers, students, scholars and researchers in the developing field of Catholic Education Studies internationally.

In the process of bringing this project to fruition, I have had numerous conversations and discussions with Gerald Grace. I have greatly enjoyed this opportunity to collaborate with him. It has been both fascinating and rewarding to learn so much more about this leading advocate of Catholic education. When I first met Gerald, at the start of my doctoral studies at the Institute of Education, London, in 2008, our conversation was engaging and wide ranging. I recall vividly how our dialogue led onto the need for more conferences and events for bringing together researchers in Catholic education. I remember well how Gerald set me the challenge of organising these once I had completed my doctorate. There have now been many such events and Gerald has frequently been the keynote speaker at them. It has been a pleasure to work alongside Gerald, particularly in my role as a Research Associate at the CRDCE.

None of my work with Gerald and in editing this volume would have been possible without the constant support and love from my wife, Bernie Whittle. It is only through having her by my side, offering me the encouragement and practical help that I need, that I have been able to bring this project to fruition. Thank you for this and for all that you do for me.

Sean Whittle

Introduction to *New Thinking, New Scholarship and New Research in Catholic Education: Responses to the Work of Professor Gerald Grace*

Sean Whittle

Introduction

Since 1997, there has been a steady growth in new thinking, new scholarship and new research about Catholic education, most of which has been influenced by the work of, and role played by, Professor Gerald Grace. This volume presents thoughtful and critical responses to Grace's work over this period. This is an important and exciting volume because it brings together a very strong collection of accomplished scholars in the field of Catholic education, from both the UK and internationally, who have taken the opportunity to engage specifically with the work and contribution of Gerald Grace. This edited collection of carefully commissioned contributions will serve as a very good introduction to *Catholic Education Studies* in the future because each chapter weaves together many different aspects of its history and development. This volume also provides an engaging yet critical platform from which to celebrate the work and achievement of Gerald Grace in relation to Catholic education.

Moreover, this volume provides readers with the opportunity to take stock of the current state of research into Catholic education, which has benefitted from both the writings and innovative work of Gerald Grace. The latter includes the creation of the *Centre for Research and Development in Catholic Education* (CRDCE) and his role as the founder and inaugural Chief Editor of the journal *International Studies in Catholic Education* (ISCE). Rather than engaging with all of Gerald Grace's work as an educator with a career spanning the best part of six decades, this volume puts the spotlight on his work in more recent years in relation to Catholic education. However, it will be suggested that it is in part his earlier career accomplishments that have provided an ideal basis from which to nurture the field of Catholic Education Studies both nationally and internationally.

This introduction will begin by putting Gerald Grace's work since the mid-1990s into context, before describing what he was able to achieve since the creation of the CRDCE in 1997. In this period, two notable publications stand out, but by far the most important contribution is Grace's achievement in creating the journal ISCE in June 2009. This is quickly followed by

DOI: 10.4324/9781003171553-1

his outstanding success in editing the journal for nearly fifteen years. Over this time, he has skilfully used his editorial role to nurture and promote new thinking and new scholarship in Catholic education.

Context: Gerald Grace and Catholic Education Studies

It was not until 1993 that Professor Gerald Grace turned his attention to what was happening in Catholic education. This was towards the end of what had been a successful career as an academic, working in the fields of the History and Sociology of Education. Grace worked extensively in education teaching, carrying out research and writing, and holding posts in leading institutions. These included King's College (London), the Institute of Education (London), the University of Cambridge and Durham University. He ended this part of his career as the Head of the School of Education at Durham University. He had firm plans to retire at the age of 60 at the start of 1996, with the intention of living serenely in Brighton in East Sussex. However, his plans for a quiet retirement in leafy Sussex were significantly disrupted by the stirrings that were taking place in relation to Catholic education in the early 1990s.

It was in 1993 that Grace attended a two-day seminar at St Edmund's College Cambridge, organised by his friends and colleagues Dr Terry McLaughlin and Dr Bernadette O'Keeffe. This seminar had been convened to consider the newly published work *Catholic Schools and the Common Good* by Anthony Bryk and his team at Chicago University. This book presented in-depth empirical research into a small number of American Catholic high schools. It was fruitful research that demonstrated how Catholic education contributes much to the Common Good of society at large. At the seminar, the scholarly excellence of the text triggered rich discussion among the participants, which also included Richard Pring from Oxford, Joseph O'Keefe SJ from Boston College and an up-and-coming doctoral researcher, James Arthur. This academic gathering had a profound impact on Gerald Grace, one that he would compare to a Damascene moment that thoroughly reorientated his academic interests and passions. Grace wanted to try to emulate the achievements of Bryk's work and extend its influence beyond the USA. In effect, he had a growing conviction, that could be likened to an academic *calling* or *mission*, to develop an international field of Catholic education scholarship and research. Grace had discovered in 1993 what would be the driving passion during his retirement. In retrospect, this moment of academic conversion was the start of what has become a second academic career for Gerald Grace, which in many respects has eclipsed and surpassed his pre-retirement one.

What Grace quickly realised was that the American research provided an obvious model that could be replicated in other parts of the world, including the UK. It demonstrated the value of in-depth fieldwork analysis of even a small number of schools, as a lens for researching the religious, spiritual and social justice principles of Catholic education. In addition, access to so-called 'big data' was shown to be a platform for statistical co-analysis of Catholic education and state/public schools in the USA. This high-quality analysis gave the Bryk research the solid foundation to be able to argue that there is an *inspirational ideology* that Catholic schools share and that this is part of the forces that contribute to the overall effectiveness of Catholic schools. As his retirement project, Gerald Grace wanted to develop an international field of Catholic education scholarship and research which could aspire to reproduce some of the quality of analysis that is exemplified in the Bryk model. Grace has always argued that high-quality empirical work from the USA was his initial inspiration.

Developments after 1997

Shortly after retiring in 1996, Grace set about the founding of a *Centre for Research in Catholic Education* (the CRDCE) in order to give himself a research base and way of collaborating with others interested in Catholic education. To fund this centre, Grace approached a range of donors to request donations, most notably Religious Congregations with a mission or charism in education. He was successful in gaining a sufficient amount of funding and was able to keep the running costs to a minimum by being given the free use of an office at the Institute of Education (London) by the director, Professor Peter Mortimore. Grace's CRDCE received initial crucial support from two members of staff at the Institute of Education, Professor Denis Lawton and Dr Paddy Walsh. What is today the UCL Institute of Education in London, thanks to the creative leadership of Peter Mortimore, is where his mission began.

In its initial stage of development, the CRDCE concentrated upon providing material that might encourage continuous professional development (CPD) sessions in Catholic schools in the UK and Ireland. This resulted in a professional focus series of booklets, ranging from the *Catholic School and the Common Good*, to *Can there be a Catholic Curriculum?*. These were sent out to schools in the period between 1997 and 2008. The second stage was when Grace, as director of the CRDCE, secured funding to undertake fieldwork in sixty Catholic, inner-city secondary schools. This ground-breaking empirical research was published in 2002, under the title *Catholic Schools: Mission, Markets and Morality*, by the publisher Routledge. This book is now rightly viewed as a seminal text. It is referred to by each of the contributors to this volume. It also marked a profound shift in research into Catholic schools in the UK, which had up to this point had a low level of empirical investigation, opting instead for theological reflections or historical surveys. It set the benchmark for subsequent research into Catholic education in the UK and, as many chapters in this volume demonstrate, its influence spread far and wide. Not long after 2002, Grace's work was translated into Spanish, making it even more widely accessible, particularly in South America. Grace's 2002 study shared the same high quality that was evident in Bryk's 1993 study and this meant the scene was set to take on a more international perspective to researching Catholic education. To help bring this about, Grace began a collaboration with Professor Joseph O'Keefe SJ (Boston, USA). They shared the concern that international studies in Catholic education was a relatively neglected field. To begin rectifying this they established a joint research project, starting in 2001, to attempt a worldwide survey of existing Catholic education research. This took in over thirty countries and jurisdictions in the five-year project. It was apparent that research into Catholic education was beginning to emerge in many more parts of the world and that this deserved to be brought to the attention of more people. Grace and O'Keefe decided to publish a 'Handbook' that would present much of what was going on. The result was the publication of a two-volume work, published by Springer (2007), titled the *International Handbook of Catholic Education*. This important work helped to demonstrate that the field of Catholic Education Studies was firmly establishing itself. This was the first ever international survey of research and scholarship in Catholic education.

By 2007, the CRDCE, thanks to the dedicated hard work of Gerald Grace, had contributed two very important publications to the field and had helped to shape the nature of the research being undertaken. Grace realised that it was not occasional bigger publications that were needed but an ongoing forum for bringing together up-to-date research and scholarship. What was needed was a journal devoted to international studies in Catholic education. Grace set himself the challenge of bringing this journal into existence, basing it firmly within the CRDCE. This was an ambitious endeavour because he was calling for the first ever *international* journal devoted to Catholic education. It was a daunting prospect to convince the leading publisher of such journals, Routledge, to commit to such a project. Their concern was over the 'market' appeal of such a journal and if there would be sufficient interest in it. Grace successfully managed to convince them by arguing that Catholic education is, at the global level, the largest provider of faith-based education and as such there ought to be a journal that takes on an international perspective. In 2008, Routledge agreed to launch the journal with Gerald Grace being the first executive editor of *International Studies in Catholic Education* (ISCE). The journal began its life tentatively in 2009: it was accessed by readers in forty countries and in total there were a reported 354 full-text downloads of articles. Today, ISCE is accessed by readers in 112 countries and in excess of 17,000 full-text downloads take place annually. The journal has grown from strength to strength and this demonstrates Grace's vision and astuteness in creating it. The journal ISCE has provided a much-needed forum for educators working in schools, colleges and universities to engage in dialogue with each other internationally.

The move to St Mary's University, London

Following an invitation from the Vice Chancellor of St. Mary's University, London, in 2016 (Professor Francis Campbell), Grace moved the CRDCE and the editorial office of ISCE away from the Institute of Education to St Mary's University. Through this move, Grace was able to support the goals of this new university to raise its international profile. Grace was happy to do this, and he took up the honorary position to become a Visiting Professor at St Mary's. The move to St Mary's provided an opportune time to strengthen the support team for the journal, drawing on the increasing number of researchers at St Mary's who work in the field of Catholic Education Studies. In less than two decades Gerald Grace has, through the CRDCE, been able to demonstrate obvious success in fulfilling the mission he embraced following his Damascene experience back in 1993. He has made a significant contribution to international studies in Catholic education. The CRDCE has found its home in a university which aspires to be a leading and innovative Catholic university in London and the journal he created is now firmly established. All the indicators are that St Mary's is fully committed to nurturing and enhancing both the CRDCE and the journal ISCE well into the future. There is a solid legacy to Grace's work.

It is also important to appreciate that Gerald Grace has played an important role in being heavily involved in giving talks, presenting at conferences and undertaking research activity in relation to Catholic education over a sustained twenty-five-year period. This is both internationally and also throughout the UK. Over the years, his presence at a seminar or conference was enough to raise the profile of the event. He is an adept, engaging and highly entertaining speaker. Crucially, he also brings an important air of gravitas to even the humblest of seminars or conferences. Gerald's seal of approval has been important in allowing other initiatives to flourish, for example the formation of the *Network for Researchers in Catholic Education* (NfRCE). The emergence of this network, which grew out of the various Catholic education conferences and initiatives organised by the Jesuit-founded *Heythrop Institute of Religion and Society*, enjoyed the full support of the director of the CRDCE. The NfRCE, which formally began in 2016, is also an important testimony to the way in which the field of Catholic Education Studies has grown since the mid-1990s throughout the UK and Ireland. There is no mere coincidence that this has been the time throughout which Grace has been hard at work bringing about his mission. He has successfully cleared the path for other researchers to enter this field of study. If it were not for Grace's work, it would be highly improbable that the NfRCE would have been able to come into existence.

The structure of this volume

There are two main parts to this book. Part I presents ten contributions from Gerald Grace's colleagues in the UK. Some are very long-standing associates, going right back to his *moment of academic conversion*, including those such as Professor James Arthur, Professor Richard Pring, Dr Paddy Walsh and Professor John Sullivan. Other contributors have worked closely with him particularly on editing or supporting the work of the journal ISCE, such as Dr John Lydon and Dr Ann Casson. Others have either worked alongside Gerald or been inspired by his practical encouragement and guidance; these include

Professor Meg Maguire, Dr Helena Miller, Dr Caroline Healey and Dr Sean Whittle. In Part II of this book, there is a firmly international flavour, with a further ten contributions. This is fitting recognition that Gerald Grace's influence extends well beyond the UK. Moreover, it is a tribute to the vigour of the international scholarship in the field of Catholic Education Studies that Gerald Grace has sought to bring into dialogue. There are contributions from the USA (Professor Quentin Woden), Chile (Professor Cristobal Madero SJ), Australia (Professor Graham Rossiter), Kenya (Dr Jacinta Adhiambo), France (Professor Francois Moog), Ireland (Dr Marie Griffin), Scotland (Professor Stephen McKinney), Thailand (Dr Theresa Punnachet), Malta (Professor Mary Darmanin) and the Philippines (Joanna Oliva). Rather than presenting a summary of each of the twenty contributions here, an abstract is supplied at the start of each chapter. The final point in this introduction is to thank each of the contributors for the high quality of their chapters. Taken together, the contributions in this volume give a powerful testimony and set of reflections about the influence of Gerald Grace and the numerous ways in which he has contributed to new thinking, new scholarship and new research in Catholic education.

References

Bryk, A. et al. (1993). *Catholic Schools and the Common Good*. Cambridge, MA: Harvard University Press.
Grace, G. (2002). *Catholic Schools: Mission, Markets and Morality*. London: Routledge.
Grace, G. and O'Keefe, J. (Eds) (2007). *International Handbook of Catholic Education*. Volumes 1 and 2. Dordrecht: Springer Publishing.

Part I

Gerald Grace's influence in the UK

Chapter 1

The 'calling' of Professor Gerald Grace

James Arthur

Introduction

In the UK it is hard to think of a more significant figure in the academic study and research field of Catholic education since Arthur Beales (1905–1974). Gerald Grace has not only contributed noteworthy research in advancing the field of Catholic Education Studies but he has also helped shape its contours both in the UK and internationally. His contribution to Catholic Education Studies in the UK has no equal in modern times. At his professorial inaugural lecture on 7 November 2016 at St. Mary's University (I have lost count of the actual number he has given at various universities), he celebrated the fact that:

> The academic and professional field of Catholic Education Studies has now achieved international recognition. This has been established by the contributions of Theologians, Philosophers, Historians, Social and Economic Scientists, Natural Scientists, Education scholars and researchers, School leaders and teachers and members of Religious Congregations with missions in education who have written about Catholic education, in all its forms, across the world in recent decades.
>
> (Grace 2016b, p. 1)

This statement is no exaggeration and only Gerald Grace had the credibility to have made it because he created the conditions that made it so. With unceasing dedication and without remuneration, Gerald has spent the last 25 years building a field of study that others had simply neglected or ignored. We need to remember that Gerald already had enjoyed a very successful and eminent academic career as historian and sociologist in a number of distinguished education faculties. He has taught Education at King's College, University of London and the University of Cambridge, together with serving as Head of the Schools of Education at Victoria University of Wellington, New Zealand and Durham University. In September 1996, he retired early from Durham University with a clear purpose and hence began his second academic career, or perhaps more appropriately, mission, that has born much fruit and spanned the last 25 years.

DOI: 10.4324/9781003171553-3

I first met Gerald Grace at an important conference on Catholic education in Cambridge in 1993 and have been a friend ever since. This seminal conference was organised by Terry McLaughlin, a friend of Gerald's from the days when they were the only two Catholic lecturers in the Faculty of Education at the University of Cambridge. Terry brought together academics from the USA, Australia, Ireland and the UK and the conference was entitled 'The Contemporary Catholic School and the Common Good'. The conference was sponsored by the Von Hügel Institute, Cambridge and Boston College, and was held at St. Edmund's Hall in Cambridge. While there had been many professional Catholic education conferences, academic conferences focused on Catholic educational research were extremely rare. It is therefore hard to overstate the significance of this conference since there had been no serious contributions to this academic field since the publication of a collection of papers in *Catholic Education in a Secular Society* edited by Bernard Tucker (1968). Tucker's contributors included his fellow ex-seminarian Richard Pring and the theme of the book was generally critical, revolving around the statement 'There is a growing minority in the Church which finds the common Catholic position on education questionable'. McLaughlin's conference was more positive and in many ways ground-breaking, but critically it influenced Gerald Grace and the purpose for which he was to later give himself. Many of the conference papers were published in *The Contemporary Catholic School* (McLaughlin, O'Keefe and O'Keeffe 1996). Gerald contributed a chapter.

Gerald expressed his admiration for the research on Catholic education that was being undertaken in the USA, particularly the work of Anthony Byrk (1993) and his colleagues from the University of Chicago. Byrk gave the keynote speech on the theme of his new book, *Catholic Schools and the Common Good*. It was at this conference that I first met Gerald and we discussed a number of themes around Catholic education. We both noted with some concern that UK Catholic education had attracted relatively little attention from educational researchers and that while there had been Catholic researchers in the field, they had largely ignored the Catholic educational contribution. We found this state of affairs also remarkable considering the size and significance of the Catholic network of schools in the UK. While the USA had major Catholic universities with important Catholic University Schools of Education, the UK had only Catholic Colleges of Education in which there was little, if any, research into Catholic education. We noted the work of Arthur Beales (1963), Anthony Spencer (1971), Michael Hornsby-Smith (1973) and Alan McClelland (1973, 1992) in Catholic education, but also recognised that this research was generally non-empirical and increasingly dated. We also observed that all four of these Catholic professors worked in secular institutions. We agreed that there was an urgent need for research, beginning with an examination of the goals of Catholic educational policy and measuring how effective these goals had been in schools. Gerald returned to Durham at the conclusion of the conference with a renewed mission, something he later termed a 'calling' to renew the field of

Catholic education. He simply thought that there was no use complaining about the state of Catholic educational research; it was time for action.

The Ebbing Tide

My own research, published as a substantial book in 1995 (Arthur 1995), was the focus of many discussions between Gerald and I, particularly the basic theme and argument of the text: the ebbing of Catholicity from Catholic education. The text posits various models of Catholic schooling, which serve to demonstrate the stages along which Catholic education has been eroded and demonstrates how educational philosophy, psychology, management, curriculum theory and policy studies had all developed in the mainstream of educational research, to the neglect of the Catholic dimension in education (Arthur 1995, p. 247). Gerald professed that the research by Bryk and myself had inspired him and that many of the themes I addressed Gerald was to revisit in his own empirical research in the following years. Later in 1995, and while still serving as Head of the School of Education at Durham University, Gerald published *School Leadership: Beyond Education Management*, in which he inserted a chapter on 'The Dilemmas of Catholic Head Teachers'. Gerald had already begun to speak about the obvious gaps in addressing Catholic education in mainstream studies. This chapter identified that there was a real danger of the depletion of the historical deposit of spiritual capital in Catholic schools and of the gradual incorporation of Catholic schools into a secularised and marketised contemporary educational culture. In terms of school leadership, he wrote:

> There is evidence that many candidates for the headship of Catholic schools in England can now talk confidently about achievements in test scores and examination results, business planning and budgets, marketing and public relations but are relatively inarticulate about the spiritual purposes of Catholic schooling. This is a major contradiction in a system of schooling which exists to give the nurture of spirituality a top priority.
>
> (Grace 1995, p. 237)

Later, in an endnote (Grace 2010: endnote XVI), he repeated this full quotation and agreed that such an outcome was predicted in my book *The Ebbing Tide* (1995). While not endorsing all of my suggestions about a weakening culture of Catholicity in schools, Gerald's own research pointed to problems at the level of school leadership and on this issue he supported my general thesis.[1] This is why it is important to read Gerald's endnotes for a full understanding of what he is conveying to the reader. However, another interesting observation is that while Gerald's book received warm reviews described variously as 'excellent' and commended for its accessible and elegant style of writing, few, including David Halpin (2007), felt qualified to comment on the Catholic leadership chapter – this particular chapter received no commentary in most reviews.

Mission integrity

It was at this time that Gerald developed some early ideas about 'mission integrity' being the greatest single challenge facing Catholic school leaders across the world. Gerald was aware that the Catholic education mission is at the service of nearly 52 million students in more than 200,000 schools and colleges across the world. It is the largest faith-based international educational system, but he believed that perhaps because it has not been researched in detail, it is often misunderstood and misinterpreted. Gerald knew that ignorance was the biggest enemy of understanding what Catholic education sought and he ambitiously wanted to do something about this. This mission ought not to be confused with a 'retirement project' because what he did was systematically embark upon a second career and he achieved far more than what some educationalists achieve in one career.

After leaving Durham, Gerald was ideally placed to move to the Institute of Education in the University of London and to persuade Peter Mortimer, the then Director and himself the alumnus of a Catholic teacher education, to provide him with a room and visiting professor status in order for him to establish a new Centre. Gerald offered his services freely and received no salary while endlessly writing letters to various Religious Congregations for much-needed funding. He received many positive responses and some money for which he has always been most thankful, acknowledging the help he received at every opportunity. He consequently founded the *Centre for Research and Development in Catholic Education* (CRDCE) in September 1997 and became its Director – the first Centre in Europe of its kind. The Centre later moved to St. Mary's University in 2016 and he currently remains the Director of CRDCE. The Centre was significant because it made a clear statement that Catholic education was a credible area for research, housed in the world's leading educational research institution, i.e. UCL/IOE. The Centre sought to encourage and support research and scholarly writing in the field of Catholic Education Studies as well as to support the work of Catholic schools and colleges, nationally and internationally, by the publication of staff development texts on various themes. Gerald offered the Centre as a place for consultancy to the bishops in England and Wales and as a place to support the work of graduate students undertaking doctoral research on various aspects of Catholic education.

Gerald wasted no time and began his own research in four areas:

- the challenges of faith and moral leadership
- the challenge of academic success as the dominating goal of the mission
- the struggle between market values and Catholic values in education
- the challenge of maintaining 'Catholicity' in changing conditions.

His Centre became the focus for annual conferences, and he began a long series of visiting lecture tours, providing workshops and forming networks around the UK and internationally. Gerald was concerned with researching the 'successes', 'failures' and 'uncertainties' of Catholic schooling and he used his considerable academic standing and influence to carve out a place for Catholic educational research in the heart of the mainstream of the educational establishment. Gerald was increasingly in demand. His after-dinner speech at the BERA Annual Conference dinner on 4 September 1999 was unprecedented by the fact that he was the first professor of education ever to talk openly about his research in Catholic education to such a gathering. He was normalising the study of Catholic education and I have always thought of the famous Heineken advert when thinking of Gerald – 'Grace reaches the parts others cannot reach'. His growing influence, that he undoubtedly accrued, was illustrated once again by an article in the *Guardian* newspaper published on 6 April 2002 entitled 'Holy Spirits in the Classroom'. The *Guardian* is not a newspaper overly sympathetic to the educational work of the Catholic Church, but Gerald was able and unafraid to write that:

> One of the prime purposes of Catholic schooling is to keep alive, and to renew, the culture of the sacred in a profane and increasingly secular world – a daunting challenge since the nature of the sacred is not easily articulated and represents "a struggle to conceive the inconceivable, to utter the unutterable and to long for the Infinite".
>
> Catholic schools and colleges are expected to be cultural and educational relays between the sacred and the profane – to be successful in league tables, while still keeping young people in a living relationship with a Christian sense of the sacred, and of the obligations that flow from this. The big question for the Catholic community in this country is, are the schools as effective in a religious context as they clearly are in the academic one?

In early 2002, Gerald defined *mission integrity* as 'fidelity in practice and not just in public rhetoric to the distinctive and authentic principles of Roman Catholic education' (2002a, p. 498) and *mission drift* was defined as 'an unintentional historical process which causes a school in its practices to move away from its foundational mission principles'. I would have perhaps questioned whether in fact that 'mission drift' was always 'unintentional'.

Grace's achievements

His first major text on Catholic education was *Catholic Schools: Mission, Markets and Morality* published in 2002, based on ground-breaking empirical research at the time. This book was the outcome of five years of interviewing 60 Catholic secondary head teachers in London, Birmingham and Liverpool. The research was part of a project within CRDCE, 'Catholic Secondary Schools in the Inner City: Challenges and Responses', and was funded by the Leverhulme Trust. We know that the empirical research base of Catholic education is limited and by publishing this single text Gerald extended its base considerably.[2] The book has been widely reviewed and universally praised in the academy and by no less than Hornsby-Smith, Walford and Davies (2003) in their detailed review in the *British Journal of the Sociology of Education*. These reviewers (2003, p. 112) remind us that Gerald's 'endnotes are often illuminating' – a fact we should not forget! I also had the privilege to review it in the *British Journal of Educational Studies*. For me, his focus in the book on the renewal of 'spiritual capital and the critique of the secular world' was central. Gerald maintains that the Catholic schooling system internationally has benefitted from the presence of significant spiritual capital among its school leaders. He specifically lists priests, sisters and lay men and women formed by their vocation as Catholic teachers and through their own spiritual formation in Catholic schooling. I believe this insight is vital because Gerald then, through solid empirical data, shows that future generations of school leaders and teachers in Catholic education are unlikely to benefit from these sources of spiritual capital. In other words, spiritual capital is ebbing out of Catholic schooling. It is a declining asset, and Gerald makes clear that the renewal of this spiritual capital is crucial for the continuance of the mission of Catholic schooling. The *transmission of the charism* is in danger, as is the Catholic critique of the secular. Gerald revisits his earlier research with Catholic school leaders and discusses the *transmission processes* by which new Catholic leaders can develop the spiritual capital enjoyed by previous generations. He provides a detailed definition of what constitutes spiritual capital in the context of Catholic school leadership and primary among them is *vocational commitment* and *empowerment*. The Church is responsible for ensuring that this spiritual capital is renewed in its teachers, and Gerald is clear that failure to do so would mean surrendering to the secularism of the age. His concluding message in the book is unequivocal: 'The Catholic Church at various levels has to resist these strategies to compromise the mission integrity of its schools, colleges, and universities. It has to hold fast to the teaching of Jesus Christ'. He offers the insight that: 'using their understanding of the fundamental principles of the Catholic faith and of its associated moral and value positions, the Catholic head teachers of this study have, in the main, attempted to maintain the mission integrity of Catholic schooling in the face of many external pressures which could compromise that integrity' (2002b, p. 237). Gerald immediately began to disseminate his key messages from the book at numerous conferences and in May 2003 the *Times Educational Supplement* reported that he had addressed the Catholic Secondary Head's Conference of that year, asking:

How do Catholic high schools manage simultaneously to achieve relatively high levels of student learning, distribute this learning more equitably with regard to race and class than in the public sector and sustain high levels of teacher commitment and student engagement?

(TES, 16 May 2003)

Gerald was able to provide answers to guide schools with a strong sense of purpose and drive and a commitment to social justice, as an essential part of the Catholic faith.

The premature death of Terence McLaughlin in 2006 came as a devastating shock to many of his friends, but none more so that Gerald. It was only fitting that Gerald wrote the first chapter in Graham Haydon's book, *Faith in Education*, that celebrated Terry's contribution to Catholic education. Gerald Grace opens the volume with a short chapter that thematises McLaughlin's scholarship into three areas: parental rights and religious upbringing, the distinctiveness of Catholic education, and a defence of faith-based schools. This chapter gives a clear and sympathetic overview of McLaughlin's scholarship. What is important here is that the work of Terry and Gerald speaks to their deep religious faith, something they often brought to bear explicitly in their scholarship.[3]

In 2007, Gerald co-edited with Joseph O'Keefe, SJ an impressive collection of chapters in two volumes entitled the *International Handbook of Catholic Education*. Again, I had the privilege to review the book as Editor of the *British Journal of Educational Studies* (Arthur 2009). Knowledge of Catholic educational scholarship and research has traditionally confined itself to specific national settings and these two volumes brought together for the first time this scholarship in an international Handbook. The Handbook provides detailed accounts of how the principles of Catholic mission are being worked out in practice in the Catholic schools and colleges from Argentina to Zambia. The Handbook, with its 45 chapters, has certainly provided a stimulus for scholarly thinking about Catholic education and for more empirical research studies to evaluate its practice internationally.[4] The then Secretary of the Congregation for Catholic Education, Archbishop Michael Miller, CSB, wrote in his contributory chapter:

> Since research should serve the human person, it is altogether fitting that the Church's institution of higher education take up the pressing challenge of fostering serious studies that further the common good of Catholic schooling. This research should include longitudinal, cross-cultural and interdisciplinary studies that would enable educators to gain a more international and empirically based perspective on the strengths, weaknesses, opportunities and challenges faced by Catholic schools across the globe.
>
> (Grace and O'Keefe 2007, pp. 477–478)

This publication certainly confirmed the place of Catholic education as a distinctive academic and policy-related field. So significant was the publication that Gerald received an invitation to present a copy of the *International Handbook* to Pope Benedict XVI in December 2007, such was his growing international reputation in the field. Gerald, by his sustained efforts, ensured that Catholic educational research has achieved international recognition.

In 2000 at a conference in Johannesburg, South Africa, Gerald, James Conroy and I first discussed the need for a Catholic journal in education. After a huge amount of preparatory work on the part of Gerald, in March 2009, he established the journal, *International Studies in Catholic Education*, with an impressive international advisory board and with Conroy and I as 'executive editors'. The journal is both international and interdisciplinary in scope and is devoted to the systematic study of Catholic education, in all its forms, across the world.[5] The Centre moved to the School of Education, Theology and Leadership in St. Mary's University in 2016. In the same year, *Faith, Mission and Challenge in Catholic Education: The Selected Works of Gerald Grace* was published in the esteemed *World Library of Educationalists* series. Francis Campbell, Vice-Chancellor of Gerald's new home, noted in the Foreword to the book:

> This book marks Professor Grace's outstanding contribution to the Catholic Church's education mission as teacher, university lecturer, and professor...? Gerald's main theme in this book is a consideration of the purpose of Catholic education. In the introduction he identifies the key rationale of Catholic education, that it is 'to keep alive and to renew the culture of the Christian sacred in a profane and secular world' and informs us that the collection aims to stimulate further studies in the 'academic and research field of Catholic educational studies'.
>
> (Grace 2016a, p. 1)

Conclusion

Mission integrity is perhaps the most important concept that Gerald has worked on to examine the connections and disconnections between the Catholic mission of Catholic education and the practice in Catholic schools. He has consistently argued over the last 25 years that in Catholic education maintaining mission integrity is an imperative; it is non-negotiable. As he says: 'Mission integrity is defined here as fidelity in practice and not just in public rhetoric to the distinctive and authentic principles of Catholic education' (Grace 2016b, p. 194). I could not have said it better myself. It is important to note that Gerald always gave attention in his research and scholarship to the challenge of striving for the common good and social justice in education and society, but from a Catholic perspective informed by his faith.

Gerald's leadership and vision have provided educationalists, and the Catholic Church, with a prominent university-based Centre, a prestigious academic international journal and two significant international volumes together with his own ground-breaking and extensive publication list, which clearly place the academic study and research of Catholic education on an international footing. Gerald's calling has been to ensure that Catholic education, as a field of study, takes its rightful and respected place in the academy. It is an extremely impressive story and one that ought to be more widely recognised and celebrated. Pope Francis in

October 2014 awarded Gerald a Papal Knighthood (KSG) 'for services to Catholic education, nationally and internationally'. It is time the bishops of England and Wales recognised his success in this venture by calling for the British Honours system to acknowledge his achievement and unfailing service.

Notes

1 In 1997, Gerald Grace was invited to write a review of James Arthur's text, *The Ebbing Tide: Policy and Principles of Catholic Education* (1995). The invitation came from a newly launched theological journal in the Netherlands. Grace wrote the review but it was never published because the journal failed to receive enough subscriptions. While Grace commended Arthur for writing a scholarly and provocative analysis of the contemporary challenges for Catholic education in England and for his call for more systematic research in the future, Grace made the point that we had to wait for more research, before we could say explicitly that Catholicity was an 'Ebbing Tide' in Catholic schools. Perhaps it was taking new forms? Professor Grace intends in the future to publish this 1997 review in *International Studies in Catholic Education* and to update this in the light of the new evidence now available.
2 It was later translated into Spanish.
3 When they were both lecturers in the Cambridge University Faculty of Education in the 1980s, a critical college referred to them as 'the agents of the Vatican'!
4 A recent report from the publishers of the Handbook, i.e. Springer, Dordrecht, The Netherlands, shows that as of August 2020 over 100,000 downloads of chapters have been recorded across the world.
5 This was the first ever international and interdisciplinary journal devoted to the systematic study of Catholic education. It began in March 2009 taken by only 40 countries and with article downloads below 500. In 2020, Routledge the publisher reported access to *ISCE* in 112 countries and article downloads of 15,000.

References

Arthur, J. (1995). *The Ebbing Tide: Policy and Principles of Catholic Education*, Leominster: Gracewing.
Arthur, J. (2003). Review of Grace, G. R. (2002) *Catholic Schools, Mission, Markets and Morality*, British Journal of Educational Studies, 50: 4, 503–504.
Arthur, J. (2009). Review of Grace, G. R. and J. O'Keefe, *International Handbook of Catholic Education: Challenges for School Systems in the 21st Century* (2 Volumes), British Journal of Educational Studies, 57: 3, 343–344.
Beales, A. C. F. (1963). *Education Under Penalty: English Catholic Education from the Reformation to the Fall of James II, 1547–1689*, London: London University Press.
Byrk, A., Lee, V. and Holland, P. (1993). *Catholic Schools and the Common Good*, Cambridge, MA: Harvard University Press.
Grace, G. R. (1995). The Dilemmas of Catholic Head Teachers, in Grace, G., *School Leadership: Beyond Education Management: An Essay in Policy Scholarship*, London: Falmer Press.
Grace, G. R. (1996). Leadership in Catholic Schools, in McLaughlin, T., O'Keefe, J. and O'Keefe, B., *The Contemporary Catholic School*, London: Falmer Press.

Grace, G. R. (2002a). Mission Integrity: Contemporary Challenges for Catholic School Leaders, in Leithwood, K. A. and Hallinger, P., *Second International Handbook of Educational Leadership and Administration: Part 1*, Dordrecht: Kluwer Academic.

Grace, G. R. (2002b). *Catholic Schools, Mission, Markets and Morality*, London: Routledge.

Grace, G. R. (2003). Educational Studies and Faith-Based Schooling: Moving from Prejudice to Evidenced-Based Argument, *British Journal of Educational Studies*, 51: 2, 149–167.

Grace, G. R. and O'Keefe, J. (2007). *International Handbook of Catholic Education: Challenges for School Systems in the 21st Century*, 2 Volumes, Dordrecht: Springer.

Grace, G. R. (2010). Renewing Spiritual Capital: An Urgent Priority for the Future of Catholic Education Internationally, *International Studies in Catholic Education*, 2: 2, 117–128.

Grace, G. R. (2016a). *Faith Mission and Challenge in Catholic Education: The Selected Works of Gerald Grace*, London: Routledge.

Grace, G. R. (2016b). Inaugural lecture at St Mary's University: 'Catholic Education, Research and Scholarship: The Achievements of the Past and the Challenges for the Future'. St Mary's University: Unpublished

Halpin, D. (2007). Review of Grace, G. (1995) *School Leadership: Beyond Education Management: An Essay in Policy Scholarship*, London: Falmer Press, *International Journal of Inclusive Education*, 1: 3, 303–305.

Haydon, G. (2009). *Faith in Education: A Tribute to Terence McLaughlin*, London: Institute of Education.

Hornsby-Smith, M. P. (1973). *Catholic Education: The Unobtrusive Partner*, London: Sheed and Ward.

Hornsby-Smith, M. P., Walford, G. and Davies, L. (2003). Review of Grace, G. R. (2002) *Catholic Schools, Mission, Markets and Morality*, *British Journal of Sociology of Education*, 24: 1, 109–118.

McClelland, V. A. (1973). *English Roman Catholics in Higher Education*, Oxford: Clarendon Press.

McClelland, V. A. (1992). *The Catholic School and the European Context*, Hull: University of Hull.

McLaughlin, T., O'Keefe, J. and O'Keeffe, B. (1996). *The Contemporary Catholic School: Context, Identity and Diversity*, London: Falmer Press.

Pring, R. A. (1968) Aims of Education, in Tucker, B., *Catholic Education in a Secular Society*, London: Sheed and Ward.

Spencer, A. E. C. W. (1971). *The Future of Catholic Education in England and Wales*, London: Catholic Renewal Movement.

Tucker, B. (1968). *Catholic Education in a Secular Society*, London: Sheed and Ward.

Chapter 2

Gerald Grace, spiritual capital, the CRDCE and ISCE

Paddy Walsh

Introduction

This chapter is in two halves. The first reflects on how Gerald Grace's seminal conception[1] of 'spiritual capital', a variant of Bourdieu's generic concept, was formed in his analysis of fieldwork data, which he had gathered from in-depth interviews with 60 headteachers of Catholic secondary schools in poor inner-city areas of London, Birmingham and Liverpool. The second half switches the focus to Gerald's centre of operations, generally known as 'CRDCE'.[2]

The conception of 'spiritual capital' and CRDCE make a good match, the latter catalysing and disseminating the further theoretical, theological and practical developments of the former. Together, conception and Centre generate, and co-generate with other centres, a veritable mass of spiritual capital and thus help to achieve Gerald's goal of 'Catholic Education' as an established field of study. In the second section's portrayal of Gerald's CRDCE work, I have dared, as invited, to see myself as a *personal witness*. I have been at least loosely connected with it from its beginning in 1997 at the Institute of Education, University of London to its departure from there in 2016, and I have connected with it again in its more luxurious quarters at St Mary's University, in a different role. More generally, this chapter is built on many vignettes and personal experiences.

Part 1: Gerald Grace on spiritual capital

In 2002, Gerald published *Catholic School: Mission, Markets and Morality*, to wide acclaim. Its concluding chapters (9 and 10) offer a fascinating account of the design and analysis of his marathon fieldwork, and how it led him to an understanding of the central role of a form of 'spiritual capital', defined as 'resources of faith and values derived from commitment to a religious tradition' (p. 236). Since the concept emerged from the fieldwork, we should attend to it first.

His single-handed engagement with 60 headteachers is justly celebrated for its ambition, but also for its fundamental rationale, methodological structure, courage, tenacity, the readability of its write-up, and, most of all, for its

DOI: 10.4324/9781003171553-4

seriousness of purpose and import for the future of Catholic schools. It was also a source of relief for many readers, as it was for Gerald, that the headteachers and schools generally were still holding the Catholic line, and were indeed inspirationally committed to it – even if the future was found to be uncertain.

Ipso facto, the success of Gerald's research by interviews showcases and endorses the value of good fieldwork in complicated and developing social situations. It therefore had the benefit of addressing a Gerald complaint, namely that 'while a lively debate exists about the nature of spirituality and Catholicity in contemporary Catholic schooling, the amount of assertion and counter assertion is greater than the research evidence' (2002, p. 210). Moreover, it should be seen as creating a benchmark for future research – while also leaving little room for excuses should negligence allow school Catholicity to deteriorate as time goes on.

The latitude that qualitative research permits is gold in the hands of a wise researcher. Consider:

> in an attempt to obtain *further* sources of evidence on these *contested* issues the sixty Catholic secondary school headteachers involved in the study were asked to give their *considered professional judgements* about the spirituality and Catholicity of their schools and students.
>
> (2002, p. 214, my emphases)

The impression given here is of the researcher relaxing his usual controls, to see what more the heads might have to give. All the schools were 'inner city', but significant differences in other respects could be expected. The interview would probably be in the security of the particular head's own school and office. By all means then, let's have a proper conversation! Such flexibility is a major advantage of qualitative research, but it is also a tribute to Gerald's commitment, emotional intelligence and experience that many of the report's most interesting viewpoints emerged from such 'conversations'. So, regarding the central question of school 'Catholicity': '[t]he majority of the headteachers looked for "outward signs of inward grace" among their students in the realm of relationships, behaviour, and involvement in good works' (2002, p. 215). There was prayer and liturgy too, but for most of these schools in a friendlier post-Vatican II way, with 'new forms of community, of worshipping together, and new ways of being family', and (another slightly reluctant-sounding headteacher), 'now we have to accept that Catholicity is a process of growing in understanding' (2002, p. 219).

That this new Catholicity might very well not include regular Sunday Mass is put down to 'weaknesses in the liturgical articulation of secondary schools and their feeder parishes' (2002, p. 221). A particularly strong statement seemed to speak for many heads:

> ...it is not that religion is ebbing out of Catholic schools – it is something within society itself. One could reverse the statement and say that the only

hope that we have is the Catholic school... the role of the Catholic school is perhaps more important today than it ever was.

(2002, p. 223)

Others, too, observed that it is their Catholic school that is their young people's living church and parish – in regularly remarked contrast with their own Catholic schooldays. Gerald, however, holds his counsel on this feature of the 'new Catholicity'. Whereas, by contrast, his support and admiration for these 'front-line practitioners' of 'the preferential option for the poor' seep out from every reference.

In concluding this 2002 book, Gerald puts 'spiritual capital' centre-stage, as follows:

> This study argues that the spiritual capital of the Catholic schooling system in England (and by implication elsewhere) is what has provided the dynamic drive of its mission in the past and helped it to preserve, in the main, its mission integrity in the challenges of the present. The renewal of its spiritual capital thus becomes the crucial question for the continuance of its distinctive mission in the future. This is a major conclusion of the research project.
>
> (2002, p. 238)

He returned to spiritual capital in a 2010 article – presenting it now as an urgent priority for Catholic education across the world, and defining it more elaborately. 'It is a form of spirituality in which the whole of human life is viewed in terms of a relationship with God, in Jesus Christ and the saints, through the indwelling of the Holy Spirit', thus providing 'a transcendent awareness that can guide judgement and action in the mundane world', and as such, empowers educators to act not simply as professionals, but as 'professionals and witnesses'. It is something that is in urgent need of renewal for lay school leaders and teachers in an increasingly secular and materialist world, to help them to be Catholic witnesses for Christ and 'not simply professional deliverers of the knowledge and skills as required by the secular state and market' (p. 125). Also, it includes theological literacy in a pastorally effective form, but can be nicely distinguished from 'charisms', which refer to inspired new movements in the Church, compared to the humbler gift of personal empowerment and sustaining resource for everyday Christian leadership – yet still 'providing the animating force and dynamic power of Catholic schooling internationally' (p. 120).

However, his main concern in this article is 'formation', the process of the *transmission* of spiritual capital to the next generations of teachers in Catholic schools. Do we know what guidance is available on this, what should be available, what can be made available? We do know that the Catholicity built into teacher training in Catholic colleges, as experienced by most of Gerald's interviewees, is now much less available. The more flexible and dialogical forms of family religious practice bring further complications. Such considerations surely do suggest a deeper and better articulation, spiritual as well liturgical, between secondary schools and feeder parishes, with significant implications for initial and continuing clerical education, as well as for teacher education.

That in turn raises the question of the provision of such education. On this matter, Gerald engages with a recent article by the then Secretary of the *Congregation for Catholic Education* in Rome, Archbishop Michael Miller, CSB: 'To be effective bearers of the Church's educational tradition, laypersons who teach in Catholic schools need a religious formation that is equal to their... professional formation' and 'It is up to the ecclesial community to see to it that such formation is made available to all Catholic school educators.... [I]n this regard, Catholic universities have a special responsibility to assist Catholic schools' (2006, p. 5).

However, across the world of Catholic universities and colleges, Gerald could find very little evidence of genuinely formative programmes in the 45 chapters of the 2007 *International Handbook of Catholic Education*, which he had recently co-edited, other than one 'original' programme in one American university. It is important, of course, to acknowledge that relevant philosophy and theology courses, 'fundamental theology for teachers' perhaps, can indeed be perspective-changing and, as such, a pastorally effective element in theological literacy. Excepting in seminaries, however, even these courses are likely to lack a sharp enough training edge for adequate 'learning how to': how to pray or care (in their widest senses), how to lead others in praying or caring, how to teach or show others how to pray or care. In 2013 Maria Riley O.P. and Kerry Danner-McDonald proposed 'a framework for the education of older youth, young adults and their educators' that would seem both to illustrate and bridge this gap impressively. Radical across its economic, business, social and ecological goals, it roots the programme in Christology, ecclesiology and liturgical planning, without which hearts would not be shaped (p. 28).

If not, or not yet, Catholic universities, then which other part of the 'ecclesial community' should we turn to? For Gerald, it is finally the responsibility of the various Conferences of Catholic Bishops internationally, but at that time he could find no sense of diocesan coordinated policies, or even evaluation studies in this area, leaving the prospects for 'formation' alarmingly *laissez faire*. He was reduced to a broad recommendation that the Conferences of Catholic Bishops internationally should give leadership in encouraging, (and even requiring), formation programmes to be created by various agencies. Those agencies, we might suppose, should surely include members of Teaching Orders with experience and success in transmitting their Orders' charisms to lay partners and successors;[3] also those lay successors themselves, by now several generations deep, who had inherited responsibility for those charisms. The parallel task for diocesan schools will have its own typical challenges and resources, but much could be learnt from the experience, strategies and perseverance of Teaching Orders in this matter.

An example of this is found in my mid-1990s case-study of a college-preparatory (14–18) Jesuit day school for boys, in a blue-collar (poor) corner of a north-eastern American city. I was encountering continuous formation and continuous regeneration of what I could later call 'spiritual capital': in its cross-curriculum focus on social justice, supportive networking with other American Jesuit schools, a thriving 'community service' programme, and an extraordinarily rich and varied retreat programme – which has to be my focus here.

Upper school 'Emmaus retreats' based on themes from the *Spiritual Exercises* of St. Ignatius were in groups of six for three days. The great majority of 'seniors', including the non-Catholics, would opt in, and staff, parents, and 'seniors' who'd already done one would volunteer as participant-leaders. *Prayer 2000* was a current new development: a young Jesuit history teacher had proposed an adaptation of the Spiritual Exercises that would stretch them out over several months of 'normal life', and 25 seniors and 6 faculty had signed up. Also, annual faculty retreat and school subsidies for staff who wanted to do a private retreat were being seen as close to the core of staff development. And the young, lay principal was leading informal study-groups for new staff to consider the life and spirit of St. Ignatius. A final-year 'senior' questionnaire included 'their last retreat' in a series of in-school and out-of-school influences on their religious development, from which it emerged as a 'major' influence, along with 'parental lives and example', well ahead of the 'medium' influences of 'peer-group', 'Catholic schooling', and 'teachers' – not to mention 'minor' influences that sadly included 'their parish'. More than four out of five thought it at least 'probable' that their last retreat was not boring, taught them respect for the views of others, gave them a sense of self-worth, had brought them close to God at times, and had had a lasting influence on them. Remarkably, more than half were 'certain' of each of these things. (Walsh 2000)

Karl Rahner once began an address to a conference of Catholic teachers with the observation that teachers, like priests, are always concerned with the whole-person, which therefore needs to include their own whole-selves. That is a profound remark about teacher formation (Rahner 1964).

My governor experience in two Catholic secondary schools has given me an impression of newly established and promising formation initiatives at diocesan and national levels. However, it seems wise also to repeat Gerald's ten-year-old bleak warning to bishops against inaction:

> \hbox{/}\hbox{/}Failure to [prioritise] this will result in the inevitable depletion of the historical deposit of spiritual capital in our schools and the gradual incorporation of Catholic schools into a secularised and marketised contemporary educational culture.
>
> (Grace 2010, p. 124)

In recalling these vignettes, in the context of a discussion about Gerald's work on spiritual capital, it has made me convinced that 'formation' needs to be identified as the key to protecting this 'spiritual capital' over time from globa-lising, secularising and marketising forces. In the ongoing success of the CRDCE, Gerald has done much to support formation.

None of the preceding should be taken to deny that the Holy Spirit, the ultimate source of 'spiritual capital', is active in schools, including inner-city schools, those of other faiths and none – the policy and research implications of which for Catholic education deserve another paper.

Part 2: Establishing the Centre for Research and Development in Catholic Education

Meeting up: The modest room allocated to the CRDCE and Gerald when he joined the Institute of Education (IOE) in 1997 happened to be next to my modest room. We could hear the raised voices of each other's visitors and research students, often to realise the other side were also going on about Catholic education. I was indeed a natural ally for my new neighbour. I had happily participated in Catholic education as pupil, student, teacher, parent and governor, had spoken and written philosophically-theologically about it, and had supervised many masters and doctoral students working in faith education. Gradually, his research base and bold vision drew me in, though my own gen-eral work responsibilities meant my actual service and participation had to be 'occasional' and 'light', e.g. standing in for him to welcome visitors from abroad and supporting the Centre's seminars and debates. That is not to say, however, that I am short of revealing personal memories. Four revealing 'case studies' are summed up here.

Gerald, schools and teachers

Once when indisposed, Gerald asked me to take over a whole-staff evening in-service training session at a prominent Catholic school, using the formidable structure and materials he had developed for such occasions, which worked very well. But most striking was Gerald's determination to stay in touch with Catholic schools, in one of which he had started his own career and to many of which his recent research had taken him back. Similarly eloquent was his engagement in the new Continuing Professional Development courses of the time for aspiring school leaders. He contrived an invitation to offer extra lectures and seminars for the Catholic, and other interested, aspirants.

Gerald and the teaching profession

In 2011, I was his emergency stand-in at the annual conference of the *Catholic Association of Teachers, Schools and Colleges* (CATSC), an important event attended mostly by senior teachers and diocesan advisers catching up with each other, listening to distinguished speakers, enjoying opportunities to pray and to attend Mass together, and in all these ways renewing their commitment to Catholic education for another year. The point here is that if Gerald could not be there, he needed to be visibly represented – I was to be careful to explain that I was deputising for him and was charged with giving him a later account. This was reaffirming his relationship with the profession nationally, with the dioceses of the northern heartlands of English Catholicism where that year's conference was being held, as well as with London and the south, thus nicely complementing his relationship with teachers in their schools and classrooms surrounded by students.

Teaching Orders, etiquette and history

CRDCE had to pay most of its own way. A prestigious Leverhulme Fellowship (1997–2000) allowed Gerald to conduct and write up his inner-city research, and he took only personal expenses from the budget. As regards its own secretarial and scholarly work, creative fund-raising was immediately needed. Appeals to various bodies, and repeated as necessary in later years, had the overall effect that the Centre was kept going very largely by donations from over thirty Religious Congregations, female and male. There was also a side-effect. Because the original appeals to Orders had requested a representation of their founder to be displayed in the office, Gerald's desk would soon be surrounded by great saints – to the interest, mystification, delight, or consternation of new visitors, including IOE colleagues.

Were these representations, perhaps, aids to prayer? Though less pious, the answer I got was one that the founders and the Orders themselves would probably find more fitting. As originally an historian, he could only be affronted by the ignorance and condescension of contemporary educationists regarding the debt owed to Religious Orders down the ages. Having these visual aids handy in his office would encourage conversation on just that theme. Later, of course, he would combat this prejudice on a wider front by inviting and facilitating many contributions to the international journal from religious women and men.

Looking to the future

Gerald has definitely accepted and wanted both the CRDCE and the journal ISCE to flourish long after he ceased to be actively involved.[4] Succession planning has always been an important priority for the CRDCE, both during its time at the IOE and more recently at St Mary's.

CRDCE at the IOE

The arrangement between Gerald and Director Peter Mortimore was far more than a business deal. There were educational and cultural advantages that were also mutual and, for sure, also anticipated by both Gerald and Peter. The challenge offered to more dogmatic forms of secularism would be one. Courteous though it would be with Gerald in charge, the arrival and presence of an education firmly and officially rooted in Catholicism would challenge some secular assumptions and prejudices and could attract some opposition in the IOE.[5] In return, the CRDCE could then expect a better-informed secular questioning of its own assumptions and prejudices. Such ongoing arguments are of course proper in a university institution.[6] In this case, the collective stores of knowledge and experiences of Catholic schools in the IOE staff and student bodies could be expected to keep arguments civil – at the very least. And then there would be so much that was common, *nearly or actually*,[7] to talk about.

To raise the profile of the CRDCE, Gerald made astute use of well-presented notices and pithy statements, using the outside of his office door as a noticeboard until proper ones were provided. I can recall a ringing affirmation of the primacy of conscience from the young Fr. Joseph Ratzinger (later to become Pope Benedict XVI), jostling with enthusiastic references to then controversial Liberation Theology. A liberal Catholic *and* a committed socialist! This is the place, perhaps, to recall Gerald's frequent references to the advice Jesus gave to his disciples as he sent them out on *their* mission, to be 'as innocent as doves and as wise as serpents' (Matt.10: 26–33). The mixture of humour and gravity that typically accompanies the reference reminds one of the 'call' he has sometimes associated with his project. In fact, however, as an internationally experienced, clearly creative, and famously hard-working professor and leader, with a relaxed demeanour, genuine sociability and a good heart, he was always going to be at home in the IOE, given that it too has a generally good heart. Most of his work was for CRDCE from his Brighton home, of which some, alongside many other inputs, would be fed into the life of the IOE. As well as reconnecting with old friends like Basil Bernstein, he made new friends collaborating and supporting younger educational sociologists, religious studies tutors, school improvement researchers, and, no doubt, many others.

Contributions to the IOE's public occasions included a well-attended and much appreciated Inaugural Lecture and deft chairing of the Inaugural of his great friend, Terry McLaughlin. Most memorable, however, was his astonishingly fierce lambasting of invited guest speaker Chief Inspector Chris Woodhead in the IOE's largest auditorium, the Logan Hall. It was for his collaboration in the government's unpicking of the historically hard-won university role in teacher education and, as such, a particularly wretched abuse of his own noble office. Hospitable and charitable this attack was not, but few were as alive as Gerald to the threads that would consolidate this reversal with a de-culturing both of teaching itself, *pedagogy*, and what would be taught, *the curriculum* – and a 'marketisation' of all three.

By no means least, Gerald became an important rallying point for Catholic staff and students at the Institute, advertising in-house Masses, rustling up the Catholics he'd come to know, also advertising talks and services in the Gower Street Catholic Chaplaincy – of which he was a sterling supporter. He remains an honorary visiting professor at the IOE.

CRDCE achievements

What was the unfolding CRDCE agenda and how did it fare in practice? Between 1997 and 2006 the focus had been national: INSET materials and consultations; a good 'professional focus' series of ten short books (around 30 pages each), offering Catholic perspectives on some significant curriculum or policy issue – and the tenth including a small fieldwork study; and Gerald was also available for media consultations and for a Catholic contribution to important new government programmes for aspiring headteachers.

In September 2016, he used a Keynote Address (with handout) at a Heythrop Conference to present an audit of CRDCE's two later phases, both international. The first had centred on the *Handbook of Catholic Education* (IHCE), five years in the making and completed in 2007, two volumes containing 45 chapters from 30+ countries across all continents. Professors Gerald Grace and Joseph O'Keefe SJ of Boston College had organised and edited it, and in its final chapter had identified its ten main themes and challenges. He noted a strong focus on empirical research studies, but a neglect of philosophers, theologians and 'new thinking writers'. Its principal limitation, however, was to be static of its very nature in sharp contrast to the 'keeping-up' dynamic of ISCE. The creation of ISCE in 2009 'marked a key moment in the international profile of the CRDCE'.

The final part of the Address was an eloquent rallying call to the 'profound and fundamental purposes' of Catholic Education Studies, so we can show by research evidence that our institutions 'do practice servant leadership, do use a pedagogy of dialogue (and not of "indoctrination"), do serve the poor and deprived, and are in open relationship with the local community' and 'are sensitive to the existence of other faiths and those of no faith in our schools'.

The CRDCE at St Mary's University, Twickenham (from 2016 onwards)

After some years of negotiation, the CRDCE moved to a new home, in St Mary's University, Twickenham. The move began in auspicious style with Gerald's Inaugural Professorial Lecture, *The Achievements of the Past and the Challenges for the Future*. Its bold opening sentence, 'The academic and professional field of Catholic Education Studies has now achieved international recognition', reassured all present that the professor was settling in well at St Mary's. His strategy was to identify and honour St Mary's past and present achievements in Catholic education with a view to inspiring – and preparing – its leadership for the major challenges he would present at the end. For the purposes of this account, that order will be reversed.

Three expensive challenges, but apt for a new university with a Catholic heritage:

1   To establish a *Chair of Catholic Education Studies*; a major financial challenge, but a development priority.
2   To build a *Doctoral Programme in Catholic Education* to attract MA completers to more advanced scholarship and research, but requiring extra supervisor staffing.
3   To plan capacity for *large-scale studies and longitudinal investigations*, requiring resourcefulness in competing for major research funding.

Gerald had skilfully pointed out that St Mary's heritage provided a solid foundation for such investments. Throughout its Vincentian period (1925–1992), it had been a leading provider of Catholic teacher education, indeed across the whole of the UK and Northern Ireland for much of St Mary's time in charge. A distinguished Vincentian educationist, Fr Joe McCann CM, had recently described it as offering its teachers-to-be 'a spirituality of education that took account of the reconciling mission of Christians to participate in the invitation of God, the Church and its people [to the service of] the poor, the ignorant, the outcast, the stranger, the sick and the vulnerable' (McCann 2014, p. 104). That resonated strongly with Gerald's own interviews with inner-city heads and his reflective realisation of 'spiritual capital' as the resource on which they drew.

Another part of the heritage was the success of the MA in Catholic School Leadership course, running since 1997. Over 150 students had completed it, the great majority by part-time study, and another 150 were currently enrolled. Its founder and first course leader had recently described it as 'a unique M-Level programme' that combined 'a Catholic philosophy of education with the principles and practice of effective school leadership' and, through its integrated nature, encouraged participants to develop 'local workplace theology as they engaged, in balanced, subtle and creative ways, in the process of relating the Gospel to contemporary contexts, questions and perspectives' (Sullivan et al. 2015, p. 32). The course is a genuine runaway success story.

A third asset proceeded from the second, namely the 150 MA dissertations seen as a counter-cultural library resource. No other Catholic university in Europe held a library of such systematic scholarship and fieldwork inquiries in the field of Catholic education. Having conducted a 'preliminary content analysis', Gerald presented a starting list of 26 'themes for further enquiry', and with a quite different focus from MA/M.Ed. dissertations in secular universities, Catholic concepts of education and leadership being 'distinctly different'.

Gerald's presentation of his case was a *tour-de-force*, and as the then current external examiner to the MA in question (as he himself had been many years earlier), and also having taught in St. Mary's for eight years of the Vincentian period, I knew none of it was far-fetched. But it had needed his touch to expose its potential as a base and resource for a doctoral school.

Concluding observations: Gerald the scholar and editor

It is only fitting to end this chapter by recognising that over the past 25 years Gerald has been an active scholar. In 2020, the *British Journal of Sociology of Education* (BJSE) published his fine article 'Taking Religion Seriously in the Sociology of Education: Going Beyond the Secular Paradigm'. It is a stinging critique of the disappearance of religion from sociology's sight and it is so well and clearly done that it could jolt the field into reconfiguring itself. There were welcome new perspectives on the complex interactions of class, race and gender in education and other contexts, but Alistair Campbell's *'we don't do God'* would sum up its attitude to religion. Gerald speaks here of a fundamentalist secularism, which also forgets that fundamentalism represents only falsehood is its tendency to present Paulo Freire as a secular radical, ignoring the fact that he was a believing, practising member of the Catholic Church – which, how-ever, he would like to be more deeply committed to the poor. In similar vein, Gustave Gutierrez's foundational texts of Liberation Theology are neglected, although they inspire students, from Latin America to Africa, Asia, Europe and North America, to believe in the role of religion in contemporary society. The BJSE and its readers are asked to recall and emulate how the founders, Marx, Durkheim and Weber, in their different ways and regardless of their own reli-gious beliefs, all took the *causal* powers of religion very seriously. This accessible paper has something for every education professional.

Sometime after Gerald had settled in at St. Mary's and had renewed his routine of coming up from Brighton twice a week, I was invited to help him out at fortnightly intervals. This allowed me some close-quarter observation of a foundation editor of a now established and prestigious journal at work. My main role was to assist him with his items of correspondence and to ensure they were properly dispatched. Typically they contained searching and constructive comments on draft papers, proposals to potential contributors, matters of policy. The correspondents ranged from university presidents and archbishops to hopeful young doctoral students.

If I must keep what I learnt or relearnt from working with Gerald down to a couple of sentences it would be as follows: Gerald is hugely proactive, forging ahead much more than catching up, and therefore marvellously productive. He is dedicated and disciplined, and urbanely so. He is bold in his approach to senior figures, but goes the extra mile with juniors. When he has to say no, he does it gently – and blames the editorial board! He is fun and Christian in (nearly) all things.

Notes

1 Following the convention of 'conception' as a particular interpretation of a more general and widely used 'concept'.
2 CRDCE stands for the 'Centre for Research and Development in Catholic Education'.

3 I was also aware that for many excellent people the Catholic dimension of their schools had diminished or spoilt their education.

4 I recall that a 'Brief Confidential Minute' of a late 2012 'working party' to consider '*The Future of the Centre (including its work for the International Journal)*' captures Gerald at his illuminating and prophetic best, identifying two scenarios:

1. If Gerald were 'rendered unable to continue' as Director of the Centre and editor of the Journal, the other three of us present, our two Fellows and myself, would, to the best of our collective abilities, ensure the survival of the Centre and the International Journal by keeping both going in the interim and by ensuring the eventual appointment of a new Director. Keeping things going would be assisted by secretary Matt Urmenyi's expert knowledge of the bedded-down routines of the Centre and the Journal, and by Gerald's policy as editor of the Journal to maintain a stockpile of acceptable papers for several issues ahead. 2). Options through and beyond Gerald's *unforced* retirement were limited by the improbability of finding a suitable replacement who would also be willing to work 'pro bono'. In Gerald's estimate, his successor would require a salary at Senior Lecturer level for some substantial number of years – to be added to the present running Centre expenses – whether at the IOE or elsewhere. But it was not yet time to hold formal discussions with other institutions.

Gerald emerges as definitely wanting a Centre and Journal beyond his stewardship, while not planning it in a way that would tie his successors' hands.

5 This was not to be feared, because as Harvey Cox noted, 'If freedom once required a secular critique of religion, it can also require a religious critique of the secular' (Cox, 1984, pp. 170–171).

6 It helped that the IOE already had a Jewish education Centre, run by Dr. Josephine Cairns. Not much later, it would also have a thriving Centre for Islamic education led by Professor Farid Panjwani. These Centres worked well together.

7 This '*same but different*' dialectic is the legacy of the 1944 Butler Act that guaranteed public funding of faith schools – a legacy arguably much weakened now by the combination of academisation and free schools.

References

Cox, H. (1984). *Religion in the Secular City: Toward a Postmodern Theology*. New York: Simon & Schuster.

Grace, G (2002). *Catholic Schools, Mission, Markets and Morality*. Abingdon, Oxon and New York: RoutledgeFalmer.

Grace, G (2010). Renewing spiritual capital: an urgent priority for the future of Catholic education internationally. *ISCE* 2:2, pp. 117–128.

Grace, G (2020). Taking religions seriously in the sociology of education: going beyond the secular paradigm. *British Journal of Sociology of Education* 41:6, pp. 859–869.

McCann, J, CM, (2014). Contributions of the Vincentians to Catholic education in Ireland and England. *ISCE* 6:1, pp. 91–107. doi:10.1080/19422539.2013.869956

Miller, M (2006). *The Holy See's Teaching on Catholic Schools*. Manchester, NH: Sophia Institute Press.

Rahner, K, SJ (1964). The Christian Teacher: Freedom and Constraint. In *Mission and Grace*, Vol 2. London and New York: Sheed and Ward, pp. 116–144.

Riley, M and Danner-McDonald, K (2013). Seeing the world anew: educating for a just and sustainable future: new perspectives for a Catholic curriculum. *ISCE* 5:1, pp. 23–35.

Sullivan, J, Murphy, A and Fincham, D. (2015). The story of an educational innovation: the MA in Catholic School Leadership at St Mary's University College, Twickenham, 1997–2013. Principles, pedagogy and research studies. *ISCE* 7:1, pp. 28–45.

Walsh, P (2000). New Wine in Renewed Wineskins: A Jesuit School Now. In Cairns J, Gardner R and Lawton D (eds.) *Values and the Curriculum*, London and Portland: Woburn Press, pp. 134–139.

Chapter 3

International Catholic Education Studies

A new academic and professional field develops

Richard Pring

Introduction

It can be argued that the publication of the *International Handbook of Catholic Education* (IHCE) in two volumes, edited by Gerald Grace and Joseph O'Keefe SJ in 2007, marked the first ever summary of the challenges facing Catholic education in over thirty countries. IHCE was the outcome of a five-year project, jointly sponsored by the *Centre for Research and Development in Catholic Education* in London (which Grace founded in 1997) and the Lynch School of Education at Boston College, USA (of which O'Keefe was dean). One of the major challenges identified at the time was the growing influence of secularisation and of secularism, especially in the West. As the editors explained it:

> Secularism represents the denial of the validity of the sacred and of its associated cultures. It affects the worldview of many people to the religious concepts, religious discourses and religious sensitivities are regarded as simply irrelevant to the everyday business of life... if secularisation in the West presents Catholic schools and colleges with the challenge of indifference, the ideology of secularism presents stronger challenges. Secularism, in educational terms, represents an active and hostile stance towards the existence of faith-based schooling and education of all types.
>
> (Grace & O'Keefe, 2007, pp. 2–3)

In 2009, Grace launched the journal *International Studies in Catholic Education*, one of the purposes of which was to monitor, by research and academic and professional scholarship, the growing impact of secularisation and of secularism on Catholic schools across the world. The journal, accessed in 2020 in 112 countries, plays a crucial role in monitoring these challenges and the responses being made to them by Catholic and other faith educators.

DOI: 10.4324/9781003171553-5

Vatican II and education

The importance of the Centre and the journal arose partly as a result of the developments in the Church, following the Second Vatican Council (1962–1965), which made several significant proposals about the religious purpose, ethos and curriculum of its Catholic schools. There was to be greater openness to the broader religious, as well as secular, ethos beyond that traditionally sustained by Catholic education. In England certainly, the establishment of Catholic schools had been a determined policy by the Church, following the establishment of the Catholic hierarchy in 1850, to support and protect the many poor Irish immigrants who were escaping from the famine. The school was part of the parish, helping its members (so many of them poor) and providing a protective community (materially and spiritually) in an often alien world.

The emphasis of Vatican II, however, was one of the Catholic school being more missionary – to be spreading more widely the Gospel message. According to Flannery in his report on *Vatican Council II: The Conciliar and Post Conciliar Documents* (1998), a more open and liberal mode of Catholic schooling was to be promoted.

> It is... the special function of the Catholic school to develop in the school community an atmosphere animated by a spirit of liberty and charity based on the Gospel. It enables young people, while developing their own personality, to grow at the same time in that new life which has been given them in baptism... Accordingly, the Catholic school can be of such service in developing the mission of the People of God and in promoting dialogue between the Church and the community at large to the advantage of both, it is still of vital importance.
>
> (Quoted in Grace, 2002, p. 17)

The key document, therefore, emerging from the Council with regard to education was *Gravissimum Educationis*, in 1965, with special emphasis on preparing young people, upon their graduation, for a much more secular society, not just to survive religiously within it but also to help transform it into the world heralded by the Gospels, which of course would include an emphasise 'Caring for the poor, for those who are without help and affection of family and those who do not have faith' (par. 10). Indeed, following Vatican II, there was a changed conception of the Catholic school as one which should be open to members of society who were not of the Catholic Faith but who might be transformed by the spiritual ethos and humanitarian concerns of the Catholic school. Such schools were increasingly seen, therefore, to have a more open missionary spirit, not simply one of nurturing the Faith within the Catholic community, as, for example, can be seen in the later document published by the Catholic Bishops of England and Wales in 1997, called simply *The Common Good in Education*.

There are a number of key documents from the Vatican *Congregation for Catholic Education* following from the second Vatican Council, and from the Catholic education authorities in the different countries, but the general message remained constant and was articulated well by Pope John Paul II in 1994 as follows.

> Against the spirit of the world, the Church takes up each day a struggle that is none other than the struggle for the world's soul. If in fact, on the one hand, the Gospel and evangelisation are present in this world, on the other there is also present a powerful anti-evangelisation which is well organised and has the means to vigorously oppose the Gospel and evangelisation. The struggle for the soul of the contemporary world is at its height where the spirit of the world seems strongest.
>
> (quoted in Carr, 1999, p. 173)

But statements and recommendations concerning such a struggle were necessarily pitched at a fairly abstract level. Their significance and implementation required much thought and deliberation, reflecting the different national circumstances and challenges, and requiring sensitivities to those different religious and national circumstances as well as systematic empirical research into the distinctive school systems.

This chapter now moves on to describing the wider sociopolitical context against which this Catholic vision for education exists, in particular the secular paradigm which dominates. It is in this context that market forces have come to have a deeply distorting effect on education. It is this difficult situation that Grace's work has repeatedly drawn attention to.

Changing context

The early 19th century saw the beginning of the national system of education when a Christian background culture was generally taken for granted and religious teaching was based on Christian foundations. But such an assumption was gradually undermined by an increased secular culture, where religious belief could no longer be taken for granted and was increasingly treated with some hostility. The Secular Education League was formed in 1907, arguing that 'teaching of religion was not the responsibility of the State' and should not be subsidised by the rates. It called for a 'national system of education, elementary and advanced, free and secular, and under complete secular control' (*Justice*, April 1908).

Emile Durkheim (1961, pp. 48–49) spoke thus of such changes in France:

> The last twenty years in France have seen a great educational revolution which was latent and half realised before then. We decided to give our children in our state-supported schools a purely secular education [that is,

an education] not derived from revealed religion, but that rests exclusively on ideas, sentiments and practices accountable to reason alone – in short, a purely rationalist education.

Such a secular view continued to exercise its influence, reflected in Lady Olga Maitland's speech in the British Parliament's House of Commons in 1962, when she declared that 'the time has come to stop being apologetic about being a Christian country, we should not allow unbelievers to undermine our traditions'.

A part solution to the problems had been suggested in 2018 by the *Commission on Religious Education* (CoRE) for England and Wales, which reviewed the legal, education and policy framework for religious education to be studied up to the age of 16, to inform policy-makers and 'to prepare pupils for modern life in Britain'. Significantly, it recommended that the subject should be renamed as *Religion and World Views*, the content of which

> ...must reflect the complex, diverse and plural nature of world-views drawing from a range of religious, philosophical, spiritual and other approaches to life, including different traditions within Christianity, Buddhism, Hinduism, Islam, Judaism, and Sikhism, non-religious world-views and concepts including humanism, secularism, atheism and agnosticism.
>
> (CoRE, 2018, p. 11)

To this the Catholic Education Council responded in a critical way that it is 'Not so much an attempt to improve religious education as to fundamentally change its character. The quality of religious education is not improved by teaching less religion' (quoted in Whittle, 2020, p. 363).

Against these differing perceptions of religious education, it is important to ask what could be meant by 'religious character' or indeed the 'teaching of religion'? To teach a subject in an educational context is to initiate someone into a way of thinking, of appreciating, of seeing things from a different point of view. It is what Matthew Arnold referred to as the cultivation of the intellect, the insight into a cultural inheritance through which one comes to appreciate the world and one's life differently. Just to learn a few propositions about one of several religious and non-religious views of life quite clearly fails to do that. The appreciation of religion, therefore, as a way of life built on a long tradition of beliefs, which have been philosophically explored and which are expressed practically through the liturgy, requires much more careful nurturing, as will be illustrated below.

Meanwhile, one needs to be aware of the changes to religious practice partly, no doubt, arising from the failure to provide insight into a religious way of life, supported by liturgical practices and the cultivation of the religious insight. Within this more secular society and the failure to provide a solid foundation for the beliefs which would underpin religious education, there has been a revolutionary decline in the proportion of young people experiencing or participating in religious practice and worship. According to the British Social Attitude Survey (BSA, 2018), less than 2% of 18–24 year-olds now identify with the Church of England which, being the National Church, has maintained the importance of religious education in all schools. That is against the background of a general decline of the population in religious practices and commitments since the previous survey in 1983, according to which there was a decline from 66% to 38% of those identifying themselves as Christian; those claiming no religion rose from 31% to 52%; the number of Britons identifying themselves as Church of England or Anglican dropped from 40% to 14%; amongst that number, but under age 24, that figure is no higher than 2%; those claiming to be Catholic reduced from 10% to 7%. The majority of the population say that they have no religion. Similar problems have arisen in the once fervently Catholic Ireland. An article in the *Tablet* entitled 'Ireland's Vanishing Church', reported 'That schools are dropping religious education, vocations are drying up, and lay people are not being prepared to take more responsibility for the maintenance of parishes. The Irish Church faces a bleak future' (Cotter, 2018, p. 28).

However, secularisation has come to signify more than indifference to religion, but rather the view that there is a contradiction between a 'confessional education' and one based on reason, clearly put by Professor Paul Hirst: 'There has already emerged in our society a view of education, a concept of education, which makes the whole idea of Christian education a kind of nonsense and the search for a Christian approach to, or philosophy of, education a huge mistake' (1972, p. 6). This something that Pope John Paul II has drawn attention to (quoted above): 'If in fact, on the one hand, the Gospel and evangelisation are present in this world, on the other there is also present a powerful anti-evangelisation which is well organised and has the means to vigorously oppose the Gospel and evangelisation. The struggle for the soul of the contemporary world is at its height where the spirit of the world seems strongest'.

The Catholic Church, therefore, especially through the way of life and the teaching within its schools, has a major task in the 'struggle for the soul of the contemporary world'. In the following section, this chapter will outline in greater detail the characteristics of that contemporary world, before daring then to suggest possible ways forward in re-invigorating its very different conception and way forward.

A secular society

Given the changes described above, Charles Taylor (2007) contrasts two very different ways in which modern society has come to perceive the purposes and values which shape our ways of living, especially the different values as to what constitutes personal well-being. He refers to them as different 'horizons of significance', each of which reflects or incorporates beliefs about the world, the values which are seen to be worth pursuing and most obviously whether or not life has a spiritual and religious significance. The secular 'horizon of significance' in the 'post-religious revolution' may be exemplified by very different understandings of sexual relations and marital commitments, by the undermining of virtues (for example, 'modesty') which were part of the religious mode of living, and by the dominant search for material satisfaction and economic profit. For example, as Keith Joseph, founder of the influential think-tank *Centre for Policy Studies*, affirmed in 1976:

> The blind, unplanned, uncoordinated wisdom of the market is overwhelmingly superior to the well-researched, rational, systematic, well-meaning, co-operative, science-based, forward-looking, statistically respectable plans of government.
>
> (Joseph, 1976, p. 3)

As Copley (2005, p. 34) expressed it, 'economics has become the theology of a materialist society'.

The 'market' was injected into educational policy and practice. Indeed, the role of 'the market' in raising standards in State schools, was strongly advocated by the Centre for Policy Studies, the leading right-wing think-tank, founded by Sir Keith Joseph and Margaret Thatcher in 1974 to develop a new generation of Conservative thinking, built now on promoting enterprise, profit and ownership. With regard to schools, this would be helped by extending parental choice of schools, assisted by schools' greater accountability in terms of targets in order to provide evidence for such choice. There would be greater autonomy of schools, encouraged by parental choice within the more marketised system and supported by the public evidence arising from the 'national assessment of performance'. It is the recognition of the damaging effects of the market which has been a central preoccupation in the work of Gerald Grace. In more recent years, other eminent voices have drawn attention to the danger within market-based ideology. For example, Pope Francis in *Evangelii Gaudium* speaks of the need for us to assert human values *in the face of a market system* (this author's italics) which has become an 'an economy of exclusion and inequality'.

One further, if connected, aspect of the very different 'horizon of significance' in the more secularised society is what one might refer to as the 'depersonalisation' enforced by the increased 'managerialism', especially apparent in the context of 'schooling'. There we see the narrowing of educational success to attainment of targets within the ever-changing qualifications systems. Gone would seem to be the 'form of the personal' (to use John MacMurray's words from his influential *Gifford Lectures* in 1957) and gone would be the wider understanding of what it means to be and to develop as a person, which is central to the very different 'horizon of significance' promoted through religious belief and practice.

The challenges facing Catholic education

In the light of the market forces which Gerald Grace's work has drawn attention to, the concluding part of this chapter will offer some proposals about the important role that Catholic education has to play in pointing beyond this secular context towards the sacred or numinous and spiritual in the world.

One can see, therefore, how the Catholic school should be seen as central to what Pope Francis referred to as part of the struggle for the soul of the contemporary world, engaging with young people, most of whom (though by no means all) would be practising members of the Church, many others only loosely so, and others too of other religious beliefs (for example, the many Muslims who attend). In such a mixed 'congregation' it is important to see how the Faith can be seen as relevant and the basis for discussion, enlightenment and commitment. In what follows there are suggested several ways in which the Catholic school might meet the demands of Pope Francis to support 'the struggle for the soul of the contemporary world'.

In terms of Catholic education, the Church should be seen as offering an *ideal* of a contrasting view of society, in which the idea of personal development for all students (not just the academically able) would be central, and which would be embodied in the curriculum, and open to systematic deliberation by all, whether believers or not. A significant part of that ideal would be an account of the Catholic Church's teaching of the 'Common Good' as detailed in Leo XIII's encyclical *Rerum Novarum* in 1879, but with special reference to the moral teaching of the Church, recognising the dignity of each member of society, irrespective of religious or social background, and with special reference to the poor and disadvantaged, as stated by the Congregation for Catholic Education (CCE): 'First and foremost the Church offers its educational service to the poor or those who are deprived of family life and affection or those who are far from the faith' (1977, par. 58). The contrast between such an idea, inspired by traditions of the Church, would most likely challenge semi-conscious beliefs and understandings of the students, whether Catholic or not.

Pointing to the sacred or numinous or spiritual in the world

It would be important for all pupils, firm believers or not, to appreciate how, underlying the beliefs and practices of the Church, there is a sense of 'the sacred' or 'the numinous', which can be recognised through poetry, literary accounts, the arts especially music – and enhanced, if properly conducted, through the liturgy of the Church. One might reflect here upon parts of Bach's *St. John Passion* or Faure's *Requiem* (especially the *Pie Jesu*, which I sincerely hope will be sung at my Requiem Mass). But this sense of the sacred is shown in much poetry – that, for example, of Gerald Manley Hopkins as in his poem *God's Grandeur*, where he reveals what he sees to be the permeating presence of the divine in surrounding nature, despite 'man's smudge':

The world is charged with the wonder of God
It will flame out, like shining from shook foil;

Or again, as William Wordsworth writes in *Tintern Abbey* of 'a presence that disturbs me with the sense of elevated thoughts; a sense sublime of something far more deeply inter-fused whose dwelling is the light of setting suns'.

Such references and also many more are explored by Otto in *The Idea of the Holy* where he concludes that the idea of the holy is a primary datum of consciousness, but can only 'be evoked, wakened in the mind: as everything that comes of the spirit'. As he points out, such consciousness is to be evoked through the lives of holy men and women, through the displays of spiritual lives of religious people, in their rites and liturgies, and in the manifestations of religious piety and worship which have been inherited. In pursuing this development of the spiritual consciousness, the teacher would no doubt benefit from the accounts by William James in his classical study of *The Varieties of Religious Experience*, or by Eric Robinson's *The Original Vision: A Study of the Religious Experience of Childhood*.

It would be important to show how such spiritual consciousness is maintained in very different religious traditions. As Hossein Nasr (1987, p. 195) explains,

The sacred art of Islam is, like all veritable sacred art, a descent of heavenly reality upon earth. It is the crystallisation of the spirit and form of Islamic revelation dressed in the robe of a perfection which is not of this world of corruption and death.

Having a spiritual perspective on life, deeply questioning the materialism which permeates our culture, would provide a basis for, and an introduction to, the distinctive contribution of Catholic schools to the 'struggle for the soul of the contemporary world'.

Recognising a spiritual dimension to living

As Gerald Grace (2002, p. 34) argues in his paper entitled 'The renewal of spiritual capital and the critique of the secular world', such awareness can arise even amongst those of little faith from consideration of the Gospel stories or accounts of the achievements of holy people or from attention to parts of the liturgy, which themselves are but the expressions and manifestations of spiritual awareness. And the development of such awareness may not be confined to the Christian liturgy. Listening to and witnessing the Muslim call to prayer or experiencing the Jewish rituals, which have persisted and inspired the Jewish race for several millennia, would create an awareness of what the Chief Rabbi Jonathan Sacks (1997, p. 51) referred to as 'a morality received not made... embedded in and reinforced by a total way of life, articulated in texts, transmitted across the generations, enacted in rituals, exemplified by members of the community and underwritten by revelation and tradition'.

The spiritual dimension arises from the gradual awareness of there being something deeper in our relation to the world and to other people than what is immediately apparent through the senses – a view of human destiny which transcends the material world and which is captured within different religious traditions. An educational programme should reveal the meaning of such traditions and the ways in which they provide a background to the lives deemed to be worth living.

Making sense of morality and the demands of conscience

It is important to reflect upon the phenomenon of 'conscience', that 'inner voice' which warns one, with varying degrees of severity, that certain intended actions are wrong. To live a distinctively human life requires the recognition of right or appropriate actions in particular circumstances – not telling lies, not offending or hurting one's neighbour, accepting obligations to friends and acquaintances, honouring promises. That strong sense of obligation and duty suggests, according to the philosopher Immanuel Kant, the postulation of a Supreme Spirit as the author of the moral obligations and the sense of duty.

Philosophical engagement with such claims

Education, particularly Catholic education, is centrally concerned with the development of reason in its different forms, and the validity of religious claims to knowledge would therefore be one such form to be investigated. To what extent is it reasonable to hold and be committed to religious beliefs and ways of life? And in answering such a question, there would be a need to answer questions about the nature, meaning and validity of key arguments. First, however, it would be important to recognise that the Church has been the custodian of a very long philosophical tradition which has shaped its understanding of the Faith, and which thrives to this day amongst leading philosophers. Part of the religious education of young people within the Church's schools, whether active members of the Church or not, would be for them to be aware of such a tradition, going back to the very early Christianity and beyond to the influence of the Greek philosophers. The basic tenets of such a tradition might be offered for discussion, though doubtless rejected by some. One is thinking here of how to put across the various arguments from causality – efficient or final – respected by major philosophers. But this would be conducted within what Martin Lipman (2003) referred to as a 'Community of Inquiry', encouraging informed discussion rather than the 'acquisition of received knowledge', informed by examples of relevant philosophical thinking but open to objections and clarification.

It is crucial here not to be too demanding on 'proof' as that is so often conceived in the light of mathematical or scientific forms of reasoning and knowledge. As with much of our knowledge and rational appraisal of life, strict proof is not possible – either, for example, that God exists or that God does not exist, either that it is right to tell the truth or wrong not to do so. Most of the important elements in living (for example, the values to be respected or the sort of life to be pursued) are open not so much to proof but to deliberation based on evidence presented, and through experiences and criticisms which support particular beliefs and understandings. That is true of the philosophical arguments for a spiritual and religious dimension to life which have entered into the Christian tradition from the inheritance of the Greek philosophers and have evolved ever since.

What Catholic schools should do is to introduce the pupils to these deeply based traditions in order to ensure at least a sense of the ideals which are part and parcel of the Christian (and indeed other) religious traditions, a sense too of the sacred and numinous, a feeling for the spiritual dimension to living, and consideration of the formation and refinement of conscience with its distinctive religious character. And, where possible (depending on the age of the pupils), an introduction to the philosophical arguments, developed over the centuries, would do no harm!

A way of proceeding

Open and free discussion of the issues, outlined at the beginning by the teacher, should be encouraged, with the different viewpoints – whether orthodox or not – expressed and opened to discussion. Strict rules would be required concerning respect for the different speakers and their views, though open to opposition based on evidence and argument. It would help, of course, if for each topic short texts would be distributed (for example, brief philosophical texts but with indications where the arguments may be pursued further). Being open to spiritual, scriptural, philosophical and theological accounts would seem to be essential to a deepening understanding of, and eventual commitment to, a religious tradition.

References

British Social Attitudes (BSA), (2018). *British Social Attitudes Survey*, https://bsa.natcen. ac.uk.
Carr, D., (1999), 'Catholic Faith and Religious Truth', in Conroy J, (ed.) *Catholic Education: Inside Out, Outside In*, Dublin: Lindisfarne Books.
Catholic Education Service, (1997). *The Common Good in Education*, London: CES.
Commission on Religious Education (CoRE), (2018). *Religious Education for All*, London: Religious Education Council for England and Wales.
Congregation for Catholic Education, (1977). *The Catholic School*, Vatican website, last accessed 9 October 2020.
Copley, T., (2005). *Indoctrination, Education and God*, London: SPCK.
Cotter, B., (2018). 'Ireland's Vanishing Church', *The Tablet*, 22 August 2018, www.theta blet.co.uk/features/2/14213/ireland-s-vanishing-church
Durkheim, E. (ed.), (1961). *Moral Education: A Study in the Theory and Application of the Sociology of Education*, New York: The Free Press.

Flannery, A., (1998). *Vatican Council II: The Conciliar and Post Conciliar Documents, Vol.1*, New revised edition, New York: Costello Publications.

Grace, G., (2002). *Catholic Schools: Missions, Markets and Morality*, London: Routledge.

Grace, G. & O'Keefe, J. (eds), (2007). *International Handbook of Catholic Education* (2 volumes). Dordrecht: Springer Publications.

Hirst, P., (1972). 'Morals, Religion and the Maintained School', *British Journal of Educational Studies*, 14, pp. 5–18.

James, W., (1902). *Varieties of Religious Experience*, London: Gifford Lectures.

Joseph, K., (1976). *Stranded on the Middle Ground*, London: Centre for Policy Studies.

Lipman, M., (2003). *Thinking in Education*, Cambridge: Cambridge University Press.

Macmurray, J., (1957). *Self as Agent*, London: Faber and Faber.

Nasr, S.H., (1987). *Islam, Art and Spirituality*, Lahore: Subhail Academy.

Robinson, E., (1977). *The Original Vision: A Study of the Religious Experience of Childhood*, Oxford: Manchester College.

Sacks, J., (1997), *The Politics of Hope*, London: Jonathan Cape.

Taylor, C., (2007). *Secular Age*, London: Harvard University Press.

Whittle, S. (2020). 'An Evaluation of the Catholic Response to the Final Report from the Commission on Religious Education', *Journal of Religious Education*, pp. 359–369.

Chapter 4

Graceful listening and educational rhetoric

John Sullivan

Introduction

Gerald Grace is probably the person who has most mapped out and influenced the development of Catholic education as a serious field of academic study in the UK. He is someone whose work stands between the living tradition of Catholic faith and contemporary educational policy developments in order to interpret one to the other and to build bridges between them. He displays an intelligent and critical fidelity engaged in a sophisticated and nuanced way with secular and secularist trends in education. He offers realism in service of fidelity, resourced by tradition but not restricted by it. His writing fearlessly exposes the unwelcome implications of the managerialist language that has swamped the reading of school leaders. He combines a stout defence of Catholic education with a ready acknowledgement of its shortcomings. He demonstrates that faith can be expressed credibly in an academic register. He has provided a level of analysis and the development of vocabulary which assists school leaders in negotiating the dilemmas they face and as they address increasing state intervention on behalf of market approaches to education.[1]

The three main fields in which Grace has established his reputation are first, sociology of education, where he has waged a war on the distortions and omissions brought about by an excessive secularisation of consciousness; second, school leadership and management, which has been colonised by the malign forces of marketisation; and third, the theory and practice of Catholic education, which has long lacked both empirical research and philosophical muscle.[2] He has exercised a major role in developing Catholic education as a serious field of academic study, energetically fostering research, as well as conducting it, editing an influential journal, *International Studies in Catholic Education* (ISCE) from 2009, and co-editing the impressive two-volume *International Handbook of Catholic Education* (2007), producing a constant stream of articles, chapters and books and, not least, communicating his ideas about the strengths and needs of Catholic education all over the world, as he is frequently invited to serve as keynote speaker at academic and professional conferences.

DOI: 10.4324/9781003171553-6

For the purposes of this chapter, I pick out two themes that are pervasive in his work. First, he exposes the gap between the *visionary rhetoric* about Catholic education and the more mundane reality that pertains in its practice, pressing the questions about the ideals espoused: is this truly reflected 'on the ground', can we back this up in practice, and what is the evidence? Second, he places great emphasis on inclusivity[3] as a necessary feature of Catholic education, focusing often on the Church's aspiration to express a *preferential option for the poor*, not omitting from the various categories of the poor those who are 'far from the faith'. As a partial response to these two themes, in the first part of the chapter, I will develop rhetoric in a different direction from Grace's use, which adopts the common interpretation of rhetoric as unreliable, untrustworthy 'spin'. Instead, I will focus on an earlier understanding of rhetoric as the art of moral persuasion, with its (Aristotelian) constitutive elements of logos, ethos and pathos. I will suggest that rhetoric understood in this sense continues to play a vital and positive role in Catholic education, as it does in any type of education. Then, in part two, I will develop a dimension of rhetoric that has been neglected, even by scholars of rhetoric; that is, listening. I will show how listening contributes to Grace's theme of inclusivity, arguing that educational inclusivity must include (!) listening by teachers, teachers who hear their pupils into speech.

Rhetoric retrieved

Rhetoric was central to education for 1500 years. To practice rhetoric is to bring together in an act of communication three elements: first, a message, which has to be clear, thought-through and make sense; second, a messenger (in speech or in writing) who has to be trustworthy, credible and come across as well-disposed towards those he or she seeks to reach; third, the target group, taking into account the perspectives, felt needs and concerns of the people we hope to persuade (Aristotle, 1991). These three elements, which are described by Aristotle as logos, or reason, ethos, or character, and pathos, or emotion, have been labelled 'the three musketeers of rhetoric' (Leith, 2011, p. 47). Rhetoric seeks to connect and relate truth to particular times, places, personalities and problems. It may lead to a range of different effects, which may be ethical, practical, emotional and intellectual. Therefore, it is at the heart of serious communication (as in teaching or preaching). It is a practical art aimed at moving souls in some direction, with a view to make life better in some respect (For an analysis of the relevance of Aristotle's theory of rhetoric for school leadership, see Sullivan, 2003).

While logos or reason seems well enough understood, the other two constitutive components of rhetoric, ethos and pathos, do not always receive the attention they deserve in literature about teaching. If the teacher wishes to influence their audience, to render them 'benevolent, attentive, and docile', then he or she must establish his or her 'honesty, credibility, and amicability before the real issue is addressed' (Gross, 2020, p. 68). This is a matter of ethos. As Sam Leith points out, 'Your audience needs to know ... that you are trustworthy, that you have a locus standi to talk on the subject and that you speak in good faith. ... you will be seeking to persuade your audience that you are one of them: that your interests and their interests are identical in this case' (Leith, 2011, p. 48). This means that a teacher should ask herself: why should students trust or believe me or follow my instructions? How do they see me: as their helper, or enemy, as a mentor who exemplifies what they teach, or as someone who seems disconnected from their own message? And pathos relates to the state of the audience one hopes to reach out to: their feelings, hopes, fears, expectations and values. For a teacher to consider the pathos of a class is to question herself about how willing and ready her students are to be moved in some way: what is their potential for learning, action and change? 'The skill is to find' the lines of approach and of argument that will 'hold most sway with your intended audience' (Leith, 2011, p. 45). But, according to the Roman exponent of rhetoric, Quintilian, 'essential for moving the emotions of others is first to move oneself' (quoted by Gross, 2020, p. 70). And thus, there is a close link between the ethos of the teacher, as picked up by students, and their own pathos.

Traditionally rhetoric has been divided into three main types. First, it can be deliberative, seeking decisions on what should be done about a situation. This is future-oriented and applies, for example, in politics, in businesses, and in schools that are developing policies to address some issues; or, indeed within any community coming to a view on how they should respond to what their members are facing. Second, it can forensic: deciding and making a judgement about what has happened (e.g. in a court of law); this kind of rhetoric is oriented to the past. Third, it can be epideictic. This kind of rhetoric is concerned with allocating praise or blame; it occurs, for example, in speeches at weddings, at funerals, or in obituaries; it is oriented to the present. The opening paragraph of this chapter is a blend of description and epideictic rhetoric. Three purposes have frequently been taken to be the aims of rhetoric: to teach, to delight and to move. Perhaps the most effective rhetoric succeeds in combining all three.

In the education and training of would-be rhetors, and following Quintilian, rhetoric has been divided up into five parts: invention, arrangement, style, memory, and delivery. These have been crisply and vividly summarised recently in the form of: 'You think up what there is to say; you devise an order in which to say it; you light on the way in which you want to say it; you get all the aforementioned into your head; and then you get on hind legs and let rip' (Leith, 2011, p. 43).

Rhetoric applies when matters are uncertain; it relates to specific contexts and cases, even if it appeals to what are held to be universal truths and values. It is concerned with practice, not with theory. It aims to bring about change in attitude or behaviour, not merely to impart knowledge. St Augustine, who earned his living as a teacher of rhetoric before he became a Christian, and then applied his rhetorical skills in service of communicating the Gospel, described effective communication:

> A hearer must be delighted so that he can be gripped and made to listen, and moved so that he can be impelled to action. Your hearer is delighted if you speak agreeably, and moved if he values what you promise, fears what you threaten, hates what you condemn, embraces what you commend, and rues the thing which you insist that he must regret, and if he rejoices at what you set forth as something joyful. ... the purpose being not to make known to them what they must do, but to make them do what they already know must be done. Its effectiveness largely depends on the quality of the relationships pertaining among speakers and listeners.
>
> (Augustine, 1997, 4. p. 12)

Students respond in many different ways to what is put before them in their classrooms. Some are intimidated and others attracted by what they hear from their teachers. Some are confused, while others feel enlightened. Some are indifferent, while others are excited. Some are resistant to what is being put forward and reluctant to take it on board, while others warmly embrace it and are disposed to put it into practice. What can be said about speakers and writers applies equally to teachers: 'Rhetoric teaches speakers and writers that the listening or reading audience is always to be considered – for it is their reception, their reactions, their responses in affect, judgement, and decision, that complete the rhetorical process' (Hinze, 2004, p. 94). In non-inclusive language, Kenneth Burke makes the point that 'You persuade a man only insofar as you can talk his language by speech, gesture, tonality, order, image, attitude, idea, *identifying* your ways with his' (quoted by Leith, 2011, p. 49). More earthily, Will Rogers observes, 'When you go fishing you bait the hook, not with what you like, but with what the fish likes' (quoted by Leith, 2011, p. 65).

Two processes occur in the course of rhetorical communication. The first of these is identification. The second is accommodation. As with audiences in other contexts, students' responses to the communicative efforts of teachers are influenced, often without them being aware of it, by a process of identification with the teacher. There are many factors which come into play, affecting the degree to which people identify or not with a speaker. These include the influence of age, gender and ethnicity, the educational background, vocabulary, accent and tone of voice of the speaker, his or her social status, life experience, level of confidence, even his or her dress and body language. All these can either assist or obstruct a student identifying with a teacher. And most of them are out of the control of the teacher and operate involuntarily on the part of the student.

More deliberately, in advance of a class and through an actual lesson, teachers must accommodate or adapt themselves to the constraints and possibilities and the particular needs of the situation they are in; they must discern what is fitting and what would be inappropriate today, here, with this group of learners. Paul gives an example of such accommodation and adaptability in 1 Corinthians 9: 20–22:

> Though I was free of all, I enslaved myself to all so that I might win more of them. To the Jews I made myself as a Jew so that I might win the Jews; to those under the Law as one under the Law (though I am not under the Law) in order to win those under the Law; to those outside the Law as one outside the Law (though I am not outside the Law of God, but under the law of Christ) to win those outside the Law. To the weak I became weak to win the weak. To all people I became all things, so that by all means I might save some.

Deciding what is fitting at least partly echoes what Cicero meant by decorum being a factor that should guide one's communication. What is fitting in one situation might be quite unfitting for another. In Cicero's use, decorum was less to do with being delicate, polite or complying with social etiquette, and more about speakers showing discretion and judgement in how they adapt to a situation in a suitable and fitting way, so that there is a match between the nature of a topic, an audience, the occasion and the purpose of the communication. Cicero wrote several works on rhetoric, modifying his emphasis on its key elements in response to changing political conditions in Rome (see 'On the Orator' in Cicero, 1971). Thus, to speak with decorum would be to say what the moment calls for, showing sensitivity and responsiveness to their audience and both self-awareness and flexibility in the manner of their presentation. Decorum implies that one's speaking is appropriate, both apt for the context and congruent with both the needs of the audience and the goal being sought. It is not about being decorous, in an aesthetic sense; rather, it combines an ethical outlook with the exercise of *phronesis* or practical wisdom.

Clearly, rhetoric can be and has been used for both good and bad purposes. More frequently than not, the word rhetoric has negative connotations for many people. It is 'empty', 'mere', 'phoney'. It is often linked with 'spin' in politics, more concerned with presentation rather than substance, wanting to make an impression, rather than doing justice to the truth of the matter. In such usage, rhetoric is viewed as something sleazy, dubious, manipulative, seductive and posturing. It is a double-edged activity. 'Even the favourable critics recognised that in its worst forms it was one of the most dangerous of human tools, while at its best it was what made civilized life possible' (Booth, 2004, p. 4). From its beginnings, rhetoric faced hostility. 'It is seen as the tool of demagogues and liars' (Leith, 2011, p. 15). Yet, even though it has gone into decline in much higher education teaching, after having been a principal educational focus for centuries in faculties of arts, it has not disappeared entirely. Modern versions of rhetorical thinking can now be found in the worlds of advertising and business, where attempts to persuade people to buy their products draw upon logos, ethos and pathos for their effectiveness. Teachers, as part of their initial formation, and also as they reflect on how their work is being received throughout their career, would benefit from engaging with the key principles of rhetoric.

It is important to make clear that rhetorical thinking, which adjusts itself to contingent and changing circumstances, does not constitute the fullness of teaching. The attention given to contingency by teachers should be balanced and complemented by a commitment to coherence. And this means that justice must be done to the logos aspect of rhetoric, which might otherwise be lost sight of by over-emphasising consideration of pathos. If contingency is about responding to local, particular and changing circumstances, then coherence is about ensuring that what teachers offer holds together, that the parts of what is taught fit together into a unity. Rhetorical thinking, which is prompted by an awareness of contingency, will always exist in some tension with logical thinking, which concerns itself with rationality and truth. Rhetorical thinking promotes flexibility and sensitivity and takes into account persons and their needs. Logical thinking or speech, on the other hand, is strong on attending to coherence; it promotes truth; it protects itself against inconsistency and bending to the wind when that seems tempting because the truth is unpopular or uncomfortable. Both types of thinking, the rhetorical and the logical, are needed, but both are also open to abuse: rhetoric can slip into being a skilful form of manipulation, while logic can ride roughshod over people's lives. There is no magic formula for how to marry contingency and coherence, but we must not give up the attempt to achieve this marriage.

Graceful listening[4]

It is striking, even shocking, how little attention is given to listening in the literature on teaching, preaching, communication and rhetoric, or more generally in philosophy and theology or politics. I searched in vain in the index of many volumes in these disciplines to find what has been said on listening, mostly finding that this topic had been omitted entirely. Even in religious literature that does focus on listening – with the honourable exception of The Religious Society of Friends, more commonly known as the Quakers – this is often in the context of listening to God in discerning one's vocation; this is something quite different from listening to one another's stories in order to know them as persons better and thereby also to appreciate how God is at work in their lives. Yet market research, to serve business, and focus groups, to serve political advisers and campaign managers, does indicate the importance of listening to those we hope to reach and to influence. It is only very recently that the Catholic Church has recognised the vital necessity of authentic listening if the faithful are to be served by effective pastoral care, teaching that is accessible and meaningful to people in their everyday lives and if church leaders are to elicit responsible engagement by their congregations. The emphasis by Pope Francis on promoting synods on key themes – gatherings for discernment for developing church teaching and pastoral responsiveness that are preceded by wide consultation – is an example of a move towards a Church that listens more carefully to the experience of her people. However, by comparison with the sustained attention given to speaking, across many different disciplines, listening has not received sustained attention in theological reflection or in church practice.

Two major exceptions to the lack of attention given to listening can be found in the ancient world, first, Plutarch (45–120), who devoted one of his works to 'Listening to Lectures', and second, Augustine (350–430), in *Instructing Beginners in Faith* who shows considerable sympathy for those on the receiving end of catechesis (Plutarch, 1927; Augustine, 2006). Yet, despite the emphasis on speaking, in authentic and effective acts of communication both speakers and listeners play a part; their interchange involves a necessary reciprocity of giving and receiving. For teaching to be fruitful, teachers need students to work with them and to develop the difficult knack of listening carefully. Plutarch (1927, p. 257) urges students to reflect on what they have heard and

> put the rest together by their own efforts, and use their memory as a guide in thinking for themselves, and taking the discourse of another as a germ and seed, develop and expand it. For the mind does not require filling like a bottle, but rather, like wood, it only requires kindling to create in it an impulse to think independently and an ardent desire for the truth.

Listening matters, both to the one who listens, as there is much of value to learn from others, but also to those who are heard. Voice matters. It matters in politics, where it is expressed in voting, in debate and deliberation and through acts of representation of different viewpoints. It matters in music, blending physical, emotional and spiritual aspects of our humanity in multiple manners as we respond to our world and its features via our vocal cords and various instruments. It matters in writing, where authors gradually develop their own distinctive voice after a process of indwelling the voices of others and becoming familiar with these voices. It matters in education; we can only learn if our experience is treated as if it counts, if our voice is heard. It matters in everyday conversation, where we learn identity, belonging, commonality and difference.

Our story is unique – the life story of each one of us – and it is precious. Although no one else knows it from the inside, like we do, we need others to help us understand our personal story – to put it in perspective. We need their support, encouragement and affirmation. We also need their misunderstanding, their disagreement, their different perspective – if we are to grow in depth and maturity. It seems to me that many people's difficulties with religion stem not from the fact that they can't believe, but from the fact that they find they are not believed. Their voice is not heard. Repeated experience of not being listened to inevitably leads them eventually to not wanting to listen themselves.

> It is precisely because of the endless particularity of the Spirit's work in forming disciples that each member [of the Church] needs, and can expect, to *learn* from the other members, and to *go on* learning from them. ... The

Spirit's work, informing the differentiated Body of Christ, is to make each member's particular learning a gift to those around them, and to make each member receptive to the endless gifts presented by those around them.

(Higton, 2012, p. 160; emphasis in original text)

When other people give us a hearing, they help us to get a bit nearer to being able to say what we mean – and also they help us to understand more deeply what we are trying to say. And we can do the same for them. Very few things give people a greater sense of their own value and worth as individuals than being truly heard. Of course, we should be careful in our use of words. Pope Francis reminds us in *The Joy of the Gospel* that 'we need to listen to and complement one another in our partial reception of reality and the Gospel' (Pope Francis, 2013, pr40, p. 26, n.44). We learn to speak by hearing others do so. We get better at speaking if we experience ourselves being heard properly.

Offering our voice and hearing others into speech are two of the most important gifts we can give to the world; they require courage, patience, humility and a willingness to be vulnerable. This applies also to the world of faith and the Church. One's reception of the Word of God and the words of others contributes to a distinct configuration and an original expression of faith – in a unique dance between tradition, situation, conversation partner and oneself. Our reception of and response to God's Word and the words of others won't be complete; it won't be perfect; but it is needed and it does make a real difference. Thus, all of us need to speak and listen to one another in the Church. Furthermore, such listening should not be limited only to those who are comfortable with the Church; those who feel committed to it; those who are in good standing, but it should be extended to all, because, as Ormond Rush points out: 'If their perspective is sought, the inactive, the lapsed, the disaffected, and the marginalised may bring to the discourse of faith questions from the margins which are for the good of the church' (2009, p. 260).

A Presbyterian minister, writing about the power and importance of listening in mission and ministry, notes that 'loving listening encourages connection and depth, which contribute to life and health for individuals and congregations'. With regard to her work with young people, she questions herself: 'to what extent am I accurately perceiving the central issues the students are trying to talk about, particularly when I have a goal or agenda for the conversation?' 'When someone listens carefully to us, it helps us feel as if our lives matter' (Baab, 2014, pp. x, 6–7). A comment attributed to George Eliot illustrates how beneficial such being heard can feel:

Oh, the comfort, the inexpressible comfort of feeling safe with a person; having neither to weigh thoughts nor measure words, but to pour them all out, just as they are, chaff and grain together, knowing that a faithful hand will take and sift them, keep what is worth keeping, and then, with a breath of kindness, blow the rest away.

In thinking about the importance of listening in the Church, George Dennis O'Brien's book *Finding the Voice of the Church* is helpful. O'Brien reminds us that 'The key to preaching the Gospel is not first defined by how one *speaks* but how one *listens*' (2007, p. 190; emphasis in original text). Christian communication, within and beyond the Church, has to begin with deep *listening*. Such listening affirms the uniqueness and intrinsic worth of the one being listened to. 'The point is to see the person standing right in front of me, who has no substitute, who can never be replaced, whose heart holds things for which there is no language, whose life is an unsolved mystery' (Barbara Brown Taylor, quoted in Goodfellow, 2015, p. 1314).

A fine example of the importance of listening as an essential foundation for Christian communication is the story of Jesus' encounter with potential disciples on the road to Emmaus (Luke 24: 13–35). In this story, before Jesus meets the two travellers, they were already engaged in conversation with one another. He comes alongside of them, listening to what they are saying and thereby tuning in to their concerns and state of mind. Then he asks them questions, getting them to articulate their understanding of the events that bother them and the nature of their perplexity, before setting out to address their confusion and dismay by his teaching. This teaching, both in words and gestures, connects the more effectively because the preceding process of listening had clarified for him, as teacher, and for them, as potential learners, what was needed at this moment. More broadly, we might claim that, so important is listening as a preliminary step in creating the conditions for learning and teaching, what is needed for more effective communication in and for the Church, as well as in school and universities, is not a bigger megaphone but a better hearing aid.

Where we listen modifies how we listen: thus, the nature and purpose of, and the feelings associated with, listening varies according to whether it occurs in church, at home, at work, in school, on a date, as a doctor with a patient, at a concert, interviewing someone for a job, or watching a political debate on television. And who is listening to us also makes a difference: 'The ear of the king, the confessor, the judge, the spy, the actor, the lover – each is different' (Gross, 2020, p. 83, quoting Alan Gross). It would be worth asking oneself how listening to a teacher differs from these other kinds of listening. It is also important to be aware of the necessity to listen to what is not said but is present in the lives and concerns of students. Furthermore, listening to oneself, being connected to one's own core, is a necessary contributing factor that supports listening to others. To be out of touch with oneself is scarcely a good basis for attending properly to others; nor can we relate authentically to others if we are at odds with our real thoughts and feelings.

An emphasis on listening as a central element in teaching and learning makes it evident that teachers and students are mutually dependent. Without students the teacher cannot function as a teacher. If mutual graceful listening is being enacted, the relationship and interaction between students and their teacher simultaneously brings the teacher into being as a teacher and the students as students. One can also legitimately claim that, in the midst of this process, students are teaching and the teacher is learning.

In a powerfully thought-provoking book on listening and the ethics of attunement, Lisbeth Lipari deepens our understanding of how listening affects us and how it contributes to interpersonal understanding. Three points she makes are particularly relevant to the claims made in this chapter. First, that serious listening is more than merely auditory; it involves the whole person of the listener. Second, one should distinguish listening and hearing. Third, authentic listening allows the one being listened to, to enter into the listener; that is, it enables some degree of communion between them.

With regard to the first point, Lipari suggests that sound is picked up by the whole body, not merely via the ears. She asks: 'do I listen not only to words with my mind, but also to the music of the voice in my ears, the posture and gesture of the body with my eyes, the vibrational rhythm of the others' pulsations, movements, and intonations in my body?' (Lipari, 2014, p. 9). This leads into her second point, that listening and hearing are not identical.

> Etymologically, "listening" comes from a root that emphasises attention and giving to others, while "hearing" comes from a root that emphasises perception and receiving from others. ... "Hearing" tend(s) to foreground the self's experience, while the ideas of attention and obedience resonating in the word "listening" tend to focus on the other.
>
> (Lipari, 2014, p. 50)

There are two aspects of this distinction. Listening is what I do, while hearing is what happens in me, what I receive or pick up. That is, listening focuses on the active aspect, the effort we put into attending to others, while hearing attends to the passive dimension, or to the quality of our receptivity. In addition, we might say that listening is other-oriented, while hearing is self-oriented. As Lipari observes, 'While it is certainly true that we can literally shut out visual but not auditory stimuli, it is also true that we can *hear* but fail to *listen*. For just as *seeing* can occur in the absence of *looking*, so can *hearing* occur without *listening*' (2014, p. 196; emphasis in original text).

Third, Lipari proposes that listening creates the conditions for self-protective boundaries between people to be lowered and for a more intimate interaction to occur, one that facilitates each opening up to their interlocutor in a mutual sharing of their very personhood, not merely in an exchange of ideas:

> In "the listening" I create a space to receive you, letting your speech enter me, flow through me. ... "The listening," as opposed to "the heard," does not absorb the other into conformity with the self, but instead creates a dwelling space to receive the alterity of the other and let it resonate.
>
> (Lipari, 2014, p. 198)

If listening opens the door from within and allows others to enter, it is likely that there is a connection between our capacity to listen to each other and our capacity to be still and receptive before God.

Graceful listening requires attention, humility, patience, respect for the other, concentration, a desire to learn from the other, and freedom from self-absorption. It also depends upon the ability to let go of prior assumptions that might short-circuit our listening properly; to take seriously the value and significance of the uniqueness of the other; and the capacity to be self-reflexive – able to listen (graciously) to ourselves and able to question why we are hearing this person's words in particular ways – what baggage are we bringing? What filters are we using? According to Joseph Beatty, among the qualities that make someone a good listener are 'good will towards the other person, a willingness to take the time, the ability to focus and avoid distraction, some concern to understand, and a working memory' (Beatty, 1999, p. 281). The teacher who attempts graceful listening tries to step outside herself or himself in order to ask: how might they – their students – hear what I am saying? In graceful listening teachers convey to each student that, in their view, the class would not have been complete without their presence, questions, insights and involvement.

Thomas Aquinas claims that grace has five effects on us. First, our soul is healed; second, we will the good; third, we work effectively for it; fourth, we persevere; and fifth, we break through to glory (*Summa Theologiae* I–II q.111 a.3 co.). If we apply these effects to graceful listening in the context of education and as carried out by teachers, we may hope that such listening will be experienced by learners as healing rather than hurting. This entails inviting them to offer their voices, reinforcing their sense of being valued as individuals, affirming the validity of their experience, welcoming their insights, and taking seriously the weight of their questions, even if teachers cannot always answer them adequately. In this way, graceful listening by teachers conveys their benign intentions and conveys their willingness to strive with all the skill at their command, being enduring in their efforts, even in the face of reluctance to engage on the part of students. Such listening, we may hope, will be blessed by being ultimately fruitful in the lives of students, even if the glory of this outcome will often fail to be apparent to teachers.

Conclusion

For many years, Gerald Grace has been a powerful advocate, both for the cause of Catholic education in the face of criticisms from its detractors, and, most especially, for the need for more robust investigation into the degree to which the claims made on behalf of Catholic educational institutions can be substantiated by evidence. He has asked, for example, whether the mission is being carried out with integrity, whether spiritual capital is being replenished and whether Catholic teachers and leaders are being sufficiently inclusive of those for whom they are providing an education. Inevitably, for individuals and for communities, there is always a gap between ideals and reality, between aspirations and achievement. The challenge that Grace poses to defenders of Catholic education to take the trouble to check out the nature of this gap – and then to reduce it – deserves to be taken up more widely by both researchers and practitioners. Stimulating awareness of the gap, creating a sense of urgency about it, and galvanising the motivation and energy to address it, all depend heavily on the kind of graceful listening and rhetorical skill that builds bridges and fosters collaboration between people with different experience, perspectives and skills, qualities winsomely displayed by Gerald Grace and which others now need to take forward.

Notes

1 Examples of terms used by Grace that have been picked up by practitioners include 'mission integrity', 'mission drift', 'the strategic subsidy' provided by Religious Congregations in the past and the concept of 'spiritual capital' and its role in Catholic education. See Grace (2010).
2 The phrase 'philosophical muscle' is borrowed from Mario D'Souza, whose tragically early death deprived the Catholic educational community of seeing more of his nuanced and soundly scholarly retrievals of previous Catholic philosophical thinking on education, such as that of Jacques Maritain and Bernard Lonergan (D'Souza, 2016). Grace has sought to champion the cause of Philosophy in the *ISCE* journal, commissioning a sequence of contributions from Brendan Carmody (2011), Sean Whittle (2014) and Paddy Walsh (2018) to address the philosophy of Catholic education. For a fuller discussion of this, see Chapter 10 of this volume.
3 In addition to the pervasive concern throughout Grace's work to question how effectively church schools address the needs of the poor (interpreted broadly), the marginalised, the 'sinners' as well as the 'saints', and those 'far from the faith', he encouraged contributions to *ISCE* articles that were designed to improve better understanding of Jewish–Catholic relations, for example Miller (2013), Jardine and Brittain (2015) and Wansbrough (2016); and invited contributions on both sides of the debate on the ordination of women (Bourgeois, 2015; Droste, 2015; Grey, 2016).
4 The term 'graceful listening' seems apt because a constant feature in Grace's approach to exploring Catholic education is his commitment to 'listening to the voices of students and teachers'.

References

Aristotle (1991). *The Art of Rhetoric* trans by Hugh Lawson-Tancred. London: Penguin.
Augustine (1997). *On Christian Teaching* trans. by R.P.H. Green. Oxford and New York: Oxford University Press.
Augustine (2006). *Instructing Beginners in Faith* trans by Raymond Canning. New York: New City Press.
Baab, Lynne M. (2014). *The Power of Listening*. Lanham, MD: Rowman & Littlefield.
Beatty, Joseph (1999). 'Good listening', *Educational Theory*, 49, 3, pp. 281–298.
Bourgeois, Roy (2015). 'The ordination of women in the Catholic Church: arguments for teachers and students in Catholic schools to consider – Part 2 the case for', *International Studies in Catholic Education*, 7:1, 15–27.
Booth, Wayne C. (2004) *The Rhetoric of RHETORIC*. Oxford: Blackwell.

Carmody, Brendan (2011). 'Towards a contemporary Catholic philosophy of education', *International Studies in Catholic Education*, 3, 2, pp. 106–119.

Cicero (1971). *'On the Orator'* in *On the Good Life* trans by Michael Grant. London: Penguin.

D'Souza, Mario O. (2016). *A Catholic Philosophy of Education*. Montreal and Kingston: McGill-Queen's University Press.

Droste, Catherine J. (2015). 'The ordination of women in the Catholic Church: arguments for teachers and students in schools to consider – Part 1 the case against', *International Studies in Catholic Education*, 7:1, pp. 4–14.

Goodfellow, Judith et al. eds. (2015). *Celtic Daily Prayer*. Book Two. London: William Collins.

Grace, G (2010). 'Renewing spiritual capital: an urgent priority for the future of Catholic education internationally', *ISCE*, 2, 2, pp. 117–128.

Grey, Mary (2016) 'The ordination of women in the Catholic Church? New considerations', *International Studies in Catholic Education*, 8, 2, pp. 216–230.

Gross, Daniel (2020). *Being-Moved. Rhetoric as the Art of Listening*. Oakland, CA: University of California Press.

Higton, Mike (2012). *A Theology of Higher Education*. Oxford and New York: Oxford University Press.

Hinze, Bradford E. (2004). 'Theology as communication: revelation, faith, and the Church as ongoing dialogues' in David S. Cunningham, ed. *To Teach, To Delight, and To Move*. Eugene, OR: Cascade Books, pp. 85–108.

Jardine, Clare and Brittain, Teresa (2015). 'Teaching about Catholic-Jewish relations: some guidelines to assist the work of teachers in Catholic schools', *International Studies in Catholic Education*, 7, 1, pp. 46–60.

Leith, Sam (2011). *You Talkin' To Me?* London: Profile Books.

Lipari, Lisbeth (2014). *Listening, Thinking, Being*. Philadelphia, PA: University of Pennsylvania Press.

Miller, Helena, (2013). 'The *International Handbook of Jewish Education* (2011): Developing a Dialogue between Jewish and Catholic Educators', *International Studies in Catholic Education*, 5:2, 113–126.

O'Brien, George Dennis (2007). *Finding the Voice of the Church*. Notre Dame, IN: University of Notre Dame Press.

Plutarch (1927). *Moralia* Vol. 1, trans by Frank Cole Babbitt. Cambridge, MA: Harvard University Press.

Pope Francis (2013). *Evangelii Gaudium/The Joy of the Gospel*. London: Catholic Truth Society.

Rush, Ormond (2009). *The Eyes of Faith. The Sense of the Faithful and the Church's Reception of Revelation*. Washington, DC: Catholic University of America Press.

Sullivan, John (2003). 'Leading values and casting shadows in church schools', *Journal of Religious Education*, 51, 1, pp. 44–49.

Walsh, Paddy (2018). 'From philosophy to theology of Catholic education, with Bernard Lonergan and Karl Rahner', *International Studies in Catholic Education*, 10, 2, pp. 132–155.

Wansbrough, Henry (2016). 'Teaching about Catholic-Jewish relationships: interpreting Jewish hostility to Jesus in the gospels', *International Studies in Catholic Education*, 8, 1, pp. 18–28.

Whittle, Sean (2014). 'Towards a contemporary philosophy of Catholic Education: moving the debate forward', *International Studies in Catholic Education*, 6, 1, pp. 46–59.

Chapter 5

Researching spiritual capital in Catholic education

On the need for theoretical frameworks and more empirical work

Ann Casson

Introduction

It was an honour to be asked to contribute a chapter to this volume of work. Gerald Grace had been a significant influence on my work in empirical research in Christian education. Three interwoven strands underpin Gerald Grace's work in the field of Catholic education. It is based on the understanding that Catholic education's fundamental rationale is 'to keep alive and to renew the culture of the Christian sacred in a profane and secular world' (Grace, 2015, p. 1). Secondly, it is motivated by an awareness of an acute need for 'an articulated theoretical framework' developed from the insights of formal scholarship (Grace, 2002, p. 17). The third strand is the call for 'systematic research' into Catholic education at a national and international level, empirical research that can inform and shape evidence-based policy and practice for Catholic educators in schools, colleges, and universities. This chapter considers the value of one critical element of Grace's theoretical framework, his articulation of the concept of spiritual capital, embedded in the Catholic faith tradition, and supported by empirical research. This encompasses all three strands. The chapter's focus is primarily on Catholic education within England and Wales. However, many of the themes highlighted will be recognised as relevant to an international audience. The first part offers an analysis of Grace's development of the spiritual capital, from its roots in Bourdieu's theory.[1] The second part considers the significance and impact of empirical research of spiritual capital in Catholic education, which has the potential to illuminate the changing Catholicity of school and inform policy and practice. The chapter concludes with a look at some examples of empirical research, and highlights areas still in urgent need of research.

Spiritual capital

Gerald Grace defines spiritual capital as 'resources of faith and values derived from commitment to a religious tradition'. It is a 'source of empowerment because it provides a transcendent impulse which can guide judgment and

DOI: 10.4324/9781003171553-7

action in the mundane world'; it empowers educators to act as professionals and witnesses (Grace, 2002, p. 236). In this definition, he builds Pierre Bourdieu's concepts of field, habitus, and symbolic power and, in particular, his articulation of religious capital. Pierre Bourdieu's work on the concept of capital (economic, social, and cultural) has been a highly influential and invaluable tool in analysing education systems.

> Economic capital, whose effects are mediated by social class inequalities in the lives of students; social capital, constituted in different access to supportive social networks; and cultural capital, viewed as resources of knowledge, language, and appropriate social relations differentially available to students in their homes.
>
> (Grace, 2010, p. 118)

Religious capital for Bourdieu (1991, cited in Dillon, 2001) is an issue of power between religious specialists and laity. The former are 'exclusive holders of the specific competence necessary for the production and reproduction of a deliberately organized corpus of secret (and therefore rare) knowledge' (Dillon, 2001, p. 414), while the laity is dispossessed, recipients rather than generators of religious capital. Agency is limited to religious professionals, who struggle to control access to 'the goods of salvation' (Bourdieu, 1991 cited in Grace, 2010, p. 118). Religious capital is thus understood in organisational terms (Verter, 2003, p. 151); it is about knowledge and competence that sustains the distinction between priest and laity (Guest, 2007, p. 188). In the Catholic context, religious capital is generated and held in the hierarchical institution of the Church.

Gerald Grace's development of the concept of spiritual capital broadens and sharpens Bourdieu's religious capital. Grace (2002, 2010) defined spiritual capital with specific reference to the context of Catholic education. His initial definition (2002), as described above, was refined and clarified in 'Renewing spiritual capital: an urgent priority for the future of Catholic education internationally' (2010). For Grace (2002, 2010), spiritual capital is a source of empowerment; Grace argues 'that those who acquire spiritual capital act as professionals within Catholic education and as a personal witness to faith in practice, action and relationships' (2010, p. 120). Spiritual capital is 'resources of faith and values derived from vocational commitment to a religious tradition'. It is a 'source of vocational empowerment' as it provides a transcendental awareness that guides judgement and a form of spirituality where life is viewed in terms of relationship with God (2010, p. 125).

Grace's definition of spiritual capital crucially diverges from Bourdieu's work concerning the laity's role in generating capital; he moves away from focusing on the power of a necessarily limited number of religious professionals within the Church to recognise the agency of the individual lay Catholic. Spiritual capital consists of a 'deregulated exchange and empowerment of individuals' (Guest, 2007, p. 190). Bourdieu's development of the concept of religious capital is centred on the power of a select number of individuals. Within Grace's interpretation of spiritual capital, 'symbolic power is instantiated in individual school leaders' (2010, p. 119). It is individual spiritual capital – a source of personal 'power to maintain' rather than 'power over'. This idea to maintain or sustain is critical to Grace's spiritual understanding; its presence and generation sustains a sense of mission, purpose, and hope. He differentiates it from charism as understood by Weber, insisting it is not found in the expression of exceptional leadership but is a sustaining resource for everyday leadership. Grace does not just transfer the power from religious professionals to school leaders; he develops the idea further to explain that spiritual capital is not held merely within the leadership but is with 'school governing bodies, in classroom teachers, in priests, in school chaplains, in parents and not least in the students themselves' (2002, p. 238). This is of crucial relevance when we later consider applying the concept in Grace's work and the potential for further empirical research in Catholic education.

Grace's focus on laity in his definition of spiritual capital is not unique. The concept of spiritual capital as distinct from religious capital has been developed independently by several scholars, for example, Verter (2003), Guest (2007), and Baker and Skinner (2006). In his article 'Theorising religion with Bourdieu against Bourdieu', Verter (2003) argues for the adoption of the term spiritual capital, identifying it as ritual capital, a form of cultural capital, and that 'spiritual knowledge, competencies, and preferences may be understood as valuable assets in the economy of symbolic goods' (p. 152). Critically, Verter (2003, p. 164) moves away from the idea of religious capital held by professionals to that held by the laity; he argues that this threatens the autonomy of the religious field, for spiritual capital may be of value in other fields, and lay people may exercise spiritual power because of capital gained in another field. Spiritual capital with its focus on the individual and looser ties to institutional religion could be seen to reflect the more fluid nature of religion in the twenty-first century.

Grace (2010) also employs spiritual rather than religious, but in a different sense to that adopted by Verter. Spiritual is often seen as a vaguer, weaker term than religious as it is often employed in common parlance in 'I am spiritual but not religious'. Nevertheless, the concept of spirituality, of humans as spiritual, has deep roots within Christianity (Giordan, 2007) and Grace's definition of spiritual is not a weaker version of religion. It is a move from institutional to personal power, but within the context of the Catholic faith tradition.[2] There is an assumption that being spiritual within a Catholic school context refers to 'to the regular sacramental, prayer-life, moral and ecclesial dimensions and expressions of one's faith as a Catholic teacher or educator, both individually and communally' (D'Souza, 2012, p. 94). Grace (2010) does not limit spiritual capital to this, arguing that it cannot be reduced to theological literacy, as integral to it is a personal witness in practice, action, and relationships. As D'Souza (2012, p. 101) explains, Catholic education is focused on human development, 'not just human development with a few churchy pieces tacked on, but, to use the language of St Paul, Christian development means progressively becoming a new creation in Christ' (2 Corinthians 5: 1). It is this understanding that better encapsulates the nature of spiritual capital.

Grace's interpretation of spiritual capital is distinct in that it retains strong links to the religious institutions. Other scholars' interpretation of the concept of spiritual capital such as Verter detailed above reflect much weaker links with the religious institution, a more fluid and free-flowing notion. For example, Davies and Guest (2007) define spiritual capital as a capital 'that is not possessed or defined by the hierarchy of the religious tradition but acknowledges the "believer" as an agent, not just a passive recipient' (2007, p. 129). Their interpretation resonates with Grace's focus on spiritual capital being a more fluid resource, an understanding of the believer as an agent, moving away from capital held by professionals within the institution. They differ in their understanding of the links to the tradition. Davies and Guest interpret spiritual capital as an 'eclectic appropriation of religious resources, chosen and adapted to meet the individual's subjective needs' (2007, p. 129). One major criticism of spiritual capital is that unlike religious capital, where there is a gold standard held by the institution (Verter, 2003), there is potentially no clear boundary to the concept. It is necessarily interpreted and adapted as it moves from one generation to the next. Davies and Guest (2007) identified a fluid process of transmission. They termed this 'transformed retention', which is a 'critically creative process of adaptive change by which beliefs pass from parents to children or mentors to those they influence' (2007, p. 170). In their research with children of Anglican Bishops, the spiritual capital they identified had in some cases tenuous links to that of the institution of the Anglican Church. Their interpretation strays too far from Grace's understanding of spiritual capital, which is rooted within the Catholic faith tradition, while avoiding a narrow focus on theological or scriptural literacy or ecclesial practices. Spiritual capital is a force that animates Catholic education and is sustained by personal witness to the faith tradition.

Grace (2010) argues that within Catholic education, spiritual capital was previously held and acquired through Religious Orders. Within the Catholic tradition, spirituality has often flourished within religious communities (Giordan, 2007). It was the contribution of the Religious Orders, 'the transmission of distinctive religious charisms' (Lydon, 2009, p. 51), that was the driving force of sustaining the Catholic Church's educational mission. The 'transmission of charism reflected an openness to the reception; to receiving from those who have encountered, or are encountering, it' (Lydon, 2009 p. 52). Religious Orders' role in the transmission of spiritual capital took place within the context of the Orders' foundation in the Catholic faith tradition. Grace argues that spiritual capital declined within Catholic education as Religious Orders have disappeared from most Catholic schools in the UK. The transmission of spiritual capital generated within Religious Orders maintained the close link to the institutional Church. In his empirical research with head teachers in England, Grace (2002) found that many head teachers' vocation had been shaped or influenced by Religious Orders in their Catholic school days. He argued that these head teachers were in the first stage of the transmission of spiritual capital (2010, p. 123). They transmitted their spiritual capital to staff who had no contact with the resource present within Religious Orders. It does raise an urgent question: as spiritual capital is reconstituted, what is happening to this spiritual capital in subsequent transmission processes? (Grace, 2010, p. 123).

An integral element of Grace's interpretation of spiritual capital is that 'those within education whose own formation has involved acquisition of spiritual capital do not act simply as professionals, but as professionals and witnesses' (Grace, 2002, p. 236). The key term here is witnesses; there is a clear implication that those working within Catholic education have the potential to become 'witnesses' to the faith, to maintain the educational mission, and animate and inspire others to do so.[3] In *Lay Catholics in Schools Witnesses to Faith*, the Congregation for Catholic Education (1982) recognised that with a decline in the number of Religious Orders in school there was an increased role for lay Catholics within education.

> The Catholic educator must be a source of spiritual inspiration... A lay Catholic educator is a person who exercises a specific mission within the Church by living the faith... with an apostolic intention... for the integral formation of the human person.
>
> (Congregation for Catholic Education, 1982, p. 14)

The Catholic educator is thus a personal witness in words and action; they are witness to the Catholic faith as lived religion. Michael Buchanan (2020) in Australia has explored the teacher's role as a witness to faith, arguing that a Christian educator who is a witness to faith offers students a real and tangible example of Christian attitudes and behaviours. However, he has drawn attention to the challenges of this in practice. In Australia, Christian educators are reluctant to witness their faith publicly; it is not within Australian culture. Similar issues have been highlighted in the UK; the reluctance to share personal faith in the classroom for fear of indoctrination and the lack of confidence many educators have in expressing their faith. Nevertheless, personal witness to the faith, vocational empowerment, is integral to Grace's interpretation of spiritual capital and this raises the question of what is needed to empower Catholic educators to fulfil this role. For Grace, the interpretation of spiritual capital, even as it moves from Religious Orders to lay Catholic educators, is rooted in the Catholic faith tradition.

Grace draws attention to the urgent need to renew this source of spiritual capital; it is essential that school leaders can acquire spiritual capital, and sustain the educational mission.

[Spiritual capital is] in urgent need of renewal in the contemporary world of Catholic education faced with growing secularisation, ideologies of secularism, global marketisation and materialism, and the decline of Religious Congregations in the field of education

(Grace, 2010, p. 125)

The need for renewal that Grace described in 2010 still exists acute as ever at the time of writing this chapter in 2020. The external and internal pressures on Catholic schooling have only increased, challenges such as in England of academisation (Buck, 2018) and the declining engagement of young people in the life of the local Church (Bullivant, 2016). Grace (2010) is concerned that the field of Catholic education is responding only slowly to this call for a renewal of spiritual capital. He proposes a two-pronged approach, a practical response focused on developing formation programmes for school leaders and teachers and in-depth empirical research on the extent to which spiritual capital is in decline or evidence of its renewal.

Grace's concept of spiritual capital is more inclusive and fluid than Bourdieu's religious capital with its recognition of the agency of the individual. It is an invaluable tool in illuminating the nature of Catholicity and faith transmission in the sphere of Catholic education, illuminating the individual's role as an animator of spiritual capital. It stands in contrast to other scholars' interpretation (Verter, 2003; Guest, 2007) with its stress on the connection to the orthodoxy of the Catholic faith tradition and characterisation as a tool to re-energise the mission of Catholic education. Grace's purpose in developing spiritual capital was not solely intended for an academic audience; it was aimed at Catholic educators working in the Catholic education sector. The development of this concept is motivated by concern for the mission integrity of Catholic education. Grace's elaboration of the concept when applied in research studies has the potential to illuminate the changing nature of Catholic schools within the UK and provide evidence to initiate and sustain the renewal of spiritual capital in Catholic education.

Researching spiritual capital in Catholic education

The second part of this chapter focuses on the value and relevance of researching spiritual capital in Catholic education research. Accessible systematic research, which improves Catholic education's integrity and effectiveness, is invaluable; it is essential to know more about the mission integrity of Catholic education and effectiveness in these challenging circumstances (Grace, 2009). Research within Catholic education is critically important in a time when society is fragmenting and faced with uncertainty. Understanding and exploring how Catholic schools can facilitate and support encounters with faith is essential not only for the future of Catholic schools but also for the future of the Catholic Church. Grace's writing is motivated by a concern for Catholic education in practice; he sees the work of Catholic education as crucial to the renewal of faith and of the Church itself. Scholarly rigorous research rooted in a well-worked-out theoretical framework can 'provide a necessary intellectual and cultural defence against the challenges of secularisation in contemporary societies' (Grace, 2009, p. 8). Challenges need to be addressed with arguments, policies, and practices supported by evidence drawn from empirical research on the ground.

Through all his works, Grace emphasises the distinctive nature of Catholic education, rooted in the Catholic faith and defined as a mission activity. He has been much influenced by *The Catholic School* document (1977), for example:

> Education is not given to gain power but as an aid towards a fuller understanding of and communion with man, events, and things. Knowledge is not to be considered as a means of material prosperity and success, but as a call to serve and to be responsible for others.
>
> (CCE, 1977, par. 56)

Within England and Wales, 'Catholic schools are provided first and foremost for the Catholic community and to facilitate the right of Catholic parents to choose a Catholic education for their children' (Stock, 2012, p. 9). In 2019, there were 2117 Catholic schools in England; that is to say, 825,032 pupils are educated in Catholic schools, of which 65% of pupils and 49% of teachers are Catholic (CES, 2019). It is this steadily declining number of Catholic pupils and Catholic staff that potentially impact on the mission integrity of Catholic schools. Mission integrity describes the connection or lack of between the Catholic mission and the practice; it is fidelity in practice and not just in public rhetoric to Catholic education's distinctive and authentic principles (Grace, 2010). Grace envisages that the renewal of spiritual capital is needed to sustain mission integrity; it must necessarily be rooted 'into the distinctive and authentic principles of Catholic education' (2010, p. 194). Researching spiritual capital in schools illuminates this connection between Catholic mission and practice. Detailed empirical research in school could provide evidence of where and how spiritual capital is changing, declining, or renewed.

However, researching spiritual capital is very problematic as it is not easily measurable or quantifiable.[4] Religious capital is more easily measurable in evidence of practice, such as how closely connected individuals are through the numbers attending Sunday Mass. Spiritual capital is open to a variety of interpretations, and short-term measures are of limited use. Individuals have different interpretations of what it is to be Catholic and personal witness to the faith tradition may take many forms. Within Catholic education there exists 'an internal culture divided on the conception of a "satisfactory realisation of Catholicity in a school"' (Grace, 2010, p. 20). Grace (2002) quotes Greeley's (1998) observation that perhaps the outcome is only fully apparent in mature adult lives and behaviour. However, the qualitative case study method may be particularly appropriate in researching spiritual outcome; it is close to practice, and aims 'to understand human behaviour at ever increasing depth and to communicate this deepening understanding to others' (Nesbitt, 2004, p. 5). Research in Catholic education working in partnership with school leaders, listening to their stories and those of other members of Catholic school community, is invaluable in understanding how individuals are acquiring spiritual capital, and the processes of generation and transmission. Accepting that there are many challenges researching spiritual capital, there are some fruitful published examples, but there are also some areas in urgent need of research. To consider first examples of fruitful research with school leaders, the changes from the generation of spiritual capital by Religious Orders to lay Catholic leaders has proved a fruitful vein for research. Catholic school leaders face many challenges in today's complex, ever-changing field of education; they are involved in constant negotiations between secular and sacred interests. Grace (2010) makes it clear that Catholic school leaders have a particular responsibility to be faith leaders as well as professional leaders and guardians of the mission integrity of Catholic schools and colleges internationally. Research with school leaders offers a fruitful method of exploring how the resource of spiritual capital is changing within Catholic schools. In Grace's own research with head teachers as detailed in *Mission, Markets and Morality* (2002), he identified the change in spiritual capital as the lay head teachers drew on personal spiritual capital acquired from their education by Religious Orders. Research into the spiritual capital in school leadership undertaken by leading practising head teachers (Friel, 2018; Wilkin, 2018) has highlighted the need for renewal of spiritual capital in Catholic education. Wilkin's (2018) empirical research detailed the challenges faced by Catholic head teachers in the English education sector: the changing political priorities, market competition compounded by parental choice, and the accountability to Ofsted (Office for Standards in Education, Children's Services and Skills). Wilkin examined how head teachers draw on their resource of spiritual capital 'to ensure that the Church maintains its links with young people' (2018, p. 164). He identified a significant role for Catholic head teachers as 'interpreters of the Church's mission for young people, and of young people for the Church, offers an opportunity for the future' (p. 174). This idea of interpretation is key; it raises concerns, highlighted earlier, that spiritual capital is more fluid and open to interpretation than religious capital. It highlights that renewing the spiritual capital of Catholic lay educators, and ensuring it is clearly rooted in the Catholic tradition, is an urgent priority.

Friel (2018) sought to evaluate how two national initiatives in England and Wales, (the National Retreat for Catholic Head teachers and the National School of Formation) impacted on the spiritual capital of head teachers. He concluded that head teachers in his study were drawing on personal resources of spiritual capital, but there was a clear need to renew these resources, as these resources are maintaining rather than developing or deepening their spiritual lives. Friel's research found evidence that Catholic head teachers' spiritual capital was inspired by a new type of formation programme. Those who had participated saw themselves as ministers of the Gospel providing an education for young people which encourages them to be 'agents of change' and to use the qualities and skills they develop in a rich curriculum in Catholic schools for the transformational service of the world, especially of the marginalised and poor (Friel, 2018, p. 92). Such research offers a promise of evidence-based ways for the renewal of spiritual capital within school leadership. It also highlights the need for more research into other members of the Catholic school community.

Grace's concept of spiritual capital has the potential to illuminate where spiritual capital is held by other members of the school community such as 'school governing bodies, in classroom teachers, in priests, in school chaplains, in parents and not least in the students themselves' (Grace, 2002, p. 238). While there has been limited research in this area, Catholic schools ideally work with home and parish to transmit the faith tradition to the next generation; both these areas are potential contributors to the renewal of spiritual capital in schools. Research is required into a variety of key contributors to the Catholic mission of the school; the parish priest, chaplain, or lay workers in retreat centres, foundation governors, and the family. For example, foundation governors, often parents, or grandparents and members of the local parish could have a critical role in renewing spiritual capital. In English and Welsh Catholic schools, foundation governors are appointed by the Bishop, or Religious Order, to represent their interests and those of the Catholic community. They are expected to implement the Bishop's policies on education and promote the distinctive nature of Catholic education (CES, 2020). There is a paucity of research on the role of Foundation Governors in English Catholic schools. Storr (2009) undertook a study of 100 foundation governors, which highlighted their perception that spiritual capital is declining in Catholic schools. Storr's finding that the governors made little or no reference to teachings of the Catholic Church from the Congregation for Catholic Education or the Bishops' Conference (p. 225), in their work of promoting the distinctive nature of Catholic education, suggests there is potential here for research into ways of renewing spiritual capital of school governors.[5]

That has been little research into the renewal of spiritual capital in young people, perhaps because of the difficulty of 'measurement', but also because it is often unclear how to approach this research area. This neglect needs to be addressed. It is vital to understand the effect of renewal of spiritual capital within Catholic school leadership on the student population, but also to investigate how young people acquire and generate spiritual capital rooted in the Catholic faith tradition. Young people are active agents, potential generators of spiritual capital.

One study that did seek evidence of spiritual capital within the Catholic student community analysed students' experience of Mass in English Catholic secondary schools through the lens of religious and spiritual capital. Casson (2013) differentiated between religious and spiritual capital, with the former seen as a means of ensuring attachment to the Catholic faith tradition, while the latter focused on students' expression of personal rather than 'institutional spirituality'(Rossiter, 2010, p. 130). Reconsidering the findings from this research, it could be argued that they suggest evidence of Grace's interpretation of spiritual capital and that students' experience of Mass within the secondary school can be a source of spiritual capital. However, further research is needed into the extent to which this spiritual capital animates and empowers young people to be witnesses to the Catholic faith tradition. There is potential to explore how spiritual capital as vocational empowerment to witness and animate Catholic education is received by Catholic students, how they acquire and generate spiritual capital, and how does spiritual capital within the student body function to sustain the Catholic mission. There is a need to undertake research in programmes directed at the formation of young people, or investigate the areas that young people identify as potential sources of their spiritual capital.

Without doubt, the work of Gerald Grace has had an impact on Catholic education research in the UK. The articulation of a theoretical framework for research in Catholic education offers Catholic education the opportunity to present the necessary intellectual and cultural defence. In this context, the concept of spiritual capital, rooted in theory, but with a focus on relevance and application in practice has been invaluable. This reflects a key focus of Grace's work, that of Catholic education in practice; in what ways does an understanding of theories and concepts such as spiritual capital illuminate how Catholic schooling functions in changing and challenging circumstances, and make visible the Catholic mission of Catholic education in practice in Catholic schools, colleges, and universities?

Grace has also actively encouraged empirical research within Catholic schools, actively supporting researchers in the field, for example practising school leaders. Research in Catholic school leadership is providing vital insights into the changes that are taking place within Catholic schools. However, there is an urgent need for further research into to what extent spiritual capital is transforming or is in decline and how successful programmes of renewal within Catholic education are. Spiritual capital research needs to widen in scope; investigation of other sections of Catholic school communities could provide a rich source of data on the nature of spiritual capital in Catholic education. The legacy of Gerald Grace's work on spiritual capital is invaluable, sparking continuing empirical research in the field of Catholic education.

Notes

1 See Bourdieu (1986) and (1991).
2 Grace makes an important qualification that states 'Spiritual Capital in this definition is a resource of faith and values possessed by *all* faith-based schools and not only by Catholic ones' (see Grace (2002) p. 262, Note 1).
3 This does not imply 'indoctrination' of students, it rather refers to a Christian 'way of being' in the classroom, e.g. social relations and care of students.

4 Sustained efforts are needed in the future from interdisciplinary teams including education researchers, theologians, religious studies specialists and in-service teachers of religious education (and school chaplains) to find sensitive ways of evaluating 'spiritual growth' in our secondary schools.
5 This is a crucial area for development. School governors (with headteachers) are the ultimate source guarding the mission integrity of Catholic schools. The spiritual capital resource of governors needs more attention from the Church.

References

Baker, C., and Skinner, H. (2006). *Faith in Action: The Dynamic Connection between Spiritual and Religious Capital*. Chester: The William Temple Foundation.

Bourdieu, P. (1986). The forms of capital. In *Handbook of Theory and Research for the Sociology of Education* (Ed. J. Richardson), pp. 241–255. New York: Greenwood Press.

Bourdieu, P. (1991). Genesis and structures of the religious field. *Comparative Social Research*, 13, pp. 1–44.

Buchanan, M. T. (2020). Teacher education: What Australian Christian schools need and what higher education delivers. *International Journal of Christianity & Education*, 24:1, pp. 96–107.

Buck, M. (2018). The ambiguous embrace: The pros and cons of accepting government funding. In *Researching Catholic Education* (Ed. S. Whittle), pp. 127–138. Singapore: Springer.

Bullivant, S. (2016). Catholic disaffiliation in Britain: A quantitative overview. *Journal of Contemporary Religion*, 31:2, pp. 181–197.

Casson, A. (2013). 'Religious' and 'spiritual capitals: The experience of the celebration of Mass in the English Catholic secondary school. *International Studies in Catholic Education*, 5:2, pp. 204–217.

Catholic Education Service (CES) (2019). *Census Digest*. Available from www.catholiceducation.org.uk/images/CensusDigestEngland2019.pdf.

Catholic Education Service (CES) (2020). *Governance of a Catholic School: A Clarification of Roles and Responsibilities for England & Wales*. Available from www.catholiceducation.org.uk/guidance-for-schools/governance/item/1003612-governance-of-a-catholic-school.

Congregation for Catholic Education (CCE) (1977). *The Catholic School*. Available from www.vatican.va/roman_curia/congregations/ccatheduc/documents/rc_con_ccatheduc_doc_19770319_catholic-school_en.html.

Congregation for Catholic Education (CCE) (1982). *Lay Catholics in Schools: Witnesses to Faith*. Vatican: St. Paul.

D'Souza, M. O., CSB. (2012). The spiritual dimension of Catholic education. *International Studies in Catholic Education*, 4:1, pp. 92–105.

Davies, D. J., & Guest, M. (2007). *Bishops, Wives and Children: Spiritual Capital across the Generations*. London: Routledge.

Dillon, M. (2001). Pierre Bourdieu, religion, and cultural production. *Cultural Studies? Critical Methodologies*, 1:4, pp. 411–429.

Friel, R. (2018). Renewing spiritual capital: The National Retreat for Catholic Headteachers and the National School of Formation: The impact on Catholic head teachers in the UK. *International Studies in Catholic Education*, 10:1, pp. 81–96.

Giordan, G. (2007). Spirituality: From a religious concept to a sociological theory. In *A Sociology of Spirituality* (Ed. P. C. Jupp and K. Flanagan), pp.161–180. London: Routledge

Grace, G. (2002). *Catholic Schools: Mission, Markets, and Morality*. London: Routledge.

Grace, G. (2009). On the international study of Catholic education: Why we need more systematic scholarship and research. *International Studies in Catholic Education*, 1:1, pp. 6–14.

Grace, G. (2010). Renewing spiritual capital: An urgent priority for the future of Catholic education internationally. *International Studies in Catholic Education*, 2:2, pp. 117–128.

Grace, G. (2015). *Faith, Mission and Challenge in Catholic Education: The Selected Works of Gerald Grace*. London: Routledge.

Guest, M. (2007). In search of spiritual capital: The spiritual as a cultural resource. In *A Sociology of Spirituality* (Ed. P. C. Jupp and K. Flanagan), pp. 181–200. London: Routledge.

Lydon, J. (2009). Transmission of the charism: A major challenge for Catholic education. *International Studies in Catholic Education*, 1:1, pp. 42–58.

Nesbitt, E. (2004). *Intercultural Education: Ethnographic and Religious Approaches*. Brighton: Sussex Academic Press Parker-Jenkins.

Rossiter, G. (2010). Perspective on contemporary spirituality: Implications for religious education in Catholic schools. *International Studies in Catholic Education*, 2:2, pp. 129–147.

Stock, M. (2012). *Christ at the Centre: Why the Church Provides Catholic Schools*. London: Catholic Truth Society.

Storr, C. (2009) Governing Catholic schools: An English case study, *International Studies in Catholic Education*, 1:2, pp. 214–227.

Verter, B. (2003) Spiritual capital: Theorizing religion with Bourdieu against Bourdieu. *Sociological Theory*, 21:2, pp. 150–174.

Wilkin, R. (2018). Interpreting the tradition. In *Researching Catholic Education* (Ed. S. Whittle), pp. 169–178. Springer: Singapore.

Chapter 6

Professor Gerald Grace and the concept of 'spiritual capital'

Reflections on its value and suggestions for its future development

John Lydon

Introduction

In so far as Religious Orders were responsible for promoting education for all from the 18th century to Vatican II, teaching was synonymous with professed members of Religious Orders dedicated to teaching the poor after the pattern of Christ (Wilson, 1883, p. 34), who demonstrated 'ardour and fervent dedication' (Congregation for Catholic Education (CCE), 1997, par. 15). *The Catholic School on the Threshold of the Third Millennium* refers specifically to four Religious Orders as setting the standard for the Church's mission, particularly to the marginalised.[1] Rather than 'hoarding the precious treasure as though obsessed with the past',[2] Gerald Grace (2002), developing from the sociological constructs of Pierre Bourdieu, speaks of the significance of the spiritual and cultural capital of Religious Orders in providing a significant dynamic in the development of Catholic education.

The nature and definition of spiritual capital

In *The Forms of Capital* (1997), Bourdieu begins by arguing for an inclusive rather a reductionist view of 'capital', defining the concept as a reality broader than a reserve of wealth in the form of money or property owned by a person or business and human resources of economic value. He suggests that capital presents itself in three further fundamental guises beyond the narrow confines of accumulated pecuniary assets available for use in the production of further monetary assets to embrace social, cultural and religious capital. Bourdieu defines social capital as made up of social obligations ('connections') which is convertible, in certain conditions, into economic capital, thus reflecting a funda-mental Bourdieusian belief in an interdependent relationship between the three forms of capital: economic, social and cultural. He also, in 1991, developed a fourth form of capital, i.e. 'religious capital', against which Grace developed spiritual capital.[3]

In the context of Grace's use of Bourdieu, the concept of cultural capital is more germane. Bourdieu argues that cultural capital exists in three forms:[4]

DOI: 10.4324/9781003171553-8

- Embodied state – in the form of long-lasting dispositions of the mind and body
- Objectified state – in the form of cultural goods
- Institutionalised state – in the form, for example, of educational qualifications.

Bourdieu claims that he developed the notion of cultural capital to explain the unequal academic achievement of students from different social classes rather than uphold the traditional view that academic achievement was simply the consequence of innate ability or aptitude. In a tangential attempt to explain why some schools appear to have maintained a distinctive Catholic ethos it would, presumably, be possible to include mission statements and written accounts of distinctive charisms of, for example, Religious Orders, in the 'objective state' category in so far as they constitute an articulation of the lived reality (an 'embodiment' of) of such charisms. With regard to the institutionalised state, the schools which have emerged as a result of the long-lasting dispositions of members of Religious Orders could be regarded as having accrued cultural capital in this context, representing the expression of the distinctive charism or ethos by a living institution or community.

Of the three forms of cultural capital, the 'embodied state' resonates most distinctively with Grace's use of Bourdieu who, in articulating the concept of cultural capital, refers to the renunciation and sacrifice that may be involved in acquiring it. He recognises that embodied cultural capital is, to an extent, conditioned by a person's social background. He also recognises, however, that such capital can be acquired by access to education and that such acquisition will be critically dependent on the extent to which an individual can gain access to education. Bourdieu suggests that a family 'endowed with strong cultural capital' is a necessary 'precondition for the fast accumulation of cultural capital', thereby highlighting the importance of the family in promoting the acquisition of cultural capital (1997, pp, 48–50). Bourdieu also articulates the link between strong cultural capital and the building up of economic capital.

Tom Inglis (1998), in his book on the rise and fall of the Catholic Church in the Republic of Ireland, applies Bourdieusian principles to the way in which religious capital was built up by Catholics in order to guarantee access to other forms of capital. Developing Bourdieu's fundamental principle regarding the interdependence of the different forms of capital, Inglis demonstrates that the most successful people, socially and politically, in the Ireland of the 19th and the 20th century up to the 1960s, ensured that they embodied the Church's teaching and traditional rituals, recognising that such an embodiment was important in being socially accepted and gaining respect.

Like Inglis, Grace builds on Bourdieu's concept of cultural and religious capital in his adoption of the term 'spiritual capital'. Having interviewed sixty Catholic headteachers in three different cities in the United Kingdom, in the final chapter of his book Grace provides the first formal definition of spiritual capital: 'Spiritual capital is defined here as resources of faith and values derived from commitment to a religious tradition' (2002, p. 236).

Grace is, in effect, expressing a certain embodied quality which he had encountered when interviewing his sample of headteachers, a quality which becomes a 'source of empowerment because it provides a transcendent impulse which can guide judgement and action in the mundane world' (2002, p. 236). He maintains this spiritual capital is derived from the prior formation experienced by those headteachers in their secondary schools and teacher training colleges, with a particularly powerful influence arising from the various Religious Orders present in these institutions. His assertion that the building up of such capital has a positive effect on the maintenance of Catholic distinctiveness in schools is analogous to Inglis' assertion regarding the positive effect of religious capital on the maintenance of distinctive Catholic communities in Ireland in the period under review. Linking with Grace's *resources of faith* idea, Michael O'Sullivan (2012) includes Religious Congregations in his list of 'resources of faith' alongside the Bible, Church traditions, the resources of theology and spirituality, Christian scholars, practitioners, practices, publications, martyrs, missionaries and international networks of Christian faith-based organisations. O'Sullivan's definition of spiritual capital as 'a society's capacity for authentic social change' links spiritual and religious capital, reflecting Inglis' description of the Ireland of the 19th and 20th centuries referenced previously (1998, p. 45).

The embodiment of spiritual capital

While Grace recognises that the building up of spiritual capital will, in the first place, involve a knowledge of the deposit of, in this case, the Catholic faith, the crucial nature of such capital resides in the ability of school leaders to embody such capital. He refers to this specifically in his enriched definition of spiritual capital (Grace, 2010, p. 120) encompassing personal witness to faith in practice, action and relationships. In other words, the extent to which spiritual capital constitutes a source for empowerment will be in proportion to the extent to which headteachers embody such a resource by demonstrating a personal faith commitment together with an ability to make that which is spiritual and transcendent a living reality in dealing the mission of everyday life in schools. In the context of Grace's work in general, the efficacy of such capital will be tested most rigorously by the extent to which schools are able to maintain a distinctively Catholic culture in the face of the relentless challenges posed by the pervading culture of consumerism, which Grace highlights as a potentially corrupting influence (see Grace, 2002, pp. 180–204). In 2010, Grace published an article giving a more detailed analysis of spiritual capital, and his position can be summed in these terms:

- resources of faith and values derived from a vocational commitment to a religious tradition (in this case the Catholic tradition);
- a source of vocational empowerment because it provides a transcendent awareness that can guide judgement and action in the mundane world so that those whose own formation has involved the acquisition of spiritual capital do not act in education simply as professionals but as professionals and witnesses;
- a form of spirituality in which the whole of human life is viewed in terms of a conscious relationship with God, in Jesus Christ and the saints, through the indwelling of the Spirit;
- a form of spirituality which has been the animating, inspirational and dynamic spirit which has empowered the mission of Catholic education internationally largely (although not exclusively) through the work of Religious Congregations with missions in education in the past;
- a form of spirituality now in urgent need of renewal in the contemporary world of Catholic education faced with growing secularisation, ideologies of secularism, global marketisation and materialism and the decline of Religious Congregations in the field of education;
- a form of spirituality which needs to be reconstituted in lay school leaders and teachers by formation programmes which help them to be Catholic witnesses for Christ and not simply professional deliverers of knowledge and skills as required by the secular state and the secular market.

Grace's emphasis on empowerment reflects definitions of spiritual capital in other contexts which resonate with concepts explored in this chapter. For example, D'Souza suggests that spiritual capital means 'power, influence and disposition [habitus] created by a person's or an organisation's spiritual belief' (2012, p. 160) while Baker (2012, p. 7) speaks of the transformative influence of spiritual capital. In reviewing and contrasting research in Catholic education in the pre- and post-Vatican II periods, Grace articulates findings which point to the extent to which a distinctive Catholic ethos has had a positive influence on behaviour and academic outcomes. He does not, however, explore in any depth specific characteristics in respect of individual leaders in relation to the resources of faith that contribute to such an ethos or culture, the latter being Grace's preferred term. It could also be argued that Grace focuses on the influence of headteachers as opposed to leadership teams or core groups of committed teachers. He does, in fact, recognise this in asserting that 'the resources of spiritual capital in Catholic schooling extend well beyond the that possessed by individual headteachers' (2002, p. 38). He goes onto to suggest that senior leaders can be, in some schools, embodiments of spiritual capital (Grace, 2008).

Links with Aquinas, Groome and Flynn: *Habitus*, depth structures and culture

Notwithstanding these limitations, the concept of spiritual capital as articulated by Grace is regarded by James Arthur as 'a major insight or thesis in the context of maintaining the mission and integrity of Catholic schooling' (2002, p. 1). In attempting to draw out what is constituted by the concept of 'spiritual capital' in relation to the individual headteacher, Grace draws on Bourdieu's (1990) use of the term *habitus* by which he means a lasting, general and adaptable way of thinking and acting in conformity to a systematic worldview. In defining *habitus* as deep-structured cultural dispositions within a community or institution, Grace's use of the term disposition resonates not only with Bourdieu's ideas but also with Aquinas' concept of habitus or disposition as an abiding characteristic in relation to the individual person.

The theme that *habitus* is a perennial as opposed to a transitional reality constitutes a seamless connection between the work of Bourdieu and Grace on the one hand and Aquinas on the other. Grace's use of the term 'deep-structured' further resonates with Groome's concept of the depth structures of Catholicism. Groome (1998) argues that the most effective schools have a characteristic set of ideals, most notably that they value people, they are optimistic about people and society, they promote community and relationships, they help to develop spirituality, they emphasise issues of justice and peace, they respect diversity, and they teach critical thinking. For Groome, these values arise out of the *depth structures* or *core-convictions* of Christianity and they are embedded deeply in the ethos and style (what can be called the total culture) of the school.

The connection between Grace/Bourdieu's use of the term *habitus* and that of Aquinas is encapsulated by Groome when he suggests that the characteristics of the depth structures of Catholicism 'often exist beneath Catholic Christianity's institutional expression or accidental features. *Much as the deep structures of people's characters shape who they are*, so the depth structures of Catholicism combine as its distinctiveness, albeit with varied expressions' (1998, p. 56; emphasis added).

The concept of *habitus* is linked intimately with that of school culture since the latter derives from the collective contributions of members of a particular school community. Cook (2003) makes the claim that when religious communities staffed Catholic schools, socialisation of teachers occurred naturally as the religious communities went about their work. He then goes on to emphasise the significance of communities of religious in designing and building Catholic culture in the Catholic schools of the USA.

While a full discussion around the nature of culture is beyond the scope of this chapter, it is interesting to note that the following definitions of culture, on the one hand, and Catholic culture on the other are linked in that both emphasise the importance of 'embodiment'. One definition of culture is 'the system of values, symbols and shared meanings of a group including the *embodiment* of these values, symbols and meanings' (Sergiovanni and Corbally, 1994, p. viii; emphasis added), echoing Groome's description of 'depth structures'. Alternatively, Flynn's (1993, p. 39) definition of Catholic school culture reflects the first definition, replacing the word 'embodiment' with a more specific reference to the activity of the members of the school community and its formative influence:

The culture of a Catholic school expresses the core beliefs, values, traditions, symbols and patterns of behaviour which provide meaning to the school community and which help to shape the lives of students, teachers and parents. In short it is the way we do things round here.

(Flynn, 1993, p. 39)

Spiritual capital and vocation

Grace argues cogently that spiritual capital is derived from the past school leaders and teachers who have been immersed in the *habitus* of the depth structures of the Catholic school system, particularly that found within schools sponsored by Religious Orders. Such spiritual capital has, according to Grace, benefitted the Catholic educational mission internationally, particularly in the context of Catholic school leadership. He then goes on to suggest that the leadership modelled by members of Religious Orders has led to the promotion of a sense of vocation among Catholic school teachers and leaders and, as a result of programmes of formation, led to the realisation that the mission of a teacher constitutes being both a 'professional and a witness' (Grace, 2002, p. 134). The sense in which having a vocation and being a professional are, in essence, simply aspects of the pathway of discipleship seems to be encapsulated in the two references to the word 'vocation' found in Vatican II's Declaration on Christian Education:

> Beautiful indeed and of great importance is the vocation of all those who aid parents in fulfilling their duties and who, as representatives of the human community, undertake the task of education in schools. This vocation demands special qualities of mind and heart, very careful preparation, and continuing readiness to renew and to adapt.
>
> (*Gravissimum Educationis*, 1965, par. 5)

The notion of witness reflects the sacramental perspective, that all ministry should be modelled on that of Christ, in the context of discipleship and the call to all the baptised to share in His divine life. While the sacramental perspective in general is rooted in the Incarnation and expresses the belief that God is encountered in the world through the mediated presence of Christ and the Church, more specifically in the context of Catholic education this perspective focuses on the person of the teacher who, in essence, models his or her ministry on that of Christ. Both Cook and Grace recognise that the intensive formation programmes of Religious Orders ensured that teachers were immersed in the culture of their particular Congregation and, while there were distinctive characteristics within such cultures, the notion of modelling or emulation constituted a consistent paradigm.

Spiritual capital: Going beyond Gerald Grace

Scholarship around the concept of spiritual capital has been referred to in this chapter. This section of the chapter will focus on recent articles published in *International Studies in Catholic Education*. In an article entitled 'Religious and 'Spiritual' Capitals: The Experience of the Celebration of Mass in the English Catholic Secondary School' Casson argues that the celebration of Mass in school may function as a means of maintaining the memory of the Catholic faith tradition. Casson refers to Grace twelve times in the article, acknowledging the cogency of his enriched definition of spiritual capital and noting his assertion that 'in twenty-first century England, the transmission of the Catholic faith through family and parish is considerably weakened, and in many cases not there at all' (Grace, 2002, p. 237). Casson examines the experience of Eucharistic liturgy in three Catholic secondary schools through the lens of religious and spiritual capital. She found that all of the students in the schools participated in the celebration of the Eucharist and regarded it as being for all members of the school. The view that the Eucharist contributed significantly to the building of community within the schools was expressed frequently by both students and staff involved in the study:

> A view expressed frequently by all participants was that the celebration of Mass within school engendered a 'sense of community' within the Catholic school. A 'sense of community' is a key factor in the development of social capital. The findings discussed here suggest that the community was focused solely on the Catholic school, rather than the traditional trinity of school, parish and family. Nevertheless this 'sense of community' enabled these Catholic secondary schools to maintain a Catholic ethos within the school; it enabled Catholic liturgies to take place and gave students space and time to encounter Catholicism.
>
> (Casson, 2013, pp. 211–212)

It could be argued that Casson is responding to one of the criticisms of Grace's work expressed earlier by citing the celebration of Mass as a specific characteristic of a *resource of faith*. She concludes by suggesting that celebrations of the ritual of Mass are still occurring in Catholic secondary schools and could be viewed as a source of spiritual capital for many students. The Catholic school does appear to generate spiritual capital, giving young people a resource of Catholic beliefs, Catholic values and attitudes that they can use and develop in their future lives (Casson, 2013). The centrality of the celebration of the Eucharist in generating spiritual capital permeates Casson's article but much more research will need to establish if this is the case for all Catholic schools.

In 'Renewing Spiritual Capital: The National Retreat for Catholic Headteachers and the National School of Formation: The Impact on Catholic Headteachers in the UK', Raymond Friel (2018) explores the concept of 'spiritual capital' among the headteachers and to evaluate the impact of two major new initiatives in England and Wales: the National Retreat for Catholic Headteachers and the National School of Formation He cites Grace twenty-three times, arguably the most cogent being his connecting the work of Grace and Richardson:

> The need was for more spiritual resources to support Catholic headteachers in the ministry of leadership, to help them grow in holiness. Richardson (2014) in his research into the theological dispositions of Catholic head-teachers concluded that their dominant disposition was 'relational', very much in line with Grace's (2010) expanded definition of spiritual capital. They have a relationship with God and other people. One of the main traits associated with this disposition was 'less concern with being faithful to a set of beliefs and more concern with living faithfully in the light of the teaching of Jesus Christ under the guidance of the Church'.
>
> (Richardson, 2014, p. 69)

In focusing on the impact of the National School for Formation (NSF) on nurturing spiritual capital among headteachers, Friel refers to what he sees as a pedagogy in the CCE's 1988 document *Lay Catholics in Schools: Witnesses to Faith*, which he suggests focuses on the relational aspects of spiritual develop-ment as opposed to the doctrinal. Such points of reference included, classically, upbringing, which has been a feature of the Church's education mission since the time of St Thomas Aquinas[5] and featured prominently in Grace's 2002 study. Friel goes on to describe a small-scale research study (built around a questionnaire to twenty headteachers, effectively mirroring Grace's methodol-ogy in 2002). Friel's analysis of his results indicates that the respondents tended to emphasise the positive impact of local and global Catholic social action as resources for faith development as opposed to the Church's teaching on educa-tion or doctrinal issues. One headteacher respondent explained that the goal of Catholic education is to produce good Christians who go on to make the world more peaceful. This chimes well with the seminal aim of the Salesian educa-tional system, which permeates the primary and secondary Salesian sources, with Bosco's axiom honest citizens and good Christians.[6] Marketisation and the hegemony of performativity feature among the challenges expressed by head-teachers in Friel's research and have featured prominently in Grace's writings since his decision to devote his life to researching Catholic education principles.

I would add two further observations, first in relation to the 'anchor' of this emphasis on the relational, without which a degree of subjectivity could emerge in relation to the axiomatic characteristics of a Catholic spirituality for head-teachers. It could be argued that being 'anchored' in a particular tradition has served the Church's education mission well since the emergence of mass state-funded education in the modern period, reflected strongly in Grace's scholarship on spiritual capital. Second, a greater emphasis on the way in which headteachers might model this relational spirituality for the benefit of their school communities would be illuminative, reflecting the point made above, regarding the realising in practice of a spiritual and transcendent reality. This could relate, for example, to appointments to key positions within the school and the extent to which performance management is engaged through a Catholic lens.[7]

Spiritual capital: Contemporary challenges

Part of Grace's 2002 analysis was to draw attention to the significant decline in members of Religious Congregations and Orders working in Catholic schools, and to dwell on possible implications for spiritual capital. However, two decades on, the issue has shifted to the decline in the numbers of baptised Catholics attending Catholic schools. Some, such as Arthur (2013), question whether or not there is still a critical mass of English Catholic parents, teachers and pupils associated with Catholic schooling who are able and willing to sustain and ensure the Church's unique teaching on the educational purpose of presenting a Catholic worldview to children. The last part of this chapter will focus on Catholic teachers and the extent to which spiritual capital is being accrued among a critical mass in order to sustain the Catholic Church's distinctive educational vision.

Defining a *critical mass* presents the first challenge. The *Catholic Education Service* (CES) insists that, in primary and secondary schools, the headteacher, deputy heads and the head (co-ordinator) of religious education 'are to be filled by baptised and practising Catholics' (McMahon, 2009, p. 1). This must constitute a minimum and one would presume that the School Chaplain would also be included in this category. The CES, in its latest published census (2019, p. 5), reports that overall 49% of teachers in maintained schools in England and Wales are Catholics, constituting 55.5% of primary teachers and 40% of secondary teachers. The statistics do not, however, affirm whether or not these teachers are practising Catholics.[8]

If Grace Davie (1994) is right in suggesting that Europe is marked by a culture of 'believing without belonging', characterised by a profound mismatch between religious values that people profess (believing), and actual churchgoing and religious practice (belonging), it has a challenge for Catholic education. Not least, it could be postulated that the religious lives of a proportion of the overall 49% of Catholic teachers will not be practising Catholics (as defined by Stock, 2012)[9]. While it may be an overstatement to suggest that the majority have moved from an institutionally Catholic identity to a more autonomous search for spirituality, one of the key questions for Catholic school leaders revolves around the promotion and maintenance of spiritual capital as an empowering and motivating reality. In other words, perhaps a critical moment has been reached. The priority now is to move from defining spiritual capital to researching effective means of sustaining it.

Conclusion: Spiritual capital – The primacy of witness

I have argued elsewhere (see Lydon, 2009) that, for schools with Religious Order trusteeships, it is possible to transmit the distinctive charism of the Order to committed lay people, primarily by the modelling of that charism by both religious (when present) and committed lay people. Evidence suggests (Lydon, 2009) that the majority of teachers in networks of schools founded by Religious Congregations are dedicated to maintaining the charism. They can do this in a way which retains a school's Catholic mission, despite being in a culture marked by an ever-increasing emphasis on performativity.

A second strategy could focus on a reservoir of recently retired Catholic headteachers who possess this capital. This could involve the creation of a project, ideally organised by the *Catholic Education Service*, within which such headteachers could have a critical influence on their successors. This might be an effective way of ensuring that future Catholic school leaders are theologically literate. Moreover, this could open a window for the formation of aspiring deputy heads involving recently retired heads.

It is apparent that headteachers place a greater deal of emphasis on the impact of modelling Catholic identity rather than formation programmes for aspiring heads. This point is deeply relevant to spiritual capital and Catholic schools and resonates with this author's previous research (2009) in which headteachers in Salesian schools were convinced that their distinctive ethos would be maintained by living it rather than talking about it. Talk, rather than action, is significant only in a supportive sense, contributing to solidarity around a common witness modelled on the lives of teachers themselves. This resonates with the key themes discussed throughout this chapter: community, embodiment and witness.

Going beyond Grace's emphasis on the role of headteachers in sustaining spiritual capital, I would argue that it will ultimately be maintained through the empowering witness of a core group of committed teachers. In fact, these will not necessarily all be Catholic, who have themselves been empowered to model what Flynn and Mok (2002) describe as the core beliefs, values, traditions, symbols and patterns of behaviour which provide meaning to the school community. Such example, more than words, will ensure that spiritual capital will remain a source of empowerment, helping Catholic school leaders to act as professionals *and* witnesses.

Notes

1 *The Catholic School on the Threshold of the Third Millennium* (1997) refers specifically to four Religious Orders: De La Salle Brothers, Piarists, Salesians and Ursulines
2 Quotation of Pope John XXIII in Hebblethwaite P., (1994), *John XXIII*, London: Harper Collins, p. 431.
3 Grace makes a strong distinction between Bourdieu's concept of 'religious capital' which equals 'power over' and his concept of 'spiritual capital' which equals 'power

to animate others in mission. This is a facilitating capital rather than a dominating one. See Grace (2010).

4 For further development of the relationship between the three forms of capital see Silva and Edwards, (2005).

5 In this context, it is also worth noting that the CCE's reference to forming young people to be 'agents of change' being part of the NSF pedagogy has, in fact, been the *raison d'être* of teaching Religious Congregations from the outset. This is reflected in the CCE's affirming comments about the impact of religious in schools and its profound regret regarding the diminution of the presence of teaching religious (see CCE, 1982, par. 4 for more details).

6 See Lydon (2009: 168ff) where he discusses the role of parents in Catholic tradition. He makes the point that Aquinas speaks of parental responsibility as a lifelong obligation extending beyond economic support to include all aspects of formation. In this regard, Aquinas appears to use the terms 'nurture', 'upbringing' and education as synonyms, implying that education transcends the boundaries of academic and technical education to encompass formation in virtue, which Aquinas refers to as the formation of the mind and the soul. He concludes by suggesting that, since the raising of children is a challenging process, particularly in regard to moral formation, both parents are required and this is a major reason, or *the* major reason, why marriage should be a permanent union.

7 Whilst teaching on the MA in Catholic School Leadership at St Mary's University, London, I lead discussions on the nature of a Catholic perspective in relation to performance management. In essence, staff should experience the dignity spoken of in the Bishops' Conference of England and Wales 1996 document ('Principles, Practices and Concerns') in terms of the relationship between staff and students. The experience should always be intrinsically positive.

8 A definition of practising Catholic is 'someone who has been sacramentally initiated into the Catholic Church and who adheres to those substantive life choices which do not impair them for receiving the sacraments of the Church and which will not in any way be detrimental or prejudicial to the religious ethos and character of the school' (Stock, 2009, p. 1).

9 Stock, now Bishop of Leeds, repeats this definition in his revised (2012) publication, *Christ at the Centre* (London, CTS).

References

Arthur, J., (2013). The De-Catholicising of the Curriculum in English Catholic Education, in *International Studies in Catholic Education* 5, 1, pp. 83–98.

Arthur, J., (2002). Review of *Catholic Schools: Mission Markets and Morality*, in *British Journal of Educational Studies*, 50, 4, pp. 503–504.

Baker, C., (2012). Exploring Spiritual Capital: Resource for an Uncertain Future. In O'Sullivan, M. & Flanagan , B. (Eds.), *Spiritual Capital*. Farnham: Ashgate.

Catholic Education Service (CES), (2019) *CES Digest of 2019 Census Data for Schools and Colleges in England*, London: CES.

Congregation for Catholic Education, (1982). *Lay Catholics in Schools: Witnesses to Faith*, London, CTS.

Bourdieu, P., (1997). The Forms of Capital. In Halsey, A. H., et al (Eds.), *Education: Culture, Economy, Society*, Oxford: Oxford University Press.

Bourdieu, P. (1990). *The Logic of Practice*, Cambridge: Polity Press.

Casson, A., (2013). 'Religious' and 'Spiritual' Capitals: The Experience of the Celebration of Mass in the English Catholic Secondary School, in *International Studies in Catholic Education*, 5, 2, pp. 204–217.

Congregation for Catholic Education (CCE), (1997). *The Catholic School on the Threshold of the Third Millennium*, London: CTS.

Cook, T., (2003). *Architects of School Culture*, Washington, D.C.: National Catholic Educational Association.

Davie, G., (1994). *Religion in Britain since 1945: Believing without Belonging*, Oxford: Blackwell.

D'Souza, S., (2012). Gardening as a Source of Spiritual Capital, in O'Sullivan, M. & Flanagan, B. (Eds.), *Spiritual Capital*, Farnham: Ashgate.

Flynn, M., (1993). *The Culture of Catholic Schools*, Homebush, NSW: St Paul.

Flynn, M. & Mok, M. (2002). *Catholic Schools 2000: A Longitudinal Study of Year 12 Students in Catholic Schools, 1972–1982–1990–1998*. Sydney, NSW: Catholic Education Commission.

Friel, R., (2018). Renewing Spiritual Capital: The National Retreat for Catholic Headteachers and the National School of Formation: The Impact on Catholic Headteachers in the UK, in *International Studies in Catholic Education* 10, 1, pp. 81–96.

Grace, G. (2008). Changes in the Classification and Framing of Education in Britain, 1950s to 2000s: An Interpretive Essay after Bernstein, in *Journal of Educational Administration and History* 40, 3, pp. 209–220.

Grace, G., (2010). Renewing Spiritual Capital: An Urgent Priority for the Future of Catholic Education Internationally, in *International Studies in Catholic Education* 2, 2, pp. 117–128.

Grace G., (2002). *Catholic Schools: Mission, Markets and Morality*, London: Routledge Falmer.

Gravissimum Educationis (1965). In Abbott, W., *Vatican Council II*, London: Geoffry Chapman.

Groome, T.H., (1998). *Educating for Life*, Allen, TX: Thomas More Press.

Inglis, T., (1998). *Moral Monopoly*, Dublin: University College Dublin Press.

Lydon, J., (2009). Transmission of the Charism: A Major Challenge for Catholic Education, in *International Studies in Catholic Education* 1, pp. 42–58.

McMahon, M. (2009). *Memorandum on Appointment of Teachers to Catholic Schools*, published on the Catholic Education Service website: www.cesew.org.uk/.

O'Sullivan, M., (2012) Spiritual Capital and the Turn to Spirituality, in O'Sullivan, M. & Flanagan, B. (Eds.), *Spirituality in Practice in Christian Perspective*, Farnham: Ashgate.

Richardson, C., (2014). The Theological Disposition of Lay Catholic Headteachers, in *International Studies in Catholic Education* 6, 2, pp. 60–74.

Sergiovanni T.J., & Corbally J.E., (1994). *Leadership and Organizational Culture*, Chicago: University of Illinois Press.

Silva, E.B., & Edwards, L. (2005). *Operationalizing Bourdieu on Capitals: A Discussion on 'The Construction of the Object'*, Manchester: Economic & Social Research Council.

Stock, M., (2012). *Christ at the Centre: Why the Church Provides Catholic Schools*, London: CTS.

Stock, M., (2009). *Catholic Schools and the Definition of a Practising Catholic*, Birmingham: Archdiocese of Birmingham Schools Commission.

Wilson, R.F., (1883). *The Christian Brothers*, London: Kegan Paul.

Chapter 7

Sociology and Catholic education

The contribution of Grace

Meg Maguire

Introduction: Understanding the social

In 1984, Gerald Grace published a set of essays in a collection called *Education and the City: Theory, History and Contemporary Practice*. In the first chapter he set out a challenge to sociologists of urban schooling where he foregrounded a central dilemma that continues to bedevil the sociology of education more widely; that is, should the focus be with a 'policy science' approach and improving practices and provision through the generation of 'constructive programmes' or rather, should the emphasis be on 'critical scholarship'?[1] Grace included an extract from C. Wright Mills to illuminate his response to this question – a perspective that he has refined over time and permeated into all of his writing and research. It is worth including this long extract right at the start of this chapter because it exemplifies the way in which Grace has always addressed innumerable educational matters through a social science and historical lens. It is the *leitmotif* in all he has done and in all he continues to do.

> Certain types of critics, by the way, judge work in social science according to whether or not its conclusions are gloomy or sunshiny, negative or constructive. These sunshine moralists want a lyric upsurge, at least at the end: they are made happy by a sturdy little mood of earnest optimism, out of which we step forward fresh and shining. But the world we are trying to understand does not make all of us politically hopeful and morally complacent, which is to say, that social scientists sometimes find it difficult to play the cheerful idiot. Personally I happen to be a very optimistic type, but I must confess that I have never been able to make up my mind about whether something is so or not in terms of whether or not it leads to good cheer. First, one tries to get it straight, to make an adequate statement – if it is gloomy, too bad; if it leads to hope, fine. In the meantime, to cry for the 'constructive programme' and the 'hopeful note' is often a sign of incapacity to face facts as they are even when they are decidedly unpleasant – and it is irrelevant to truth or falsity and to judgements of *proper work in social science*.
>
> (Mills, 1973, p. 89 cited in Grace, 1984, p, 43, my italics)

DOI: 10.4324/9781003171553-9

In *Faith, Mission and Challenge in Catholic Education: The Selected Works of Gerald Grace* (2016), a collection of Grace's highly influential writings in the area of Catholic Education Studies, a field which he has pioneered, this approach to 'proper social science' is powerfully evidenced. For example, influenced by the work of French sociologist Pierre Bourdieu, a theorist to whom he has returned many times, Grace identified and named the power and place of 'spiritual capital' in Catholic schools.[2] Through his interviews with sixty head teachers of Catholic schools, he illustrated the ways in which their vocational work was inspired by an 'animating form of spirituality' (Grace, 2010, p. 125). In this way, he took up and extended the theoretical frame of Bourdieu's notion of capitals, that is, various forms of assets, placing this approach firmly in the field of the Catholic school. While this feature of headship may seem *obvious* today and a core feature of positive leadership in any school, Grace combined sophisticated theoretical social science approaches with a grounded empirical exploration that recovered an ethical-moral pedagogical commitment in order to 'get things straighter' and clearer about Catholic headship. A feature of Grace's work has always been to relate theoretical ideas to empirical fieldwork in ways accessible to a wide range of readers.

Getting things straight

As I have already indicated, Gerald Grace has been writing and researching in the areas of educational policy, practice and provision for a considerable number of years. During this time, he has produced a substantial number of books, papers and reports. His contribution to the sociology of education has been wide ranging and inclusive but always with a central concern for the common good. His work has included some provocative challenges to educational thinking, particularly in some of his earlier work in urban sociology. His scholarship in the area of leadership in schools, while concentrating on the previously under-researched Catholic school system in England, has much to say to leaders of all schools everywhere concentrating as it does on matters of an ethics and morality that underpins headship. Those charged with leading other teachers and with the task of making wise choices and decisions have had their work celebrated as being centrally connected with a moral agenda (Grace, 2000). Grace has charted the complexities of headship and leadership with a specific focus on this work as one of 'mission integrity' in the Catholic school. However, he has always centred on the role these schools have to play in maintaining the common good and serving the needs of the poor – an interest reaching right back to his urban sociology of the 1970s onwards (Grace, 1978, p. 1984).

In preparing this chapter about aspects of the diverse and wide contributions made by Gerald Grace, as I have said, there are many different strands to his work that I could have selected for further discussion. However, what I want to do is concentrate on and explore his fascination both with Catholic education and the social sciences and the insights that social science can lend to the study of Catholic education. For this reason, in what now follows I will centre on one piece of his work that combines these two facets; a chapter entitled 'The Field of Catholic Education: Perspectives from Bourdieu and Bernstein' (Grace, 2002). In drawing on one piece from his vast set of publications, my intention is to foreground Gerald Grace's commitment to 'judgements of proper work in social science'.

Catholic education and the work of Bourdieu and Bernstein

In this chapter, Grace argues that the sociological study of Catholic schools and education provision has been 'relatively undeveloped and marginalised' (2002, p. 25). More specifically, he claims that at the time of writing (2002), very little work exploring the 'particular aspects of social theory to a deeper understanding of the field of Catholic education' had been undertaken, other than some keynote work in the US.[3] His argument is that ignoring the contribution that can be made through drawing on social theory may serve to position Catholicity in an ahistorical manner and reduce the capacity to produce a more powerful and reflexive account of the role and practices of Catholic education.

In the chapter, Grace draws on the work of Pierre Bourdieu and Basil Bernstein. I will start, as Grace does, by detailing the insights that he has taken from the work of Bourdieu and that he has applied to Catholic education. Bourdieu is perhaps most celebrated for his concepts or method of analysis; namely, his interwoven concepts of field, habitus and capital. Starting with 'field', Grace explains this concept as denoting 'a social and cultural space characterised by a particular activity' (2002, p. 26). So, for example, a school or a church can be a 'field'. Drawing on Bourdieu, Grace makes the case that any field constitutes a setting where power relations are struggled over and where symbolic power is exercised. As Grace points out, the history of the Catholic Church is replete with instances of power struggles and contestations between different factions, different popes and different anti-popes. He also claims that over time, despite any contradictory evidence, the overt discourse of the Catholic Church has stressed 'vocationalism, idealism, consensus, service and unity' (2002, p. 26). In this way, the Catholic Church has marginalised and erased any internal debates and contestations or any other 'difficulties' in case they 'disturbed' the faithful. The point and value of using the concept of field is that it 'compels' (2002, p. 27) Catholic educationalists to face up to these struggles and contestations as part of the real, agentic and sometimes messy social worlds of all institutions, organisations and fields. Reading this argument in 2020, with the knowledge of the abhorrent abuse of power underpinning international and institutionalised child sexual abuse cases in the Catholic Church now well established, even if not always dealt with fully and openly, demonstrates the need for honesty, dialogue and an admission of the dangers of power and an uncritical stance to ecclesiastical hierarchy. Situating the Church as a *field* where power relations and struggles over status and control characterise the struggle that takes place in order to appropriate various forms of capital (such as the power to define and shape the social order) provides an account that allows for a richer and more robust account of contestations and a way in which to understand the social world in a more analytical rather than a 'received' and static manner.

Power, control and Bourdieu

Grace selects a number of key areas for consideration that come out of his application of a Bourdieusian perspective to Catholic education. He writes of 'legitimation struggles' and of 'symbolic power' and 'control struggles'. Starting with his argument around legitimation, he writes about how some critics challenged the validity of the separate Catholic education mission in the UK, especially after the radical proposals of Vatican II. Essentially the point was made that if Catholic schools and Catholic education were to become more inclusive, then these schools would have to be abolished. Catholic schools should change to become 'a "leaven" in the secular world' (Grace, 2002, p. 28). This argument was confined in the main to a small group of intellectual Catholics at the time but, importantly, as Grace points out, 'neither the hierarchy nor the Catholic community in general were ready for such a debate' (2002, p. 29). The habitus of the Catholic Church, those social patterns that endure over time but that shift to accommodate to specific contexts, become set in place to support various dispositions to think and act in certain ways. *Habitus* is a set of dispositions shaped by past events and different structures that influence how the social world is produced and imagined (Bourdieu, 1984). Positioning the Catholic Church as a habitus works to reveal its way of being and ways of controlling. So, in the example of calls that challenged the legitimacy of the Catholic school to exist, there was a monumental challenge to the well-established habitus of this particular field. In the face of this powerful critique to the legitimacy of Catholic schools to exist, the hierarchy was able to sideline and disregard this debate. As Grace points out, it was easy to ignore these debates in a period where what was valued (the habitus) was consensus, order and obedience towards the leadership of the clergy. To paraphrase Grace, Bourdieu had pointed out that a habitus defends itself from challenges to its hegemony by applying sets of avoidance strategies. This is what occurred in response to the arguments being made for the closure of Catholic schools post Vatican II. In a recent paper, Grace has returned to Bourdieu's work and its resonances for understanding and illuminating the power of religion in society. Bourdieu recognised that in the field of religions 'a constant struggle was always in progress between the institutional "priests" and the radical and heretical "prophets"' (Grace, 2020, p. 865).[4]

A second strand where Grace illuminates the power of Bourdieusian theory to interrogate Catholic education relates to the concept of 'symbolic power' – which is itself part of the process of legitimation. Bourdieu claimed that symbolic power was constructed out of 'culturally significant attributes such as prestige, status and authority and it functions in practice as a powerful means of communication and potential domination' (Grace, 2002, p. 30). In the chapter under consideration, Grace argued that the Catholic Church holds considerable symbolic power, which has traditionally been wielded by the bishops who have controlled education provision. As Grace says, even so, there have been struggles and challenges to this panoply of symbolic power over time. There have been differences of opinion as to what Catholic schools and Catholic education should look like. He cites some of the early struggles between Rome and certain Religious Orders (and makes the point that the Jesuits have always been able to steer their own ship to a large degree). His point is that even in periods where symbolic power has dominated, there have always been struggles over points of definition and provision. However, he does say that the Church has taken the position that 'it has been unedifying to draw attention to them' (p. 30) but that the existence of challenges and political struggles demonstrate the reality that there is no 'simple' account of consensus or unity. Things in reality have always been a little more vexatious and contentious. He picks out for further examination clergy–laity relations in Catholic educational settings as well as the tensions that exist in the policy landscape.

One of the fundamental features of the Catholic Church in the UK is that it has been patterned by strong and clearly delineated hierarchical relationships between the clergy and laity. As Grace says, this relationship has been mediated by social class hierarchies since the beginning of urbanisation in the UK. Many of the large number of migrants coming into the newly emerging cities were working-class families of Irish Catholic heritage. While religion provided a buttress against the vicissitudes of urban life, it was a very top-down arena where priests and their bishops' authority was rarely if ever challenged. Grace believes that this power-hierarchy continued well into the twentieth century. However, by the 1970s in the UK, there was a move to engage more directly with parents in a new education policy settlement where older partnerships between state and churches were dissolving to some degree, where parents were moving into the driving seat, in theory at least, through tactics such as choice of schools. It was a time where the Catholic Church had 'to conform its educational arrangements to policies devised by governments strongly influenced by New Right ideologies of market forces, competition, individualism and consumer choice in schooling' (Grace, 2020, p. 32).

'Parent power' was and is a 'complex phenomenon which can be appropriated to serve various social and political ends' (Grace, 2002, p. 34). For example, parents could decide to change their school's status to become 'grant-maintained',[5] which would effectively remove the traditional voice of the bishopric in these schools. Parents could even choose to change the character of the school in new ways that 'could oppose diocesan reorganisation plans' (p. 32). For example, if a small Catholic school were being threatened with closure, parents could organise to 'save' their school by opting out of diocesan control through becoming grant maintained. Grace details some of the *cause-celebres* of the period, most notably the struggle round Cardinal Vaughan School in London and others 'who defied episcopal authority by voting for grant maintained status' and, in the case of Cardinal Vaughan, threatened to take Cardinal Hume to court to assert their legal rights to control and manage the school and to take decisions that may well have been in their own interests but were seen as not in the interests of the wider Catholic community. It is worth citing Grace at some length here:

> The socio-cultural struggle within the Catholic community was large. Not only had a group of Catholic headteachers, school governors and parents defied the advice of their Cardinal and their bishops on a key issue of educational policy but some of them had been prepared to 'take the Cardinal to court' on the issue. Such events were unprecedented within the English Catholic community and they made visible the limitations of clerical symbolic power when faced by the alliance of 'strong state' and 'strong parentocracy'.
>
> (2002, p. 37)

While this is a significant moment in the history of Catholic schools in England, here this example is cited to illustrate a challenge to the older habitus and symbolic power of the Catholic Church and its educational provision. Being able to 'read' these events through a stronger theory-driven lens using the concepts of habitus and symbolic power affords a more critical and analytical understanding of Catholic education over time and in its current formation too (see Byrne and Devine, 2017; Grace 2020).

Pedagogy, knowledge and Bernstein

According to Gerald Grace, a second major social theorist whose work can provide a powerful and critical 'intellectual resource' (Grace, 2002, p. 25) for understanding Catholic education at a deeper level is Basil Bernstein. Grace claims that, as with Bourdieu's analysis, the application of Bernstein's work to Catholic education theory and practice has also remained underdeveloped. He concentrates on two core strands of Bernstein's work around pedagogy as well as knowledge and the curriculum. Starting with pedagogy, Grace claims that Bernstein's work on what he termed 'visible' and 'invisible' pedagogy 'have proved fruitful in empirical research in various educational settings' (2002, p. 49).

Bernstein saw visible pedagogy as being a concentration on the 'performance' of the learner; 'where the pedagogy is visible, it is likely to be standardised and so schools are directly comparable as to their successes and failures' (1975, p. 31). For instance, visible pedagogy is reflected in concerns with outcomes and attainment, with league tables and scholarly achievements; with aspects of the neoliberal market form. In contrast, invisible pedagogy refers to those processes involved in socialisation and the construction of desired dispositions and behaviours. As Grace says, 'at the most general level, invisible pedagogy is designed to be person forming whereas visible pedagogy is designed to be product forming' (2002, p. 49).

Now when it comes to applying these concepts to an analysis of the field of Catholic education, Grace makes the point that the schooling of young people has always involved *both* of these approaches. And it is important to underline his argument (made in 2002) that many headteachers of the period when he wrote this chapter attended schools that had foregrounded visible pedagogies and 'were themselves socialised within ... the visible pedagogies of traditional schools'. Thus it could be predicted that they would reproduce 'aspects of this academic culture within contemporary schooling' (p. 50). However, Grace argues that this approach simultaneously still valued the sacred and 'concepts of service to community and the public good' (p. 50). What Grace was concerned about was the stronger emphasis on visible pedagogy that was an intrinsic part of the insertions of market forces into all forms of education. Again, it is worth citing Grace in full in order to convey his concerns and also to illustrate the power of his contention; that drawing on social science theory really can help researchers move to a deeper understanding of educational change, the deep structure and not only the surface structure.

> The danger of this new dominant form is that it dislocates knowledge from a relation to the sacred or to the community and replaces it with a utilitarian, commodified and individualistic relation. While Catholic schools may be 'successful' and 'effective' within this new visible pedagogy, such success will not articulate well with the principles enshrined in their mission statements.
>
> (Grace, 2002, p. 50)

While Grace warned about schools valorising visible pedagogical outcomes at the expense of their spiritual mission, a stress in policy that came from central governments, he was far more concerned about the threats inherent in aspects of the invisible pedagogy and its focus on the formation of the person. Invisible pedagogies have, he claims, always been central to the mission of the Catholic school. To paraphrase his words, while these schools have had a visible pedagogy of direct religious teaching, alongside this there has been a central commitment to support and develop the 'good Catholic'; a less tangible and less visible outcome altogether. Grace warns of what he sees as the inherent danger of Catholic schools taking on the need to do well in the market place and assert themselves as bastions of academic excellence rather than a more traditional concern with what he sees as the primary purpose of the Catholic school: the production and nurture of good people.[6] The trick perhaps is to be able to hold on to both visible and invisible pedagogies in the pursuit of Catholic education: a concern that has been a significant endeavour over time on the part of Gerald Grace.

Drawing on some of the substantive debates about knowledge that are central to Bernstein's work, Grace believes that the main threat is a dehumanisation of knowledge. He cites Bernstein (1996, p. 87) in order to highlight the dangers implicit in moves towards a marketised form of knowledge.

> Knowledge should flow like money to wherever it can create advantage and profit. Indeed knowledge is not like money, it is money… Once knowledge is separated from inwardness, from commitments, from personal dedication, from the deep structure of the self, then people may be moved about, substituted for each other and excluded from the market.
>
> (Bernstein, 1996, p. 87, cited in Grace, 2002, p. 46)

Bernstein also generated two key concepts, *classification* and *framing*, that helped to unpack some of the complexities of curriculum studies. By classification, Bernstein was referring to the boundaries that support and maintain subjects and practices. He argued that where boundaries were strong and there was insulation between subjects, this generated distinctive aspects of the curriculum, for example mathematics or biology. Where the boundaries were less well insulated, 'subjects' became more diffuse and less distinctive, for example environmental education perhaps. Grace takes this set of ideas and argues that historically Catholic education has been strongly classified and bounded and 'insulated from the secular world' (2002, p. 47). Since Vatican II, these boundaries have been weakened, he believes, by contextual shifts in ideology, politics and other social changes. Grace adds that this weakening has been forced upon Catholic schools because of other factors such as the reduction in priests and Religious Orders in schools and a major shift in the 'distinctive habitus which they represented in schools' (2002, p. 47). Also there have been systemic policy reforms that have eroded the autonomy of Church schools to a large degree, certainly since the 1980s onwards in the English setting.

Bernstein's second major curriculum concept is that of 'framing'. This refers to the power relations that shape what is to count as knowledge, the curriculum, pedagogy and assessment – the message systems of the curriculum. Historically, the curriculum of the Catholic school was determined by the diocese or the teaching order that provided schools even before the state took up this responsibility. When the state took over the responsibility for education provision, initially as Grace notes (2002, p. 48), 'the degree of relative autonomy for a distinctively Catholic framing of priorities was large'. From the 1980s onwards, however, in the light of a massive shift in England where the 'secret garden' of the curriculum was opened to the control of the educational state, what ensued was a 'strong framing regime on all schools regardless of religious character' (2002, p. 48). This incursion has continued and currently in England is driven by a (traditional) knowledge-based approach that stresses the need for tightly classified (traditional) subjects as well as a discourse of the need to meet global market demands and be wealth producing. In these contexts, and drawing on issues of curriculum framing, Grace (2002, p. 48) believes that this approach can drive research questions such as 'what remains distinctive in the cultural messages carried by Catholic schools'?

New thinking, new scholarship and new research in Catholic education

At the end of the chapter that I have concentrated on here, Grace finishes with a return to the central question of 'social theory and the study of Catholic education'. He makes his case cogently:

> Aspects of social theory applied to Catholic education have the potential to illuminate the field, to provide greater in-depth analysis of issues and to generate fruitful theoretical frameworks for future research and enquiry.
>
> (2002, p. 51)

Through using some of the key concepts in Bourdieu's writing (field, habitus, capital and symbolic power) as well as Bernstein's key concepts of visible and invisible pedagogy and the classification and framing of knowledge, Grace demonstrated that this sort of *'proper work in social science'* could be extremely valuable in extending the study of Catholic education through critical scholarship. While this chapter was written some time ago, the relevance of its argumentation to a collection entitled *New Thinking, New Scholarship and New Research in Catholic Education* is still significant. In the examples that Grace has provided of the application of these key concepts from Bernstein and Bourdieu, it is possible to identify and articulate some key analytical questions that are central to this academic endeavour. Questions about the relevance of faithed schooling in a secularising society. Questions about what should count as knowledge in these complex and ever-changing times. Questions about power, hierarchy and influence – still central issues in unpacking educational policy and provision. In arguing for proper work in social science, Grace believes that the study of Catholic education can benefit from this approach. As he details in a more recent piece, 'contemporary sociologists of education should "take religion seriously" and go beyond their own personal paradigms in future research' (Grace, 2020, p. 867). Finally, I wonder if Gerald Grace would still select Bourdieu and Bernstein's writings as being his choice of social scientists whose work demonstrates the contribution that sociology can make to understanding and theorising Catholic education. I rather suspect that he might!

Notes

1 At the time, Grace also used the term 'policy scholarship' because he believed that policy needed an interdisciplinary approach, using history, sociology, economics and politics to obtain a more comprehensive understanding of policy.
2 He first defined 'spiritual capital' (2002, p. 236) as 'resources of faith and values derived from commitment to a religious tradition'. This was not limited only to Catholic religious tradition but applied to all religious traditions.
3 Grace argues that he became 'converted' to the serious study of Catholic education following his reading of Anthony Bryk, Valerie Lee and Peter Holland's (1993) brilliant research *Catholic Schools and the Common Good* from the USA.

4 This raises the question, was Jesus Christ perceived as a radical or heretical prophet by the 'institutional Church' of his time.
5 'Grant-maintained schools' were an educational innovation in England, introduced by a Conservative government to encourage schools to 'opt out' of the relationship with the Local Education Authority (LEA) and make a direct financial arrangement with central government in the 1980s.
6 Catholic schools before the Second Vatican Council (1962–1965) had a primary aim of forming 'Good Catholics'. In more recent years, in a more pluralist social context, contemporary Catholic schools have a primary aim of forming 'Good People' who may be Catholic but who may not be, i.e. a more inclusive and open access principle now characterises many Catholic schools in England.

References

Bernstein, B. (1975). Class and pedagogies: Visible and invisible, *Educational Studies*, 1:1, pp. 23–41.

Bourdieu, P. (1984). *Distinction: A Social Critique of the Judgement of Taste*, London, Routledge.

Bryk, A., Lee, V. and Holland, P. (1993). *Catholic Schools and the Common Good*, Cambridge MA, Harvard University Press.

Byrne, R., and Devine, D. (2017). Theorising Catholic Education through the lens of Bernstein and Bourdieu. *International Studies in Catholic Education*, 9:1, pp. 29–44.

Grace, G. (1978). *Teachers, Ideology and Control: A Study in Urban Education*, London: Routledge and Kegan Paul.

Grace, G. (1984). *Education and the City: Theory, History and Contemporary Practice*, London/Boston, MA: Routledge and Kegan Paul.

Grace, G. (1993). On the study of school leadership: Beyond education management, *British Journal of Educational Studies*, 41:4, pp. 353–365.

Grace, G. (2000). Research and the challenges of contemporary school leadership: The contribution of critical scholarship, *British Journal of Educational Studies*, 48:3, pp. 231–247.

Grace, G. (2002). *The Field of Catholic Education. Perspectives from Bourdieu and Bernstein, in Catholic Schools: Mission, Markets and Morality*, London/New York: RoutledgeFalmer, pp. 24–52.

Grace, G. R. (2010). Renewing Spiritual Capital: An Urgent Priority for the Future of Catholic Education Internationally, *International Studies in Catholic Education*, 2:2, 117–128.

Grace, G. (2016). *Faith, Mission and Challenge in Catholic Education: Selected Writings of Gerald Grace*. London: Routledge, World Library of Educationalists.

Grace, G. (2020). Taking religions seriously in the sociology of education: Going beyond the secular paradigm, *British Journal of Sociology of Education*, 41:6, pp. 859–869.

Chapter 8

May 'Grace' be with you always

Gerald Grace and Jewish education

Helena Miller

Introduction

When I was training to be a teacher at Goldsmiths' College, quite coincidentally, all three of my teaching practices took place in Catholic primary schools in London – St. Joseph's on Deptford High Street, Our Lady of Lourdes in Wanstead, and St. Anne's off Whitechapel Road. They were all well out of the comfort zone of a young Jewish student from a north-west London suburb. Those experiences, however, were the best training I could have had. The staff in these schools really showed me how a Catholic religious ethos and religious values could take centre place in a school environment. The dedication of those te achers ensured that their pupils were instilled with a love of their religion as well as the very best of progressive education of the late 1970s.

Fast forward fifteen years. After many years of a most rewarding career in schools, I found myself training Jewish teachers, and running a Master's degree in Jewish education for the Leo Baeck College in London. I was involved at the time with RESQUJE (Research and Quality in Jewish Education), headed by Dr Jo Cairns, then senior lecturer in education at the Institute of Education, University of London. I was interested to have someone from the Institute come along to the College to talk to my students about teaching in a Christian faith school – a comparison with their own experiences in the Jewish faith sector. Jo introduced me to her colleague, Professor Gerald Grace, and a collegial relationship began which has been maintained over decades. Gerald has influenced Jewish education initiatives in specific ways, and I wonder whether he even realises how important his interactions have been over the years.

In the early 1990s, Jewish schools in the UK spent very little or no time considering religions other than Judaism. Consequently, when my colleague Rabbi Dr. Michael Shire and I designed a Master's degree in Jewish education for Leo Baeck College, London, our focus was entirely on Jewish teachers and Jewish education. Gerald Grace was, for many of our students, the first visiting professor who allowed them to think about and discuss Jewish education in relation to Catholic education and Catholic schools. Gerald's insight and breadth of experience, as well as his very well-developed and singular sense of

DOI: 10.4324/9781003171553-10

humour, made him a very popular guest speaker, and thereafter we prevailed on him annually to teach our postgraduate students. There is a generation of graduates of that MA in Jewish education who will never forget the opportunities that Professor Grace gave them to understand the dilemmas that religious schools face through the lens of contemporary Catholic schools and education.

The *International Handbook of Jewish Education* (IHJE) adds to a growing list of substantial volumes that inform and debate issues within religious education traditions and frameworks. The starting point for the book was a conversation in 2007 with Professor Gerald Grace, who was then editing *The International Handbook of Catholic Education* (IHCE) (Grace and O'Keefe 2007). Gerald sat in my office and, in his usual serious and enthusiastic manner, convinced me that a sister publication for, and by, the Jewish education community would be a valuable addition to this family of Springer publications, stimulating exchange of knowledge between two religious cultures and traditions. Before an hour had passed, he had also somehow managed to persuade me that, despite having a more than full-time job, I would be the person to make this huge project happen. And, being Gerald, he was right. One of the things he also stressed was the importance of working with others to make this happen. And so, together with two wonderful colleagues, Lisa Grant and Alex Pomson, four years later, our two-volume edition of the IHJE was published. I hope that in the introduction to our edited volume, I managed to do justice to Gerald's part in instigating the Handbook.

During those years when I was busy working on the IHJE, Gerald's publishing career was taking him in the direction of journal editing; since 2009, he was the senior editor of *International Studies in Catholic Education*, a role he relinquished at the end of 2021. Gerald came back to me in 2012, the year I thought I was going to have a rest from writing and publishing, and invited me to contribute an article to his journal. The original reason for this contact in 2012 was that I had invited Gerald to be the keynote speaker at the annual Research in Jewish Education Conference in London. Gerald took the conference by storm. He was able to give the participants at that conference the opportunity for deep reflection and analysis of our Jewish education settings and contexts through his examination of Catholic schools and education. And once again, after that conference, a short conversation in the hallway, as Gerald was getting ready to leave, had me agreeing to write an article for him on how Jewish education and Catholic education inform each other, through the lens of the respective books and journals we had edited.

The article that I wrote for Gerald (Miller 2013) interrogated the various themes and chapters of the IHJE in relation to chapters in Gerald's IHCE and also to articles in *International Studies in Catholic Education* (ISCE). Some of the highlights of that article are considered again here.

Vision and practice

The concept and content of educational vision has been a key component in thinking about knowledge and the imparting of that knowledge through time.

Chapters in the IHJE explore educational thinking which has had an influence on Jewish educational thought and practice. Vision is of utmost importance within a volume that not only reviews the current state of Jewish education and Jewish education research, but also looks to the future. But vision on its own, while it sets the scene and provides an underpinning for the ends and means of a Jewish education, is not enough. The articulation of vision has to relate to practice – it forms the rationale for what takes place within the educative process. And there is a third strand which connects the two elements of vision and practice, and that is policy. Together with planning, policy is a process for guiding change towards desired ends. These concepts are not particular to the Jewish educational world. Brendan Carmody SJ explores many of the same issues as he writes about a contemporary Catholic philosophy of education in ISCE, Volume 3 (October 2011).

Michael Rosenak explores basic distinctions in the philosophy of education, and concludes by surveying some of the key questions asked by philosophers of Jewish educators, namely, What? How? Why? The influence of Rosenak's writings go far beyond the content of his chapter in the IHJE. Within the bibliographies of those who contributed to this section, as well as throughout the rest of this publication, Rosenak features repeatedly, reinforcing his position as one of the most influential Jewish educational thinkers of his generation.[1]

A characteristic of the chapter bibliographies within this section is their emphasis on both Jewish and non-Jewish visions and philosophies. Hanan Alexander, in his chapter, which explores contemporary Jewish education from a post-modern perspective, draws upon, amongst others, Scheffler, Buber, Levinas, Oakeshott and Kant. Buber and Levinas are two of a range of philosophers whose ideas are applied by Jonathan Cohen in his chapter on Jewish thought (pp. 219–236). Cohen illustrates how insights from modern Jewish thought can enrich discourse and reflection on issues of principle in Jewish education. His focus on education for spirituality should be read together with the chapter by Michael Shire, who reviews the research into the spiritual lives of children. Shire's interest is in exploring how faith can be formed in children by means of a Jewish religious education. This interest leads Shire to identify important questions of purpose and practice for Jewish educators hoping to incorporate visions of the child as a spiritual being.

Spiritual life and the development of faith resonates strongly with Catholic educators and Graham Rossiter addresses the needs of contemporary youth spirituality in his article in ISCE (2011), and in the journal a year earlier, Gerald Grace explored the renewal of spiritual capital as a priority issue in the future of Catholic education (2010). Faith formation is also explored in the IHCE (2007), for example in Sister Lydia Fernandes' chapter 'Faith formation in Indian Catholic schooling'.

Religious identity

Religious identity development characterises the agenda of both Catholic and Jewish educators and researchers. Didier Pollefeyt and Jan Bouwens (2010) explore the Catholic identity of an educational institute and in the IHJE (2011), Gaby Horenczyk and Hagit Hacohen Woolf examine the basic assumption that Jewish education is widely perceived as one of the major means for strengthening Jewish identity and identification. They suggest that a multifaceted approach to the mapping of Jewish attitudes and behaviour – mapping what Jewish identity might mean – can help better define the goals of Jewish education. Stuart Charme and Tali Hyman Zelkowicz also approach Jewish identity formation from multifaceted and multiple-process formulations in their chapter, in which they argue for a shift in thinking towards conceiving of identities as being multiple and shifting.

Steven Cohen and Judith Veinstein's chapter on Jewish identity shifts the focus of the discussion onto policy and practice. Their chapter examines the impact of Jewish social networks on identity outcomes. The authors argue for educators and policy makers to recognise and value the nurture of Jewish friendship networks as an explicit act of Jewish education. With social scientific research having repeatedly demonstrated that well-connected individuals exert more influence on others than do social isolates, the challenge for educators and policy makers is to locate such influential youngsters (and others) and mobilise them on behalf of Jewish interests and Jewish engagement – both for their own benefit, and for that of their surrounding circles of contacts and intimates.

Jewish schools: UK

My own chapter, which focuses on the changing nature of how Jewish schools relate to, and integrate with, their local and wider communities, takes a different view of policy and planning. I highlight how the prescriptive policies of government and education agencies can strongly influence educational practice. This chapter, which is one of the few in the Handbook to use Britain and British schools as the lens through which to explore Jewish educational issues, should be read in conjunction with David Mendelsson's chapter on Anglo-Jewish education, found in Part IV of the Handbook. The *Catholic Education Service* of England and Wales works closely with other denominations in the UK, particularly on issues related to government and faith schools. In recent years, the Jewish and Catholic communities have spoken with one voice on a number of issues, including schools admissions processes and inspections of schools, both topics which equally concern Jewish and Catholic schools.

Janush Korczak, who is well known for his heroic stand against Nazism during the Holocaust, left a lasting legacy to Jewish and general education.[2] In his chapter, Marc Silverman explores Korczak's legacy to Jewish education. His is the first of several chapters in IHJE which relate to the Holocaust in some way. While the modern relationship between Jews and Catholics should not be defined by the Holocaust, it owes its repair to a large extent to that dark time in Jewish history.

Teaching and learning

Teaching and learning are the essential processes of education. There is a strong thread running through these chapters which show the relevance of curriculum as process. Curriculum is not just a physical set of objectives but rather the interaction of teacher, learner and knowledge. While the emphasis throughout is on current educational models, these chapters also look at the possibilities and challenges of change and development. Throughout, the chapters explore teaching and learning through the lens of Jewish educational research.

A recurring theme in these chapters is the impact of aspects of teaching and learning on the individual lives of the learners. Whether it is through learning a language with the intent to facilitate integration into society, as Nava Navo explores, or through the growing interest in Jewish life cycle education, as examined by Howard Deitcher, it is clear that the themes in these chapters play a critical role in shaping individual Jewish lives. As both Navo and Deitcher show in their analyses of subject matter structured by shared commonplace components but conceived for widely different curricular purposes, the context of Jewish education (in Israel and the Diaspora, in Orthodox and liberal religious settings) makes as sharp a difference to the content of Jewish education as do the needs of the learners in view, whether children or adults. Rito Baring explores a new approach to catechetical Catholic education in his article (ISCE, 2010) and teaching and learning in context with local environments feature strongly throughout the IHCE (2007).

The relationship to community is also explored in other chapters of this section of the IHJE. Several authors touch upon the relationship between Jewish travel education and community. Travel as a Jewish educational tool in contemporary Jewish education is explored by Erik Cohen. More specifically, Scott Copeland observes the centrality of Israel travel in the development of Jewish communal life. Similarly, in another chapter on travel, Jeremy Leigh draws on empirical research to address elements of community. This perspective is challenged by David Mittelberg, who argues for Jewish peoplehood education, asserting that today, Jewish youth seem to feel little existential need to belong to the Jewish collective, whether local or national.[3] Hence, he argues for focused attention on Jewish peoplehood education in order to cultivate a stronger sense of belonging. Mittelberg's peoplehood paradigm has some resonance with Leigh in that both consider how travel can instil in young people a need for belonging. Jewish peoplehood fuels the continuing search for shared meaning within the current ambiguity and ambivalence that Jews face in both Israel and abroad.

Holocaust education is frequently placed within the history curriculum, although it is considered a field of inquiry on its own. In her chapter, Simone Schweber explores the current state of Holocaust education and asks what might Holocaust education do if conceptualised not from the standpoint of building nations or concretising collective memory but as a project of global citizenship and human understanding. Again, the notion of what it means to be part of the Jewish people and where Jews situate themselves amongst other peoples resonates with themes explored by Mittelberg, Cohen and Leigh. The Holocaust is also part of the Catholic past, and bound up with the Jewish-Catholic narrative. Can a Jewish narrative on the Holocaust help a Catholic educator towards an understanding of the complexities of the topic?

Both Catholics and Jews share a common text. Barry Holtz explores the nature of Bible education in contemporary Jewish education through an examination of the history of Jewish Bible interpretation, reflecting the content of scripture teaching. He explores these distinctions by researching various curricular projects and pedagogies. His chapter concludes by looking at research which draws upon work in pedagogical content knowledge and specific orientations to subject matter, exploring the implications of this scholarship for Bible teaching.

Arts education

While cognitive curricular areas traditionally focus on intellectual growth, as expounded by Holtz, Lehmann, and Gillis, the Arts provide questions and concerns for both Jewish education and Jewish educational research. In this section of the International Handbook, two chapters explore contemporary issues relating to Jewish Arts education. In the first, Robbie Gringras explores what he terms as the 'seam-line' between education and art. He explores the questions and concerns that engage educators interested in creating culturally significant meaning, encoded in an affecting and sensuous medium. Using song, literature and poetry to illustrate his argument, Gringras suggests that art can be a significant aspect of any Jewish curriculum, particularly in the informal sector. Ofra Backenroth takes a different, and Diaspora-oriented, perspective as she focuses on the value of the Arts in the formal Jewish education system, where, in the context of a dual curriculum, they must wrestle for time and budget. She examines the goals, content and methodology of how the Arts are being taught in today's Jewish day schools in North America. Both she and Gringras call for a continuum of curricular integration, where the teaching of the Arts ranges from arts as discrete disciplines to multidisciplinary integration. The Arts, particularly through the visual arts and music, have a long and serious tradition in Catholicism and in Catholic education.

The IHJE focuses on two aspects of teaching and learning that are very much twenty-first-century additions to the field, namely the environment and technology. Of course, an interest in caring for the environment has been a religious concern since the earliest times. In the Bible, (Genesis 2:15), humanity is called upon as stewards put on this earth to look after it, but in the twenty-first century, caring for the environment has taken on new and acute significance. For Eilon Schwartz, that there is only a nascent academic field of Jewish environmental education today mirrors the peripheral status of environmentalism within the Jewish educational establishment, and within society in general. Shwartz proposes that like so many shifts in educational theory and practice, change in public consciousness and political will do not come from the top-down, but from the bottom-up. It will come from a growing field of educational innovators whose central challenge will be to take their intuition as to what needs to change, and transform it into a reflective educational practice. The Jewish future, he suggests, depends on the collective ability to re-imagine educational and communal institutions, and to build a Jewish community where continuity does not begin and end at the Jewish doorstep as if Jewish existence lives apart on the only planet on which humanity has been created to live.

Brian Amkraut's chapter is no less grounded in a sense of the current historical moment. Amkraut writes about the digital era and shows how perspectives on Jewish continuity in general and approaches to Jewish education in particular are now, and will continue to be, shaped by a new world in which traditional notions of authority, community and identity are challenged and redefined. As Schwartz does in his chapter with reference to environmentalism, Amkraut argues that embrace of new technologies does not only call for extending the subject matter of Jewish education, it calls for thinking anew about its purposes and practices, texts and contexts.

A regret is that the IHJE did not manage to explore the growing field of social justice education. Catholic educators are ahead of us in this respect, as I noted in Cardinal Renato Raffaele Martino's article 'What Catholic schools can do to advance the cause of justice and peace in the world' (ISCE, 2010).

Jewish day schools

The chapters in the IHCE and the articles in the ISCE (2009–11) primarily focus on schools and congregations. Three authors in the IHJE investigate the world of Jewish day schools. Alex Pomson focuses on how the historical tensions between survivalist and integrationist impulses in Jewish day school development account for some of the most intense contemporary debates surrounding liberal day school education worldwide. As with Aron's findings in congregational education, Pomson points to a shift in the aims of liberal day school education from a paradigm of instruction (concerned with helping children acquire knowledge of the ideas and skills that society values) to one of enculturation (the more broadly conceived task of initiating children into a culture to which they may not already be committed).

A different challenge exists in Orthodox Jewish day schools as described by Shani Bechhofer who presents a rich description of the changing landscape of

Orthodox education in America. She argues that a variety of institutional and educational pressures upon schools result in institutions that are more diverse, more competitive, more ideologically differentiated, and also more innovative than ever before.[4]

Two complementary chapters explore the sub-field of informal and experiential education from very different perspectives. First, by means of two case studies Joseph Reimer describes the potentially profound impact creative collaborative partnerships between business-oriented philanthropists and Jewish educational leaders can have on the field of informal Jewish education. David Bryfman then explores both the theoretical and practical aspects of experiential education and how it has shaped the field of Jewish education in general (pp. 767–784). He suggests that experiential education is poised to reach a tipping point in the Jewish communal landscape and offers both a language and strategies for helping experiential education to further impact the Jewish identity development of Jewish youth and young adults.

The robust growth of Jewish studies in North American universities is the focus of the chapter by Judith Baskin. She reports that over two hundred and thirty endowed chairs of Jewish studies exist at eighty colleges and universities with many other positions and programmes in Jewish studies present at other North American institutions that are funded internally without outside support. As early as 1974, the *Guidelines for Implementation of the Nostra Aetate* recommended that chairs of Jewish studies be established in Christian institutions and collaboration with Jewish scholars encouraged.

Shira Epstein's chapter focuses on gender issues, another relatively new area in Jewish education. Epstein documents how formerly evaded topics such as body image, sexuality, healthy relationship building and sexual violence have become normative parts of many North American Jewish educational programmes and professional development initiatives. She also describes how participatory action research between Jewish educators and cohorts of adolescents can transform the landscape of gender in Jewish education. The changing role of women is explored by Mary Darmanin (ISCE, 2009 and IHCE, 2007), who looks at the contribution of contemporary Catholic schools to the empowerment of girls and young women, specifically in Malta.

A different perspective on adolescents is explored by Evie Levy Rotstein in her chapter on children of intermarried parents. Rotstein's research reveals a variety of factors that motivate such teens to continue their Jewish education into their high school years, including family life, parental commitment to Jewish education, a positive religious school experience, and the students' own involvement in the decision to continue. Her case is supported by drawing on a broader literature relating to 'resilient youth'.

Just as parental involvement is key in the decision of adolescent children of intermarried parents to continue their education, so too is it central to virtually all aspects of Jewish educational engagement, as documented by Jeff Kress. In his chapter, Kress shows how North American parents today are much more active in choosing educational settings for their children than in past generations. Indeed, individualisation results in a range of educational choices within the same family. As Kress shows, the ways in which parents relate to other Jewish organisations, particularly synagogues, impacts their experiences and expectations of Jewish education regardless of setting.

Choice also appears as a key theme in the chapter on adult Jewish learning by Lisa Grant and Diane Tickton Schuster. Here they present how contemporary social forces have led to new developments in the field and what changes and priorities appear to be shaping the vision and decisions of adult education planners and policy makers today. They provide a conceptual framework moving away from a primary focus on literacy-based learning to a more diversified niche-marketing approach for situating the *where, when* and *what* of different types of learners and the learning programmes and experiences that will meet their interests and needs.

The education of clergy

Another emerging field of study is addressed by Lisa Grant and Michal Muszkat-Barkan in their chapter on the professional identity formation of rabbi-educators working in a variety of settings. This cross-cultural research explores how Conservative and Reform rabbi-educators in Israel and North America describe their roles and goals based on their rabbinic and education training. This small study urges further investigation to determine whether the professional identity of rabbi-educators is indeed distinct from that of educators or rabbis who perform similar functions. It would be interesting to know what research has been undertaken on the education and formation of Catholic priests.

A broader view of professional development of Jewish educators is taken by Gail Dorph in her chapter. Dorph's exploration of this topic centres on key questions about the principles and challenges in creating and sustaining effective professional development. She then offers three case studies that provide images of effective professional learning that can impact the capacity of teachers to enhance student learning in Jewish schools. Roisin Coll (2009) explores Catholic school leadership and its impact on the faith development of probationer teachers in Scotland. Teacher development is approached by Sharon Feiman-Nemser's chapter in the IHJE. She presents two examples in which she describes how both trends in general education and the emergence of a new kind of Jewish school influenced the creation of these programmes of Jewish teacher development.

This section closes with a chapter by Leora Isaacs, Kate O'Brien and Shira Rosenblatt on the challenges, successes and potential facing the field of Jewish education as it moves to recruit, retain and provide excellent professional development for Jewish educators. The authors assert the need for a systemic approach in linking excellence in teaching and student outcomes. They explore levers for change that directly impact the complex environment that influences teaching and learning in Jewish day and congregational school settings.

Geographical range

This final section of the IHJE reveals the extent to which Jewish education emerges at an intersection between the global and the local. The chapters in this section provide an opportunity to explore questions in the study of Jewish education regarding the influence of factors in the local environment and of international Jewish cultural patterns on the norms, modalities and goals of Jewish education.

While other sections of the Handbook gravitate mostly around the State of Israel and the United States, the contributors to this section provide an opportunity to appreciate nuances in communities that lie outside the orbit of these two major centres of Jewish education. What emerges is a sense of the varieties of Jewish education; how the push and pull of localised forces – community demographics, history (and particularly the twin upheavals of the Holocaust and communism), the relationships between church and state, and those between Jews and the local majority – have developed diverse narratives of Jewish education.

It is this section of the Handbook that appears to provide the most direct parallel with the IHCE (Grace and O'Keefe 2007). Both Jewish and Catholic handbooks have chapters on the USA, Canada, the UK, Australia, Latin America, and several aspects of education in different parts of Europe. The reader will have to decide to what extent the geographical context does provide any useful comparisons or whether the preceding sections on vision, policy, teaching and learning in Jewish educational contexts actually resonate more helpfully with issues in Catholic education.

Yet, for all of the differences brought in to view in this section, these chapters provide evidence, first, of certain phenomena that challenge most if not all Jewish communities whatever their circumstances, and, second, of a general tendency to pursue certain common educational solutions to these challenges. Thus, in all Diaspora Jewish communities, there are doubts about the sustainability of systems for intensive Jewish education because of a declining demographic base, and because of doubts about the capacity of these systems to graduate future generations of knowledgeable educational leaders. These concerns have led almost everywhere to a concentration of investment in all-day Jewish schools, summer camps and Israel trips; these being the few educational experiences that are viewed as having a better than even chance of sustaining Jewish identification and cultural creativity.

David Mendelsson, in his chapter on Jewish education in the UK, makes evident that acceptance of Jewish day schools by British parents since the Second World War occurred most directly in response to cultural and demographic changes in English society and to changes in government educational policy that democratised state schools. The turn to day schools, such that today more than 50% of Jewish children ages 5–18 attend such schools, was not, what he calls, internally driven; it was an unintended side effect, brought about in large part because of parental flight from state schools.[5]

Forgasz and Munz's chapter on Australia indicates that the founding of Jewish schools was galvanised and then sustained by waves of Jewish immigrants, first from post-war Europe and then more latterly from South Africa, who have displayed a strong desire to replicate the intensity of the Jewish life they experienced in the places from which they came. These internal drivers explain some of the highest rates of day school enrolment in the world.

It is fascinating to compare these two chapters with the sections of Bouganim's chapter on France that are also concerned with day school education. In all three contexts, as with Catholic schools, the government is deeply implicated in the certification and supervision of school programmes, and provides substantial support for Jewish schools. But the cultural context in France – where there is such a contested relationship between religion and the state – has until recent times strongly deterred the widespread development of parochial Jewish schooling in that country. The French context provides a setting for observing how the development of Jewish education is so much coloured by local context.

It is geographic singularities such as this that make readers wonder what might be inferred or applied from a particular instance to other, different, settings. Barbara Lerner-Spectre details the development of a programme at Paideia, the European Institute for Jewish Studies in Sweden that responds to a phenomenon she coins 'dis-assimilation', a pattern in which 'young adults who, before the fall of communism, were unaware of their Jewish heritage but who, in confronting this disclosure, choose to identify themselves as Jews' (pp. 1155–1166). She asks us to consider how her programme can have implications for contemporary religious adult education outside of Europe.

Similar questions about applicability are provoked by Bar-Shalom and Ascher-Shai in their chapter on innovations in secular schooling in Israel. The cases they present from schools in Israel derive from the absorption of diverse minorities into the only public Jewish school system in the world, and, as in the best instances of case study, these cases provoke more general questions. They challenge the reader to think about the potential forms and content of secular Jewish education, and its capacity to engage Diaspora communities, to make intensive Jewish education meaningful to secular Jews. Understanding the challenges of secularisation, in a Catholic context, is explored by James Arthur (2009).

Goldstein and Ganiel, in their chapter on Latin America, a part of the world with a strong Catholic tradition, highlight how different Jewish education looks in the largest communities of the region, in Argentina, Brazil and Mexico (pp. 1253–1270). They advance a set of models – pragmatic change, spiritual renewal, and insularity – that can be observed as common responses to the forces of democratisation and globalisation across the continent. Further, they argue strongly that these models can help make sense of developments in Jewish education elsewhere.

By contrast, Michael Brown demonstrates how, in Toronto and Montreal, the vigour and stability of Jewish education derives from special features in the Canadian context: Canada's bi-national structure; public attitudes to religion and state; the Jewish community's relatively recent arrival. These factors have produced institutional diversity, high levels of participant enrolment, innovative research, and strong central education bureaus. Ironically, while it will be difficult, as Brown implies, to reproduce such outcomes elsewhere, he indicates that in recent years these distinctive strengths have been eroded by forces that are more global in nature.[6]

These global forces are detailed by Wertheimer in his chapter on the United States.[7] He points to heightened consumerism on the part of families, rising rates of intermarriage, and severe time constraints limiting the availability of children and their families. These trends have led to a decline in the numbers of children receiving a Jewish education and to a shift towards providing immersive educational forms to a shrinking minority of consumers. In turn, these developments have driven a wave of experimentation funded in large part by private foundations.

A mark of the globalisation of Jewish educational patterns is best appreciated by comparing these American trends with what has emerged over the last twenty years in the former Soviet Union. Of course, the social and historical backdrop in Russia and parts of Eastern Europe could not be more different, and as Markus and Farbman show in their chapter, there are some especially challenging problems that derive from the Communist past, most obviously the absence of the synagogue as a support for Jewish community. The effects of Communism on the Catholic communities in Eastern Europe parallel these issues.

If and how communities might be created anew is the central thread that connects the chapter on the Former Soviet Union with chapters about smaller Jewish communities in Europe and the chapter about the Netherlands. In Eastern Europe, as Steve Israel indicates, the residential camp – a total Jewish environment for children, young adults and for families – seems to have been more successful than any other educational intervention. They have served as incubators for resuscitating communities that have lost much of their memory, and most of the elements, of Jewish life. It would be interesting to know what are the threads that connect the small and emerging communities in the Catholic world?

Conclusion

The IHJE set out to produce a record of the state of Jewish education in its widest number of contexts and forms at a particular moment in time. The intention was that the resulting book would find its place where there is interest in how Jews engage with Jewish education. For the Catholic education world, I hope that elements of the book spark debate, make connections, and most of all that it stimulates further questions and dialogue.

This book would not have come about without the influence of Gerald Grace. The Jewish educational world is in his debt.

In 2002, one of Gerald's most important works, *Catholic Schools: Mission, Markets and Morality*, was published. During one of our meetings together soon after the book was published, Gerald presented me with a copy of the book. Inside the front cover, he had written (in his distinctive handwriting!):

> To Helena,
> May "Grace" be with you always.
> Yours ever,
> Gerald
> 17.02.2002

Gerald Grace has indeed been with me always, in what he taught me about education and being an educator, and most importantly, in what he has given more broadly to the world of Jewish education.

Notes

1 Examples of Rosenak's contribution to the philosophy of Jewish education can be found in Rosenak (1987, 1995).
2 Janusk Korczak (1878–1942) is renowned worldwide for refusing to abandon the hundreds of children and staff at the Jewish orphanage in Warsaw, which he had headed since 1912, remaining with them to their end in the Nazi death camp of Treblinka.
3 Mittelberg (IHJE, p. 515) suggests that Jewish '...youth are relatively ignorant of, uneducated about, and unaffected by each other, suggesting that the goal of global solidarity of the Jewish people is constantly challenged. Increasingly, the paradigm of Jewish peoplehood is being offered as a framework to address this problem'.
4 Bechhofer (IHJE, p. 743) argues that 'a diverse and competitive market exists...' which has 'allowed for the flourishing of diversity. This has enriched the field and increased options for parents choosing schools for their children'.
5 Mendelsson (IHJE, p. 1111) states: 'In the immediate post-war years, Independent schools were beyond the means of most Jews ... Grammar schools were seen as the best choice. Two decades later, changes to the education system, particularly the phasing out of Grammar schools, impelled parents to seek alternatives ... Jewish schools attracted growing numbers of parents'.
6 Brown (IHJE, p. 1147) states that 'global forces' refers to 'societal shifts that are worldwide. One of these is the alienation of increasing numbers of Jews from Judaism, Jewish life and institutions, including schools ... also a reflection of the general weakening of faith in the Western world...'.
7 Wertheimer's (IHJE, p. 1096) examples of 'experimentation' include '...new national educational programs ... independent worship communities ... ecologically oriented groups ... service programs, cultural gatherings ... a broad array of affinity groups that attend to the needs of sub-populations...'.

References

Arthur, J. (2009). Secularisation, secularism and Catholic education, in *International Studies in Catholic Education* Volume 1: 2, pp. 228–239.

Baring, R. (2010). A new approach to catechesis: Involving students in catechetical education in the Philippines, in *International Studies in Catholic Education* Volume 2: 2, pp. 176–192.

Carmody, B. (2011). Towards a contemporary Catholic philosophy of education, *International Studies in Catholic Education* Volume 3: 2, pp. 106–119.

Coll, R. (2009). Catholic school leadership: Exploring its impact on the faith development of probationer teachers in Scotland, in *International Studies in Catholic Education* Volume 1: 2, pp. 200–213.

Darmanin, M. (2007) Catholic schooling and the changing role of women: Perspectives from Malta, in Grace G., O'Keefe J., *The International Handbook of Catholic Education*. Heidelberg: Springer.

Darmanin, M. (2009). Empowering women: The contribution of contemporary Catholic schools, in *International Studies in Catholic Education* Volume 1: 1, pp. 85–101.

De Souza, M., Engebretson, K., Durka, G., Jackson, R., McGrady, A. (2006). *The International Handbook of the Religious, Moral and Spiritual Dimensions in Education*. Netherlands: Springer.

Fernandes, L. (2007). Contemporary challenges to faith formation in Indian Catholic schooling, in Grace G., O'Keefe J., *The International Handbook of Catholic Education*. Heidelberg: Springer.

Grace, G., O'Keefe, J. (2007). *The International Handbook of Catholic Education*. Heidelberg: Springer.

Martino, R. R. (2010). What Catholic schools can do to advance the cause of justice and peace in the world, in *International Studies in Catholic Education* Volume 2: 2, pp. 212–216.

Miller, H. (2013). *The International Handbook of Jewish Education* (2011): Developing a dialogue between Jewish and Catholic educators, in *International Studies in Catholic Education* Volume 5: 2, pp. 113–126.

Miller, H., Grant, L. D., Pomson, A. (2011). *The International Handbook of Jewish Education*. Mahwah, NJ: Springer.

Pollefeyt, D., Bouwens J. (2010). Framing the identity of Catholic schools: Empirical methodology for quantitative research on the Catholic identity of an educational institute, in *International Studies in Catholic Education* Volume 2: 2, pp. 193–211.

Pomson, A., Deitcher, H. (2009). *Jewish Day Schools, Jewish Communities*. Portland: Littman Library of Jewish Civilization.

Pope Paul VI (1965). *Nostra Aetate*. Rome: Libreria Editrice Vaticana.

Rosenak, M. (1987). *Commandments and Concerns: Jewish Religious Education in a Secular Society*. Philadelphia: Jewish Publication Society.

Rosenak, M. (1995). Roads to the Palace: Jewish Texts and Teaching. Providence, Oxford and London: Berghahn Books for the Institute of Education, University of London.

Rossiter, G. (2011). Re-orienting the religion curriculum in Catholic schools to address the needs of contemporary youth spirituality, in *International Studies in Catholic Education* Volume 3: 2, pp. 57–72.

Chapter 9

Catholic education and a new Christian humanism

In honour of Grace

Caroline Healy

Introduction

Gerald Grace has throughout his body of work examined the interface of Catholic virtues and the challenges to them with ever-shifting contemporary educational policy developments.[1] He has remained an unwavering advocate of these perennial virtues in Catholic education, which can be located broadly under the concept of Christian humanism and include the preferential option for the poor (education for all); contributing to the common good; the importance of solidarity and community around the education mission and academic education as a means, not an end. Last, he considers the formation of the whole person as vital work of Catholic schools and the essentialness of the role of school leaders and teachers in this regard, who lead by example living virtuous lives, reflecting a sacramental vision articulated in this chapter.[2]

Educating to fraternal humanism[3]

In the view of the *Congregation for Catholic Education* (CCE), the following is required to:

> …humanise education, that is, to make it a process in which each person can develop his or her own deep-rooted attitudes and vocation, and thus contribute to his or her vocation within the community. 'Humanising education' means putting the person at the centre of education, in a framework of relationships that make up a living community, which is interdependent and bound to a common destiny. This is fraternal humanism.
>
> (CCE, 2017, para. 8)

In describing current scenarios, the document echoes Pope Paul VI's 1967 Encyclical *Populorum Progressio*, which at the outset stated that:

> The contemporary world, multifaceted and ever changing, is hit by multiple crises of different kind: economic, financial, labour; political crises

DOI: 10.4324/9781003171553-11

including within participatory democracy; environmental and natural crises; demographic and migratory crises...

(CCE, 2017, para. 3)

In the section on Humanising Education, the significance of the role of the teacher is alluded to:

A humanised education, therefore, does not just provide an educational service, but deals with its results in the overall context of the personal, moral and social abilities of those who participate in the educational process. *It does not simply ask the teacher to teach and students to learn* [*emphasis is my own*], but urges everyone to live, study and act in accordance with the reasons of fraternal humanism.

(CCE, 2017, par. 10)

The highlighted words reflect John Sullivan's (2001, pp. 134–135) concept of 'reciprocity and mutuality' and 'charismatic circularity', the term used by the *Congregation for Catholic Education* in its *Consecrated Persons and Their Mission in Schools* (2002), in the context of the transmission of distinctive charisms. In essence, this perspective claims that learning is a two-way process and the teacher is enriched to the extent to which he/she is open to the possibility of learning from recipients, in this case students. Parker J. Palmer (1998) also places a good deal on emphasis on the appropriateness of the 'space' in which the vocation of the teacher is nourished. Resonating with Sullivan's (2000, p. 185ff) concept that schools should primarily be 'hospitable spaces for learning', Palmer articulates the nature of the space in a series of paradoxes, for example bounded yet open, welcoming yet challenging and inviting both the voice of the individual and the group.

Humanism: Historical context

Franchi (2014) makes the point that no contemporary reference to humanism can omit reference to the historical notions of humanism exemplified in the work of Francesco Petrarcha (1307–1374) and Desiderius Erasmus (1466–1536). Bowen (1975, p. 337) makes the point that, in essence, these Renaissance humanists were inspired by classical antiquity, access to which emerged from the time of St Thomas Aquinas (1227–1274) onwards. In what amounted to a return to the sources of the Hebrew and Greek scriptures alongside key philosophical texts such as those of Plato and Aristotle from the 4th century BC, these scholars focused on an orientation towards the Good, encompassing a positive attitude towards the human as opposed to a perspective of the human blocked by the twin barriers of frustration and sin: 'freedom of the will' as opposed to 'bondage of the will' in the classical binary of Erasmus and Luther.

In his book, *The Crisis of Western Education*, Christopher Dawson speaks of the 'age of humanism' as:

> ...inspired by an intense devotion to classical culture but not conscious of any disloyalty to the Christian tradition. The great humanist educators... were themselves devout Christians who wished to unite the intellectual and aesthetic culture of Hellenism with the spiritual ideals of Christianity.
>
> (1961, p. 31)

This unity between classical culture and Christian tradition is exemplified in the work of Aquinas, particularly in the context of Natural Law and conscience, which will be referenced subsequently. Since the early 1980s, there has been renewed scholarly interest in the concept of Christian humanism. A number of official Catholic documents have stressed the importance of 'Christian humanism', as a vehicle of Christian social teaching and, indeed, as a key principle of Catholic education with a holistic approach to education. This can be regarded as an architectonic concept.[4] In *Re-Envisioning Christian Humanism* (2016), Jans Zimmermann endeavours to *recover* a Christian humanist ethos in our contemporary context. In a related work, Zimmermann (2012) argues for an incarnational humanism built around the person of Christ in his uniting in His own person the divine and the human. Zimmerman's work encapsulates the view that any version of Christian humanism must include an openness to the transcendent as one of its constituent features and an anthropology that is deeply influenced by Christology.

In an ecclesiastical context, Pope Benedict XVI's 2007 address to the first European Meeting of University Lecturers in Rome is particularly germane. Reflecting the dialogue between classical culture and Christian tradition alluded to earlier, he suggests that:

> Historically, it was in Europe that humanism developed, thanks to the fruitful interplay between the various cultures of her peoples and the Christian faith. Europe today needs to preserve and re-appropriate her authentic tradition if she is to remain faithful to her vocation as the cradle of humanism.
>
> (2007, p. 1)

Rooting his presentation in the centrality of the person of Christ, Pope Benedict goes on to voice his conviction that 'unless we do know God in and with Christ, all of reality becomes an indecipherable enigma' (2007, p. 1). It is worthy of note in this context that fruitful dialogue requires a clear understanding of one's own philosophical, cultural and theological traditions and a commitment to present this worldview to a variety of audiences. The sacramental perspective, in framing all Christian ministry around the person of Jesus, reflects Pope Benedict's conviction.

The sacramental perspective

The idea of Christ as a primordial sacrament first became popular with the work of Otto Semmelroth, a German Jesuit who, in 1953, published *The Church as the Original Sacrament*. It was Karl Rahner's writings, together with those of Edward Schillebeeckx, that brought the idea of Christ as the primordial sacrament and the Church as a basic sacrament into international prominence. In 1961, Rahner published *The Church as Sacrament* while Schillebeeckx had published *Christ, the Sacrament of the Encounter with God* in 1964. In these writings, the idea of the Church as a basic sacrament and Jesus in his humanity as a fundamental or primordial sacrament are seen to be critically interdependent.

The sacramental perspective in an educative perspective

According to Lydon (2011, p. 80ff), in the context of the Catholic school the sacramental perspective is a dominant paradigm within the theological framework of the Second Vatican Council. By engaging in the ministry of teaching, the individual Christian is responding to his or her primary call to be a disciple of Jesus in a distinctive manner, reflecting the notion of charisms being a concrete realisation of the universal gift of God through Christ to all the baptised explored earlier. This fundamental calling demands that all teachers model their ministry on that of Christ. Teachers are, in effect, signs of the presence of Christ within their educational community. As Parker J. Palmer (1998, p. 2) puts it, they 'teach who they are'. The notion that the Christian educational vision is 'passed on in the very lives of the teachers themselves', in the view of Grassi (1973), constitutes a key theme in many post-Vatican II documents.

The sacramental perspective and dialogue

Earlier in this chapter, I hinted towards a dialogue, principally in the context of the relationship between student and teacher, seminal in the context of a holistic perspective. In terms of the sacramental perspective, in his article 'Faith and the Catholic Teacher' (2012), Lydon uses the term 'witness' sixteen times in support of his argument that the whole tone of post-Vatican documents published by the *Congregation for Catholic Education* is dominated by the theological idea that Christ is the foundation of all educational enterprises and that commitment to modelling their lives on Christ is the only effective way in which teachers can translate this vision into practice.

By modelling her ministry on Christ, the teacher will reflect the key aspects of that ministry which encompass many qualities: an invitational and inclusive approach to all, effective presence, respect for an individual's discernment and challenge, reflected in the response of the first disciples. Each of these aspects is underpinned by a commitment to the building of community, which is a central feature of the sacramental perspective, both being linked integrally in all post-Vatican II documents on Catholic education.

Christians and the followers of other religions can work together via inter-religious dialogue to address issues of social responsibility that they have in common to create a new humanistic ethos. The Second Vatican Council presented a ground-breaking document, *Nostra Aetate* (the Declaration on the Relation of the Church to Non-Christian Religions), on the relationship between the Catholic Church and other religions.

> The Church, therefore, exhorts her sons, that through dialogue and colla-boration with the followers of other religions, carried out with prudence and love and in witness to the Christian faith and life, they recognize, preserve and promote the good things, spiritual and moral, as well as the socio-cultural values found among these men.
>
> (*Nostra Aetate*, 1965, par. 2)

Meeting God in Friend and Stranger is the 2010 teaching document on inter-religious dialogue from the Catholic Bishops' Conference of England and Wales. It reminds Catholics that they are called by their baptism to engage in dialogue with others, and specifically with people of other religions. This is part of the Church's task of continuing the dialogue that God engages with His Church, and of reading the signs of His will in our times. The document stresses that this dialogue is not restricted to academics, but takes place where everyday life is shared in an atmosphere of respect and openness. Shared experiences of worship – where the worship takes the form not of coming to pray together, but of coming together to pray, is also a valuable aspect of dia-logue, and one which meets appropriately the desire to share occasions of grief, joy and remembrance (see also Whittle, 2018). The document recognises also that most young people will not enter into interreligious dialogue in a formal academic or theological context. Christians are, however, called to live inter-religious dialogue in practice by building community with people of other faiths and belief-systems. Catholic schools are challenged 'to prepare for that lifetime of interreligious dialogue' (Catholic Bishops' Conference of England and Wales, 2010, p. 85). This latter statement resonates with the mutual respect, and tol-erance, *of those with* different faiths and beliefs spoken of in discussions around the concept of British Values.

Christian humanism: A return to the virtues

In the context of advocacy for people across the world described by Pope Francis as being 'on the peripheries', Catholic-inspired organisations were called to 'move toward a more inclusive society' (2017) and later to position themselves as 'Promoters of Humanity' (Pope Francis, 2019).[5] Yet, perhaps few when asked would be able to define the term 'humanism', even recognised experts. This signifies an inherent challenge of reducing the term 'Christian humanism' to a slogan, analogous to the overuse of the term 'Gospel values'.

Gospel Values is a term used often but only makes sense within the matrix from which it emerges. According to Lydon (2011), virtue is a stronger term than values. He holds the view that virtues dwell in us whereas values, possibly, are more peripheral, analogous to the contrast between ethos and culture. Virtues involve training, apprenticeship, community, communication, self-subordination, disposition, happiness, building on Thomas Aquinas' treatise on virtue, whereas the term 'value' tends to be contingent and in danger of becoming particularly subjective. Gertrude Himmelfarb in *The De-Moralisation of Society* (1995) distinguishes between virtue and values, possibly over-emphasising the dichotomy. She claims that Victorian virtues/values were very strong then, highlighting the strength of the family in transmitting virtues. However, she maintains this strength has been eroded by a greater emphasis on economics and a utilitarian approach:

> ...in this scientific century, morality, virtue and character gradually but steadily became verbal artefacts of an age of religion and superstition. *Values* brought with it the assumptions that all moral ideas and rules are subjective and relative, and in effect, that all human behaviour is socially, economically or genetically determined.
>
> (1995, p. 138)

Scholars such as Boland (2007) argue for a return to the virtues, significant in the context of the classical and medieval roots of humanism, referred to above. Perhaps the most extensive treatment of the concept of virtue, built upon by successive generations of scholars, is contained in Aquinas' *Summa Theologica*, written in 1265–1274 and originally published in 1485.

In articulating the virtue of prudence, Aquinas refers to the Aristotelian concept of *phronesis*, 'practical wisdom', which, again, is particularly relevant to the notion of character or disposition. Terence McLaughlin (1999) invokes the idea of *phronesis* when exploring the concept of 'the reflective practitioner' and argues that the development or formation of character is central to such a concept. This is a different emphasis for reflection, putting the focus on professional competencies. McLaughlin describes *phronesis* as 'a major ordering-agency in our lives generally' (1999, p. 120).

The significance of tradition and community is, undoubtedly, an integral prerequisite to growth in virtue, in the mind of Aquinas. Moral development is always within communities and traditions whose narratives teach the virtues and so provide a model of character that is worthy of emulation and resonating. According to Lydon (2011), this chimes with a key theme from the Pauline corpus in the NT.

A new humanism that is timely in our contemporary global context

The term 'anchorless deliberator' is particularly pertinent in the context of the call for 'a new Christian humanism'. Following Frankfurt (1971), Charles Taylor (1985) draws a distinction between weak evaluation and strong evaluation. Frankfurt distinguishes between two kinds of desires. We experience first-order desires such as hunger along with other animals. However, second-order desires, in which we evaluate other desires – I am hungry but should watch my diet – are unique to human beings. Taylor (1985) elaborates with a distinction between two sorts of second-order, evaluative desires. Weak evaluation entails desires about matters based on mere feeling. Strong evaluation, in contrast, entails desires that define the very person you choose to be. To choices concerning desires of this sort, Taylor argues, entail values that originate outside of yourself, in community, tradition, nature, or God. In other words, to exercise what Taylor calls human agency a person needs strong values, and these can surely be drawn under the appropriate circumstances from faith traditions.

Terence McLaughlin (1985), building on Taylor's distinction, speaks of *autonomy via faith*. In his view, an upbringing in a living (or what he calls a thick) tradition can lead to a strong sense of personal autonomy. When this is accompanied by a good understanding that comes from maturity, young people should take increasing control of their own lives. Religious traditions can in this way be regarded as a source, not a hindrance to, of moral independence. This is because the values one learns through religious instruction could become the basis upon which one makes independent choices.

To say that autonomy can be achieved or enhanced via faith presupposes an individual who is embedded in tradition, history, culture and language. Secularism or comprehensive liberalism is not neutral, in this view, but constitutes a tradition (or more precisely, a variety of traditions) in its own right into which a child may be initiated. To be sure, people raised in different ethical and religious traditions may share many things in common, including almost certainly some common rational grounds for shared discourse and disputation. However, these rational capacities are shaped and moulded by tradition, culture, history and language as a child matures. McLaughlin's position resonates with that of Bryk *et al.*'s (1993) concept of 'openness with roots' that emerged from their empirical research concerning the impact of Vatican II on Catholic secondary education in the US. It involves thus maintaining a balance between some form of critical intelligence and serious religious commitment. This is reflected in the whole tenor of Vatican II, which sought to offer, rather than impose, a distinctive Catholic education project.

This chapter concludes by returning to the *Congregation for Catholic Education*'s document:

> It [fraternal humanism] does not aim to create division and divergence, but rather offers places for meeting and discussion to create valid educational projects. It is an education – at the same time – that is sound and open, that pulls down the walls of exclusivity, promoting the richness and diversity of individual talents and extending the classroom to embrace every corner of social experience in which education can generate solidarity, sharing and communion.
>
> (para. 10)

This sums up most effectively what Grace's work has aimed to achieve[6].

I wish to acknowledge, with much gratitude, my colleague John Lydon, in the preparation of this chapter.

Notes

1 Relevant examples would be Grace (2002), Grace (2007), Grace (2010), Grace (2013) and Grace (2016).

2 A tradition of Catholic theology which proved itself particularly amenable to the Christian mindset.

3 John Sullivan's work has a series of references to 'reception' within Catholicism, in what is, essentially, a critique of the work of Maurice Blondel (1995) on 'living tradition'.

4 See, for example, Congregation for Catholic Education (1977) *The Catholic School*, London: CTS, where reference is made to 'the formation of the whole person' twelve times.

5 Pope Francis speaking at the Catholic-Inspired Non-Governmental Organisations (NGO) Forum, Rome December 2017 and December 2019.

6 Overall, it can be seen that the contribution of Gerald Grace's work in the period 2002–2016 can be interpreted as an early statement of Christian humanism. He did not use this term himself, but close analysis shows that he wrote in the spirit of Christian humanism before the Congregation for Catholic Education formally defined it in 2017.

References

Aquinas, St T. (2006). *The Summa Theologica of St. Thomas Aquinas*. Second and Revised Edition 1920. Literal translation by Fathers of the English Dominican Province (Kevin Knight), Online Edition.

Blondel, M. (1995). *Complete Works*, Paris: Universities of France Press.

Boland, V. (2007.) *St Thomas Aquinas*, London: Continuum.

Bowen, J. (1975). *A History of Western Education: Volume III Civilisation in Europe*, London: Methuen.

Bryk, A., V.E. Lee & P.B. Holland (1993). *Catholic Schools and the Common Good*, Cambridge, MA: Harvard University Press.

Catholic Bishops Conference of England and Wales (2010). *Meeting God in Friend and Stranger*, London: CBCEW.

Congregation for Catholic Education (CCE) (2002). *Consecrated Persons and Their Mission in Schools*, London: CT.

Congregation for Catholic Education (CCE) (2017). *Educating to Fraternal Humanism*, London: CTS.

Dawson, C. (1961). *The Crisis of Western Education*, London: Sheed & Ward.

Franchi, L. (2014) 'The Catholic School as a Courtyard of the Gentiles'. *Journal of Catholic Education*, Vol. 17, No. 3, Article 4, pp. 57–76.

Frankfurt, H. (1971). 'Freedom of Will and the Concept of a Person'. *Journal of Philosophy*, Vol. 67, No. 1, pp. 5–20.

Grace, G. (2002). *Catholic Schools: Mission, Markets and Morality*, London: Routledge Falmer.

Grace, G. (2010). 'Renewing Spiritual Capital: An Urgent Priority for the Future of Catholic Education Internationally', *International Studies in Catholic Education*, Vol. 2, No. 2, pp. 117–128.

Grace, G. (2013). 'Catholic Social Teaching Should Permeate the Catholic Secondary School Curriculum: An Agenda for Reform', *International Studies in Catholic Education*, Vol. 5, No. 1, pp. 99–109.

Grace, G. (2016). *Faith, Mission and Challenge in Catholic Education*, London and New York: Routledge, World Library of Educationalists.

Grace, G. R. and O'Keefe, J. (2007). *International Handbook of Catholic Education: Challenges for School Systems in the 21st Century*, 2 Volumes, Dordrecht: Springer.

Himmelfarb, G. (1995). *The De-Moralisation of Society*, New York: Alfred A. Knopf.

Grassi, J. (1973). *The Teacher in the Primitive Church and The Teacher Today*, Santa Clara, CA: University of Santa Clara.

Lydon, J. (2011). *The Contemporary Catholic Teacher: The Reappraisal of the Concept of Teaching as a Vocation in a Catholic Christian Context*, Saarbrucken: Lambert Academic Publishing.

Lydon, J. (2012). 'Faith and the Catholic Teacher', *The Pastoral Review*, Vol. 8, No. 5, pp. 36–41.

McLaughlin, T.H. (1985). 'Religion, Upbringing and Liberal Values: A Rejoinder to Eamonn Callan', *Journal of Philosophy of Education*, Vol. 19, No. 1, pp. 119–127.

McLaughlin, T.H. (1999). 'Beyond the Reflective Teacher', *Educational Philosophy & Theory*, Vol. 31, No. 1, pp. 9–25.

Palmer, P.J. (1998). *The Courage to Teach*, San Francisco: Jossey-Bass.

Pope Benedict XVI (2007). *Address of His Holiness Benedict XVI to the Participants in the first Meeting of University Lecturers*, Rome: LEV.

Pope Paul VI (1967). *Populorum Progressio*, Encyclical Letter 'On the Development of Peoples' promulgated by Pope Paul VI on the Feast of Easter.

Rahner, K., S.J (1961). *The Church as Sacraments*, Freiburg: Herder.

Second Vatican Council (1965). *Nostra Aetate/Declaration on the Relation of the Church to Non-Christian Religions*, London: CTS.

Semmelroth, O., S.J. (1953). *The Church as the Original Sacrament*, Frankfurt: Main Knecht.

Schillebeeckx, E., O.P. (1964). *Christ, the Sacrament of the Encounter with God*, London: Sheed and Ward.

Sullivan, J. (2000). *Catholic Schools in Contention*, Leamington Spa: Veritas.

Sullivan, J. (2001). *Catholic Education: Distinctive and Inclusive*, Dordrecht: Kluwer Academic Publications.

Taylor, C. (1985) (ed.). *Ethics, Ethnicity and Education*, London: Kogan Page.

Whittle, S. (2018) (ed.). *Religious Education in Catholic Schools*, Oxford and Bern: Peter Lang.

Zimmermann, J. (2016). *Re-Envisioning Christian Humanism: Education and the Restoration of Humanity*, Oxford: Oxford University Press.

Zimmermann, J. (2012). *Incarnational Humanism: A Philosophy of Culture for the Church in the World*, London: IVP Academic.

Chapter 10

Gerald Grace and the philosophy of Catholic education

Sean Whittle

Introduction

This chapter will tease out Gerald Grace's relationship with the philosophy of Catholic education.[1] At the outset, it is essential to note that Grace would be the first to point out that he is firmly an historian and a sociologist of education and he would delineate a sharp distinction between these disciplines and that of the philosophy of education. Respecting his firm distinction, this chapter will present its analysis in three stages. First, it will demonstrate that Grace has repeatedly drawn attention to there being a contemporary need for a clear articulation of the philosophy of Catholic education. Second, praise will be given to the way that Grace has skilfully used his role as editor of the journal *International Studies in Catholic Education* (ISCE) to foster and promote fresh debate and clarification around the philosophy of Catholic education. A brief overview of this debate will be presented. The third stage of the analysis will focus on identifying what would amount to Grace's stance on the philosophy of Catholic education. It will be explained that for Grace this philosophy is built around the imperative of serving the educational needs of the poor. This is, of course, somewhat different to the typical approach, defended in Church teachings, which has traditionally built the philosophy of Catholic education around parental rights. By way of conclusion, the analysis will briefly take up Grace's stance on the philosophy of Catholic education and point out the potentially far-reaching impact it could have on Catholic schooling and educational policy. It will be proposed that, perhaps, Gerald Grace could be regarded as being prophetic in his convictions about how the Church in the modern world ought to be framing its philosophy of Catholic education around the option for the poor.

On the contemporary need for a philosophy of Catholic education

Grace's seminal work, *Catholic Schools: Mission, Markets and Morality* (2002), draws attention to the paucity of contemporary work on the philosophy of Catholic education. This book presents ground-breaking empirical research

DOI: 10.4324/9781003171553-12

about the nature and effectiveness of Catholic schooling in secular Britain. Grace found the relative underdevelopment of a philosophy of Catholic education 'surprising' and that a suitable defence of it might have been expected, one 'constructed by Catholic philosophers' (2002, p. 16). He concurred with others (notably Carr *et al* 1995) that new efforts are needed to produce a contemporary philosophy of Catholic education. In calling attention to this situation, Grace was not alone. Others, such as Elias (1999), had pondered over the decline of formal Catholic philosophies of education. Elias mused on the number of works in the middle of the twentieth century that had deployed Neo-Thomism to frame, justify and conceptualise Catholic education, yet none of these had been updated or had remained in favour after Vatican II. In a roughly similar vein, Kelty (1999) describes how following Vatican II the attention shifted away from formulations of the philosophy of education to the theology of Catholic education.

According to Grace, in the absence of a fully articulated philosophical framework, advocates of Catholic education have used the various publications from the *Congregation for Catholic Education* as a source of guiding principles. He points out that

> In so far as contemporary Catholic schooling, in England at any rate, can claim to be an articulated theoretical framework, it has been derived from these "documents for guidance" rather than from the developed insights of formal scholarship.
>
> (2002, p. 17)

This careful and measured assessment indicates that Grace shares the concerns raised by McLaughlin (1996), who drew attention to the tendency to use phrases such as *Gospel values* or statements from the various education guidance documents to act as a proxy for a properly developed philosophy or theory of Catholic education. The problem with them is two-fold. First, such theological slogans give the false impression that there is a clearly worked-out account of what they actually involve or refer to. Second, they have stifled the task of developing a robust theory of Catholic education because they are repeatedly not recognised for what they actually are. As McLaughlin observes, 'such phrases are primarily useful as spurs to a deeper discussion, not a substitute for it' (1996, p. 138). Far too often these, theologically inspired, slogans or expressions of piety are treated as if they summarise all that needs to be said to frame and justify Catholic education. According to McLaughlin, too often the education documents are 'mined' for such phrases in a rather eclectic way (p. 138).[2]

Thus, in order to justify and frame Catholic education, Grace had little option but to focus on the insights of two key education documents. The first is Vatican II's *Declaration on the Extreme Importance of Christian Education* (*Gravissimum Educationis*, 1965). This relatively short statement is part-and-parcel of the *aggiornamento* or updating of the second Vatican Council (1962–65), when the leaders of the Catholic Church sought to engage with what it means to be the Church in the modern world. According to Grace:

> The declaration, *Gravissimum Educationis* (1965), was therefore calling for a new mode of Catholic schooling to meet the challenges of a modern and secular culture and the needs and expectations of young people growing to maturity in such a culture.
>
> (2002 p. 18)

In addition, the declaration calls attention to members of the Church enabling Catholic schools to become better in 'Caring for the poor, for those who are without the help and affection of family and those who do not have the faith' (*Gravissimum Educationis* par. 9). This sentence reflected a recalibration of the mission of the Catholic school, reaffirming a tradition of attending to the poor and responding to those who face family breakdown, but also introducing a recognition about the mixed nature of the contemporary Catholic school. The bishops at Vatican II were aware that in many parts of the world, Catholic schools are not primarily full of Catholic children. Formally recognising this, even in this fleeting manner, was a significant point of departure for reframing and challenging assumptions about who and what the Catholic school is for. This tacit modification of the philosophy of Catholic education is part of how Vatican II achieved some *aggiornamento* in relation to Catholic education.

The second education document was issued twelve years after the close of the Council. It was promulgated as a guidance document issued by the Vatican's *Congregation for Catholic Education* and it had the title *The Catholic School* (1977). According to Grace, it is this document which

> ...reasserted the role of education as part of the saving mission of the Church to reveal to all ages the transcendent goal which alone gives life its full meaning (p. 13). The influence of Catholic social teaching is particularly evident in this document where the principle of special concern for the deprived in education and again it is emphasised: "First and foremost the Church offers its educational service to the poor" (The Catholic School, 1977 par. 58).
>
> (Grace, 2002, p. 19)

For Grace, more so than *Gravissimum Educationis*, this document gives an emphatic focus on Catholic education being primarily a service to the common good of society and firmly directed at serving the poor.[3] This document had the benefit of being composed in the first flush of Vatican II's reception.[4] There was already, just twelve years after the final session of Vatican II, a growing sense of the Church's 'option for the poor' and the realisation that its priority is not in supporting the status quo but in clearly being on the side of the poor. The 1977 document applied this insight to Catholic education. For Grace, this emphatic alignment between the Catholic school and serving the poor gives the 1977 guidance an importance that supersedes the Council's declaration. This means that the educational mission of the Catholic school can be summed up as serving the poor. For Grace, this pithy summary of the philosophy of Catholic education was able to serve as the starting point for his empirical research into the situation facing headteachers leading Catholic schools in England.

In *Catholic Schools: Mission, Markets and Morality* (2002), Grace reported the finding of his field work in sixty inner-city schools. He draws out the extremely difficult situation which Catholic education in England finds itself in because of explicit government policies to create a market place within educational provision. Grace described the tortuous situation that Catholic headteachers find themselves in because of the huge changes in government-led educational policies over a twenty-year period. There is quite literally a deep tension between the mission of Catholic schools and the educational market place that they have been forced to operate within. As Grace explains:

> If schools in a market economy in education must show good company results in academic success and growing social status, what becomes of the Catholic school principle of 'preferential option for the poor'?
>
> (Grace, 2002, p. 181)

In order to survive there have had to be compromises and accommodations. Grace is maintaining that Catholic education has had to adapt to making academic achievement and league table position an ever-increasing priority. Given this, Catholic schools are being deflected from their primary mission. Grace's 2002 work is a rallying cry to take urgent action to ensure that there will be sufficient *Spiritual Capital* [5] to allow future Catholic school leaders to maintain the core mission of Catholic education, particularly in the face of market values dominating education. A key part of the action needed is the development of a fully worked-out philosophical framework, to underpin the successful transmission of Spiritual Capital.

Gerald Grace's role in promoting debate about the philosophy of Catholic education

Having drawn attention in 2002 to the urgent need for a contemporary robust and developed philosophy or theory of Catholic education, Grace was able to play a role in fostering debate around it. This came about from 2009 onwards, as a direct result of his work as the editor of ISCE. As the founding editor of this international journal, Grace has been able to kick-start a dialogue about a contemporary philosophy of Catholic education. It was in volume 3 of ISCE that he presented the first article that dealt specifically with the contemporary philosophy of Catholic education, written by Professor Brendan Carmody (2011). Grace's firm hope was that 'this contribution will stimulate a debate and further articles on this crucial subject' (2011, p. 2). His astute observation was correct, because it resulted in, to date, three other contributions that have sought to take further this formal philosophical reflection over the aims and justification of Catholic education.

There is richness to the debate and dialogue that Grace's editorship of ISCE has gifted to the field of Catholic Education Studies that deserves to be briefly summarised here. In Carmody's original article (2011), the argument is built around the proposal that the Jesuit philosopher Bernard Lonergan's account of self-transcendence could provide the framework for a contemporary philosophy of education. The mission of Catholic education is to foster a religious conversion through schools that are inclusive but are also 'distinctive, where faith, reason and life are brought into an integrated relationship as a holistic education experience' (Carmody, 2011, p. 113). Given this, the mission of Catholic education can be characterised as being concerned with ensuring or promoting a real assent among students. This could be taken as a partial response to those who would be critical of the place of religion (or theology) in the curriculum. Carmody skilfully indicates how general themes in Lonergan's philosophy could be used to inform or frame Catholic education. This involves a commitment to social justice and to dialogue with all others, including those who belong to different religions. Catholic education sets out to be open to other faiths and is able to challenge the materialism and self-centred attitudes that can dominate contemporary life. In response to Carmody's position, I offered an alternative way of framing the philosophy of Catholic education around insights from another leading Jesuit scholar, the theologian Karl Rahner. This contribution (Whittle 2014a) describes how at the heart of Rahner's theology is an insistence about the significance of mystery in human life, and it is this theological insight which can be used to inspire and stimulate a range of educational arguments that provide the basis for a contemporary theory or philosophy of education. When developed with reference to Rahner's method, Whittle is even able to provide a theological justification for a non-confessional account of Catholic education.[6] As part of this, it can be argued that the curriculum as a whole has a central role to play in bringing pupils to what Rahner described as the threshold of theology. It is the whole curriculum, rather than just Religious Education, that has a role to play in ensuring that pupils recognise the mystery within human existence.

In 2018, two further contributions to the debate appeared in ISCE. The first, by Mario D'Souza, sought to offer further reflections on the philosophy of Catholic education through a critical scrutiny of the contributions from Carmody and Whittle. Although he could see merits in both, his analysis leads on to a detailed argument that favours the relevance of both Lonergan and the neo-Thomist philosopher Maritain, for framing and justifying Catholic education. In the second part of volume 10 (2018), an important contribution from Paddy Walsh appeared that returned to an analysis of how both Lonergan and Rahner are able to reconfigure the contemporary philosophy of Catholic education. Walsh skilfully sought to demonstrate that there is a significant level of complementarity in what these truly great thinkers can together offer as a philosophy of Catholic education fit for our times. In particular, he wanted to combat a tendency in Whittle's contribution to the debate, which championed Rahner over Lonergan. Walsh neatly encapsulates the movement away from drawing a sharp distinction between the 'philosophy' as opposed to the 'theology' of Catholic education. Spelling this out in the detailed way that Walsh does amounts to an important contribution to the contemporary philosophy of Catholic education. Theology and philosophy are inextricably interwoven within the philosophy of Catholic education, particularly in the light of Vatican II's *aggiornamento*.

Nestled alongside these more formal contributions, Grace's editorship of the journal ISCE has, over the past twelve years, sought out further opportunities to put the spotlight on the philosophy of Catholic education. For example, in the inclusion of works in the book review section, the editor of ISCE has always opted to offer readers detailed and high-quality book reviews, which feature very few works – typically just two or three per edition. Crucially, books about the philosophy of Catholic education have been included in this highly select review of works in the field of Catholic Education Studies. For example, Professor Richard Pring's philosophical analysis, *The Future of Publicly Funded Schools* (2017), was afforded two reviews in the same edition (ISCE 2019, issue 1). Similarly, one of the only book-length monographs from the past decade dealing with the theory or philosophy of Catholic education was given a lengthy review by Dylis Wadman (2015). [7] Moreover, other contributors such as Carmody (2017) have explored issues which are central to philosophical debates within the philosophy of Catholic education. In this article, Carmody critiques the very idea of there being a non-confessional Catholic education and takes issue with using Rahner to avoid the spectre of indoctrination from Catholic education.

In all this, Grace as editor of ISCE has performed an important service in nurturing debate and dialogue surrounding the contemporary philosophy of education. In October 2020 (ISCE 2020, p. 129), it was announced that Grace would be relinquishing his editorial role at the end of 2021. It is vital that the same level of attention will be given to fostering and nurturing the much-needed contemporary philosophy of education within the pages of ISCE under new editor(s). Having begun this commendable work, it will be incumbent on others to build on what Grace has achieved in this aspect of Catholic education scholarship.

Grace's stance on the philosophy of Catholic education: An assessment

Having described how Grace has made both a strong case for the contemporary need for a philosophy of Catholic education and then outlining the steps he has taken to promote it, attention can now shift to teasing out Grace's own take on what it involves. This is to return to the observation made above, about the way in which Grace embraced the alignment between the Catholic school and serving the poor in the 1977 document on *The Catholic School*.

In latching upon paragraph 58, which includes the sentence that emphatically declares 'first and foremost' the Church is making its educational provision available to the poor, Grace has identified an embryonic philosophy of Catholic education. It is one that characterises the Church's education work as something which is depicted as both an *offer* and a *service* to those who are poor, deprived of family help and affection and those who are far from the Catholic Christian faith. In being an *offer*, Catholic education is not being framed in terms of the rights of the Church or as something that could be imposed on others. As an *offer*, it has the quality of being 'gift-like' and like all genuine offers it comes without any strings or conditions attached. In addition, in being a *service*, Catholic education is something openly or freely available to those who are in need of it. In that sense, it is not a commodity which can be traded or bought. This is a point emphasised in paragraph 58, when it lists those for whom a Catholic education is intentionally and primarily seeking to serve – those who are poor or are in significant need. These are the marginalised or underclass of society and as such, they are the least able to pay and stand in most need of the *offer* and *service* afforded in a Catholic education. Another facet of this embryonic philosophy of Catholic education is the clause of the sentence which declares that the *offer* and *service* is specifically extended to those who are 'far from the faith'. This means a Catholic education is not, first and foremost, something that is exclusively for the children of Catholic parents. Thus, it is possible to draw out from this embryo the central elements of a highly inclusive and socially just philosophy of Catholic education.

This conclusion is powerfully reinforced when paragraph 58 of *The Catholic School* is read as a whole, rather than just the sentence that Grace hones in on.

> Since it is motivated by the Christian ideal, the Catholic school is particularly sensitive to the call from every part of the world for a more just society, and it tries to make its own contribution towards it. It does not stop at the courageous teaching of the demands of justice even in the face of local opposition, but tries to put these demands into practice in its own community in the daily life of the school. In some countries, because of local laws and economic conditions, the Catholic school runs the risk of giving counter-witness by admitting a majority of children from wealthier families. Schools may have done this because of their need to be financially self-supporting. *This situation is of great concern to those responsible for Catholic education, because first and foremost the Church offers its educational service to "the poor or those who are deprived of family help and affection or those who are far from the faith".* Since education is an important means of improving the social and economic condition of the individual and of peoples, if the Catholic school were to turn its attention exclusively or predominantly to those from the wealthier social classes, it could be contributing towards maintaining their privileged position, and could thereby continue to favour a society which is unjust.
>
> (*The Catholic School*, 1977, par. 58, emphasis added)

There is a strong sociological analysis built into this paragraph. It begins from a global awareness for the need for social justice, which needs to be built into both what is taught and lived out in the daily practice of the Catholic school. Whilst the text recognises the need for Catholic schools to be financially viable, there is a real danger they could actually give a counter-witness by favouring children from wealthier families. In fact, the paragraph hinges on sociological arguments about education being a powerful engine of social improvement and a way of bringing about social justice. Thus, Catholic education has an important role to play in transforming socio-political relationships within societies across the world. The Church has to ensure its educational provision and service are put to work improving social justice throughout society, rather than (inadvertently) maintaining the power or privilege of the wealthy in society. This is a philosophy of Catholic education that puts the pursuit of social justice at the centre stage of its work. With this level of sociological analysis, it is hardly surprising that Grace, given his grounding in the sociology of education and his practical commitment to inclusive and socially just education practices, would have been drawn to the significance of paragraph 58.

However, it is important to acknowledge that Grace's recognition of this embryonic philosophy of Catholic education is a significant break from the typical ways of justifying and framing Catholic education. For almost a century, the standard way to justify and frame Catholic education was through the lens of 'parental rights', following the pattern of arguments presented in Pius XI's encyclical of 1929. To date, this is the only papal encyclical about Catholic education and as such it stands out as an important statement of official Church teaching on Catholic education. This encyclical, known under its Latin name of *Divini Illus Magistri*, is about the Christian education of young people. The encyclical reaffirms the right of the Catholic Church to be involved in education and schooling. To do this, *Divini Illus Magistri* employed a rights-based argument that employed the scaffolding provided by Natural Law principles.[8] It assigned three levels to socio-political relationships.[9] The encyclical maintained that whilst the family comes first, it is dependent on the wider civil society if it is to achieve its purpose. One of the important roles of civil society is to support families in various ways, including educational provision and ensuring that the rights of families are met. The encyclical also maintained the prerogative of families to exercise their legal rights to bring up their children in their religion. The encyclical argued that, as a consequence, the Catholic Church has both a right and a responsibility (towards families) to be involved in the provision of State education. The encyclical argued that the State must recognise the rights of the Church in this area and that it ought to be contributing financially to support Catholic schools.

Gravissimum Educationis deliberately sought to reaffirm much of what Pius XI had stated in 1929. However, notably, this Vatican II declaration recast the language and tone of the encyclical in the way it explained the Church's ongoing commitment to Catholic education and schooling. Crucially, it affirmed the importance of parental rights to justify Catholic education and the political right of the Church to be involved in State education. This rights-based argument (built on the rights of parents as the primary educators) for Catholic education is also enshrined in Canon Law and as such, it has endured as the typical or default way of summing up the philosophy of Catholic education. However, this is significantly different to the position outlined in paragraph 58 of *The Catholic School*, which just does not utilise the concept of parental rights. It might well be that there is a way of synthesising these competing approaches to underpin the philosophy of Catholic education; however, this has not yet been identified. Grace, and those who are persuaded by his arguments around the importance of *The Catholic School* guidance document, is eschewing the typical approach, defended in key Church teachings, which builds the philosophy of Catholic education around parental rights alone.[10]

Concluding observations

By way of conclusion, it is interesting to speculate, albeit briefly, on what the potential impact might be if Grace's stance on the philosophy of Catholic was to be widely taken up and put into practice, particularly in the UK.[11] First, there would be a significant readjustment of admission policies for those seeking a place in Catholic schools. Typically, in English Catholic schools, baptised Catholic children are prioritised for admission. However, Grace's philosophy of Catholic education would mean also prioritising poor and socially disadvantaged students.[12] It is important to reiterate that it is for *all* who are poor and needy, rather than just poverty-struck or disadvantaged Catholic children. Almost inevitably this would lead to a further decline in the proportion of Catholic children in English Catholic schools.[13]

In addition, those who are 'far from the faith' need to be able to find a welcome in Catholic schools. This firm inclusion of those who are 'far from the faith' has some wide-ranging implications for the intentions and goals of a Catholic education. For example, no longer can the fostering or reinforcement of Catholic identity be a central goal. Trying to inculcate a Catholic identity in those children who are 'far from the Catholic faith' would sound alarm bells about the risk of indoctrination, or just the simple failure to welcome these students without wanting to convert them. Thus, Grace's stance allows us to envision a highly inclusive Catholic school, in which there may well be only a minority of students from Catholic families, and because it welcomes those who are far from the faith, it does not impose the Catholic faith on its students. Presumably this would call for a reconfiguration of Religious Education in Catholic schools, moving away from overtly Catholic content and embracing the need to teach a range of worldviews. This sounds very much like the non-confessional account of Catholic education that others have argued in favour of (such as Whittle, 2014a, 2014b).[14]

When it comes to specific education policies, the stance Grace adopts towards the philosophy of Catholic education challenges educational policy in a number of ways. At the obvious level, it would seriously challenge the existence of private or fee-paying Catholic schools, which in the UK are known as independent schools. Given that education is a service to society, it ought not to be reduced to a commodity which can be purchased by the wealthier members of society. As such, it becomes incredibly difficult to justify the existence of Catholic independent schools. At the less obvious level, another but perhaps far more wide-reaching educational policy that is called into question is the drive towards 'academisation', in which schools in England can be directly funded by the Department for Education.[15] The Academy agenda has been highly disruptive, in particular allowing 'market forces' and competition between schools to increase way beyond those worrying levels which Grace first described over two decades ago in *Catholic Schools: Mission, Markets and* Morality (2002). A situation where Catholic academies are in open competition with other Catholic schools goes directly against the primary mission of serving those who are most in need of a Catholic education. Perhaps the only way of justifying the academisation of Catholic schools would be through a radical reconfiguration of *Catholic academies* into schools that are exclusively for poor and socially disadvantaged students. Thus, an educational landscape where Catholic independent schools have a changed role and Catholic academies are first and foremost for the poor and deprived, irrespective of faith tradition, would be one that stands in marked contrast to the current situation. Grace's promotion of the embryonic philosophy of Catholic education found in paragraph 58 of *The Catholic School* is allowing him to be prophetic in his convictions about the aims and content of Catholic education in the twenty-first century. In the light of this prophetic voice, the challenge now is to nurture this stance and develop in more robust terms what it means to frame the philosophy of Catholic education around the *option for the poor*. There is thus a striking convergence between what Grace has been calling for over the past twenty-five years and what has come to the fore with the papacy of Pope Francis.

Notes

1 In this chapter, the focus will be on the 'philosophy of Catholic education', rather than the notion of a 'Catholic' philosophy of education. Whilst there are a number of theorists who employ this ambiguous phrase, such as D'Souza (2018), Hunt and Nuzzi (2004) and Carmody (2011), making the case for a separate version of a specifically Roman Catholic version of every discipline within the field of philosophical studies is fraught with conceptual and epistemological issues.

2 It is interesting to note that Grace has deliberately eschewed McLaughlin's pejorative description of this as '*Catholic edubabble*', despite his long and close working relationship with him. Presumably this is because it sounds as if McLaughlin is being unhelpfully dismissive of educational theory. I have argued more recently in Whittle (2021) that McLaughlin is actually seeking to safeguard the need for a properly worked-out theory of Catholic education, rather than relying on theological slogans and statements of piety.

3 Grace's preference for the 1977 *The Catholic School* over Vatican II's Declaration is something I have challenged (most notably in Whittle, 2016). This is because Vatican II opted to produce a pastorally aware document that deliberately sought to tone down many aspects of Pius XI's encyclical. In contrast to subsequent documents by the *Congregation for Catholic Education*, the declaration has the advantage of saying less rather than more about Catholic education and schools. For a fuller defence of the superiority of *Gravissimum Educationis* over other post-conciliar education documents, see Whittle (2016).

4 It is important to appreciate the close relationship between Vatican II and the subsequent education documents published by the *Congregation for Catholic Education*. When *Gravissimum Educationis* was being considered by the then bishops at the council, they wanted to make a set of positive statements about education, both in the Catholic school and the university, rather than present a fully worked-out treatment of Catholic education. Moreover, the bishops clearly regarded these matters as important and in need of further treatment. One of the pivotal parts of *Gravissimum Educationis* is actually found in the introduction, which explains that there will be a special post-conciliar commission to develop and apply the fundamental principles identified in the declaration. *Gravissimum Educationis* is important both in itself and for bequeathing to the Church agenda a forum in which matters of Catholic education are to be further considered. Rather than being the definitive word on education from a Catholic perspective, *Gravissimum Educationis* is important because it is the beginning of an ongoing discussion about it. This discussion or dialogue has been unfolding in the decades after Vatican II in the various documents issued by the *Congregation for Catholic Education*, beginning with *The Catholic School* (1977). It is interesting to note that the 1977 document deliberately returned to the title that had been abandoned in the earlier draft versions because of the pressures of time.

5 Grace's distinctive development of the theme of spiritual capital is explored and analysed in Chapter 5 of this volume, by Casson ('Researching Spiritual Capital in Catholic Education: On the Need for Theoretical Frameworks and More Empirical Work').

6 The term 'confessional education' is a shorthand way of depicting what Hirst (1972) describes as a primitive or tribal education, where the primary goal of education and upbringing is to hand on the traditions, beliefs and wider cultural life of the tribe. Advocates of faith-based education systems can be characterised as sharing the same confessional desire of the tribal or primitive approach to education. A Catholic education which is aiming to hand on the faith traditions, beliefs and wider cultural life of Catholic Christianity could be described as confessional. In contrast, a non-confessional approach is one which is not in its aims and practices seeking to be confessional or tribal in its approach to education.

7 This is 'A Theory of Catholic Education', Sean Whittle, 2014, London: Bloomsbury.

8 Throughout the twentieth century, the Natural Law political philosophy of Thomas Aquinas was regarded as authoritative within Catholic practice. Given this, it is hardly surprising that *Divini Illus Magistri* couches the discussion of parental rights in these terms.

9 At the primary level are to be found families, and these are the fundamental units of society. In the secondary supporting level there was the State. In essence, the State exists to help families fulfil their *telos*, which is the generation of children and their formation or education within families. There was a third level that came about when individuals joined the Church. This is a supernatural order in which there is a superiority to the natural order afforded by the State.

10 In a personal interview with Professor Grace, whilst writing this chapter, I sought to clarify his position on the status of parental rights in accessing Catholic schools. His answer was 'that parental rights are guaranteed not only by the Church but also by

the United Nations Declaration on Human Rights. However, there is some evidence that the number of baptised Catholic students is reducing over time and a number of secondary schools have, in practice, a category of *other students*. A Governing Body which took seriously the Church's public commitments to the preferential option to the poor and those that are far from the faith might decide to use these principles in admitting *other students* from the local community. We need to be more inclusive of local communities than we are at present'. Grace's careful answer here, whilst not formally rejecting the Church's championing of parental rights alone, indicates how in the local context Governing Bodies could modify this official position and use the insights of Paragraph 58 to achieve the goal of Catholic schools being more inclusive of their local communities.

11 Here attention will be on the situation in England, given that this was the context of Grace's original research. However, Grace's stance on the philosophy of Catholic education would have serious practical implications for Catholic education internationally.

12 In this paragraph, I am suggesting that the thrust of Grace's stance would mean the priority for admission to a Catholic school ought to be around the principles of paragraph 58, rather than on those who have been baptised. In a situation where there are limited spaces available, it might well be that more affluent baptised Catholic children will not gain a place in a Catholic school. This is because socially disadvantaged children, who are perhaps also far from the faith, will be prioritised and be given admission.

13 The annual *Catholic Education Service of England and Wales* census data shows how, over many years, for increasing proportions of the Catholic community, choosing a Catholic school is no longer the default position. Overall, the data for 2019 shows that 68% of children at Catholic schools came from Catholic families. However, there are more than enough baptised children in the UK to fill all the spaces in Catholic schools; it is just that these families are choosing non-Catholic schools to educate their children. The cause of this is largely rooted in the sociological changes that have occurred among the Catholic community in Britain. The drift towards the adoption of middle-class values and attitudes, which the Catholic sociologist Michael Hornsby-Smith drew attention to in 1978 has continued apace (see Hornsby-Smith, 1999). Thus, it would appear that there are fewer poorer and socially disadvantaged Catholic families in England, and this would indicate that there ought to be fewer of these children at Catholic schools.

14 In the personal interview (see endnote 10), I asked Professor Grace about his stance on non-confessional Catholic schools. His answer was that he had been strongly influenced by the counter-argument to non-confessional Catholic schools written by Brendan Carmody SJ in ISCE (2017). Grace is convinced that post-Vatican II Catholic schools have moved from an indoctrinatory pedagogy to a dialogic pedagogy which respects the integrity of the student. As Carmody says 'the Catholic church sees its Catholic schools as *confession* but at the same time *truly educative*' (see *The Catholic School*, 1977). As paragraph 31 puts it, 'Catholic schools must develop people who are responsible and inter-directed, capable of choosing freely in conformity of their conscience'. Although Grace's answer is a rejection of non-confessional Catholic education, this does not detract from my concluding observation that his stance sounds very similar to the position I have argued for (Whittle, 2014a, 2014b) and described as non-confessional Catholic education.

15 For a fuller discussion of the issues surrounding academies and Catholic education, see Buck (2019) and Whittle (2020).

References

Buck, M. (2019). *Renewing the Church-State Partnership for Education*. Oxford: Peter Lang.

Carmody, B. (2011). Towards a Contemporary Catholic Philosophy of Education, in *International Studies in Catholic Education*, 3:2, pp. 106–119.

Carmody, B. (2017). The Catholic School: Non-confessional?, in *International Studies in Catholic Education*, 9:2, pp. 162–175.

Carr, D., Haldane, J., McLaughlin, T. and Pring, R. (1995). Return to the Crossroads: Maritain Fifty Years On, in *British Journal of Educational Studies*, 43:2, pp. 162–178.

Congregation for Catholic Education. (1977). *The Catholic School*. London: Catholic Truth Society.

D'Souza, M. (2018). Further Reflections on a Catholic Philosophy of Education, in *International Studies in Catholic Education*, 10:1, pp. 2–14.

Elias, J. (1999). Whatever Happened to the Catholic Philosophy of Education?, in *Religious Education*, 94:1, pp. 92–110.

Grace, G. (2002). *Catholic Schools: Missions, Markets and Morality*. London: Routledge.

Grace, G. & Lydon, J. (2020). Editorial, in *International Studies in Catholic Education*, 12:2, p. 129.

Gravissimum Educationis, in Abbott, W. (Ed.) (1966). *The Documents of Vatican* II. New York: Herder and Herder.

Hirst, P. (1972). Christian Education: A Contradiction in Terms, in *Learning for Living*, 11: 4, pp. 6–11.

Hornsby-Smith, M. (1999). *Catholics in England 1950–2000: Historical and Sociological Perspectives*. London: Cassell.

Hunt, T. & Nuzzi, R. (Eds.) (2004). *Handbook of Research on Catholic Education*. New York: Greenwood Press.

Kelty, B. (1999). Towards a Theology of Catholic Education, in *Religious Education*, 94:1, pp. 6–23.

Pius XI, (1929). *Divini Illus Magistri* [On Christian Education of the Youth]. Papal Encyclical available at Vatican official website: Online at www.vatican/va.

Pring, R. (2017). *The Future of Publicly Funded Schools*. London: Routledge.

McLaughlin, T. H. (1996). The Distinctiveness of Catholic Education, in McLaughlin, T. H., O'Keefe, J. M. & O'Keefe, B. (Eds). *The Contemporary Catholic School: Context, Identity and Diversity*. London: Falmer Press.

Wadman, D. (2015). Book Review of *A Theory of Catholic Education*, in *International Studies in Catholic Education*, 7:2, pp. 247–250.

Walsh, P. (2018). From Philosophy to Theology of Catholic Education, with Bernard Lonergan and Karl Rahner, in *International Studies in Catholic Education*, 10:2, pp. 132–155.

Whittle, S. (2014a). Towards a Contemporary Philosophy of Catholic Education: Moving the Debate Forward, in *International Studies in Catholic Education*, 6:1, pp. 46–59.

Whittle, S. (2014b). *A Theory of Catholic Education*. London: Bloomsbury.

Whittle, S. (Ed.) (2016). *Vatican II and New Thinking about Catholic Education*. London: Routledge.

Whittle, S. (Ed.) (2020). *Conference Report from the First National Conference on Academisation*. Whitehaven: Networking Education Trust Ltd.

Whittle, S. (Ed.) (2021). *Irish and British Reflections on Catholic Education: Foundations, Identity, Leadership Issues and Religious Education in Catholic Schools*. Singapore: Springer.

Gerald Grace's influence internationally

Chapter 11

Measuring the contributions of Catholic schools globally

Quentin Wodon

Introduction

About two and a half years ago, I had the opportunity to meet Professor Gerald Grace for the first time in Rome. We both participated in a conference on Catholic education organised by the University of Notre Dame and were on the same panel. Right after the panel, he asked me to draft an article for the journal he had created a decade earlier – *International Studies in Catholic Education* (ISCE). His request was for me to use some of the data I had compiled from household surveys and other sources to provide a quantitative assessment of the extent to which Catholic schools were reaching the poor in Africa. The issue of whether Catholic schools were successful in reaching the poor was one that he deeply cared about. More generally, his intent was to promote robust empirical work on the contribution of Catholic schools, given that much of the existing literature tended to be conceptual or theological, or based on small datasets. He felt that if the contributions of Catholic schools to students and their families, as well as communities and societies, were to be better recognised, they had to be documented quantitatively using robust, nationally representative data. Over the last two years, he has encouraged me to pursue work in this area, especially in developing countries where fewer studies have been conducted so far on Catholic schools than is the case in high-income countries.

The second time I met Professor Grace was in London a year later, again thanks to a conference on Catholic education organised by the University of Notre Dame. I have two vivid memories of Professor Grace from that week. The first memory is when he asked to comment on one of the issues being discussed at the conference, and therefore needed the microphone. A friend of his brought the microphone on a small red cushion (if I recall properly) and gave it to him saying 'Your Grace'! This was a playful mark of respect not only for Professor Grace's ability to inject crucial substance into virtually any discussion, but also for the way in which he did so, using an orator speaking style that was reminiscent of a previous era. Combined with his vast knowledge and the fact that he was always impeccably dressed, you had the feeling of being in the presence of a type of scholarship that has become rare these days. A second memory from that

DOI: 10.4324/9781003171553-14

same week is when I gave a lecture at Saint Mary's University Twickenham (London) at Professor Grace's invitation. He simply organised everything with perfection, from the choice of the venue (the Senior Common Room) which was beautiful, to his introductory remarks and the reception afterwards. He even went through the trouble of dropping me back by car in London at my hotel after the event. Truly, he was a wonderful host. Apart from his scholarship, his personal qualities and the friendship he extended to others, this, I suspect, is also a reason why his work on Catholic education has been so influential internationally. He is also generous with his time – when I asked him to answer a few questions for an interview for the *Educatio Si Bulletin* that I am co-editing for the International Office for Catholic Education (*Office International de l'Enseignement Catholique* or OIEC[1] in French), he agreed right away (Grace, 2020).

As I thought about the focus of a chapter for this Festschrift, I faced a bit of a dilemma in terms of the choice of topic to focus on. Should I try to write an essay on some of the areas that Professor Grace worked on himself, and in particular the concept of spiritual capital (e.g., Grace, 2002a, 2002b)? Or should I focus more on some of the areas on which he thought I might be able to contribute some new insights because of my training as an applied economist? As I am still very much of a novice in the field of research on Catholic education, I feel that I do not yet have the depth of knowledge needed to tackle properly the 'big issues' related to the identity of Catholic schools, how to foster spiritual capital,[2] and how to build 'fraternal humanism', to borrow the term used by the Congregation for Catholic Education (2017). So allow me to focus on the area on which I have done more work – trying to measure, albeit imperfectly, some of the contributions of Catholic schools globally. This is in fact also an area in which Professor Grace was a pioneer, including through the comparative analysis of Catholic education he provided in his two-volume handbook on international Catholic education (Grace and O'Keefe, 2007).

Rather than focus on any one particular contribution of Catholic schools globally, it seems more useful for a Festschrift to go a bit broader, and provide an overview on the topic at hand. For this reason, the analysis in this chapter is adapted from the first chapter of the *Global Catholic Education Report* (Wodon, 2020a) I wrote recently for OIEC. This analysis has not been published formally in book format, so I thought it might be appropriate to include it in this Festschrift, especially since Professor Grace encouraged me to work in this area. For this chapter, I updated the data on enrolment trends to reflect the latest available data from the Secretariat of State of the Vatican (2020), reorganised some of the components of the analysis, and shortened it to fit within the allocated word limit. Finally, in the conclusion, I added a few personal thoughts on the inspiration that we can all derive from Professor Grace's leadership in this field of research.

The main message from this chapter is that Catholic schools contribute in a very significant way to achieving the fourth of the Sustainable Development Goals (SDGs) – ensuring inclusive and equitable quality education and promoting lifelong learning opportunities for all. To show how this is the case, I will first document trends in enrolment in Catholic schools using data from the annual statistical yearbooks of the Church. Thereafter, I will discuss some of the specific contributions made by Catholic schools that benefit students and their families, as well as communities and broader societies. Finally, in my conclusion, I will briefly mention some of the concerns that are emerging from the COVID-19 crisis.

Trends in enrolment

Data on the number of students in K12 Catholic schools are available in the Catholic Church's annual statistical yearbooks, with the most recent data available for 2018.[3] The yearbooks provide data by country on enrolment in K12 schools by level, considering separately preschools, primary schools, and secondary schools for each country and some territories. Data are also provided for enrolment in institutions of higher learning, but this is not considered in this chapter (for trends in enrolment at the tertiary level, see Wodon, 2020b; for a more detailed analysis of K12 trends, see Wodon, 2018a).

Figures 11.1 through 11.4 provide estimates of enrolment in Catholic schools for preschools, primary schools, and secondary schools, as well as total enrolment for all three levels combined. Trends are visualised for five regions: Africa, the Americas, Asia, Europe, and Oceania. The analysis is kept at that level to keep the figures manageable, but data are available at the country level in the statistical yearbooks as well as in the statistical annex of the *Global Catholic Education Report 2020* (in that report with data over time in five-year intervals up to 2017). For primary and secondary schools, data are provided in Figures 11.2 and 11.3 from 1975 to 2018. For preschools, data are not available for 1975, so the series starts in Figure 11.1 in 1980. More detailed breakdowns for sub-regions could be constructed, but the regions included in the figures are sufficient to establish stylised facts on broad trends in enrolment globally and regionally.

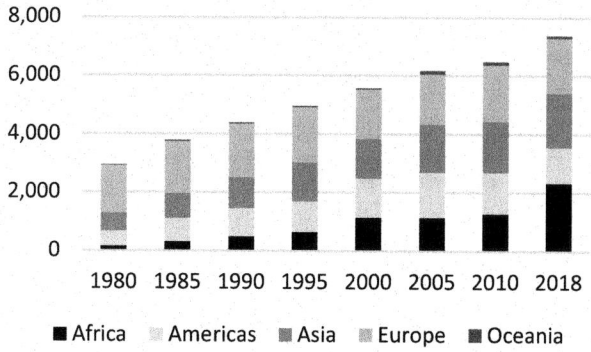

Figure 11.1 Enrolment in Catholic preschools (thousands)

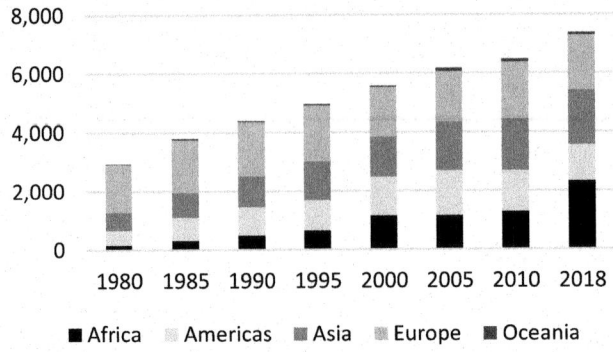

Figure 11.2 Enrolment in Catholic primary schools (thousands)

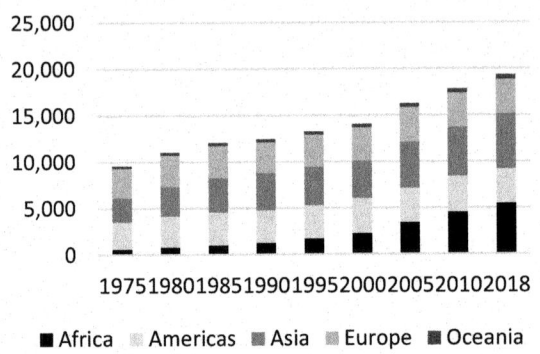

Figure 11.3 Enrolment in Catholic secondary schools (thousands)

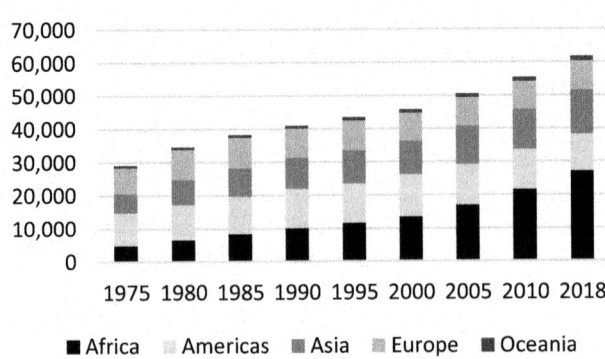

Figure 11.4 Total enrolment in Catholic K12 schools (thousands)
Note: Preschools not included in 1975
Source: *Statistical Yearbook of the Church*

In 2018, according to the latest statistical yearbook, 7.4 million children were enrolled in Catholic preschools globally, 35.0 million children attended primary schools, and 19.3 million children attended secondary schools, for a total across the three levels of more than 62.1 million children. Overall, the Church managed more than 100,000 primary schools, close to 50,000 secondary schools, and over 70,000 preschools. In some countries such as India that are large and complex, estimates of enrolment in Catholic schools could be on the low side due to the difficulty of collecting comprehensive data from multiple organisations managing Catholic schools beyond Dioceses. While additional work could be conducted at the country level to check estimates with other data sources country by country, this would be a major undertaking beyond the scope of this chapter.

Despite necessary caution about the data, a number of stylised facts emerge. First, trends in enrolment suggest healthy growth over time. Total enrolment in K12 education more than doubled between 1975 and 2018 globally, from 29.1 million to 62.1 million students. Most of the growth was concentrated in sub-Saharan Africa. This is not surprising, given the region's high rate of population growth and its gains in enrolment thanks to the 'education for all initiative'. As a result, by 2018, the Africa region had 27.2 million children enrolled in Catholic K12 schools. Of those, 19.4 million were in primary schools. This accounted for 55.1 percent of all children enrolled in Catholic schools at that level globally. The other region with a large increase in enrolment in absolute terms over time is Asia, mostly due to gains in India, especially at the secondary level.

Second, there are differences between regions in the share of students by level. Globally, primary schools account for 56.22 percent of total enrolment in K12 Catholic schools in 2018, versus 32.1 percent for secondary schools, and 11.7 percent for preschools. In Africa, however, primary schools still account for 71.3 percent of total enrolment, mostly because the transition to secondary schools is still weak in many countries (only four in ten students in sub-Saharan Africa complete their lower secondary school according to the World Bank's World Development Indicators). Globally, there has been a progressive decline in the share of students enrolled at the primary level globally given gains in educational attainment and more opportunities for children to benefit from pre-primary education.

Third, in proportionate terms, as a percentage change from the base, the highest growth rates are observed for Africa, as was the case for absolute gains in enrolment. But growth rates are also high in Asia and Oceania. By contrast, in the Americas (and especially the US) and in Europe, growth rates tend to be much smaller, and in some cases are negative. If those trends continue, Africa will represent in the future an even larger share of all students enrolled in Catholic schools globally (Wodon, 2019a).

Fourth, the share of students enrolled in Catholic schools globally has remained somewhat stable over time. To compute this share, estimates of enrolment in

Catholic schools can be compared to data on the total number of pupils enrolled in school from the UNESCO Institute of Statistics. This can be done for primary and secondary schools as data for preschool enrolment are less reliable. Globally, just under five percent of all students at the primary level are enrolled in Catholic schools. For secondary school, the proportion is a bit smaller. Over time, this share has decreased slightly at the secondary level, but it has increased slightly at the primary level. In Africa, however, these shares are much higher.

Fifth, there is a lot of heterogeneity between countries in the size of their Catholic school networks. Together, the top 15 countries in terms of enrolment in K12 Catholic schools account for about two-thirds of global enrolment. Enrolment is largest in absolute terms in India due in part to the sheer size of the country. But many of the other countries with large enrolment are from sub-Saharan Africa, including the Democratic Republic of Congo, Uganda, Kenya, and Malawi. Three of these four countries are classified as low income by the World Bank, with Kenya classified as lower-middle income, as is the case of India. In other words, many of the largest Catholic school networks are located in countries with substantial poverty, contributing to the mission of Church to serve the poor.

Sixth, the fact that the highest growth rate in enrolment over the last four decades is observed for preschools is good news. Early childhood is a critical period in the life of children and investments at that age tend to have high returns. This is the case especially for the first 1,000 days in the life of children when brain development occurs, but also later, including to make sure that children are ready to enter primary school (Black et al., 2017). Early stimulation and preschools are among key programmes that governments should promote to invest in human development (Denboba et al., 2014).

Contributions to education systems

By enrolling 62.1 million students globally, Catholic schools clearly make a contribution to education systems in the countries where they operate. But what about the quality of the education being provided? It is often believed that Catholic schools perform comparatively well in terms of learning outcomes. In the United States where much of the research has been conducted, multiple studies have suggested positive outcomes for students attending Catholic schools (see among others Coleman et al., 1982; Greely, 1982; Coleman and Hoffa, 1987; Bryk et al., 1993; Evans and Schwab, 1995; Evans et al., 1995; Sander and Krautman, 1995; Sander, 1996; Neal, 1997; Altonji et al., 2005; Carbonaro, 2006; Hallinan and Kubitschek, 2013; and Freeman and Berends, 2016). Whether the schools themselves perform better than other types of schools remains debated, and a few studies have suggested that this may not be the case (see for example Jepsen, 2003; Elder and Jepsen, 2014). Yet overall, the evidence points to a Catholic school advantage possibly linked to core values espoused by the schools such as an emphasis on the community, high expectations for students, and a concern for social justice leading schools to reach out to low-income and minority students. In developing countries, the evidence on the performance of Catholic schools is less extensive in part due to lack of data, although there are exceptions. Yet, it cannot be denied that in many countries there is a strong demand from parents for a Catholic education related at least in part to a perception of academic strength.

The ability of Catholic schools to empower principals and create a positive school culture may be one of the reasons why they seem to perform well.[4] This relates to conditions for school autonomy and accountability emphasised in the literature (Demas and Arcia, 2015). The importance of school leadership and management can be illustrated with the case of Fe y Alegría schools in Latin America (Wodon, 2019b). Evidence in Peru suggest that the schools perform well (Lavado et al., 2016). See also the essays in Parra Osorio and Wodon (2014). According to focus groups and interviews (Osorio and Wodon, 2014), factors contributing to the good performance of Fe y Alegría schools include a high degree of independence at the school level for generating and managing resources, a favourable institutional climate, an emphasis on the proper selection, tutoring, supervision, and training of teachers, autonomy and authority for school principals, and the capacity to adapt to local realities. Principals convey 'the mission of the schools' in order to engage students, teachers, and the whole community. Fe y Alegría teachers are motivated by the sense of purpose they witness in the schools and experienced teachers enjoy the opportunity to coach and mentor younger teachers. These various elements of the culture of the schools are mutually reinforcing, leading to better teaching and student learning.

Contributions to communities

As mentioned earlier, Catholic schools and the Church more generally have a long tradition of serving the poor (e.g. Pontifical Council for Justice and Peace, 2004; Francis, 2015; McKinney, 2018). Today, implementing the preferential option for the poor is challenging for many schools. Congregations which used to be able to provide quasi-free education a few decades ago may no longer have the personnel and resources to do so today. In the absence of state support, cost recovery may lead the schools to be unaffordable for the very poor. These pressures are unlikely to change, and may become more severe. One of the ways to reach the poor is to locate schools in poor areas, but this is not necessarily where new schools are being built (Wodon, 2020c). Still, even if Catholic schools are not primarily serving the poor today as is the case for most other types of schools, they do reach millions of children in poverty (on sub-Saharan Africa, see Wodon, 2014, 2015, 2019c, 2020d).

Catholic and other faith-based schools also provide options for parents, thus contributing to healthy pluralism in the educational choices available to them. One benefit is that parents may be more comfortable with faith-based schools for their adolescent girls (Gemignani and Wodon, 2017; see also Gemignani et al.,

2014, on parental perceptions of schools.). Another benefit relates to the concepts of integral growth or integral human development used in Catholic social thought to refer to the growth of the whole person, including in terms of the values that the person acquires. By emphasising those aspects, even if the evidence to that effect remains limited, Catholic schools may help build stronger communities with higher levels of civic participation from their members.

Education systems should help children to become engaged citizens who are respectful of others and of the earth. This was recognised in Article 29 of the Convention on the Rights of the Child (on the crucial importance of the right to education for other human rights and the Sustainable Development Goals, see Wodon, 2019g). It is also recognised by most school networks, whether of public, private, secular or faith-based nature. What exactly the call for promoting values and character education in educational systems entails may differ depending on the school system considered. But respect for others and for pluralism (which does not imply relativism) should be one of the core values being taught.

According to the Congregation for Catholic Education (2017), Catholic schools should strive towards the development of a person's psychological and moral consciousness. The Congregation defines 'a school as a place where integral formation occurs through a living encounter with a cultural inheritance'. Given the pluralism that characterises today's societies and the fact that many students in Catholic schools are not Catholic, the Congregation calls for an education that leads to 'fraternal humanism and a civilization of love' (p. 532). Ensuring that education is provided 'in a Catholic key' should be a key aim of Catholic schools (DelFra et al., 2018). Such an education is based on a personal encounter with others who pass on faith and wisdom; it is sacramental, permeated by an intentional culture; it is Eucharistic in affirming the communal nature of the person; and it is unitive, combining faith and reason. When they are successful, the schools create an environment that fosters not only academic excellence, but also spiritual growth – for children who are Catholics and those who are not, so that all can pursue their own journey towards the fullness of human flourishing. The respect for faith, including other faiths than the Catholic faith, and the emphasis on values may again contribute to civic engagement (Dee, 2005; see also Green et al., 2018a, 2018b) and help build stronger communities (Brinig and Garnett, 2014). To put this in Professor Grace's own terms, as schools invest in the spiritual capital of staff, teachers, and principals, this may have lasting benefits for the schools and their students (Grace, 2002a, 2002b).

Economic contributions

There is a debate in many countries as to whether states should provide funding for low-cost nonprofit 'private'[5] schools, which would include Catholic schools. Discussing arguments related to this debate is beyond the scope of this chapter, but it should be noted that a robust network of Catholic schools, whether they benefit from public funding or not, may be beneficial to societies in several ways. One of them relates to savings for state budgets since in many countries parents pay some or all the cost of sending their children to Catholic schools. When this is the case, enrolment in Catholic schools reduces budget outlays that states must finance to provide basic education to children. These savings represent a shift of the economic burden of providing education to households.

To estimate education budget savings for governments from Catholic schools, information is needed on the number of children enrolled in Catholic schools and the level of funding per student provided by states to Catholic schools in comparison to funding provided to public schools. As noted earlier, information on enrolment in Catholic schools is available from the annual statistical yearbooks of the Church. Information on state funding for private and public schools is available for OECD and partner countries through data collected for *Education at a Glance* reports. Assuming for simplicity that Catholic schools are funded by states at the same level as other private schools (in some countries such as the United States, funding for Catholic schools is lower), the data can be combined with data on enrolment in Catholic schools to measure budget savings for states generated by Catholic schools.

Estimates for 38 OECD and partner countries suggest that, overall, budget savings from Catholic schools in these countries are valued at US$ 63 billion per year in purchasing power parity terms (Wodon, 2019d). When comparing those estimates to those for private schools overall, Catholic schools account for 35.4 percent of the total budget savings from private schools at the primary level, and 19.2 percent at the secondary level. The country that accounts for the largest budget savings from Catholic schools is the United States, with savings valued at US$ 12 billion for primary schools and US$ 7 billion for secondary schools. Similar analysis for Catholic colleges and universities suggests that Catholic tertiary education institutions help generate in the same set of countries another $43 billion in savings for state budgets versus a situation in which the students were to enrol in public institutions instead (Wodon, 2018b; see also Wodon, 2019e for estimates for all private schools as opposed to only Catholic schools).

Another way to show the economic contribution of Catholic schools is to compute the share of 'human capital' wealth created by the schools using recent World Bank data on the changing wealth of nations.[6] Wealth is the assets base that enables nations to generate future income. Human capital wealth is defined as the present value of the future earnings of a country's labour force. The other two main sources of wealth are produced capital and natural capital, but human capital wealth accounts for a much larger proportion of total wealth than natural capital and produced capital (Lange et al., 2018).

To estimate the contribution of Catholic schools globally to human capital wealth, analysis can rely on an assessment of the share of human capital wealth attributed to educational attainment, and in turn the share of the contribution of Catholic schools to educational attainment. Such an analysis for 141 countries accounting for 95 percent of the world's population suggests that Catholic schools may contribute globally US$ 12 trillion to the changing wealth of nations (Wodon, 2019f). The main objectives of Catholic schools are not economic, but their economic contribution for societies' development is substantial.[7]

Conclusion

Building on the pioneering work of Professor Grace in exploring the role played by Catholic schools in many countries (Grace and O'Keefe, 2007), the purpose of this chapter was to document some of the contributions made by Catholic schools globally. After a brief review of global and regional trends in enrolment in K12 Catholic schools, this chapter considered three key contributions by Catholic schools: their contribution to education systems, their contribution to communities, and finally their economic contribution. These contributions are substantial and need to be better recognised.

In many ways, Catholic schools appear to have done comparatively well. But we should not forget that doing well in comparison to other types of schools does not imply doing well in absolute terms. Especially for student learning, much remains to be done, as noted by the World Bank (2018) report on the learning crisis and companion studies such as Bashir et al. (2018) for sub-Saharan Africa. In the developing world, many education systems, including in all likelihood many Catholic schools, have not yet succeeded in ensuring that all the children enrolled in school actually learn effectively. These education systems were already facing a learning crisis before the COVID-19 crisis. The challenges brought about by the current crisis on top of those that prevailed before the crisis hit are daunting. Catholic schools in countries that do not provide financial support to the schools are especially vulnerable, because the economic crisis has weakened the ability of parents to pay for the education they want to give to their children. In these countries, there is a high risk that many Catholic schools may have to close (on the threats from the current crisis and potential responses, see the analysis in Wodon, 2020e, 2020f).

It is too early at the time of writing to assess how adequate Catholic school responses as well as broader national policy responses will be to mitigate the effects of the COVID-19 crisis. For developing country contexts, which is where enrolment in Catholic schools is growing fastest, useful reviews of options for schools and education systems to cope with the current crisis have been published (see for example World Bank, 2020). Some of the lessons from those reviews are valid for developed countries as well, even if the challenges are different. Those reviews emphasise the idea of 'rebuilding better' after the crisis, for example through blended learning mixing in-person teaching with online materials. While rebuilding better will not be easy, it will be needed. Ensuring that Catholic schools can pursue their mission will be challenging, but the benefits of doing so will be reaped for many years to come.

In concluding this chapter, let me mention one last thought about Professor Grace's contribution to research on Catholic schools. At one of our meetings in

London, I asked him why he launched ISCE in 2009. He mentioned that as he was driving one night, he had an inspiration that promoting research on Catholic schools should be his 'calling' in retirement. I guess that at the time he was still serving as Head of the School of Education at Durham University after a long teaching career among others at Kings College (London), the University of Cambridge, and Victoria University of Wellington. It seems fair to say that he never retired. Apart from founding ISCE, he remained very active in managing the *Centre for Research and Development in Catholic Education*, publishing books and articles, speaking on Catholic education, and even serving as a Consultor to the Congregation for Catholic Education for several years. This level of dedication to the cause of Catholic education is a great example for all of us, and especially those (including myself) who may be starting to think about 'what next' when planning their future retirement!

Notes

1 OIEC is a nonprofit that federates globally national Catholic education associations and congregations running schools, and helps represent Catholic education in international fora, including at the United Nations.

2 In the interview I did with Professor Grace for the *Educatio Si Bulletin*, I asked what was 'spiritual capital'. He answered that he thought about the concept after interviewing 60 Catholic headteachers working in challenging inner-city Catholic secondary schools in London, Birmingham, and Liverpool. As he explained it, 'the majority of them were possessed by what can be called a "vocation" or an "inner spiritual strength" which sustained them in the day to day challenges of their work. They characteristically related their Catholic faith to their practice in schools. As a background to my fieldwork, I had read the important work of the French social theorist Pierre Bourdieu and his valuable analytical concepts of "Social capital", "Cultural capital" and "Religious capital". However, my participants seemed to have a form of capital which was different from these and in the last chapter of my book I expressed this internal resource which they possessed as "Spiritual Capital". This was not Bourdieu's religious capital. I defined it as: "Resources of faith and values derived from commitment to a religious tradition"' (Grace, 2002b, p. 236).

3 K12 refers to education from Kindergarten (pre-school) to the 12th grade or completion of high school.

4 This could be related to Grace's hypothesis about the presence of Spiritual Capital and its motivating consequences for teachers and school leaders, but more research would be needed before this relation could be demonstrated empirically.

5 Some Catholic researchers object to the use of the label 'private' for Catholic schools. Many Catholic schools began historically as 'voluntary schools'. Education was provided by religious congregations at minimal cost to parents. Today, in many countries, in part because of reductions in the numbers of Religious available as teachers, many Catholic schools are compelled to charge fees in order to survive. But they aim to maintain those fees as low as possible and they have an identity that differs substantially from traditional private schools which tend to be socially exclusive and charge high fees (although there is today also an increase in low-cost private schools especially in the developing world).

6 Human capital wealth can be estimated using household surveys by computing and discounting the stream of earnings that individuals are expected to accrue over the

remainder of their work life, with earnings themselves modelled as a function of the individual's level of educational attainment and their work experience.

7 It is important for the Catholic Church, working through its conferences of bishops and national Catholic education associations across the world, as well as the Congregation for Catholic Education and organisations such as OIEC and the International Federation of Catholic Universities (IFCU), to bring this type of data to the attention of global leaders. This can help demonstrate how Catholic schools are contributing to the common good of the societies in which they are located. This is one of the reasons why I wrote for OIEC the first *Global Catholic Education Report* in 2020. The next report is planned for release in March 2021.

References

Altonji, J. G., T. E. Elder, and C. R. Taber, (2005). An Evaluation of Instrumental Variable Strategies for Estimating the Effects of Catholic Schooling, *Journal of Human Resources* 40, pp. 791–821.

Bashir, S., M. Lockheed, E. Ninan, and J. P. Tan, (2018). *Facing Forward: Schooling for Learning in Africa.* Washington, DC: The World Bank.

Black, M. M., S. P. Walker, L. C. H. Fernald, C. T. Andersen, A. M. DiGirolamo, C. Lu, D. C. McCoy, G. Fink, Y. R. Shawar, J. Shiffman, A. E. Devercelli, Q. Wodon, E. Vargas-Barón, and S. Grantham-McGregor, (2017). Early Child Development Coming of Age: Science through the Life-Course, *The Lancet*, 389 (10064), pp. 77–90.

Brinig, M. F. and N. S. Garnett, (2014). *Lost Classroom, Lost Community: Catholic Schools' Importance in Urban America.* Chicago: The University of Chicago Press.

Bryk, A. S., V. E. Lee, and P. B. Holland, (1993). *Catholic Schools and the Common Good.* Cambridge, MA: Harvard University Press.

Carbonaro, W., (2006). Public-Private Differences in Achievement among Kindergarten Students: Differences in Learning Opportunities and Student Outcomes, *American Journal of Education*, 113, pp. 31–65.

Coleman, J. S., T. Hoffer, and S. Kilgore, (1982). *High School Achievement: Public, Catholic, and Private Schools Compared.* New York: Basic Books.

Coleman, J. S. and T. Hoffer, (1987). *Public and Private High Schools: The Impact of Communities.* New York: Basic Books.

Congregation for Catholic Education, (2017). *Educating to Fraternal Humanism: Building a "Civilization of Love" 50 Years after Populorum Progressio.* Vatican City: Libreria Editrice Vaticana.

Dee, T. S., (2005). The Effects of Catholic Schooling on Civic Participation, *International Tax and Public Finance*, 12 (5), pp. 605–625.

Delfra, L. A., W. C. Mattison, S. D. McGraw, and T. S. Scully, (2018). Education in a Catholic Key, in W. H. James, editor, *The Handbook of Christian Education.* Hoboken, NJ: Wiley Blackwell.

Demas, A. and G. Arcia, (2015). *What Matters Most for School Autonomy and Accountability: A Framework Paper.* SABER Working Paper Series Number 9. Washington, DC: The World Bank.

Denboba, A., R. Sayre, Q. Wodon, L. Elder, L. Rawlings, and J. Lombardi, (2014). *Stepping Up Early Childhood Development: Investing in Young Children for High Returns.* Washington, DC: The World Bank.

Elder, T., and C. Jepsen, (2014). Are Catholic Primary Schools More Effective than Public Primary Schools? *Journal of Urban Economics*, 80, pp. 28–38.

Evans, W., and R. Schwab, (1995). Finishing High School and Starting College: Do Catholic Schools Make a Difference? *Quarterly Journal of Economics*, 110, pp. 941–974.

Francis, (2015). *Encyclical Letter Laudato Si' of the Holy Father Francis on Care for Our Common Home*. Vatican City: Libreria Editrice Vaticana.

Freeman, K. J., and M. Berends, (2016). The Catholic School Advantage in a Changing Social Landscape: Consistency or Increasing Fragility?, *Journal of School Choice*, 10 (1), pp. 22–47

Gemignani, R., and Q. Wodon (2017). Gender Roles and Girls' Education in Burkina Faso: A Tale of Heterogeneity between Rural Communities, *American Review of Political Economy*, 11 (2), pp. 163–175.

Gemignani, R., M. Sojo, and Q. Wodon, (2014). What Drives the Choice of Faith-inspired Schools by Households? Qualitative Evidence from Two African Countries, *Review of Faith & International Affairs*, 12 (2), pp. 66–76.

Grace, G., (2002a). *Catholic Schools: Mission, Markets and Morality*. London and New York: Routledge Falmer.

Grace, G., (2002b). Mission Integrity: Contemporary Challenges for Catholic School Leaders. In K. Leithwood and P. Hallinger, editors, *Second International Handbook of Educational Leadership and Administration*. Dordrecht: Kluwer Academic Press.

Grace, G., and J. O'Keefe, (Ed.), (2007). *International Handbook of Catholic Education: Challenges for School Systems in the 21st Century*, two volumes. New York: Springer.

Grace, G. (2020). Meet Professor Gerald Grace, Editor of International Studies in Catholic Education (Interview by Q. Wodon), *Educatio Si Bulletin*, Issue 3, Winter 2020, pp. 30–33.

Greeley, A. M., (1982). *Catholic High Schools and Minority Students*. New Brunswick, NJ: Transaction Books.

Green, B., D. Sikkema, and D. Sikkink, (2018a). *Cardus Education Survey 2018: British Columbia Bulletin*. Ottawa: Cardus.

Green, B., D. Sikkema, and D. Sikkink, (2018b). *Cardus Education Survey 2018: Ontario Bulletin*. Ottawa: Cardus.

Hallinan, M. T., and W. N. Kubitschek, (2013). School Sector, School Poverty, and the Catholic School Advantage, *Journal of Catholic Education*, 14 (2), pp. 498–518.

Jepsen, C., (2003). The Effectiveness of Catholic Primary Schooling, *Journal of Human Resources*, 38, pp. 928–941.

Lange, G. M., Q. Wodon, and K. Carey, (2018). (Eds.). *The Changing Wealth of Nations 2018: Sustainability into the 21st Century*. Washington, DC: The World Bank.

Lavado, P. et al. (2016). *The Effect of Fe y Alegría on School Achievement: Exploiting a School Lottery Selection as a Natural Experiment*. IZA Discussion Paper number 10431. Bonn, Germany: IZA – Institute of Labor Economics.

McKinney, S., (2018). The Roots of the Preferential Option for the Poor in Catholic Schools in Luke's Gospel, *International Studies on Catholic Education*, 10 (2), pp. 220–232.

Neal, D., (1997). The Effects of Catholic Secondary Schooling on Educational Achievement. *Journal of Labor Economics*, 15 (1), pp. 98–123.

Parra Osorio, J. C., and Q. Wodon, (2014). *Faith-Based Schools in Latin America: Case Studies on Fe y Alegría*. Washington, DC: The World Bank.

Pontifical Council for Justice and Peace, (2004). *Compendium of the Social Doctrine of the Church*. Vatican City: Libreria Editrice Vaticana.

Sander, W., (1996). Catholic Grade Schools and Academic Achievement. *The Journal of Human Resources*, 31 (3), pp. 540–548.

Sander, W. and A. Krautmann, (1995). Catholic Schools, Dropout Rates and Educational Attainment. *Economic Inquiry*, 33 (2), pp. 217–233.

Secretariat of State of the Vatican, (2020). *Annuarium statisticum Ecclesiae 2018 / Statistical Yearbook of the Church 2018 / Annuaire statistique de l'Eglise 2018*. Vatican City: Libreria Editrice Vaticana.

Wodon, Q., (2014). *Education in sub-Saharan Africa: Comparing Faith-based, Private Secular, and Public Schools*. Washington, DC: The World Bank.

Wodon, Q., (2015). *The Economics of Faith-based Service Delivery: Education and Health in sub-Saharan Africa*. New York: Palgrave Macmillan.

Wodon, Q., (2018a). Enrollment in K12 Catholic Schools: Global and Regional Trends, *Educatio Catholica*, IV (3), pp. 189–210.

Wodon, Q., (2018b). Enrollment in Catholic Higher Education across Countries, *Educatio Catholica*, IV (4), pp. 173–195.

Wodon, Q., (2019a). Implications of Demographic, Religious, and Enrollment Trends for the Footprint of Faith-Based Schools Globally, *Review of Faith & International Affairs*, 17 (4), pp. 52–62.

Wodon, Q. (2019b). Catholic Schools in Latin America and the Caribbean: Enrollment Trends, Market Share, and Comparative Advantage, *Estudios sobre Educación*, 37, pp. 91–111.

Wodon, Q., (2019c). How Well Do Catholic and Other Faith-based Schools Serve the Poor? A Study with Special Reference to Africa, Part I: Schooling, *International Studies on Catholic Education*, 11 (1), pp. 4–23.

Wodon, Q. (2019d). Pluralism, the Public Purse, and Education: An International Estimate of Savings to State Budgets from K-12 Catholic Schools, *Review of Faith & International Affairs*, 17 (2), pp. 76–86.

Wodon, Q., (2019e). Budget Savings from Private Primary and Secondary Schools in OECD and Partner Countries, *International Journal of Education Law and Policy*, 15, pp. 29–36.

Wodon, Q., (2019f). Measuring the Contribution of Faith-based Schools to Human Capital Wealth: Estimates for the Catholic Church, *Review of Faith & International Affairs*, 17 (4), pp. 94–102.

Wodon, Q. (2019g). Editorial: Education, The Rights of the Child, and Development, in A. de La Rochefoucauld and C. M. Marenghi, editors, *Education as a Driver to Integral Growth and Peace – Ethical Reflections on the Right to Education*, The Caritas in Veritate Foundation Working Papers. Chambésy, Switzerland: Caritas in Veritate Foundation.

Wodon, Q., (2020a). *Global Catholic Education Report 2020: Achievements and Challenges at a Time of Crisis*. Rome: International Office of Catholic Education.

Wodon, Q., (2020b). Enrollment in Catholic Higher Education: Global and Regional Trends, *Journal of Catholic Higher Education*, 39 (1), pp. 87–104.

Wodon, Q., (2020c). Are New Secondary Schools Built Where They Are Needed Most? Comparing Catholic with Public and Other Private Schools in Uganda, *Review of Faith & International Affairs*, 18 (2), pp. 44–60.

Wodon, Q., (2020d). How Well Do Catholic and Other Faith-based Schools Serve the Poor? A Study with Special Reference to Africa, Part II: Learning, *International Studies on Catholic Education*, 12 (1), pp. 3–20.

Wodon, Q., (2020e). Covid-19 Crisis, Impacts on Catholic Schools, and Potential Responses, Part I: Developed Countries with Focus on the United States, *Journal of Catholic Education*, 23 (2), pp. 13–50.

Wodon, Q., (2020f). Covid-19 Crisis, Impacts on Catholic Schools, and Potential Responses, Part II: Developing Countries with Focus on sub-Saharan Africa, *Journal of Catholic Education*, 23 (2), pp. 51–86.

World Bank, (2018). *World Development Report 2018: Learning to Realize Education's Promise*. Washington, DC: The World Bank.

World Bank, (2020). *The COVID-19 Pandemic: Shocks to Education and Policy Responses*. Washington, DC: The World Bank.

Chapter 12

Catholic schooling in Chile
The need for rebuilding spiritual capital within the rules of the market culture

Cristóbal Madero S.J.

Introduction

It is difficult to make a fair reading of education in Chile without pointing to what the Catholic Church has meant institutionally and symbolically in its history. Formal schooling in Chile bears the profound mark of the Catholic Church's participation as a provider of education. Even though the Chilean society is experiencing an accelerated process of secularization,[1] the Church's weight cannot be overlooked by anyone. The Catholic school is an institution with a long history since before Chile was established in an independent Republic in 1810. It lives within a tension, on the one hand benefitting from the rules of the market and the favourable treatment by the Chilean state, and on the other hand, compromising its mission because of playing precisely with rules of the market culture.

The work of Gerald Grace is fundamental for approaching that tension because he has critically observed how Catholic schools deal with two impactful processes. One of these processes is secularization. The other process is the hegemony of capitalism and its logic in the realm of education.

In this chapter, I aim to offer a view on the current state of Catholic education at the school level in Chile using Grace's key concept of spiritual capital and the market. With those concepts, I plan to show the present and envision the future of Catholic schools in Chile.[2]

Spiritual capital and its values

Grace uses the concept of spiritual capital, meaning the 'resources of faith and values derived from a commitment to a religious tradition' (Grace, 2002, p. 236), in very secularized contexts. I propose here that he understands that we live, in his own UK, elsewhere in the West, and in countries like Chile, in a secular age (Taylor, 2009). In a secular age, we have experienced the process of secularization as a cultural phenomenon in which we do not live in a transcendental frame, but within an immanent frame. For an organization like the Catholic school, and for the actors involved in that organization, to start living within an immanent frame

DOI: 10.4324/9781003171553-15

has affected and continues to affect how it understands itself. That is why the notion of spiritual capital, which I consider to be Grace's most significant contribution to the field, turns out to be of relevance within the context of secularization. As Grace claims:

> ...the spiritual capital of the Catholic schooling system in England (and by implication elsewhere) is what has provided the dynamic drive to its mission in the past and helped it to preserve, in the main, its mission integrity in the challenges of the present. The renewal of its spiritual capital thus becomes the crucial question for the continuance of its distinctive mission in the future.
>
> (Grace, 2016, p. 35)

Spiritual capital at the level of the leaders, the schools, and the system provides both a lifeguard and a lighthouse for a Catholic education that navigates in a secular ocean. Grace is conscious that "the crucial question for the future is: are the reserves of spiritual capital in the Catholic school system being renewed or is the system in contemporary conditions living on a declining asset?" (Grace, 2016, p. 43) Catholic schools are good for societies' pluralism and diversity. If they want to continue or to recover their relevance, they have to assume the new immanent frame, commit to their mission and do whatever they can to increase their spiritual capital.

Educational markets in capitalist societies

In capitalistic societies, for Catholic schools to succeed at the same time as staying faithful to their mission, it is not easy. To run a school with Catholic values and principles in a capitalistic society means to live in the tension between being faithful to the Gospel's principle of the option for the poor and surviving in a market of different educational values where the option of shutting down the school is around the corner. How does one understand Catholic education in this context? How does one keep a school Catholic in this tension? This question requires a reflection at the level of the Church hierarchy. In this respect, Grace poses the question about why the post-Vatican Council II Church calls Catholics to *embrace* almost unreflectively *Humane Vitae*, but only to *consider* the document, *The Catholic School* (1977), which includes norms and inspirations for creating a more just society. Such a question reveals that Grace's concern for the future of Catholic education relies not only on the practice of millions of Catholic teachers and leaders around the world but also on the leadership at the highest level in the Church.

Grace knows that capitalism and the forces of the market impose pressure over the school system in general, and over the Catholic school in particular. That is why his reflection upon the market has been so present in his research work. Just considering his 20 most referenced articles on Google Scholar, it is seen how prevalent the topic of the market is. Using the Q.D.A. software Nvivo, I studied the frequency and the context where the concept of the market is used in the 20 articles. As Table 12.1 shows, the use of the concept is used in connection to several topics ranging from teachers' marketplace to culture, passing through curriculum and values.

In what follows, I present the Chilean education and the types of Catholic schools within that system, using the concepts of spiritual capital and market provided by Grace in his writings between 1985 and 2013.

The Chilean educational subsystem

Before the institutional frameworks that would lead to talk of an educational system in Chile, Catholic missionaries carried out formal education in the colonial period—c. 16th to 18th centuries—creating schools. Schools proved to be successful institutions for the transmission of the faith. Behind that function, there was, and there remains an undoubtedly evangelizing impetus. The Catholic school is proposed as an institution for the service of letters, but also

Table 12.1 Presence of the concept of market and related themes in 20 most-cited articles

Article	No.	Themes
(Grace, 1985)	4	Teacher labour market
(Grace, 1989)	12	Market place-system
(Grace, 1991b)	1	Teacher labour market
(Grace, 1991a)	18	Education as a commodity, market culture
(Grace, 1991c)	9	Education as a commodity, market culture
(Grace, 1993)	17	Education as a commodity, market relations of schooling
(Grace, 1998)	39	School choice, market culture, Free market provision of education
(Grace, 2000)	22	Marketing, managerialism
(Grace, 2001)	25	New right market doctrines, market relations of schooling
(Grace, 2003a)	9	Market values, market practices
(Grace, 2003b)	13	Market values, market materialistic culture
(Grace, 2004)	4	Market and secular curriculum
(Grace, 2006)	5	Market forces
(Grace, 2008)	26	The market-driven education system, market values
(Grace, 2009c)	6	Market values
(Grace, 2009b)	2	Market values
(Grace, 2009a)	1	Market values
(Grace, 2010)	6	Secular market, marketing
(Grace, 2012)	3	Market-dominated consumer culture
(Grace, 2013)	8	Market idolatry, market competition

of piety. In more up-to-date language, Catholic schools were a fundamental piece of the Chilean education system, and at the same time, one of the few formal spaces where the teaching and transmission of faith and values can remain possible.

It has been studied how Catholic schools have an institutional relationship more or less coupled with the Catholic Church in their contribution in forming the religious consciousness of their students and, in that sense, contribute to social pluralism as a democratic value (Smith, Longest, Hill, & Christoffersen, 2014). Catholic schools are also relevant in being more effective in standardized test results, graduation rates, and promotion to tertiary education than non-denominational public schools with equal resources (Coleman, Hoffer, & Kilgore, 1982; Neal, 1995; Ravitch, 2013). Catholic schools can also create community environments that would promote learning (Bryk, Lee, & Holland, 1993), citizen security, and even social cohesion (Brinig & Garnett, 2014).

In Chile, the tendency has been to understand Catholic schools as depending on the Catholic Church in terms of their property, operation, and funding. Male and female Religious Congregations as school owners have been understood in the history of Chile as the image of what the Catholic school consists of (CIDE, 1971).[3] This image mutates from the reforms of the 1980s. At the beginning of that decade, a comprehensive reform took place. With the coup d'état of 1973, a process of making education less segregated by implementing the *Escuela Nacional Única* (E.N.U) was interrupted. The socialist ideology underneath that project was replaced with one of the most radical neoliberal reforms in education in the world. Inspired by a group of students who had studied in the School of Economics at the University of Chicago, the military government implemented several neoliberal policies. In particular, decentralization policies took away power from the central government, privatization policies empowered private citizens and intermediate groups (like the Catholic Church) to erect schools, and a financing system was created in the service of financing the demand on the side of families via school vouchers.

New actors entered the system to carry out Catholic educational projects. Until that time, the schools in Chile consisted of two types of dependency: (a) municipal, where 100% of the funding is public, or (b) private schools paid by individuals with no public funding. Since 1980, subsidized private schools have joined the two other types of schools. In these schools, the funding was mixed, i.e., public and private, but 100% public funding predominated. This new type of school gave rise to the creation of Catholic schools, explosively, not only for an elite but for all kinds of families.

This trend starting in the 1980s and that stopped, in terms of the number of elite schools, came as a result of the two ideas that concerned Grace's work. One is that market rules, market values, and marketing make it possible for Catholic schools to offer Catholic education in more places, to more students. On the other side, without spiritual capital deposited in the laity, it would have been impossible to make it grow in the way as it did.

Types of Catholic schools in Chile[4]

Currently, the Chilean education system is composed of three types of schools: municipal, private subsidized, and private. At the same time, when thinking about their relationship to the Catholic Church, three types of Catholic schools emerge: oriented, recognized, and sponsored by the Catholic Church. These three types of Catholic schools intercept with the three types of dependency in Chile, creating an educational subsystem with varying degrees of institutional coupling (Weick, 1976) to the Catholic Church (see Figure 12.1).

Under the prism of religious orientation (oriented schools), in Chile, schools of all dependencies can declare to have a religious orientation, including a Catholic orientation. Therefore, for the state, schools that receive full funding, and are owned and operated by municipalities, can be considered Catholicly oriented, just as those that receive funding are owned and are privately operated, as is the case of the private subsidized and private (Celis & Zárate, 2015). Halfway between these two realities are schools that receive full or partial state funding, and those that are privately owned and operated.

From the perspective of the direct or indirect responsibility of the Catholic Church over schools, the above situation changes in two ways. On the one hand, there will be schools that are recognized by the Church (recognized schools), thus receiving a seal of catholicity on the part of the ecclesiastical authority. This process is carried out in each diocese of the country and represents both for the Catholic Church and for schools, a light coupling (Weick, 1976). However, it is not as light as in the case of oriented schools. The Church is not related either financially, or legally to the schools she recognizes (Secretary Status Rationarium Generale Ecclesiae, 1970). On the other hand, some schools are sponsored by the Catholic Church directly through dioceses or Religious Congregations and foundations (sponsored schools).

According to the Ministry of Education's directory of educational schools, considering religious orientation, in Chile, one in four educational schools defines itself as Catholic (27.2%). In the case of schools operating under a

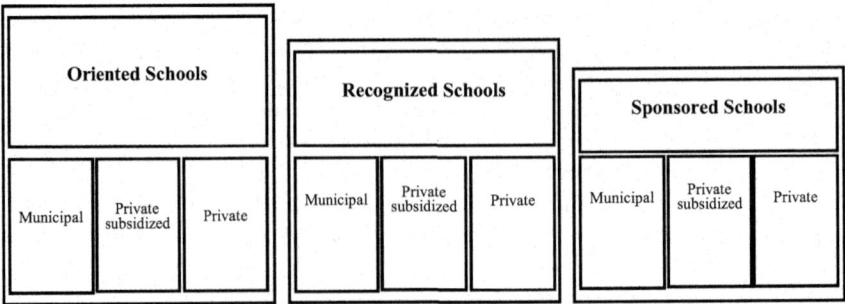

Figure 12.1 Catholic schools subsystem. Types of schools depending on their relationship to the Catholic Church

private subsidized dependence, this proportion increases slightly (28.5%). The proportion decreases slightly for municipal schools (25.1%). Considering enrollment, one in six students in Chile attend a Catholic school (16.6%), one in four in private subsidized (26.3%), and one in three in private (39.4%) (Passalacqua, 2006).

Benefitting from the rules of the market

Given the picture described above, it can be seen that the school education provided by the Catholic Church in Chile enjoys the sympathy of the state. The Church receives essential degrees of freedom and autonomy in the educational system, which operates as a market. In specific terms, Catholic schools, in all of the three types identified here (oriented, recognized, or sponsored), receive a subsidy from the state. In most cases, this is 100%. In return, the state exercises control over the school, but not because the school is Catholic, but because it is a school receiving a state grant.

The accountability mechanisms that exist in Chile are robust and put pressure on the school (Falabella, 2016). They are mechanisms installed since the neoliberal reform of 1980 in the middle of the military dictatorship. Neither at that time nor today has there been in Chile a movement against the Catholic schooling mission. If a school is categorized as insufficient for four years in a row by the Education Quality Agency,[5] that school will be closed, just like any school, confessional or not. If a school performs poorly in national standardized tests, or if it is denounced for anti-inclusion practices, or for altering student attendance against which the voucher is paid, it will be punished by the Ministry of Education. It is unthinkable to believe that the Catholic character of the school would cause this.

Given the equal treatment in the market, Catholic schools, and for this purpose, all the confessional schools, enjoy a benefit that can be perceived as an additional grant. Every school in Chile, confessional or not, has to provide Religious Education. Students can exempt themselves from enrolling in religion classes. Their parents just have to express that desire. However, the school is obliged to offer the religion class. For a public school, oriented or not by the Catholic Church, this is an obligation: it is the law. In the case of schools oriented, recognized, or sponsored by the Catholic Church, offering religion classes is a duty and, therefore, the state matches its responsibility with the mission of the Church. It is the state that pays for such religious formation. Despite this being the case today, such religious formation is called into question by many sectors in Chile that propose alternatives to the subject (Montecinos, Moya, Vargas, Berkowitz, & Cáceres, 2017).

In the case of the Catholic Church, it is the ecclesiastical authority that declares the suitability of a teacher to teach religion in a Catholic school. For many years (only since 2019 has this finished being the case), it was the ecclesiastical authority that could give the authorization of a religious teacher to teach in a public school not oriented by the Church. This attribution is a further example of what I stated at the beginning of this chapter that the symbolic and institutional footprint of the Church is deeply imbued in the Chilean education system.

The future of Catholic schools in Chile

The Catholic Church in Chile is going through what is probably the greatest crisis in its history. The institutional decline is added to the crisis caused by abuse, especially sexual, conscience, and power abuse perpetrated by representatives of the Catholic Church. In concrete terms, in the last 15 years in Chile, 80 clerics have been accused, of whom 34 had minors as victims. A total of more than 100 people have been affected. One in four accused and convicted sex abusers served as teachers or chaplains in Catholic schools, mostly diocesan, but also in Religious Congregations such as the Marists, Salesians, Jesuits, Legionries of Christ and others (Labrín & Sallaberry, 2018).

Although a majority of cases correspond to events that occurred 20, 30, and up to 40 years ago, that the proportion of abusers does not reach 3% of the total number of religious, and that the massive majority of school personnel are laypeople, the magnitude of the abusive acts themselves at the school level raises the relevant question about the effect that these facts have on the Catholic school. In the words of Grace, how much spiritual capital do the Catholic schools in Chile need to achieve so they can continue navigating as schools with a definite mission, in a turbulent market with some doubts about student care?

In this sense, the Catholic school faces in Chile a crisis caused by its leaders. The schools lost freedom and autonomy not by an oppressive or anti-clerical state, but because of the lack of accountability within the Church itself. The Catholic school in Chile today is looked upon with suspicion by the institution that has oriented, recognized, and sponsored it. It is the hope of educators and formators in school, for the sake of a quality education focused on the values of the Gospel whose message is more necessary than ever before, that the Catholic Church is up to the tremendous challenge that the school takes in times of convulsion.

Grace is a reminder that to be meaningful and helpful, Catholic schools in today's society need to have types of ministers, teachers, and leaders who conceive of the school and its role not only as a creator of social, economic, or cultural capital but also as a mentor of spiritual capital. It needs people who do not avoid living in the tension of the secular and capitalistic, but who learn how to live fruitfully in such tension. Gerald Grace invites the world of Catholic education to consider, again, the heart of teaching and leading in a Catholic school today, i.e. that they should 'render to God as well as to Caesar'.

Notes

1 Between 1998 and 2018, the proportion of Catholics in Chile decreased from 73% to 55%, and those who say they have no religious denomination grew from 7% to 24% in the same period, and to 36% in those under the age of 35 (CEP, 2018). The same

study indicates that in 1998, 91% of the population believed in God, and that in 2018 86% of the population did. Thus, over the course of 20 years there was a 5% decrease in belief in God, and a 18% adscription to the Catholic Church institution.

2 Catholic school means here the different institutions that group from the preschool or pre-primary level (4–5 years of age) to the last level of secondary education (17–18 years of age).

3 Being a holder refers in Chile to those who own the school, and therefore enjoys its legal representation.

4 Parts of this section are also present in Madero, C. (2020). Libertad, autonomía, y accountability en la escuela Católica en Chile, in *Contemporary Issues Facing Catholic Schools* [Special Issue], *Educatio Catholica VI* (1), pp. 155–161.

5 The Education Quality Agency, established in 2011, has the mission to hold schools accountable, so the education system can achieve educational quality.

References

Aldo Passalacqua. (2006). *Catastro colegios católicos*. Santiago, Chile: Conferencia Episcopal de Chile. Área Educación.

Brinig, M. F., & Garnett, N. S. (2014). *Lost classroom, lost community: Catholic schools' importance in urban America*. University of Chicago Press.

Byrk, A., Lee, V., & Holland, P. (1993). *Catholic schools and the common good*. Cambridge, MA: Harvard University Press.

Celis, A. M., & Zárate, S. (2015). *Libertad de enseñanza y libertad religiosa: Los establecimientos escolares con orientación religiosa en Chile* (No. 10/84; Temas de agenda pública, p. 18). Centro de Políticas Públicas UC.

CEP. (2018, January 12). *Encuesta CEP: tema especial religión*. www.cepchile.cl/estu dio-nacional-de-opinion-publica-octubre-noviembre-2018-tema/cep/2018-2012-18/093906.html [last accessed 15 January 2019].

CIDE. (1971). *La educación particular en Chile*. CIDE.

Coleman, J. S., Hoffer, T., & Kilgore, S. (1982). *High school achievement: Public, Catholic, and private schools compared*. New York: Basic Books.

Congregation for Catholic Education. (1977). *The Catholic school*. London: Catholic Truth Society.

Falabella, A. (2016). ¿Qué aseguran las políticas de aseguramiento de la calidad?: Un estudio de casos en distintos contextos escolares. *Estudios pedagógicos (Valdivia)*, 42(1), pp. 107–126.

Grace, G. (1985). Judging teachers: The social and political contexts of teacher evaluation. *British Journal of Sociology of Education*, 6(1), pp. 3–16.

Grace, G. (1989). Education: Commodity or public good?. *British Journal of Educational Studies*, 37(3), pp. 207–221.

Grace, G. (1991a). The New Right and the challenge to educational research. *Cambridge Journal of Education*, 21(3), pp. 265–275.

Grace, G. (1991b). The state and the teachers: Problems in teacher supply, retention and morale. *Evaluation & Research in Education*, 5(1–2), pp. 3–16.

Grace, G. (1991c). Welfare Labourism versus the New Right: The struggle in New Zealand's education policy. *International Studies in Sociology of Education*, 1(1–2), pp. 25–42.

Grace, G. (1993). On the study of school leadership: Beyond education management. *British Journal of Educational Studies*, 41(4), pp. 353–365.

Grace, G. (1998). Scholarship and ideology in education policy studies. *International Studies in Sociology of Education*, 8(1), pp. 135–140.

Grace, G. (2000). Research and the challenges of contemporary school leadership: The contribution of critical scholarship. *British Journal of Educational Studies*, 48(3), pp. 231–247.

Grace, G. (2001). The state and Catholic schooling in England and Wales: Politics, ideology and mission integrity. *Oxford Review of Education*, 27(4), pp. 489–500.

Grace, G. (2002). *Catholic schools: Mission, markets, and morality*. Routledge.

Grace, G. (2003a). "First and foremost the church offers its educational service to the poor": Class, inequality and Catholic schooling in contemporary contexts. *International Studies in Sociology of Education*, 13(1), pp. 35–54.

Grace, G. (2003b). Educational studies and faith-based schooling: Moving from prejudice to evidence-based argument. *British Journal of Educational Studies*, 51(2), pp. 149–167.

Grace, G. (2004). Making connections for future directions: Taking religion seriously in the sociology of education. *International Studies in Sociology of Education*, 14(1), pp. 47–56.

Grace, G. (2006). Urban education: Confronting the contradictions: an analysis with special reference to London. *London Review of Education*, 4(2), pp. 115–131.

Grace, G. (2008). Changes in the classification and framing of education in Britain, 1950s to 2000s: An interpretive essay after Bernstein. *Journal of Educational Administration and History*, 40(3), pp. 209–220.

Grace, G. (2009a). On the international study of Catholic education: Why we need more systematic scholarship and research. *International Studies in Catholic Education*, 1(1), pp. 6–14.

Grace, G. (2009b). Reflections on Allen and West's paper: 'Religious schools in London: school admissions, religious composition and selectivity.' *Oxford Review of Education*, 35(4), pp. 495–503.

Grace, G. (2009c). Faith school leadership: A neglected sector of in-service education in the United Kingdom. *Professional Development in Education*, 35(3), pp. 485–494.

Grace, G. (2010). Renewing spiritual capital: An urgent priority for the future of Catholic education internationally. *International Studies in Catholic Education*, 2(2), pp. 117–128.

Grace, G. (2012). Faith schools: Democracy, human rights and social cohesion. *Policy Futures in Education*, 10(5), pp. 500–506.

Grace, G. (2013). Catholic social teaching should permeate the Catholic secondary school curriculum: An agenda for reform. *International Studies in Catholic Education*, 5(1), pp. 99–109.

Grace, G. (2016). *Faith, mission and challenge in Catholic education: The selected works of Gerald Grace*. Routledge.

Labrín, S., & Sallaberry, J. P. (2018, September 1). Las 80 denuncias por abuso sexual que ha enfrentado la Iglesia en Chile. *La Tercera*. www.latercera.com/noticia/las-80-denuncias-abuso-sexual-ha-enfrentado-la-iglesia-chile/#.

Madero, C. (2020). Libertad, autonomía, y accountability en la escuela Católica en Chile, *Contemporary Issues Facing Catholic Schools* [Special Issue], *Educatio Catholica*, VI(1), pp. 155–161.

Montecinos, C., Moya, L., Vargas, F., Berkowitz, D., & Cáceres, P. (2017). *Caracterización de la enseñanza de la religión a partir de la implementación del Decreto 924/1983 en las escuelas públicas de Chile* (No. 309/2015). PNUD.

Neal, D. (1995). *The effect of Catholic secondary schooling on educational attainment* (No. w5353). National Bureau of Economic Research.

Ravitch, D. (2013). *Reign of error: The hoax of the privatization movement and the danger to America's public schools.* Alfred A. Knopf.

Secretaria Status Rationarium Generale Ecclesiae. (1970). *Statistical yearbook of the Church.* Libreria Editrice Vaticana.

Smith, C., Longest, K., Hill, J., & Christoffersen, K. (2014). *Young Catholic America: Emerging adults in, out of, and gone from the Church.* Oxford University Press.

Taylor, C. (2009). *A secular age.* Harvard University Press.

Weick, K. E. (1976). Educational organizations as loosely coupled systems. *Administrative Science Quarterly*, 21(1), pp. 1–19.

Chapter 13

The future trajectory of the narrative of Catholic school Religious Education

Graham Rossiter

Introduction: Gerald Grace and Catholic Religious Education

This chapter, in a book acknowledging and honouring the scholarship of Gerald Grace, provides a timely opportunity for looking at a sub-narrative of Catholic education – Religious Education in Catholic schools. Arguably, Religious Education is the most distinctively religious and Catholic aspect of Catholic schools.

Grace has not studied Religious Education (RE) in detail, but has always recognised its important place and role in Catholic schooling. When I spoke with him in 2001 at the *Centre for Research and Development in Catholic Education* (CRDCE) in London, I found him quick to acknowledge the contemporary issues for RE and to discuss wide-ranging implications – even some humorous ones deriving from his lateral thinking. For example, when talking about problems with professional language in education generally and in RE in particular, he recalled with humour how his doctoral research supervisor, the well-known sociologist and linguistics scholar Basil Bernstein, was surprised, disappointed and somewhat annoyed when someone reported that on reading one of his papers he understood it perfectly at first reading. Apparently, for Bernstein, being abstruse and not easily accessible seemed to be essential ingredients in good academic writing. Gerald and I were 'on the same page' in having a different view. Accessibility, clarity and focus on significant issues have always been characteristic of Grace's writings on Catholic education.

Over the years of his editorship of *International Studies in Catholic Education* (2009–2021), Gerald Grace examined many articles for publication. For him, 'examination' was the appropriate word to use – with connotation from the examination of research theses – because he scrutinised the material, often suggesting where further clarification was needed and where 'explanatory endnotes' would enhance readability. From this work, he built up professional familiarity with developments and issues in Catholic education in many contexts around the world. Also, he looked at RE carefully, appreciating its pivotal role in Catholic education, especially in Catholic schools.

DOI: 10.4324/9781003171553-16

Both Grace's professional dealings with RE[1] as well as the contribution of *International Studies in Catholic Education* (ISCE) to international discussion of RE are evident in the published ISCE articles, as well as in book reviews and editorials. While only 18 (7%) of the 256 articles published (up to Volume 12, Issue 2) are specifically concerned with RE, this measure tends to under-rate its presence and significance. The most web-viewed article in the journal is on secondary curriculum implications for Catholic social teaching by Gerald Grace (7,757 views, October 2020).[2] Of the top ten most viewed articles, the second, third and ninth-placed articles were on RE, and overall, six of the top ten had significant implications for RE. A good proportion of all the journal articles have some implications for RE.

The rest of this chapter will be concerned with reviewing the current discourse or narrative for Catholic RE in schools, proposing a way forward.

Problems with the language in the discourse of Religious Education in Australian Catholic schools

This material will focus specifically on the Australian Catholic school context. This specificity can be taken into account by educators concerned with evaluating the situation of Catholic RE in other countries.

The *discourse* of RE is made up of the words and ideas used by educators to articulate underlying assumptions, purposes and practices, and for the evaluation and development of the discipline. A synonym for the discourse is the *narrative* for RE where the nuanced connotation refers to the 'storyline' that is used to give an account of RE, its history and progress, how it is understood today and how it might change and develop in the future.

The particular words used by educators when talking about RE are important because they 'frame' the aims, content and pedagogy. In 1985, Crawford and Rossiter argued that there was a need to evaluate the language of Catholic RE because the multiplicity of ecclesiastical terms being used was confusing for teachers, students and parents; it tended to create ambiguity and distract from the task of articulating a meaningful and relevant RE for contemporary youth. This task is even more critical for Catholic RE now than it was then.

> The language of Religious Education structures the discussion of the subject. In effect, it determines many of the possibilities that will emerge; it has a formative influence on teachers' expectations and on what and how they teach; it influences presumptions about the types of responses they will seek from students; it provides criteria for judging what has been achieved; it influences teachers' perception and interpretation of problems in religious education; it even influences the way teachers feel about their work – "Am I a success or a failure?" This language can be oppressive if it restricts

religion teachers to limited or unrealistic ways of thinking and talking about their work.

(Crawford & Rossiter, 1985, p. 33)

In 1970, in the article *Catechetics RIP*, US scholar Gabriel Moran was one of the first to comment on an emerging problem within the language of Catholic RE. Where idiosyncratic, ecclesiastical terms were used exclusively, the discourse became 'in house' and relatively closed to outside ideas and debate. Since 1981, publications by Crawford and Rossiter collectively (1981, 1985, 1988, 2006, 2018) drew attention to various aspects of this problem, including the multiplicity of ecclesiastical terms as well as the way that devotional and emotional titles, and presumptive language had negative effects on religion curricula and teaching.[3]

More recently, Rossiter (2020), in the current issue of ISCE, explained the problem he labelled as 'ecclesiastical drift'. It is said to occur where the discourse about the purposes and practices of RE has gradually and incrementally come to be dominated almost exclusively by constructs like faith development, faith formation, Catholic identity, new evangelisation and Catholic mission. There is evidence (in diocesan and school documents/websites and in the re-naming of former diocesan RE departments, as well as in the rise of new religious leadership roles in Catholic schools) that these ecclesiastical terms have been replacing the word Religious Education. For example: in one instance, the re-badged, advertised role description of the former diocesan RE Director did not include any direct mention of RE. Also noted in this study, has been a deleterious effect on RE as an academic discipline in Catholic tertiary institutions.[4]

Only some conclusions from the study will be noted here where the focus will turn towards what might be done to address this ongoing question, which I consider to be *the* major ongoing problem for the future of Australian Catholic RE.

- Excessive use of ecclesiastical language, at the expense of the word 'education', turns the focus *inwards* towards Catholicism – at the very time when more of an *outwards* focus on the shaping influence of culture is needed.
- Ecclesiastical language dominance eclipses the educational dimension to RE and what suffers is thinking about what it means to *educate* today's young people spiritually and religiously.
- If students, teachers and parents are inclined to see RE as an *ecclesiastical* rather than as an *educational* activity, then increasingly they are less likely to see it as a meaningful part of school education.
- Special attention given to 'Catholic identity' gives the impression of exclusiveness that can make the 30% of students who are not Catholic, as well as the non-religious Catholic students, and non-Catholic and non-religious teachers, feel uncomfortable and perhaps marginalised.[5]

What might be done to address the problem of 'ecclesiastical drift' and to create a more meaningful and relevant narrative for, and practice of, Religious Education

The remainder of the chapter will summarise principles/issues as part of an overall strategy that might help bring more balance to the discourse of Catholic school RE by emphasising its educational value and processes. Hopefully, this can assist in re-configuring the creative tension that needs to exist between legitimate ecclesiastical and educational perspectives on RE. And in turn, this can flow through into enhancing classroom practice.

What follows is in one sense not anything new. It is proposed simply as putting a spotlight on current best thinking and practice. This could be affirming for religion teachers as well as more inviting to teachers who are considering involvement. Detailed academic references related to the items have been omitted. This does not mean that they lack academic roots and credibility. The list of principles/issues may well be 'old hat' for many religion teachers – if this is the case, and if a high proportion are 'on the same page', then I would see this as 'good news'. Inevitably, there are different and conflicting estimates of the nature and purposes of school RE, and individuals will disagree with, and diverge from, the value positions stated here. But as well as proposing emphases that will address ecclesiastical drift, this material will help readers identify more readily which are the issues that they consider still remain controversial and open to debate. It can serve as a 'checklist' of issues on which religious educators need to take some stance.

In brief, this is about building a narrative for RE that can give a *meaningful account of the educational value of this core spiritual/moral subject* in the curriculum which can *resource the spirituality of young people* for life in the 21st century, whether or not they are formally religious or Catholic. Hopefully, this narrative can enhance both the perceptions RE as well as its classroom practice. In turn, this might help 'put Religious Education back on the Catholic schools map' – because in recent years there seems to have been a discernible loss of focus for RE, especially in the language used for articulating its purposes.

Firstly on the broad canvas, the narrative of RE needs to emphasise its three main functions.

- Giving young people substantial access to their Catholic religious heritage with knowledge (and experience where relevant) of theology, scripture, liturgy, prayer, morality, Church history etc.;
- Some knowledge of other religious traditions that are present in Australia[6] and of their complex interactions with society;
- Skills in the critical evaluation of the shaping influence of culture on beliefs, values and lifestyle, together with study of contemporary spiritual/moral issues. This aspect needs to have more prominence in the senior classes.

Elements in a 'revitalising' strategy for the narrative of Religious Education

I Avoiding ecclesiastical drift language and restoring balance by giving more attention to educational and psychological accounts of Religious Education

Because ecclesiastical terms are so deeply embedded in the current discourse of RE, it has become difficult for educators to articulate its purposes without recourse to them (Rossiter, 2018, p. 132). But it is educationally rewarding to try to do so – re-formulating one's understanding of RE in terms that are meaningful and relevant for students and teachers.

2 Enhancing students' perceptions of the educational and potential personal value of the subject Religious Education

The narrative for RE needs to give more attention to explaining for both students and teachers its educational values. It is the only core subject that is directly concerned with the spiritual/moral dimension to life. It can cover this content to help *resource the personal spirituality* of young people no matter what their religious disposition. Children have a *right* to an informative education in their own cultural religious tradition; at their own personal level they will respond differently and not all will become active members of the church. But all need to become properly *educated* citizens, and this includes systematic knowledge and understanding of religion.

In addition to the above educational values of RE, attention can be given at different places in the religion curriculum to highlighting the following.

- While RE is about *educating* young people spiritually, morally and religiously, the process hopefully will enhance their capacity to find meaning and value in life, and in decision-making, while trying to navigate a happy life in a challenging culture, in difficult times. The current pandemic has amplified the uncertainty and fears that many young people were already experiencing; previously secure and stable presumptions about lifestyle, freedom, career, travel, media, communications, peak experiences etc. now seem more contingent and fragile, making it more pressing to give attention to clarifying personal values and goals in life. Education cannot make young people wise – but it can *resource their wisdom*. Hopefully, the knowledge and skills gained from RE can help them become more capable of learning from their life experience.
- Students' awareness of contemporary spiritual/moral issues and the value of analytical and interpretative skills for their evaluation. Growth in confidence that they can research important questions and make better-informed decisions.

- Research indicates that young people with reasonable theological backgrounds are less likely to be 'conned' into joining religious cults.
- As noted in the UK in the 1970s, being educated in religions has been a valuable background for people engaged in various roles of public service (e.g. doctors, nurses, paramedics, teachers, police, health care, lawyers, etc.).

3 The importance of a core spiritual/moral subject in the school curriculum

This is a long-held key element in Catholic educational philosophy and the most distinctively religious aspect of Catholic schooling.

Catholic educational philosophy has always upheld the principle that *any school curriculum (even in state schools) that does not have a learning area that attends specifically to the spiritual/moral dimension would be judged as deficient.* This is the rationale for having RE as a core element in the curriculum of Catholic schools since their origins in Australia in the early 1800s.

This argument suggests that RE should be regarded as philosophically the most important subject in the curriculum. The fact that it has low status and how this fuels students' dislike of RE will be considered later (Item 5).

4 Religious Education as a challenging academic subject across the school curriculum

RE should be an academic subject, which in no way suffers by comparison with the academic demands made by other regular subjects. For this principle to work, it has to apply from the earliest primary school years. What is considered to be 'academic' will naturally be different depending on the age and level of maturity of the students. For example, in the early years a literal 'hands-on' approach is a part of being 'academic'.

This principle means that RE should abide by all the standard protocols for student study, assignments and examinations and assessment procedures. Where challenging academic study is not experienced by students, they are more likely to consider RE as of little consequence in their schooling.

What happens in religion classes should be comparable with what happens in other standard academic subjects in the school curriculum. Hence, there should be a transfer of good teaching methods and skills into religion lessons.

5 Acknowledging and addressing the problem of negative student perceptions of religion and Religious Education

Because of the relatively low cultural regard for religion in secularised Western countries, it is inevitable that this will flow over into poor perceptions of RE by Catholic school students and their parents. While RE is philosophically the most important life-related subject in the curriculum, its perceived life-relevance is 'subverted' by a number of socio-cultural and educational factors. This is explained in detail in Crawford and Rossiter (2006, ch. 14, especially pp. 307–309; see also Middleton, 2001).[7]

There is no formula that will completely solve this problem. Even where students have said they 'like RE' and acknowledge that they can learn something valuable about life from it, they will still feel that it is of little importance by comparison with the subjects that 'count' like English, Maths etc. Acknowledging the problem as a sort of 'natural' one these days is important for RE teachers – and for their mental health. Anything that can be done to enhance students' experience and perceptions of the subject, including the proposals here, will be helpful.

6 The potential place for the teachers' own beliefs and commitments in classroom interactions: The ethics of teaching

This and the following four sections as a block deal with questions that have significant ethical implications for teachers as well as students. They are concerned with the interactions and learning transactions that occur in the classroom. They have a considerable bearing on both content and pedagogy, and on expectations of what should be achieved in RE. For many years, I have been puzzled why diocesan RE documents in Australia do not address these questions in any depth. While I believe that most religion teachers follow their own healthy professional instincts on these questions, there remains some ambiguity and uncertainty that, in my view, have been created and sustained by the ongoing problem of ecclesiastical drift, which affects teachers' understanding of the nature and purposes of RE.

This topic is an issue at the heart of the educator's ethics of teaching. One of the best and most useful accounts of the question has been in the writings of Australian philosopher of education and Christian education scholar Brian Hill. A detailed presentation of his views is provided on the ASMRE (2020) website. The code of ethics for teaching referred to below is derived from Hill (1981).

The teacher's personal and professional commitments should not be confused. The teacher is to help students engage with the content. Teachers may refer to their own personal views only if, and when, they judge that this makes a valid educational contribution to classroom transactions – and the same applies to the students. Their personal views are content along with the other provided content and should be subject to the same sort of academic class evaluation. The teacher should not 'privilege' their own personal views. Neither should they compromise Church teachings and other content by substituting their own idiosyncratic interpretation.

Pope John Paul II made a strong statement about this potential problem in *Catechesi tradendae* in 1979.

[The religion teacher/catechist] will not seek to keep directed towards himself and his personal opinions and attitudes the attention and the consent of the mind and heart of the person he is catechising. Above all, he will not try to inculcate his personal opinions and options as if they expressed [adequately] Christ's teaching and the lessons of his life.

(# 6)

No one (teacher or students) should ever be made to feel any psychological pressure to reveal their own personal views. Anyone can 'pass' if they do not want to talk about them. If any personal sharing occurs naturally in class, that is fine and it should be valued and acknowledged. But personal testimony is not the purpose of classroom RE (while it is often more natural and prominent in voluntary religious commitment groups). Content needs to be presented impartially. The teacher should be able to model responsible, respectful, critical evaluation.

Evidence suggests that such an ethical regime in the classroom not only protects students and teachers' privacy and personal views; it makes it more likely that personal statements may be made comfortably, precisely because of the ethically respectful class environment (cf. Item 7).

Christian witnessing in the classroom? It is pertinent here to note the problem sometimes caused by misunderstanding of the implications of the teacher being a Christian witness. Christian witnessing is about how Christ-like individuals are in the way they relate to other people and the environment etc. This is about how the core values in a person are manifested. Witnessing goes on all the time both inside and outside the classroom. But 'witnessing' is not a classroom pedagogy.[8] And it is not an un-ethical licence to purvey one's own views in the classroom. See also Item 8 below.

The place for personalism and relevance in Religious Education (Items 7–10)

7 Personalism: What does making RE personal mean? What is healthy, authentic personal sharing in the classroom? What is faith sharing? How does personal sharing foster personal and spiritual development? What ethical caution is needed to prevent manipulation?

The stance that teachers take on the issues signposted here strongly influences what they will try to achieve in their classroom interactions with students and in interactions between students. A more detailed discussion of 'The quest for personalism and relevance in Religious Education' is given in Crawford and Rossiter (2006, ch. 17, pp. 391–408.)

Since the 1960s, one of the principal driving motifs in Catholic RE was the intention to make it more *personal* and *life relevant* for young people (Buchanan, 2005; Rossiter, 1999; Ryan, 2013). Not all the efforts in this direction were successful. In particular, where so-named 'personal sharing' discussions came to dominate RE, they were perceived by students as contrived rather than authentically personal; they felt uncomfortable with any perceived psychological pressure to reveal the inner self. This same problem exists to some extent in contemporary RE when too much attention is given to 'sharing your personal story' or 'witnessing your faith journey' (cf. Item 8 below) – an approach which is more relevant in retreats than in the classroom; but even in retreats it causes problems (Rossiter, 2016).[9]

The desirability of healthy personalism and relevance in RE has never been in question. Perhaps now they are more pertinent and important than at any previous time. The critical questions are about *how much* and *what sort* of personalism and relevance are desired, and how do teachers and the RE curriculum promote this in healthy and ethical ways.

Crawford (1982), in a seminal article, showed that it was really *informed debate* rather than *personal sharing* that was 'at home' in RE; and that a challenging academic study with the right sort of content provided the best natural context not only for such debate, but also for personal insights from students when they felt comfortable enough to contribute freely to the learning process in this way. Her study also showed how wrong it was to claim that RE could not be *personal* if it was *academic*; the two are in no way incompatible. See also Items 9 and 10 below, especially the need for personal/life-related content.

There is an interesting parallel evident in the discussion approach to British state school RE in the mid-1960s. It was influenced by the writings of Loukes (1961, 1965, 1973). But what proved problematic in both the UK and in Catholic school discussion-oriented RE was the pedagogy. Uninformed discussion could amount to little more than sharing ignorant opinions. And the intention of having 'deep' personal discussion was usually counter-productive. It could not sustain student interest for too long. Also, this approach was perceived by students as a low-grade pedagogy in a subject that had little academic status; the crucial missing ingredient was a high-grade pedagogy – a serious study of the issues, in the light of up-to-date expert information. Here, dialogue or discussion was one useful part of the whole study exercise – like an informed debate – and not like a time-filling, non-directed, relatively purposeless activity.

8 The relevance of 'sharing your personal story' and 'witnessing your faith journey'

The religion programme *Sharing Our Story* originated in the Parramatta diocese (1999) and was adopted or adapted in some other dioceses. It was based on Groome's (1980) Shared Christian Praxis approach. There were also references in diocesan and other literature stating or implying that 'personal faith sharing' was a fundamentally important process in RE. It was regarded as the transaction in RE in which personal faith 'developed'.

The interest in personal sharing spread widely in RE in the 1970s following the impact of Carl Rogers' (1961, 1969) relationship-centred, humanistic psychology where the idea of intimate personal sharing in encounter groups became popular with the religious personnel who accounted for most of the Catholic school religion teachers at the time. It influenced their thinking about, and practice of, personalism in the RE classroom. And in the next decade, this morphed into the idea of personal, *religious* faith sharing in the wake of the great popularity of Fowler's (1981) *psychological* faith development theory. The term faith development still remains prominent in contemporary Catholic RE discourse.

From 15 years of conducting adult retreats, I have regularly experienced and valued the sharing of personal insights in groups. No doubt it was important for the participants and they would see it as helpful for their own lives. Whether it was the participants' fundamental faith/fidelity relationship with God that was being shared or a 'lesser' personal matter, I was never interested in wanting to know. I could comfortably leave all the details of personal faith in the hands of God and the believer. I also have first-hand experience of young people sharing personal insights in voluntary commitment groups and camps, and to a lesser extent in school retreats. In these settings, especially where participation was voluntary, there seemed to be an unspoken acceptance that sharing of personal insights was natural and healthy. But it could not be authentic if there was any psychological pressure to contribute at this level.

The religion classroom in Catholic schools is a type of public educational forum. It is not like the voluntary retreat. Hence, I take the position that 'sharing of personal/faith insights' is not a principal, or even a desirable, activity to try to make happen in this setting. The ethical principles noted in Item 6 above should apply to both students and teachers in the classroom – in RE and all other subjects. It is not that personal sharing is wrong. It is not banned. It is good and healthy when free, authentic and not contrived. And as noted in Item 7, it often occurs naturally within a sound academic study; but this is a valuable, somewhat serendipitous event. It is an unintended healthy by-product of academic study and a respectful, accepting class climate, and not a programmed or expected outcome that is essential for RE. In most cases, how young people integrate learning in RE within their own beliefs, values and lifestyle will happen privately and slowly over many years.

Problems with misunderstanding of 'witnessing' were noted in Item 6. In a study of retreats in Catholic secondary schools, Rossiter (2016) cautioned about the strategy of teachers (and others) telling their 'personal faith journey' as a stimulus to get students to do the same. While students naturally are voyeuristically interested in any personal details volunteered by their teachers, the faith journey approach can be counter-productive, particularly if it appears contrived and rehearsed, and if there is unwelcome psychological pressure on young people to make revelations about their personal thinking and values. I expect that adolescents are uncomfortable if they feel the teacher is manoeuvring them towards talking about their 'faith journey'. I heard a report from some students recently who have labelled teachers who tried this as 'over-exposures' or 'over-sharers'. There are related difficulties where a student personal RE journal or diary is required and even more so where this is to be inspected by teachers.

9 Relevance in pedagogy: The need for critical, evaluative research-oriented pedagogy, especially in the senior classes

Brian Hill described the mission of education as 'resourcing the choosing self'; RE could make a special contribution through helping students 'to *interrogate their own cultural conditioning* and reach a position of being able to develop an adequate personal framework of meaning and value' (Hill, 2006, p. 55, emphasis added; Hill, 2004).

Hill took for granted that the sense of freedom and individuality permeating Westernised cultures would ensure that young people will eventually construct their own meaning, values and beliefs – even if for some (or perhaps many?) this will not be a conscious, reflective process but more a popular, cultural socialisation. Nothing could stop the 'choosing'; but their choosing could be better *educated*. Hence, knowledge of contemporary issues and critical thinking would be important for informing life decisions, as well as knowledge of what one's own and other religious traditions were saying about meaning in life. The religion classroom should be the very place where one might expect that students could learn how to appraise the shaping influence of culture.

A critical pedagogy and issue -related content can be a part of RE across the whole curriculum. How it is employed will depend upon the age and academic maturity of the students. The same style of pedagogy can and should be applied when teaching formally religious topics.

A good student-centred RE always includes the following pedagogical elements in an age-appropriate fashion: information-rich study; knowledge of traditions; critical interpretation; informed debate; the experiential dimension; student research.

Much more detail on an inquiring, evaluative pedagogy is provided in Rossiter (2018). Examples of presentations from students, as well as from postgraduate RE teachers that illustrate mini-research projects on contemporary spiritual/moral issues, are posted on the ASMRE (2020) website.

10 Relevance in content: Including something on world religions and on the contemporary search for meaning, including contemporary spiritual/moral issues

It is difficult to sell the idea of a religion curriculum that is relevant to students' lives if all the content is exclusively Catholic. While in Catholic schools it is to be expected that Catholicism would be the principal content of RE, it is recognised that most of the students are not very religious and for them broader content would be beneficial. But even for the religious, regular church-going students, just studying Catholicism would be an inadequate RE. They need the second and third elements mentioned earlier just as much as the non-religious students.[10]

Attention to world religions has long been a part of Catholic RE, even if most diocesan syllabuses make little mention of it. In German state schools where denominational RE is taught by regular, trained departmental teachers, study of world religions has been for many years a mandated part of the Catholic religion curriculum.[11]

But just including some world religion content is not enough. There is a need for more issue-oriented content that is pertinent to contemporary life, including spiritual and moral issues and study of the search for meaning in a secularised, consumer society. This is important if young people are to see RE as making a valuable contribution to their education and personal development (cf. Item 2). Note for example an elective unit in the new Brisbane Catholic Education (2019) syllabus for the course *Religion, Meaning and Life* is titled 'Identity and meaning: How people construct personal identity and community in a consumerist culture'.

In Australia, academic subjects in the senior school which are accredited for contribution to students' university entrance qualifications have what is called ATAR registration (Australian Tertiary Admissions Ranking). Other non-ATAR subjects can be studied but cannot count towards university entrance scores. Because Catholic school Y11–12 students can already study state ATAR courses like *Studies of Religion* and *Religion and Society*, and non-ATAR *Religion and Ethics*, it has been acceptable to have 'other-than-Catholic' content in RE programmes at this level. So the principle of allowing for the study of spiritual/moral questions that at first sight are not formally religious can be claimed as already established in Catholic RE. At this point it is noted that in my professional opinion, the state-accredited courses can be judged not to have enough life-relevant content because they have for too long stayed with the descriptive world religions approach that dominated UK school courses in the early 1970s (Crawford & Rossiter, 2006)

11 Participation in research concerned with the discourse of Catholic Religious Education

Currently, trial data collection has commenced in a survey that investigates the extent to which teachers think that there is a problem with excessive use of ecclesiastical terms in RE (ASMRE, 2020). This is an opportunity for those engaged in RE to have their say.

Ecclesiastical terms have become so embedded in the fabric of Catholic RE that any questioning of their relevance and utility tends to be resisted because it feels somewhat uncomfortable – as you would if questioning key words in the country's founding constitution. These terms have acquired a resilience in the discourse of RE and they are likely to remain prominent for a considerable time to come. It seems unlikely then that the survey would show a high proportion of teachers who readily identified the problems in ecclesiastical drift. Hence the principal purpose of the questionnaire was to serve as an initial stimulus for religion teachers to think about the issues and potential problems. I called it the 'stop and think' or 'reflective' questionnaire. It may perhaps incline religion teachers towards a more discerning and frugal use of the ecclesiastical constructs.

The first part of the questionnaire asks for a simple valuation of various ecclesiastical and educational words for explaining the purposes of RE. This is followed by some brief narratives or scenarios for RE where an exclusively ecclesiastical narrative can be compared with others that have an educational focus.

Then questions are raised about potential problems with excessive use of ecclesiastical terms where they tend to displace the word Religious Education from the RE narrative. Attention is given to particular constructs – faith formation and Catholic identity. In addition to investigating ecclesiastical drift, the survey has items looking at the possibility of giving more curriculum space and time to critical evaluation of culture and study of the contemporary search for meaning and values in a relatively secularised society.

The questionnaire takes about 15 minutes to complete. However, some trial participants noted that it took longer because it prompted them to pause and think about the issues, resulting in some clarification of their views. The proportion of participants who choose the 'not sure' option for questionnaire items could end up being significant as an indicator of a 'stop and think' approach to the survey.

In the trial, some found it more difficult answering the initial questions evaluating the various terms; they said it was easier to answer questions that identified potential problems related to the excessive use of ecclesiastical language. While the initial trial data has not yet been analysed and while no Catholic school systems have yet participated systematically, I anticipate that the same pattern in the results of an earlier small-scale study of the views of teachers and parents by Finn (2011) would show up again. He found that teachers (more so than parents) were respectful of the ecclesiastical terms. But both groups found 'the language was generally confusing and not helpful for understanding religious education' (Finn, 2011, p. 84; cf. 89, 111).

Hopefully, it will be possible to get Catholic diocesan school systems interested in participating in the survey.

12 Taking into account the relative 'secular spirituality'[12] of most students in Catholic schools

An important 'need to know and understand' for religion teachers is the extensive secularisation of culture in Australia and elsewhere that has an inevitable bearing on how one approaches RE. Most of the pupils in Catholic schools are, or will be, non-church-going. Nevertheless, no matter what their religious affiliation and level of religious practice, RE can make a valuable contribution to their education and personal development resources (Rossiter, 2018).

Conclusion

In looking at the history of the discourse of Catholic school RE in the English-speaking world, two significant dates were 1965 and 1971. In 1965, the Second Vatican Council released *Gravissimum educationis* (Declaration on Christian

Education) in which, somewhat surprisingly, the principal focus was education and how this could enhance the personal and religious development of people. Perhaps not all the Catholic bishops at the Council appreciated the significance of choosing a word that the Catholic Church did not 'own'. This educational emphasis was both expansive and ecumenical in scope. Prior to this, much of the Catholic focus was on 'Christian Doctrine' – the most common name for religion class in Catholic schools. The educational emphasis was naturally open to dialogue with other Christian denominations where the term 'Christian education' was prominent. This also articulated with the wider, international discourse of education.

In 1963, while in a teacher education programme, I started a book of teaching notes I called 'Christian Doctrine Instructions', and we had lectures on 'Catechetics'. But by 1967, the word Religious Education had taken over (and my book of Christian Doctrine instructions was discarded because it was irrelevant). The term Religious Education had strong cultural and educational roots in the UK where RE was a well-established subject in state schools. Michael Grimmitt's famous book in 1973 was called *What Can I Do in RE?* In North America, the Religious Education Association (with its international journal *Religious Education*) had been prominent since its founding in 1903.

In February 1970, the Italian bishops published *Il rinnovamento della Catechesi* as a national Directory for Church ministry and Religious Education. It followed through in the educational trajectory of the 1965 declaration. In August 1970, the Australian bishops published a translation of the Italian document, together with a supplement on Catholic schooling, called *The Renewal of the Education of Faith*. In Australia, this publication was intended to add substance to the completion of the Australian Catholic catechisms from kindergarten to Year 12, when the Years 11–12 books *Come Alive* were released earlier in 1970. The response to the colourful magazine style *Come Alive* was mixed. The booklets, produced by practising teachers, were liberal in tone and somewhat revolutionary in format; they were not well received by the conservatives in the Church, and for some bishops the bright discussion-informing booklets were not consistent with what they thought a catechism should be like. There was much debate about where RE was headed. Brother Bourke *et al* (1971) led the conservative critique in publishing *What's Wrong with 'Come Alive'*. The liberal response promptly labelled their book '*Drop dead*' as a comic alternative name, contrasting with that of the new catechism, *Come Alive*.

The Renewal of the Education of Faith was also published in 1970 in the UK by T Shand Publications. But it is not clear what currency the document had in Catholic education there or in New Zealand.

Then came the second crucial event in 1971. That year, the Roman Congregation for the Clergy released the *General Catechetical Directory*. This signalled that the apparent 'romance with education' was over. From then on, *faith* or derivative terms (like catechesis, faith development, and more recently faith formation and Catholic identity) would gradually tend to replace the word Religious Education in the discourse of RE itself. Even though the word Religious Education remains the name of the school subject, the dominance of ecclesiastical terms (ecclesiastical drift) created ambiguity about its nature and purposes. And this has had a lasting effect on the trajectory of the RE discourse, especially in the last 15 years (Rossiter, 2018, pp. 87–93).

This chapter, as part of the volume honouring Gerald Grace, has attempted to raise awareness about what is considered to be a significant problem for Catholic school RE going forward since 1971. And hopefully it may catalyse further research and debate on the questions considered. I know that Grace wants the journal *ISCE* to be a forum for such dialogue and debate.

To address the problem of ecclesiastical drift, it has summarised a set of principles/issues considered to be in line with best practice; it is not proposing any new approach. It recommends that efforts to revitalise the narrative of RE as a particularly valuable learning area in the Catholic school curriculum should give more attention to these aspects. And to stimulate a contemporary re-configuring of the narrative of RE, it has proffered ideas and unambiguous language that may help get RE better appreciated by teachers and students for its great potential in resourcing young people's spirituality and enhancing their capacity to construct a meaningful personal narrative for their own lives.

Also, this discussion, by giving attention to the educational dynamics of RE, may help affirm what religion teachers do best – *educating*. It can help both current and prospective RE teachers by projecting more realistic *expectations* about the knowledge/skills student outcomes of RE, together with *hopes* about how it might enhance their personal spirituality. And this lessens the problem where RE is evaluated in terms of changing young people's level of religious practice. For Australia, this may help give RE a more realistic, but also prominent and important, place in the larger discourse of Catholic education. In brief, these efforts may help 'put Religious Education back on the "Catholic school map"' – front and centre. How pertinent the issues are in other countries is yet to be determined; responses to this chapter, I know, would be welcomed by the Editor of *ISCE*.

Notes

1 It must be remembered that there are a number of journals specifically dedicated to Religious Education and it is likely that RE teachers direct their articles to these journals. This tends to keep discussion 'in-house'. The ISCE journal, which is interdisciplinary in readership, opens such discussion to a larger academic and professional audience.

2 Grace has always suggested that Catholic social teaching should be interpreted within Catholic RE, on the principle that 'faith without works is dead' (St James). The number of views for this article suggests that many teachers in schools and colleges are interested in this approach.

3 Presumptive language is evident when the RE language, both in the literature and in the classroom, presumes that all students are, or should be, regular churchgoers and that they will assent to the views being presented. A common example is evident in the way the word 'we' is used as if all present agree.

4 See, for example, the account of the effects on RE in Catholic tertiary institutions in Australia in the paper at https://asmre.org/EDrift.html

5 There is anecdotal evidence of this problem in Australian Catholic schools. As noted in the chapter, empirical research on this question has been initiated, with data from a small pilot testing of the questionnaire yet to be analysed.

6 Of the just under 25 million Australians, 52% are Christian (with 23% Catholic and 13% Anglican). Other world religions represented are: Islam (2.6%), Buddhism (2.4%), Hinduism (1.9%), Sikhism (0.5%), and Judaism (0.4%). In 1911, the year of the first Australian census, the number who indicated they had no religion was 0.4%. In the 2016 census for the same question on religious affiliation, 30.1% indicated 'no religion' and a further 9.6% did not answer this census question (total of 39.7%).

7 The low status of RE in Australian schools generally is well known to both teachers and the wider community. The references cited here attempt to explain it in detail. I do not know to what extent this may be the case in other countries.

8 This is a complex question. In Catholic schools, the need for Catholic teachers who are engaged with the Church and the need for religion teachers who are believers and committed to the values in studying religion are not in question. The issue here is about cautioning those who use the idea of being a Catholic witness to justify une-thical teaching procedures in the classroom.

9 School retreats follow in the long spiritual/religious tradition for retreats in the Catholic Church. See https://asmre.org/retreats.html for an account of a recent sub-stantial research project on retreats in Australian Catholic secondary schools.

10 I know of no systematic research about how parents perceive the inclusion of some study of other religions in Catholic RE. I consider that it would be viewed as making a valuable contribution to their children's religious education.

11 There is anecdotal evidence that teachers in Catholic RE regard the inclusion of some study of other religions as a valuable part of RE. This is presumed in the general acceptance of state-developed religion studies courses available in Years 11–12 in a number of Australian states. Catholic schools provide the large majority of the candi-dature in these subjects.

12 The term 'secular spirituality' has been widely used to describe the spirituality of people who consider themselves 'spiritual' but not 'religious', and of those who are not reli-gious, but who have a non-religious spirituality 'implied' in their values and moral behaviour, as explained in detail in Rossiter (2018) and Crawford and Rossiter (2006).

References

ASMRE website. Various professional development study materials on Religious Edu-cation; also, Survey on Religious Education: The language of Religious Education and the need for more attention to critical evaluative pedagogy. https://asmre.org/, last accessed November 2020.

Australian Episcopal Conference, (1970). *The Renewal of the Education of Faith*. Sydney: EJ Dwyer.

Bourke, L. et al., (1971). *What's Wrong with 'Come Alive'*. Melbourne: Authors' publication.

Brisbane Catholic Education, (2019). *Religion, Meaning and Life: A course for Years 11–12. Elective Unit. Identity and Meaning: How People Construct Personal Identity and Com-munity in a Consumerist Culture*. Brisbane: Brisbane Catholic Education.

Buchanan, M., (2005) 'Pedagogical Drift: The Evolution of New Approaches and Paradigms in Religious Education'. *Religious Education*, 100 (1), pp. 20–37.

Catholic Education Office Diocese of Parramatta, (1999). *Sharing Our Story: Religious Education Curriculum, K-12*. Sydney: Catholic Education Office Diocese of Parramatta.

Congregation for the Clergy, (1971). *General Catechetical Directory*. Vatican City: Vatican website.

Crawford, M., (1982). 'A Year 12 Course on World Religions in a Catholic High School: Contrasts with the Regular Education in Faith Program', in R. H. Elliott and G. Rossiter, Eds., *Towards Critical Dialogue in Religious Education*. Sydney: Australian Association for Religious Education.

Crawford, M. & Rossiter, G., (1985). *Teaching Religion in the Secondary School: Theory and Practice*. Sydney: Christian Brothers Province Resource Group.

Crawford, M. & Rossiter, G., (1988). *Missionaries to a Teenage Culture: Religious Education in a Time of Rapid Change*. Sydney: Christian Brothers Province Resource Group.

Crawford, M. & Rossiter, G., (2006). *Reasons for Living: Education and Young People's Search for Meaning, Identity and Spirituality*. Melbourne: Australian Council for Educational Research.

Finn, A., (2011). *Parents, Teachers and Religious Education: A Study in a Catholic Secondary School in Rural Victoria*. EdD Research Thesis. Sydney: Catholic Schools Office, Diocese of Broken Bay.

Fowler, J. W., (1981). *Stages of Faith: The Psychology of Human Development and the Quest for Meaning*. San Francisco: Harper & Row.

Grimmitt, M., (1973). *What Can I Do in RE?* Great Wakering: McCrimmons.

Groome, T. H., (1980). *Christian Religious Education: Sharing Our Story and Vision*. San Francisco: Harper & Row.

Hill, P., (1981). 'The Ethics of Helping: A Comparison of the Role of Self-Reliance in International Affairs and Pedagogy'. *Metaphilosophy*, 12 (2), pp 181–205.

Hill, B. V., (2004). *Exploring Religion in School: A National Priority*. Adelaide: Openbook.

Hill, B. V., (2006). 'Values in Free Fall: Religious Education and Values in Public Schools'. *Journal of Religious Education*, 54 (2), pp. 51–58.

Loukes, H., (1961). *Teenage Religion*. London: SCM Press.

Loukes, H., (1965). *New Ground in Christian Education*. London: SCM Press.

Loukes, H., (1973). *Teenage Morality*. London: SCM Press.

Middleton, M., (2001). *Lutheran Schools at Millennium's Turn: A Snapshot 1999–2000 from Slab Hut to Cyberspace*. Adelaide: Lutheran Education Australia Office.

Moran, G., (1970). 'Catechetics R.I.P'. *Commonweal*, 18 December, pp. 299–302.

Pope John Paul II, (1979). *Catechesi Tradendae*. Vatican City: Vatican website.

Rogers, C. R., (1961). *On Becoming a Person: A Therapist's View of Psychotherapy*. London: Constable.

Rogers, C. R., (1969). *Freedom to Learn: A View of What Education Might Become*. Columbus, Ohio: Charles E Merrill Publishing.

Rossiter, G., (1981). 'Stifling Union or Creative Divorce? The Future Relationship between Catechesis and Religious Education in Catholic Schools', *Word in Life*, 29 (4), pp. 162–173.

Rossiter, G., (1999). 'Historical Perspective on the Development of Catholic Religious Education in Australia: Some Implications for the Future'. *Journal of Religious Education*, 47 (1), pp. 5–18.

Rossiter, G., (2016). *Research on Retreats. The Views of Teachers and Senior Students about Retreats in Australian Catholic Secondary Schools.* Sydney: School of Education, Australian Catholic University.

Rossiter, G., (2018). *Life to the Full: The Changing Landscape of Contemporary Spirituality. Implications for Catholic School Religious Education.* Sydney: Agora for Spiritual, Moral and Religious Education.

Rossiter, G., (2020). 'Addressing the Problem of "Ecclesiastical Drift" in Catholic Religious Education'. *International Studies in Catholic Education*, 12 (2), pp. 191–205. The full research study is available at https://asmre.org/.

Ryan, M., (2013). *A Common Search: The History and Forms of Religious Education in Catholic Schools.* Revised Edition. Brisbane: Lumino Press.

Second Vatican Council, (1965). *Gravissimum Educationis.* Vatican City: Vatican website.

Chapter 14

Professor Gerald Grace's innovations in Catholic education as guide for future research

Jacinta Mary Adhiambo

Introduction

I met Professor Grace at a conference that was organized on *Global Catholic Education and Integral Human Development: Setting a Social Science Research Agenda*, which took place in Rome in April 2018. In this conference, Grace gave a presentation which touched me when he said that he had developed a deep interest in Catholic education and began to research and write about it. It was at this conference that I learnt about the journal of *International Studies in Catholic Education*. Professor Grace advanced that there were many good things happening in faith-based schools that were not known and there was a need to make people appreciate what the Catholic Church does in the field of education, especially for the poor.

Having co-edited the *International Handbook of Catholic Education: Challenges for School Systems in the 21st Century* and been the Executive Editor of the journal of *International Studies in Catholic Education*, Grace is at the forefront in the discussions on Catholic education, advancing scholarship and research. This in reality is a great contribution of Grace in the understanding of issues related to Catholic education in the 21st century. In his desire to promote readership on Catholic education, he engaged different contributors from across the world: Nigeria, Kenya, Malawi, South Africa, Belgium, Australia, United States of America, Zambia, Italy, Uruguay, United Kingdom, to mention but a few.

Going through the articles in the journal which Grace edited, one identifies the different perspectives of Catholic education across cultures and religion. That is why the journal includes articles from those who deal with other forms of faith schooling (Anglican, Jewish or Muslim) and the critics of existing forms of faith schooling. Indeed, the critics help in evaluating faith-based schooling, thus giving insights for Catholic education. The articles expose the quality touch that Grace, the Editor, gave in the selection of the themes that he sent out in the call for papers.

The innovations that this chapter endeavours to discuss emerge from selected articles edited by Grace. These include *spiritual capital*, contribution of different Religious Congregations that have education as a mission and

DOI: 10.4324/9781003171553-17

understanding challenges to Catholic education in the 21st century that do need new research and scholarship. In the preface of the first issue of *International Studies in Catholic Education*, Grace states: 'A deeper understating of challenges facing Catholic education and of creative and progressive responses to these challenges need to be constructed from a variety of perspectives and case studies' (2009, p. 1). Indeed, there are now many case studies that have been published. This is why this chapter highlights Grace's special innovations that are posing a need to continuously engage with reading, searching and researching to keep abreast with the new approaches to understanding the concept of Catholic education. The following section reviews *spiritual capital*, Grace's key contribution to the understanding of Catholic education/schooling in the 21st century.

There is a need to define what Catholic education entails: the 'formation of the human person in view of his or her final end and the good of that society to which he or she belongs and in the duties of which a person will as an adult, have a share' (*Gravissimum Educationis*, 1965, par. 1). The Catholic Church's view of education is to develop a person to become an active member with a transformative role in society.

Grace and *spiritual capital*

In his contribution towards the understanding of Catholic education, Grace (2010) articulated the element of *spiritual capital* for the continuity of Catholic schools. This was one of many issues that he dealt with in the discourse on Catholic education. This is why Franchi (2017) in the review of Grace's selected works identified the themes as 'mission', 'spirituality' and '*spiritual capital*'; the 'preferential option for the poor'; 'faith-based schools', 'concepts of educational leadership'; 'concepts of educational "effectiveness" in Catholic schooling'; 'mission integrity', and 'Catholic values' among others. Grace argues that spiritual capital is important in a world where secularization has taken root.

In addition, he contends that spiritual capital is the inner dynamic that stems from the spiritual and religious power that give the impetus for the sense of mission, purpose and work. This is what Grace calls the sustaining and inspirational factor. This is what keeps Catholic education going given that Christian education is the mandate of the Catholic Church in obedience to the command of Jesus Christ to go and teach, baptize and spread the gospel.

At this stage, it is quite important that we discuss further the question: What is *spiritual capital*? There are different ways of describing or defining the concept. Moghadam and Makvandi, investigating the relationship between spiritual capital and job performance, cite Ian Marshall, who argues that spiritual capital can be measured by 'Self-awareness, vision led, positive use of adversity, compassion, holistic, diversity, independence, tendency to ask fundamental questions, spontaneity... and humility' (2019, p. 4). In the same development, Rima notes that spiritual capital is the 'Accumulated and enduring collections of belief, knowledge, values and dispositions that drive societal, organisational and inter-personal behaviour' (2020, p. 1).

Basing our discussion on the above description, it is clear that the intrinsic and inner power and voice that moves one to keep momentum is spiritual capital. The values of honesty, communion with our Creator-God in prayer, devotion to duty, self-sacrifice, serenity, peace, sense of responsibility, human dignity, to mention a few would be included in the list. This capital, just like material/cash capital that is invested to gain interest, should be continuously invested in Catholic education to sustain it in the future; this is likely to pose more challenges given the trend of materialism and secularism.

Spiritual capital is still timely for the current generation, which tends to look at spiritual values as outdated and may have nothing to offer in the technolo-gical era where there is a tendency to imagine that almost all the answers to problems can be obtained from the Google search engine with the click of a button. Adhiambo (2019) observes that social media challenges the Catholic schools in Kenya. Learners who are exposed to too much information in the media find a number of contradictions with the spiritual values that the Catholic schools propagate.[1] Grace's idea of the inner energy that emerges from spiritual and religious beliefs needs to be perpetuated in Catholic education in the world. The question to be answered here is how will the agents of Catholic education present the *spiritual capital* for its continuity? May be this an invi-tation to researchers, Catholic education practitioners and the Catholic Church to look for new ways of evangelizing in their schools. This indeed requires new research and new scholarship on how to keep God in our schools, in ways which engage modern youth.

In the same way, Groome (2014) in analysing Catholic education in terms of 'from and for faith' argues that there are children who do not attend Catholic schools because of faith but because of the quality education offered in such schools. Such students may not be involved in the practice of faith as such. However, Groome believes that the 'Catholicism of our schools is essential if they are to both serve the common good and foster the spiritual development of students' (2014, p. 114). Indeed, the *spiritual capital* that Grace talked about is advanced by the above argument. Even those students whose faith is not Catholic are to be helped to connect to that inner energy. The spiritual capital developed in the graduate enables him or her to respond to social issues in the light of faith. At this point, I would like to pose a question. Is this the reality? Don't we come by some graduates who are corrupt and dishonest? Does it mean that the Catholic education did not take place? That the spiritual capital that Grace talked about is not attainable? The answer to such questions would be obtained by doing rigorous research on the impact of Catholic education and specifically spiritual capital on the lives of graduates of Catholic schools.[2]

It is the responsibility of each graduate of Catholic education to bloom where they are planted and to propagate the Catholic tradition and faith. However, even if the opposite is the case, there is no need to panic. Even one candle lit in the darkest corner of the room brightens the room. Taking the current situation of the Covid-19 pandemic, where all the learning institutions were challenged to close down and at the time of writing reopening was being discussed, that inner energy that inspires good deeds moves students of Catholic schools to be kind, loving, caring and mindful of the needs of neighbours amidst the social distancing applied as a measure to prevent infection. The "new normal" requires true rethinking of scholarship on spiritual capital when some people's faith has been tested. Will the students who have been traumatized and others who have lost their loved ones not challenge the relevance of spiritual energy in the post–Covid-19 era?

In the discussion on the goals of education, Arrupe posits that the purpose of Catholic schools 'is not to produce pious faithful allergic to the world in which they live but incapable of responding to it sympathetically but form people who are balanced, serene, constant, open to whatever is human' (as cited by Meyo, 2014, p. 130).[3] This is the *spiritual capital* that Grace writes about – the intrinsic spiritual energy that propels one to express values of honesty, service, openness and sensitivity to what is happening now and in the future. That is why Catholic education is anchored in the Catholic traditions based on gospel values of love, mercy, forgiveness and care for each other, self-giving and sacrifice among others. In fact, Grace advances that 'education does not only refer to classroom teaching and vocational training but to the complete formation of the person' (2013, p. 105). For Grace, Catholic education is geared to the formation of people equipped with knowledge and skills to serve the common good motivated by faith and a Catholic social conscience to challenge the status quo and consistently be the voice of reason and of faiths.

The argument is not different to that in the foreword of *Policy Document for Catholic Education in Kenya* of 2013:

Catholic Schools are places where self confidence and trust are promoted and moral, spiritual and intellectual potential realized for the integral development of each person... schools as places of evangelization, socialization and places where children are helped to internalize and live the Gospel values and positive traditional values.

(Kenya Conference of Catholic Bishops, 2013, p. 5)

From the foregoing presentation I am still of the opinion that the discourse on *spiritual capital* needs to be expounded by scholars to propagate its relevance in the 21st century. The topic cannot be exhausted and Grace's legacy in this area will live on and that is one way his contribution in the field can be celebrated. A review of Grace's book on *Faith, Mission and Challenge in Catholic Education* engages readers time and again. Franchi (2017) posits that Grace challenges those who have the mission of formal education and those interested in Catholic Education Studies to gauge how they practise and dedicate themselves to faith and mission in the provision of Catholic education today.

Contributions of the Religious Congregation in Catholic education from selected works of Grace[4]

Religious Congregations have been and are agents of evangelization in the Catholic Church. The charisms of Religious Congregations or institutes are for the good of the Church. Canon 577 stipulates,

> In the Church there are a great many institutes of consecrated life which have different gifts according to the grace which has been given to them: they more closely follow Christ who prays, or announces the kingdom of God, or does good to the people, or lives with people in the world, yet who always does the will of the Father.
>
> (The Code of Canon Law, 1997, Canon 143)

In the same way, Vatican II's Decree *Perfectae Caritatis* (on the Up-to-date Renewal of Religious Life) (1965) argues that many institutes engage in a variety of apostolic work and are endowed with gifts, which vary according to the grace given to them as expressed in I Corinthians 12:4 which explains that there are varieties of gifts but the same spirit. Of course, this stand is based on what is enshrined in Canon 794, Clause 1: 'The Church has a special duty and the right to educating, for it has a divine mission of helping all to arrive at the fullness of Christian life' (The Canon Law Society, 1997, p. 183). Again, in *Gravissimum Educationis* (1965), the Council 'exhorts the sons (and daughters) of the Church to assist in a spirit of generosity in the whole field of education' (1965, para. 3). This is why the Church through the different Religious Congregations continues to play a vital part in the development and extension of education where they deem it necessary.

In the volumes of the journal that Grace has edited, there are many Religious Congregations or Orders that have been made reference to in relation to their contribution to Catholic education. Scanning through some of the articles, the list includes the Society of Jesus: Jesuits (Meyo, 2014); the Marist Brothers (Green, 2014); the Salesians of St. Don Bosco (Lydon, 2009); Spiritan Missionaries (Amadi, 2016), Society of Holy Child Jesus (Aidoo, 2016); Evangelizing Sisters of Mary, Sisters of the Blessed Virgin Mary: Loreto, Sisters of St. Joseph, De La Salle Brothers, Patrician Brothers among others (Adhiambo, 2019), to mention but a few. I imagine that Grace knew well that there was no way he would contribute to the discourse on Catholic education without involving the very agents of evangelization in the Church. No wonder, he challenged the Priests, Sisters, Brothers or collaborators of the Religious Congregations or Orders to research and share perspectives and challenges to make the readership of Catholic education aware of what exactly the Religious Congregations have achieved. It is common knowledge that if nothing is written about a given area or topic, there may be no addition of knowledge and people may remain ignorant.

Looking at Catholic education from the perspective of the Salesians, according to Lydon (2009), the Salesian educator is 'the good shepherd who knows his pupils and goes before them' (p. 48). In this case, we see the aspect of Jesus the Good Shepherd (Jn 10: 14–16) inspiring the education in Salesians' schools. The qualities of the Good Shepherd: knowing the sheep, caring for the sheep, looking for the lost sheep, leading the sheep to the greener pasture are perpetuated in the Salesian schools. This is true and just and thanks to Grace, who gave this author the opportunity to tell the world the Salesian approach to education. Lydon continues to say that for Don Bosco, the contact with the young people in the classroom and formal situation is not sufficient. This calls for the educator to develop an abiding presence with the pupils or students. The 'presence' is within and beyond the school. This is indeed a great contribution in the understanding of Catholic education from Salesians' perspectives.

Marist Brothers are also presented in the works of Grace. Green (2014) presents the life of Marists in education as the disciples of Jesus and having Mary the Mother of Jesus as their model. He posits that they set out into the 'hill Country' of the students' lives 'filled with hope and joy bringing them news of justice, mercy and faithfulness of God' (Luke: 39–56, Green, 2014, p. 151). The contribution of the Marist Brothers is a call to bring good news to the 'new normal' students at different levels. Traumatized youth due to the Covid-19 pandemic lockdown that removed them from schools, some of whom have gone through all forms of abuse: sexual, child labour, domestic violence, need the education approach of the Marist Brothers. The lessons learnt from the Marist Brothers may inspire other Catholic schools.

Many Religious Congregations with education missions provide Catholic education to the poor and needy children. Wodon (2020) observes that many of the Catholic or faith-based schools are costly to parents given that they have to pay for the tuition and other fees. Indeed, some of the schools are less affordable. But why would parents wish to take their children to schools that are based in Catholic education? Wodon reports that parents value good values instilled in the young and in some cases academic performance, teacher quality and discipline. Adhiambo (2019) argues that in Kenya, many secondary schools run by the Religious Congregations[5] and by extension the Catholic Church perform better in national examinations. However, there is a need to do an assessment of the impact of such schools on society and the Church. What about the values system that the schools are best known for? Do all the graduates of such Catholic schools practise the values that they appreciated while at school? Why do we still have some cases of moral decadence in society? Such questions call for further and new research studies to gauge the impact of the Catholic education offered in such schools.

'Preferential option for the poor' is a positive feature of the Catholic schools and was also one of the themes that Grace highlighted. Aristimuno (2020) argues that there are few Catholic schools in Uruguay that take care of the less privileged. Grace's article on faith, mission and challenges in Catholic education puts emphasis on the preferential option for the poor. Grace has understood the Catholic social teaching principle 'Option for the poor and vulnerable'. Does this have a link with the service to the poor in Catholic schools? Of course, yes, the opportunity to have basic education that prepares one to fit into society takes care of the vulnerable children who may not be able to afford an education like that of their colleagues from rich families. Especially in the education mission of the Church, the poor are to be taken care of. At this point, the question that Wodon (2020) poses remains a key area for research: How are the poor served in the Catholic schools in other parts of Africa and other developing countries? Maybe this is the right time to obtain the stories and lived experiences of the beneficiaries of such schools and to further the discussion on Catholic education and service for the poor.

Challenges facing Catholic education from selected articles

Scanning through the articles that are in *International Studies in Catholic Education*, one realizes that the provision of Catholic education encounters a number of challenges. It is paramount that these are highlighted to form a basis for future discourse on how to deal with them.

To begin with, Grace (2016) reports that there are countries where Catholic schools find themselves admitting many children from 'well-to-do' families and from other faiths because of the principle of openness. This is an issue for Catholic education, which stresses that the Church also ought to offer educational services to the poor. This does not imply that the Church does not care about children from more advantaged families. They too are to be taken care of but priority is to be given to those who cannot afford education.

Some of the highlighted challenges are unique to particular regions or countries. For example, in Kenya, Akala (2007) enumerates degenerating morals due to secularization of education because of the introduction of new subjects, reluctance of the government to enact certain laws and anti-religious attitudes by other stakeholders.[6] What is the case at the time of writing this chapter in 2020? Challenges seem to have taken on a different orientation and facets that call for more research on how to keep Catholic education relevant in the 21st century. In Ethiopia, Chernet (2007) observes recruitment, formation and retention of school leaders as the main drawbacks. In this case, the management of the said schools need to improve on the formation and retention of leadership to continue inspiring the governance of Catholic schools.

The Catholic Church cherishes collaboration among agents of evangelization. This is why, where it is not possible to have Religious Congregations continue with the governance of their founded Catholic schools, the leadership is handed over to dedicated lay faithful. Aristimuno (2020) posits that many Catholic schools in Uruguay are run by former lay collaborators although this poses a challenge in the continuation of the charism of the Religious Congregations just in case the lay people show lack of commitment to the original vision. Religious

Education coordinators are also involved in the governance of some of the schools. However, noted is a 'lack of strong faith experiences' (Rymarz & Belmonte, 2014, p. 198) in some of the coordinators. A person with such an experience may not convince the Catholic school community in matters of faith if challenged. It is therefore essential that before the Religious Education coordinators or other lay collaborators are charged with responsibility for Catholic education, they ought to be adequately prepared in matter of religious beliefs, faith and Religious Congregations' charism to ensure their continuity.

In the *International Handbook of Catholic Education*, Grace and O'Keefe (2007) give an overview of the Catholic schools facing challenges of the 21st century. They highlight secularization as posing a problem encountered in Catholic schools. These schools are expected to counteract it with the 'Sacred Culture'. In many places where secularization has taken root, there is always a feeling that there is no place for the Supernatural Being: God. In my opinion, this is why Grace calls on Catholic schools to be vigilant so that they are not taken hostage by secularization. This would render Catholic education irrelevant in the 21st century. The religious beliefs that are promoted in Catholic schools would not occupy any space in the minds of the young and this would compromise the education mission of the Catholic Church.

Conclusion

The contribution of Professor Gerald Grace to scholarship and research in Catholic education in the selected works shows the quality of time, energy and commitment with which Grace participated in the discourse. He made society and the Catholic Church aware of what the Church is doing in the education mission, thus continuing the teaching mission of Jesus Christ the Divine Master.

The selected areas of spiritual capital, the role of the Religious Congregations or Orders in the provision of Catholic education, and recurring challenges facing Catholic schools are still relevant topics of discussion and further research. Indeed, research in these areas will make the concept of Catholic education understood in different contexts and generate new ways of appreciating Catholic education when the values propagated in such education no longer make sense to a majority of people.

In my opinion, Grace is leaving a legacy of *internationality* in the understanding of the studies in Catholic education. He ensured that the contributors were sourced from different nations and states. A journey through the journal exposes insights and thoughts from the developed and developing worlds, which justifies the international nature of the journal. Grace has brought his new perspective to the discourse on Catholic education. May the ideas of Grace remain in the hearts and practice of all who hold dear Catholic education and Catholic schools.

I suggest new researchers to develop the themes that were originally present in the studies of Catholic education over the last 25 years, in order to bring new perspectives to it, particularly in the post Covid-19 context. The current situation calls for a new look at the issues related to the development of the education mission of the Catholic Church over the next 25 years.

Notes

1 Posts that encourage hatred, the dishonesty reflected in fake news, promotion of pornographic materials, materialism and individualism to mention but a few.
2 An important discussion of this challenge has been provided by Angelina Gutierrez (2012). However, further discussion could be done in different parts of the globe in the next decade.
3 Meyo in appreciating the contribution of Fr. Pedro Aruppe gives the mode of assessing the impacts of education. One who has gone through Catholic education should be seen by the good fruits that he/she produces in the society. Education that adds value to the human person.
4 It should be noted that Gerald has always made the involvement of Religious Congregations in the Catholic education mission a central feature of all his work. This can be shown by a content analysis of the articles in ISCE which shows many contributions from Religious Congregations, female and male.
5 Institute of the Blessed Virgin Mary, Sisters of Mary, Little Sisters of Francis, Franciscan Sisters of St. Ann, De La Salle Brothers, Sisters of Mary Immaculate, Nyeri, Assumption Sisters of Nairobi, Assumption Sisters of Eldoret, Missionary Congregation of the Evangelizing Sisters of Mary, Sisters of St. Joseph, Franciscan Sisters of St. Joseph, Marist Brothers to mention but a few.
6 There are cases where some argue that non-Catholic students in Catholic schools need not be subjected to attending Eucharistic Mass, and that teaching and learning Christian Religious Education should be optional in such schools, Yet the Catholic schools' management are convinced that through such activities the youth are moulded to become better citizens with moral character.

References

Adhiambo, J. M. (2019). Catholic schools in Kenya: history, achievements and challenges. *International Studies in Catholic Education*, 11 (1), pp. 159–177.
Aidoo, P. (2016). The contribution of the Society of the Holy Child Jesus to Catholic Education in West Africa. *International Studies in Catholic Education*, 8 (1), pp. 44–60.
Akala, W. J. (2007). The challenges of curriculum in Kenya's primary and secondary education: the response of the Catholic Church. In G. R. Grace (Ed.), *International Handbook of Catholic Education: Challenges for School Systems in the 21st Century* (pp. 619–635). Dordrecht: Springer.
Amadi, A. (2016). The contribution of the Holy Ghost Congregation to the educational development of Nigeria: historical and contemporary reflections. *International Studies in Catholic Education*, 8 (1), pp. 90–101.
Aristimuno, A. (2020). Challenges for Catholic schools in contemporary Uruguay. *International Studies in Catholic Education*, 12 (1), pp. 51–61.

Chernet, F. A. (2007). Catholic Education in Ethiopia: challenges and prospects. In G. Grace &. J. O'Keefe (Eds.), *International Handbook of Catholic Education: Challenges for School Systems in the 21st Century* (pp. 637–650). Dordrecht: Springer.

Franchi, L. (2017). *Faith, Mission and Challenges in Catholic Education: The Selected Works of Gerald Grace* by Gerald Grace, Book review. *International Studies in Catholic Education, 9* (2), pp. 236–239.

Grace, G. (2009). On the international study of Catholic education: why we need more systematic scholarship and research. *International Studies in Catholic Education, 1* (1), pp. 6–14.

Grace, G. (2010). Renewing spiritual capital: an urgent priority for the future of Catholic education internationally. *International Studies in Catholic Education, 2* (2), pp. 117–128.

Grace, G. (2013). Catholic social teaching should permeate the Catholic secondary school curriculum: An agenda for reform. *International Studies in Catholic Education, 5* (1), pp. 99–109.

Grace, G. (2016). *Faith, Mission and Challenge in Catholic Education* (pp. 1–15). London and New York: Routledge, World Library of Educationalist Series.

Grace, G. &. J. O'Keefe. (2007). *International Handbook of Catholic Education.* Dordrecht: Springer.

Gravissimum Educationis, in Abbott, W. (Ed.) (1966). *The Documents of Vatican II.* New York: Herder and Herder.

Green, M. (2014). New wineskins: reimaging Australia's Marists. *International Studies in Catholic Education, 6* (2), pp. 148–163.

Groome, T. (2014). Catholic education: from and for faith. *International Studies in Catholic Education, 6* (2), pp. 113–127.

Gutierrez, A. (2012). Does Catholic education have lasting effects on adult life? Reflections of alumni from Catholic colleges and universities in the Philippines. *International Studies in Catholic Education, 4* (1), pp. 16–34.

Kenya Conference of Catholic Bishops. (2013). *Policy Document for Catholic Education in Kenya*, 4th edition. Nairobi: KCCB.

Lydon, J. (2009). Transmission of the charism: a major challenge for Catholic education. *International Studies in Catholic Education, 1* (1), pp. 42–58.

Meyo, O. S. (2014). The educational ideas of Pedro Arrupe, SJ: a valuable resource for all Catholic educators. *International Studies in Catholic Education, 6* (2), pp. 128–139.

Moghadam, K. A. & Makvandi, R. (2019). Investigating the relationship between spiritual capital and job performance with organizational citizenship behaviors in employees (Evidence from Iran). *Cognet Business and Management, 6* (1), pp. 1–15. Open Access.

Perfecta Caritas in Abbott, W. (Ed.) (1966). *The Documents of Vatican II.* New York: Herder and Herder.

Rima, S. (2020, May 4). What is Spiritual Capital? Retrieved from https://scmli.com/what-is-spiritual-capital/.

Rymarz, R. & Belmonte, A. (2014). Some life history narratives of religious education coordinators in Catholic schools. *Internatonal Studies in Catholic Education, 6* (2), pp. 191–200.

The Canon Law Society. (1997). *The Code of Canon Law, New Revised English Translation.* London: HarperCollins Publishers.

Wodon, Q. (2020). How well do Catholic and other faith-based schools serve the poor? A study with special Africa: Part II: learning. *International Studies in Catholic Education, 12* (1), pp. 3–20.

Chapter 15

'Spiritual capital' and 'charisms' in the mission of Catholic schools

A dialogue between a sociologist and a theologian involved in Catholic education

François Moog

Introduction

In his research on Catholic education, Professor Gerald Grace has paid particular attention to Catholic values as expressed, for example, in the 'preferential option for the poor'. In particular, he focused on the spiritual and religious resources used by headteachers, which he referred to as 'spiritual capital' (Grace, 2010). In doing so, Gerald Grace opens up a particularly interesting and challenging perspective. However, it may be important to have a better understanding of the concept in relation to our understanding of the mission of Catholic schools.

For the theologian composing this chapter, Gerald Grace's main challenge is that he is an historian and a sociologist. How could a sociologist understand what spiritual capital is? Will not the transcendent dimension of this 'capital' only escape the sociologist? But the friendship I have with Gerald Grace and the esteem I have for his research prevents me from getting lost in judging him in this way. Gerald Grace is an atypical sociologist (everything about him is atypical, inasmuch as a Frenchman can pass judgement on the behaviour of a British scholar) and this makes him particularly open to interdisciplinary exchange. He is a man with a Catholic view of scholarship.[1]

Thus, if it is possible for the readers of this contribution to imagine a dialogue between an English sociologist and a French theologian, I intend to initiate this exchange on the basis of a specific question: Does the 'spiritual capital' of which Gerald Grace writes have something to do with the 'charisms' of which the Christian tradition speaks? For the theologian, it is a question of saying what the charismatic dimension of the mission of Catholic schools is and of verifying how this can be linked with the sociologist's reflection on spiritual capital.

For the theologian's part at the beginning of this exchange, it is appropriate first of all to pay benevolent attention to what the sociologist says, then to articulate this proposal with the notion of charisma and, finally, to look at the practical consequences for Catholic schools.

DOI: 10.4324/9781003171553-18

Gerald Grace's notion of *spiritual capital*

It is within the framework of his research on school leaders that Gerald Grace shows that headteachers are drawing upon a spiritual and religious resource which he calls 'spiritual capital' (Grace, 2002). He defines it as a sustaining and inspirational factor for the mission of these leaders, which he describes as 'resources of faith and values derived from a commitment to a religious tradition' (Grace, 2002, p. 236).[2]

The interest in the notion of *spiritual capital*

Grace's approach is interesting in many ways. The first is that, as a good sociologist, he is interested above all in the protagonists of the mission, those he calls 'front line practitioners'. This avoids an overly theoretical discourse on the Catholic school and allows for reflection on the practices of those who, in the daily life of schools, have to find resources to meet the educational challenges they encounter and thus ensure their mission. Another very enriching aspect of Grace's proposal is the consideration of the social, cultural and anthropological educational challenges that the use of this 'spiritual capital' makes it possible to face.

What is most original is that a sociologist can take an interest in these questions as they constitute a challenge to the faith, hope and charity of those engaged in educational responsibilities. On this point, Grace opens the possibility of the intervention of the theologian and seems to call for a dialogue between our two disciplines.[3] This becomes even more convincing when he qualifies the commitment of these people as a 'factor of vocational commitment' (Grace, 2010, p. 118). Above all, establishing a link between spiritual capital and vocation, as proposed by Grace, invites us to think deeply about the nature or form of this spiritual capital, if it is linked to a call and therefore of a relational nature.

Spiritual capital and charism: Initial approach

It is then that the dialogue between sociologist and theologian can become necessary and, in the final analysis, fruitful. Indeed, the sociologist's natural source, which Grace clearly states (Grace, 2010, p. 119), is Pierre Bourdieu's work on the forms of capital (Bourdieu, 1986). But while this is not unrelated to Bourdieu's research on education from 1970 onwards (Bourdieu, 1990), it remains internal to sociological thinking and is quite clearly rooted in Max Weber. However, when Weber puts forward the notion of *charisma*, always in the singular, it is to speak of a personal charismatic authority (Weber, 1954 and 1968). For Grace's reflections, this is not without consequence, because speaking of spiritual capital allows him to keep his distance from a conception of charisma as power. For Grace, it is therefore a question of looking outside the sociological 'tradition' for a foundation for the leadership of heads of schools.

It appears then that the spiritual capital put forward by Grace is not the implementation of a religious type of power, but the capacity to deploy spiritual resources in a community in the name of a common mission. As he himself says, it is not a question of a 'power over' people, in a rather clerical way, but of a 'power to maintain an educational mission and to animate and inspire others' (Grace, 2010, p. 119).

There is a shift in perspectives that leads the sociologist to distance himself from sociology alone, which leads him to consider spiritual capital, in a very evangelical way, as a treasure to be shared openly with everyone. This is why Grace's reflection leads him to two new questions. The first is that of the link between this spiritual capital and the theological literacy of school leaders. Here, it is about their 'ability to communicate knowledgeably how the faith of the Church relates to contemporary everyday experience' (Weeks and Grace, 2007, p. 8), a skill that goes to the heart of the mission of Catholic schools. The other question is precisely that of the link between this spiritual capital and the notion of charisma. With John Lydon, Grace seems to be looking for a rather extraordinary version of charisms, as appears among the great charismatic leaders (Cf. Lydon, 2009), even though he refuses to think in the form of a 'dramatic charism and charisma of exceptional leadership' (Grace, 2010, p. 120) and that he wishes to favour 'the sustaining resource for everyday leadership in Christian living and working'. It is therefore a question of introducing a notion of charisma that goes beyond Weber. For by going beyond the Weberian notion of charisma, Grace's proposal can help on the one hand to understand how the implementation of spiritual capital depends on the mission of a community more than on the power of its leader, and on the other hand to shed new light on a question addressed by Grace, that of the transmission of the spiritual capital of a Religious Congregation to a community of lay people, i.e. the renewal of spiritual capital in the next generation.

Pauline charisms and *spiritual capital*

In order for the notion of charisma to enrich that of spiritual capital, it is necessary to broaden the basis of reflection and to go beyond Weber to Saint Paul. Surprisingly enough, we have no systematic theology of charisms (see Hasenhüttl, 1970 and Gignac, 2009). But an exploration, even a quick one, of the sources of this theology in Saint Paul opens the way to a reflection which, by thinking in terms of structure and mission together, allows us to enter into a stimulating dynamic.

To the sources of a theology of charisms

The sources of a theology of charisms are easily accessible, both in Scripture and in the recent dogmatic tradition. In 1 Corinthians 12, Paul states two fundamental principles. The first principle is that of a diversity of gifts from a single donor. The second principle is that of the link between gift and mission.

In verses 4–6, charisms (*charismata*) are structurally linked to ministries (*diakonia*) and to God's ways of acting (*energemata*):

- v. 4, there is a diversity of gifts, but it is the same Spirit;
- v.5, there is diversity of ministries, but it is the same Lord;
- v.6, diverse modes of action, but it is the same God who produces everything in all.

These three aspects constitute the unfolding of the same spiritual reality and emphasise, on the one hand, the power of divine action and, on the other hand, the functions that the gifts make it possible to fulfil. It is then a question of making God's action visible in the community and, for this purpose, of looking away from the gifts themselves and focusing on the giver (origin) and on the putting into action of these gifts for the good of the whole body (purpose). This twofold concentration on the donor and on the implementation of the gifts prevents any attempt to subjectivise or substantiate the charisms and rather obliges us to an active conception according to which we should not speak of the charisms of the believer but of the charismatic dynamics of every Christian life.

The Second Vatican Council goes in the same direction, both in *Lumen gentium* 12 (henceforth *LG*) and in *Ad gentes* 28 (henceforth *AG*). In *LG* 12, the Council states that God's gifts are distributed among all the faithful and that they are distributed for the common good and for the necessity of the Church, making the charismatic dynamic a common reality for believers and placing it in a missionary perspective. In the same sense, *AG* 28 recalls that the charismatic reality spares no baptised person and that it is ordained to one end: the building of the Church. In this sense, Vatican II conceives charisms as an ordinary mode of action of the Holy Spirit.

The charismatic dynamics of the life of the Church

A number of conclusions can already be drawn from this rapid overview.

First of all, it is necessary to note the elusive character of charisms which draw their consistency only from their giver, God, and the mission in which they engage. Charisms cannot therefore be defined by what they are, but must be defined by their origin and purpose, from a purely dynamic perspective.

Moreover, charismatic dynamics is a common reality which requires the recognition of the participation of all the baptised in the life and mission of the Church. A charism cannot be an element that separates believers, but on the contrary unites them in the one Church. Thus, no one has the right to be passive in a Christian community because each one receives from God what enables him or her to participate in the building up of the Church and the implementation of its mission of salvation (Cf. Hasenhüttl, 1970).

From this, it appears that charisms are not goods to be possessed but goods to be implemented. God's gifts are not quantifiable and the quality of Christian life does not depend on the quantity or quality of these gifts, but on their fulfilment in the life of the believer and in the Church. It is here that the notion of spiritual capital can be fruitful for thinking about the mission of educational communities in Catholic schools.

Charism and *spiritual capital* in the life of Catholic schools

It appears then that in Saint Paul, charisms are not to be understood primarily in terms of leadership or personal power, but in terms of organic function within a community and with a view to the edification of that community (Gignac, 2009, p. 140).

But to say that a charismatic dynamic animates the life of the Church, and therefore of Catholic schools, is to face the difficult question of the secularisation of these schools. It manifests itself in two directions. On the one hand, secularisation in the philosophical and sociological sense of the term, when religious motivations are marginal for a family that entrusts their child to a Catholic school (religious motives are only invoked in France for 5.6% of families), raises the issue of a possible sharing of the spiritual capital linked to the Catholic dimension of the educational mission. On the other hand, this is secularisation in the religious sense of the term, when the proportion of teachers belonging to a Religious Order in France has fallen from 40% to 0.1% between 1950 and 2020, and at the same time the proportion of religious school headteachers has fallen from 100% to almost 0%.

Under these conditions, how could it be possible to take a broader view of spiritual capital by qualifying it as a common good of the community and to deal more specifically with the question of the transmission of this spiritual capital?[4]

Spiritual capital as a common good

First of all, it must be reiterated with conviction that the spiritual capital of Catholic schools, because it designates the resources of Christianity to carry out its educational mission, cannot be reduced to a catalogue of moral values. It is rather the work of faith, which must be thought of as a resource for the inventiveness and credibility of Catholic schools in pedagogical and educational matters. For this is where the usefulness, including the social usefulness of Catholic schools, comes into play: in their capacity to make faith available and effective in order to awaken freedoms, form people beyond their economic usefulness, promote growth rather than 'performance', and work towards a more just and fraternal society.

If we are indeed dealing here with spiritual capital linked to the charismatic dynamics of the Church, this calls for a serious consideration of the fact that the educational community is not a sum of individuals, but a subject in its own right which has this spiritual capital at its disposal as a common good, that is to say, as the Catechism of the Catholic Church says, to 'the sum total of social conditions which allow people, either as groups or as individuals, to reach their fulfilment more fully and more easily' (article 406).

The principle here is that the responsibility of persons is exercised in a community that is ordered by a mission. Thus, the Catholic education project is not individualistic,[5] but invites everyone to make a contribution within a community. This engages the members of the educational communities in a work of discernment of their willingness to contribute to the common project.

Setting the reflection on an institutional ground allows the sociologist to feel as comfortable as the theologian. According to this logic, if the community is a subject, then it must be taken into account that it is not the faith of those who make up the community that determines the catholicity of the Catholic school. As an ecclesial subject, the catholicity of the school is determined by its organisational form and ethos. What determines the catholicity of the school is its organisation and ethos, which guarantees the quality of relations within the community: how are decisions made? How is the differentiated participation of each individual in the common project promoted? How is the commitment and authority of each individual regulated? How is respect for each person's convictions guaranteed in the joint implementation of a Christian project? The Catholic school is not only a community of subjects: as an ecclesial subject, it is an organisation that must be thought out and evaluated in the light of the Gospel (Cf. Moog, 2020, 147 sq).

So the headteacher's leadership cannot be thought of simply in terms of a Weberian-type charisma, but must be thought of in a broader charismatic logic as an animating spirit of the community. It is therefore through the implementation of his or her responsibility that the headteacher enables the entire educational community to be the subject of an ecclesial mission. He or she is the pivot of the educational community.

In this way, school headteachers guarantee what, according to the Second Vatican Council, is the heart of the Catholic school: 'its proper function is to create for the school community a special atmosphere animated by the Gospel spirit of freedom and charity' (*Gravissimum Educationis* 8). The formulation is broad: 'atmosphere'. But it refers to what makes the community so decisive for the Catholic school and, more broadly, for Catholic education: the relationship. If it is difficult to understand what such an atmosphere is, it is useful to be guided by what qualifies it: freedom and charity. It is then the requirement of an interpersonal relationship of freedom and charity which is the place and the aim of Catholic education and constitutes, in the end, the heart of its spiritual capital.

Charism and transmission of a *spiritual capital*

Another question is that of the transmission of this spiritual capital. It is understandable that an overly personal conception of the charism causes difficulties in terms of transmission when a Religious Congregation is no longer in a position to ensure by itself the teaching and direction of a school. In a Catholic

Church which is still discovering itself to be grappling with a profound form of clericalism,[6] the ability of the lay faithful to guarantee the catholicity of a school project can sometimes give rise to suspicion. But is it so simple to make this spiritual capital depend on the structure or organisation?

In France, many Teaching Orders are questioning the sustainability of their educational works and are expressing their willingness either to associate lay people with them or to transmit them to them. This willingness is expressed in very diverse ways but often through the use of the semantic field of charism: 'to transmit the charism', 'to share the charism, 'to transmit one's charism and mission', 'to keep a spirit alive'. These expressions carry a double risk: on the one hand, the risk that the register of 'charism' is used without theological precaution, as if a charism were an objectifiable good that could be transmitted, in the same way as school buildings, for example. On the other hand, the search for a legal framework likely to guarantee this transmission risks taking precedence over the reasons why the search for a framework would be necessary. To put it another way, there is a concentration on the institutional figure of the educational work which risks overshadowing the community reality of this work. In fact, an institution in the Church is always the form taken by a community which is the subject of a mission and endowed with its own history and culture.

In the context of the transmission of an educational work of a Religious Order to lay people, it must be remembered that if we can speak of a charism proper to an institute, it is above all in the name of the community which constitutes the institute and which benefits from a system enabling it to implement it. This is a multifaceted system: figure and work (writings, social works, heritage) of a founder, history and narrative of this history constituting the narrative identity of the Religious Order, specific practices (particularly educational) linked to the institute's mission, practices regulating the life of the institute: novitiate, constitutions, chapters.

But, although multiple, this institutional structure is unified by the community which constitutes the institute and which is itself instituted by practices linked to the charismatic dynamics of all Christian life: a life of prayer, fidelity to the Word of God and fraternal communion. In this sense, the institutional structure which allows the exercise of the charism, that is to say, which, together, constitutes a verified mediation of the divine origin of the gift exercised and its missionary orientation, is not transferable outside the institute.

However, it can be said:

1   that any transmission of a missionary work, and especially an educational one, requires clarification of the institutional mechanism by which the educational work can be carried out by another group. It is the role of the ecclesial authority to verify and guarantee this.

2   that the transmission of a missionary work from one institute to others, even those close by history, intention and spiritual intuition, requires the

awareness on the part of the institute that it renounces all forms of authority and initiative. In this case, however, the modalities of communication and relationship between the new structure and the institute must be clearly envisaged so that the link maintained is clear and satisfactory for everyone.

3   that the sharing of the missionary work between an institute and another structure of the Church brings about a transformation of the institutional conditions for the exercise of the mission and requires the accompaniment of the competent ecclesiastical authority.

4   that the ecclesiastical authority, as a guarantee of communion and mission, must be able to ask an institute to give an account of the institutional arrangement by which it intends either to associate itself or to transmit to others a missionary work of its own.

This is how the institutional form of spiritual capital, conceived as a charismatic dynamic, will be honoured. For it is this institutional form that guarantees the operability of spiritual capital, so that it is not based on individual goodwill or the 'charismatic' authority of a leader, but on the structure itself. The example of the transmission of an educational work by a Religious Order shows that this requires a set of institutional mediations to be thought of, but which can be evaluated in the light of the Gospel much more easily than the commitment of individuals.

It seems then that the dialogue between the sociologist and the theologian may have enabled a further step to be taken in an issue that lies at the heart of the mission of Catholic schools. In this book recognising the contribution of Professor Grace, we can only hope that this dialogue will continue for many years to come and that the spiritual resources of Catholic schools will be replenished in various ways.

Notes

1   This is why Grace launched the journal, *International Studies in Catholic Education*, in March 2009 to be an interdisciplinary publication inviting contributions from theologians, philosophers, historians, social scientists and educational scholars and researchers, as well members of Religious Congregations with missions in education. Today this journal is accessed in 112 countries.

2   A more detailed theoretical statement of spiritual capital was written by Grace in ISCE 2010.

3   An analysis of articles in the ISCE journal (2009–2020) demonstrates that theologians have made regular contributions, e.g. Boland (2012), Droste (2015), Wansborough (2016) and Moog (2016, 2019).

4   Grace regards the transmission and renewal of spiritual capital in all forms of Catholic education as an 'urgent priority' at this time. See Grace (2010).

5   Catholic values of community and solidarity are fundamentally opposed to market values in education which emphasise individual achievement and a 'winner'/'loser' culture in society, as described by Pope Francis in *Laudato si* paragraphs 53, 108, and more especially, 215.

6   By clericalism, I mean it in the sense given by Pope Francis in his 'Letter to the people of God' (20 August 2018).

References

Boland, V., "St. Thomas Aquinas: What is his relevance to Catholic education today?", in *International Studies in Catholic Education*, 4:2 (2012), pp. 122–135.

Bourdicu, P., "The forms of capital", in J. Richardson (Ed.), *Handbook of Theory and Research for the Sociology of Education*, New York: Greenwood Press, 1986, pp. 241–258.

Droste , M., "The ordination of women in the Catholic Church: Arguments for teachers and students in schools to consider – Part 1 the case against", *International Studies in Catholic Education*, 7:1 (2015), pp. 4–14.

Gignac, A., "Charismes pauliniens et charisme wébérien, des faux-amis?", in *Théologiques*, 17 (2009), pp. 139–162.

Grace, G., *Catholic Schools: Mission, Market and Morality*, London: Routledge, 2002.

Grace, G., "Renewing spiritual capital: an urgent priority for the future of Catholic education internationally", in *International Studies in Catholic Education*, 2 (2010), pp. 117–128.

Hasenhüttl, G., "Les charismes dans la vie de l'Église", in Y. Congar (Ed.), *L'apostolat des laïcs – Décret Apostolicam actuositatem*, Paris: Le Cerf, 1970, pp. 203–214.

Lydon, J., "Transmission of the charism: a major challenge for Catholic education", in *International Studies in Catholic Education*, 1 (2009), pp. 42–58.

Moog, F., "The challenges facing Catholic education in France today", in *International Studies in Catholic Education*, 8:2 (2016), pp. 155–167.

Moog, F., "The humanistic challenge of Catholic education: an essay for Catholic educators to consider", in *International Studies in Catholic Education*, 11:1 (2019), pp. 24–36.

Moog, F., *Éducation intégrale – Les ressources éducatives du christianisme*, Paris: Salvator, 2020, p. 192.

Pope Francis, *The Encyclical Laudato Si'*, Vatican website, 2015, pp. 1–184.

Pope Francis, *Letter to the People of God*, Vatican website, 2018, p. 1.

Wansbrough, H., "Teaching about Catholic-Jewish relationships: Interpreting Jewish hostility to Jesus in the Gospels", *International Studies in Catholic Education* 8:1 (2016), pp. 18–28.

Weber, M., *Law in Economy and Society*, Cambridge. MA: Harvard University Press, 1954.

Weber, S., *Max Weber on Charisma and Institution Building: Selected Papers*, Chicago: Chicago University Press, 1968.

Weeks, N. and Grace, G., *Theological Literacy and Catholic Schools*, London: Institute of Education, CRDCE, 2007.

Chapter 16

The mission of the Catholic school and the preferential option for the poor

Stephen McKinney

Introduction

Two interconnected themes in the research of Gerald Grace are the mission of the Catholic school and the preferential option for the poor. Grace is anxious to connect these themes conceptually but also in the operation and daily life in Catholic schools. This can be discerned in the seminal *Catholic Schools: Mission, Markets and Morality* (2002) and the *International Handbook of Catholic Education: Challenges for School Systems in the 21st Century* (2007) and also in articles in the *Oxford Review of Education* (2001), *International Studies in Sociology of Education* (2003) and *International Studies in Catholic Education* (2013). This chapter examines the conceptual and practical connections between these two themes in the works of Grace and deepens and expands the discussion, drawing on scripture, theology and some key Church documents on Catholic education and schooling. The chapter argues that these two themes are key to an understanding of the authentic mission and role of Catholic schools in the 21st century, in the United Kingdom and internationally.

The preferential option for the poor in the works of Professor Gerald Grace

Professor Gerald Grace is a great advocate of the idea and practice of the preferential option for the poor in Catholic schools. He has consistently highlighted this issue in his lectures and has adopted a number of approaches to the issue in his publications and as editor of *International Studies in Catholic Education*. These approaches are interconnected, but it is instructive to separate them and provide a brief examination of each one.

First, he draws on the history of Catholic schools in England and Wales and the legacy of the 'mission' to the poor. This is exemplified in *The State and Catholic Schooling in England and Wales: Politics, Ideology and Mission Integrity* (2001) where he discusses the priority of Catholic school education over other work in the Catholic Church in England and Wales in the 19th century. The renewal of the Catholic faith depended upon good Catholic schooling in the view of the bishops.

DOI: 10.4324/9781003171553-19

Second, he argues that the preferential option for the poor is an integral part of the aim and mission of the contemporary Catholic school (Grace, 2002, 2003; Grace and O'Keefe, 2007). In a number of publications, he illustrates this by highlighting sections of *The Catholic School* document (1977), especially section 58 (see Grace, 2000, 2003, 2009; Grace and O'Keefe, 2007).[1] The highlighted part of section 58 comments:

> ...first and foremost the Church offers its educational service to "the poor or those who are deprived of family help and affection or those who are far from the faith". Since education is an important means of improving the social and economic condition of the individual and of peoples, if the Catholic school were to turn its attention exclusively or predominantly to those from the wealthier social classes, it could be contributing towards maintaining their privileged position, and could thereby continue to favour a society which is unjust.
>
> (The Sacred Congregation for Catholic Education, 1977, section 58)

Third, he uses the idea of the preferential option of the poor as a *lens* in his analysis of the theological and ecclesial integrity of the stated mission and coherence in practice in contemporary Catholic schools in England. This is observed in *Catholic Schools: Mission, Markets and Morality* (2002). This lens is extended to Catholic schools in other parts of the world in the *International Handbook of Catholic Education: Challenges for School Systems in the 21st Century* (2007) co-edited with J. O'Keefe. Grace and O'Keefe list the challenges that Catholic schools face in the 21st century in the introduction. One challenge is 'Responding to Vatican II principles of renewal of the mission e.g. with special reference to the "preferential option for the poor"' (p. 2). They invited the contributors to the *International Handbook* to report on how Catholic school systems respond to the preferential option for the poor in their national contexts. Grace and O'Keefe (2007, pp. 6, 9) are acutely aware of the complexities of funding for Catholic schooling throughout the world and they warn of the dangers of the selection of children for Catholic schools on the grounds of wealth or ability to the exclusion of other children:

> Catholic schooling internationally will be faced with a major contradiction if, despite a formal commitment to the service of the poor, it is found in practice to be largely in the service of students from more favoured sectors of society.
>
> (Grace and O'Keefe, 2007, p. 6)

This is consistent with the message of section 58 of *The Catholic School* (1977) quoted above.

Fourth, Professor Grace positions the preferential option for the poor within the wider discussion of Catholic Social Teaching (CST). He argues that CST should permeate the curriculum of the Catholic school and not be confined to the Religious Education classroom (Grace, 2013). This argument is supported by a close reading of Pope Benedict's *Caritas in Veritate* (2009) and includes a concerted focus on inequalities in wealth and resources and the possibilities of large-scale redistribution of wealth (Grace, 2013, pp. 102–103).

Fifth, he has been very proactive in promoting research into the preferential option for the poor and Catholic schools. He has consistently published articles focussed on this topic as editor of *International Studies in Catholic Education* (first issue in 2009). This can be discerned in Klaiber (2013) and Wodon (2020). This extends to publishing articles on Liberation Theology *per se* and CST and Catholic education (Torevell, 2013; Byron, 2015; Madero, 2018).

The contribution of Professor Grace to the promotion of the preferential option for the poor has been invaluable and has demonstrated a powerful and unswerving dedication to this fundamental principle. His concern for the preferential option for the poor is within the context of a deep understanding of the complexities of the relation between the Church and Catholic schools and the State and the competing demands on Catholic schools (Grace, 2001). This includes the aforementioned pressures of securing funding for Catholic schools and of the academic competition between schools that is driven by the neo-liberal marketisation of education. He has consistently warned of the dangers of the preferential option for the poor being a low priority or even being ignored, echoing the concerns raised about Catholic educational institutions straying from the preferential option for the poor in *Consecrated Persons and their Mission in Schools: Reflections and Guidelines* (Congregation for Catholic Education, 2002, sections 70, 75).

Liberation Theology and the preferential option for the poor

> Poverty is a human question, a Christian question—because poverty is death; it is inhuman; it is anti-evangelical. Theologians, among them my friends, will say, "I know you are very concerned with poverty because you are a Peruvian." I reply, "No, my friend, I am concerned because I am Christian."
>
> (Gutiérrez, 2012, pp. 5–6)

The term 'preferential option for the poor' originates in the early development of Liberation Theology. Liberation Theology emerged in the 1960s in Latin America as a response to the crippling poverty and the unjust social structures experienced by many people. There are a number of key figures associated with the rise and development of Liberation Theology in the Catholic Church, including: Jon Sobrino SJ; Leonardo Boff; Clodovis Boff; Juan Luis Segundo SJ and Gustavo Gutiérrez. Gutiérrez is the theologian most closely associated with the emergence of Liberation Theology and continues to be a powerful advocate of Liberation Theology.

The writings of Gutiérrez have been heavily critiqued: for using Marxist analysis as a scientific tool; for the use of dependency theory, especially in early works; and for being 'contextual' theology (Houtart, 1989; Groody, 2011).[2] Critics of Gutiérrez often focus on his early work, fail to discern the developments in his theology and fail to acknowledge that he has always positioned himself firmly within the Catholic Church. Gutiérrez used dependency theory in a qualified and critical manner, fully aware of the limitations of the theory and anxious about an over-emphasis on external factors and not enough on internal factors (McGovern, 1989). Gutiérrez proposed that some aspects of Marxist analysis could be used as a 'science', as an analytical tool, and not as an ideology in *Theology of Liberation*. While his use of Marxist-related analysis has been arguably exaggerated, his later theology has moved away from the use of this analysis. Liberation Theology has been categorised and almost dismissed as 'contextual theology'. Gutiérrez (2012) counter-argues that all theology is contextual. Theology should be engaged with the problems of the current context in the contemporary world. Further, Gutiérrez emphasises that the theologian is called to discipleship, like every other believer (Gutiérrez 1996). Nolan (1989) comments that Gutiérrez is considered to be a modern-day prophet because he speaks of God to the present-day context: 'All prophecy and prophetic theology speaks of, and speaks to, a particular time in a particular place about a particular situation' (Nolan, 1989, p. 433).

In recent years, there appears to have been a decline in interest in Latin American and Caribbean Liberation Theology (Müller, 2015). This is disappointing as there is much to be gained from academic and ecclesial appraisal of the contribution of Liberation Theology and its influence on Church teaching and Catholic education. The works of Gutiérrez, in particular, provide deep insights into the preferential option for the poor and its roots in the gospels. Gutiérrez argues:

> The fundamental contribution of liberation theology, it seems to me, revolves around what is called the 'preferential option for the poor' … The option for the poor is radically rooted in the gospel and this constitutes an important guideline for sifting through the fast-paced events and the intellectual currents of our days.
>
> (Gutiérrez, 2015, p. 88)

Gutiérrez has spent his life trying to talk about the love of God in 'a situation characterised by poverty and oppression' (Gutiérrez, 1989, p. xiv). The preferential option for the poor is rooted in the gratuitousness of God's love (Gutiérrez, 1996). The word 'preference' is not a negation of the universality of God's love because 'preference' does not mean that God's love for the poor is exclusive. Rather, the word preference stresses that the poor are the first, not the only persons, to receive the love of God, and it is this preference that Christians are called to follow by Jesus Christ (Matthew 11:5; Luke 4: 16–22; Gutiérrez, 1983, 2009). Gutiérrez (2012) argues that it is not enough if we are in solidarity with the poor and are critical of the causes of poverty; we have to fight against the causes of poverty.

The scriptural roots of the preferential option for the poor

This contemporary articulation of the 'preferential option for the poor' is drawn from fundamental principles in the Old and New Testaments. These begin with the God-given dignity of all people who are made in the image of God (Genesis 1:27).[3] The obligation to care for the widow, the orphan, the stranger in the Old Testament is mandated by God in the Holiness Code in the book of Leviticus (19:9–10; 23:22) and the book of Exodus (22:20–23; 23:9). The gospels provide many examples of the preference for the poor, notably in the Magnificat (Luke 1:46–55), Jesus in the synagogue (Luke 4:16–22), the parable of the Good Samaritan (Luke 10:25–37), the Beatitudes and curses (6:20–26); right use of possessions (Luke 12:13–21, 12:33–34. 14:33) and the Last Judgement in Matthew 25 (31–46). I have explored some of the major sources for the preference for the poor in the Old Testament and in Luke's gospel in other works (McKinney, 2018a, 2018b, 2018c). I now turn to further important sources. The first is a series of four key passages from the Acts of the Apostles that examine events in the early Christian community in Jerusalem. The second is a passage from Matthew's gospel and is usually called 'The Last Judgement' or 'The Sheep and the Goats'.

The Acts of the Apostles

Let us examine four key passages from the Acts of the Apostles that focus on the early Christian community and the care for the poor. The first two passages are Acts 2:42–47 and Acts 4:32–35. Acts 2:42–47 depict the early Christian community in Jerusalem that adhered to the teaching of the Apostles, lived in harmony, prayed (see also Acts 1:14) and celebrated the Lord's Supper (Fitzmyer, 1998).[4] The community is described as follows: 'The faithful all lived together and owned everything in common; they sold their goods and possessions and shared out the proceeds among themselves according to what each one needed' (Acts 2:44–45).

This may be an idealised account of the early Christian community but one that Luke wished to emphasise (Barrett, 2002, p. 34). This is revisited in Acts:

> The whole group of believers was united, heart and soul; no one claimed for his own use anything that he had, as everything they owned was in common... None of their members was ever in want, all those who owned land or houses would sell them, and bring the money from them, to present it to the apostles; it was then distributed to any members who might be in need.
>
> (Acts 4:32, 34–35)

This passage is immediately preceded by the accounts of Barnabas (4:36–37) and Ananias and Sapphira (5:1–11). Barnabas owned a piece of land, sold it and brought the money to the Apostles, acting in accordance with the representation of the community in Acts 2:42–47 and Acts 4:32–37. The story of Ananias and his wife Sapphira is one of deception and represents a fracture in the community. Ananias agreed to sell a property but held some of the money back, with the connivance of his wife. When challenged by Peter, Ananias falls down dead to the ground. Later Peter challenges Sapphira, who tries to deceive Peter about the price of the property and she too falls down dead to the ground. These two very dramatic episodes of miraculous intervention may have antecedents in examples of punitive deaths in the Old Testament, but ultimately, they serve to demonstrate that the communal life has been disrupted by evil and deception (Fitzmyer, 1998, p. 320; Harrill, 2011; O'Loughlin, 2014).

The story of Ananias and Sapphira is not couched as a direct teaching on the dangers of avarice and the renunciation of possessions that can be found in the Luke's gospel (12:13–34; 16:1–31; 18:18–30; 19:1–10; Tannehill, 2012, p. 280). Nevertheless, Luke has once again highlighted the importance of the right use of material possessions and the dangers of the wrong attitude towards money and, in this case, money that was to be used to help the poor in the community.

The final passage from Acts is Acts 6:1–6. The passage recounts another serious disruption to the harmony of the community: 'About this time, when the number of disciples was increasing, the Hellenists made a complaint against the Hebrews: in the daily distribution their own widows were being overlooked' (Acts 6:1).

The distribution of food was no longer 'according to what each one needed' as described in Acts 2:44–45. The Twelve act quickly and seven men were appointed to give out the food (6: 2–6). This lack of care appears to be a form of double discrimination. It discriminates against the Hellenists (non-Jewish Christians) and widows (some of the most vulnerable people in the community). This lack of care of the widows recalls the many times the Jews were reminded of their duty to care for the widows in the Old Testament (Fitzmyer, 1998, p. 345). Possibly the role of the Seven in waiting on the tables was to re-emphasise the importance of using table fellowship to welcome the outsider, the outcast – as Jesus had done (Luke 5:29–32; 15:1–2; Pao, 2011. p. 139). The idyllic Christian life as presented in Acts chapters 2 and 4 has been disrupted by deception and exclusion. The exclusion of the widows is only resolved by swift and decisive intervention.

Matthew 25:31–46: The Last Judgement – the Sheep and the Goats

The passage in Matthew's gospel refers to the Last Judgement and the separation of people as a shepherd separates sheep from goats, according to their care for the hungry, the thirsty, the stranger, the naked, the sick and the prisoner. The virtuous, the sheep, enter into the kingdom because they have cared for the needy and by doing so have demonstrated their care for God. The goats have not attended to the needs of these others and are to be treated harshly:

Next he will say to those on his left hand, 'Go away from me, with your curse upon you, to the eternal fire prepared for the devil and his angels. For I was hungry and you never gave me food; I was thirsty and you never gave me anything to drink; I was a stranger and you never made me welcome, naked and you never clothed me, sick and in prison and you never visited me.' Then it will be their turn to ask, 'Lord, when did we see you hungry or thirsty, a stranger or naked, sick or in prison, and did not come to your help?' Then he will answer, 'I tell you solemnly, in so far as you neglected to do this to one of the least of these, you neglected to do it to me'. And they will go away to eternal punishment, and the virtuous to eternal life.

The Last Judgment in Matthew 25:31–46 is a passage that Gutiérrez has referred to frequently in his writings (Gutiérrez, 1971, 1991, 1992, 2012). He interprets this passage in a number of ways and is influenced by the writing of Bartolomé de Las Casas (1484–1566), especially *De Unico Modo* (1537), and Pope John Paul II (Gutiérrez, 1992, 1996).[5] First, he recognises the core message of the passage: 'In Matthew 25:31–46, Jesus speaks of the last judgment and says if we give food to the least of our siblings, we give food to him. This is a very bold affirmation of the gospel writer' (Gutiérrez, 2012, p. 8).

Gutiérrez does not understand this in an allegorical manner nor in a 'spiritualizing manner'; he understands the passage as an insistence on the need for 'concrete, "material" actions towards others and especially the poor' (Gutiérrez, 1991, p. 119). Christian disciples are called to witness through these kinds of concrete actions (p. 131). This is the active discipleship of the sheep, the virtuous, in the passage and not the passivity of the goats (Carter, 2007, p. 92).

Second, Gutiérrez presents an incisive and challenging interpretation of the latter part of the passage by quoting two sources. Gutiérrez explains that de Las Casas drew on this passage to vehemently denounce the injustice enacted towards the indigenous people of the Indies in *De Unico*:

> Bartolomé returns to this Gospel passage, recalling a penetrating question posed by Augustine of Hippo: "If someone is damned by hellfire by Christ saying to him or her: 'I was naked and you did not clothe me,' to what hellfire will they be damned to whom he says, 'I was clothed and you stripped me!'" That is what is actually going on in the Indies. Not only are the naked not clothed, but, perversely, the poor of those lands are violently unclothed: the Indians are despoiled of their legitimate possession. The poor are robbed and, in them, Christ himself.
>
> (Gutiérrez, 1992, p. 64)

In a later work, Gutiérrez (1996) draws on the homily delivered by Pope John Paul II in Edmonton airport in Canada in 1984. Similar to de Las Casas, John Paul II explores some of the deeper implications of the Last Judgement in

Matthew 25: 31–46. He applies the words of Jesus to the global injustice that exists between the rich north and the poor south:

> Nevertheless, in the light of Christ's words, this poor South will judge the rich North. And the poor people and poor nations – poor in different ways, not only lacking food, but also deprived of freedom and other human rights – will judge those people who take these goods away from them, amassing to themselves the imperialistic monopoly of economic and political supremacy at the expense of others.
>
> (Pope John Paul II, 1984, section 4)

The preferential option for the poor, the fundamental contribution of Liberation Theology, is a powerful demand for justice in the world. It is at the heart of Christianity and Christian life and cannot be reduced to pious sentiments; it requires different forms of action: solidarity with the poor and fighting the effects *and* causes of poverty.

Catholic schools

The history of contemporary Catholic schools in the United Kingdom commences in the late 18th and early 19th centuries and is closely connected to the historical development of the Catholic Church.[6] Some of the prominent features of this history include (1) the arrival of Catholic migrants from Ireland in the 19th and 20th centuries and, at different times, Catholic migrants from Italy, Poland, Belgium, Ukraine and Lithuania and (2) the low socio-economic status of many in the Catholic population (Tenbus, 2010; Taylor, 2018).[7] The mission to the poor Catholic children was part of the rationale for the establishment and growth of Catholic schools. Historians recognise the role of the Religious Orders and Congregations in providing high-quality school education, notably in the advanced stages of schooling (McKinney and McCluskey, 2019). This facilitated opportunities to acquire public examination qualifications and increased the possibility of economic advancement and social mobility.

The scourge of poverty, however, remains very real in the United Kingdom and still affects children in schools. Child poverty remains a serious challenge for society and schools have limited resources to address this challenge. Many teachers work with children who suffer from the effects of poverty on a daily basis. The language of 'mission to the poor' in Catholic schools has evolved into 'preferential option for the poor', 'inclusion' and the education of the 'most vulnerable'.

I have previously highlighted the importance of the Vatican document *Consecrated Persons and their Mission in Schools: Reflections and Guidelines* (2002) because of the depth of the detail of the theological discussion on poverty and Catholic education (McKinney, 2018a, 2018b, 2018c). This document captures a real sense of the prophetic vision of the preferential option for the poor in

Catholic schools. One of the key statements is that 'The preferential option for the poor leads to avoiding all forms of exclusion' (section 69). This is further developed in the challenge of positioning the poorest at the centre of the educational endeavour:

> When the preferential option for the poorest is at the centre of the educational programme, the best resources and most qualified persons are initially placed at the service of the least, without in this way excluding those who have less difficulties and shortages. This is the meaning of evangelical inclusion, so distant from the logic of the world. The Church does, in fact, mean to offer its educational service in the first place to "those who are poor in the goods of this world or who are deprived of the assistance and affection of a family or who are strangers to the gift of Faith."
>
> (Section 70)

This passage extends section 58 of *The Catholic School* (1977).[8] This prophetic vision of the preferential option for the poor needs to be exemplified in examples of concrete witness and action. I present two case studies of concrete preferential option for the poor below, both located in Catholic schools in Scotland.

Case study 1

Case study 1 is focussed on John Ogilvie High School, a State-funded Catholic secondary school in South Lanarkshire. This Catholic school was anxious to include an increasing number of new-arrival Polish children in the life of the school (McKinney et al., 2015). The children belonged to families that had migrated to the area to work in local industries. These families were mostly at the lower end of the socio-economic scale. The school faced challenges of engaging with children with little knowledge of the English language and Scottish culture and sought the support of the Scottish research team from the European *Portfolio of Integration* Project. The *Portfolio of Integration* was designed in Italy to help new-arrival children integrate into school education and community life. The head teacher of John Ogilvie High School approached neighbouring schools to participate in specially designed training sessions. The research team identified three ways in which John Ogilvie High School and the other schools were meeting the challenges: addressing language; creating culturally relevant pedagogy and pastoral support.

John Ogilvie High School was acutely aware that the language and culture of the new-arrival Polish children were not simply to be accommodated but valued. The staff were trained in some basic Polish and school signs were bilingual. The school aimed to respect Polish traditions and celebrated Polish feasts where appropriate. It worked with parents in a home school partnership. In effect, the school made changes in the way it operated to integrate these young people within the school. The aim was to ensure that the dignity of the Polish children was respected, that they felt fully accepted and did not feel marginalised in the school. This was a form of the 'evangelical inclusion' advocated by *Consecrated Persons and their Mission in Schools: Reflections and Guidelines* (2002, section 70).

Case study 2

Case study 2 is focussed on Trinity High School, also a State-funded Catholic secondary school in South Lanarkshire. The school established a 'Nurture Group' in 2009 to provide support for the most vulnerable young people in the school (McKinney and Hall, 2016). The Nurture Group targets young people who have experienced severe social, emotional and behavioural challenges. This includes poverty and disadvantage, trauma, deep emotional upset, experience of abuse, violence and neglect (Chapman et al., 2015). These are young people who make slow academic progress, can exhibit behavioural difficulties, and are at risk of suspension or exclusion. The Nurture Group provides support to the young people in the form of a designated and carefully furnished space and selected teaching staff who have been trained to provide pastoral care. The young people begin the school day in the Nurture room and prepare for the school day. The group also depends on the cooperation of the teaching staff throughout the school, as the young people can return to the Nurture room at any point in the day if they feel undue stress in a class. The Nurture Group has been very successful in actively supporting the young people, integrating them into the school and in helping them to progress to an initial positive leaver destination at the end of formal schooling.

The school has placed the most vulnerable young people at the centre of the educational programme by providing the special support that is required by these young people. The school has made decisions about allocating significant professional and material resource to support these young people and, by doing so, acts in solidarity with the poor and the most vulnerable, the ones who could be excluded or self-exclude. This ensures that these young people remain included in the life of the Catholic school.

Conclusion

The concept and enactment of the preferential option for the poor in Catholic schools draws from the fundamental principle of the scriptures of the care for the poor and the marginalised. The message of care is quite clear, and the poor must not be excluded. The two case studies have provided two quite different examples of Catholic schools resolving to enact the preferential option for the poor in the daily life of the school. This is based on conscious and courageous decisions that are coherent with the Christian vision of the dignity of all individuals and the inclusion of all.

At the time of completing this chapter (November 2020), the world is still experiencing the effects of the Covid-19 pandemic and the subsequent series of restrictions and lockdowns. These restrictions and lockdowns have created very serious challenges for the poor in Catholic schools that include higher levels of food insecurity, digital exclusion and issues of physical and mental health and wellbeing (McKinney, 2020). We are witnessing increased levels of poverty and child poverty across the world and this will have a long-term effect on families, children and school education in the United Kingdom. It is important to be clear that the levels of poverty and child poverty were increasing before the pandemic and the lockdowns as a result of a number of factors: the changes in benefits and the introduction of Universal Credit and the increase in working poverty (McKinney et al., 2020). The pandemic, lockdowns and restrictions have extended and deepened the effects of the pre-existing poverty that was affecting increasing numbers of families. The prophetic Christian mandate of the preferential option for the poor is now more urgent than ever for children in Catholic schools.

Notes

1 Section 58 expands on an initial statement on caring for the poor in section 9 in *Gravissimum Educationis* (Pope Paul VI, 1965). The poverty experienced by the children is: '…poor in the goods of this world or who are deprived of the assistance and affection of a family or who are strangers to the gift of Faith' (Pope Paul VI, 1965).

2 Gutiérrez has been critiqued for selective use of scripture. For a discussion of his use of scripture and an extended examination of his use of Marxist analysis, see McKinney, S.J. (2021).

3 *Compendium of the Social Doctrine of the Church*, section 108 (Pontifical Council for Justice and Peace, 2004).

4 The Franciscan Peter John Olivi (1248–1298) interpreted Acts 2:42–47 and 4:32–35 within the context of his mission to renew the Franciscan commitment to poverty (Karris and Flood, 2007).

5 Bartolomé de las Casas was a Spanish Dominican priest who worked as a missionary. He became a strong defender of the poor Indians who were part of the Spanish colonies and who were deemed to be less civilised. He was an outspoken critic of slavery and later became the bishop of Chiapa in Mexico. See Gutiérrez (1992).

6 The growth and development of the Catholic Church in the United Kingdom from the 19th century to the present day is complex and has been examined using a variety of hermeneutical lenses constructed around different forms of exclusion, including: anti-Catholicism, sectarianism and socio-economic exclusion (Gheeraert-Graffeuille and Vaughan, 2020).

7 While the influx of the Catholic Irish was to have a major impact on Catholicism in the United Kingdom, it is important to recognise all Catholic migrant groups alongside the surviving Catholic communities in parts of the Highland and Islands of Scotland, old English Catholic gentry and the different waves of the influential Oxford movement in England. See Tenbus (2010) for some of the groups in England.

8 The document includes a very valuable discussion on the causes and manifestations of child poverty. Among these, destitution occupies an undisputable place. It often brings with it the lack of a family and of health, social maladjustment, loss of human dignity, impossibility of access to culture and consequently a deep spiritual poverty (Congregation for Catholic Education, 2002, section 71).

References

Barrett, C.K. (2002). *The Acts of the Apostles: A Shorter Commentary*. Edinburgh: T &T Clark.

Byron, W.J. (2015). What Catholic schools can do about world hunger. *International Studies in Catholic Education 7* (2) pp. 201–209.

Carter, W. (2007) The Gospel of Matthew. In Segovia, F.F. and Sugirtharajah, R.S. (Eds.) *A Postcolonial Commentary on the New Testament Writings*. pp. 69–103. London: Bloomsbury.

Chapman, C., Lowden, K., Chestnutt, H., Hall, S., McKinney, S., Hulme, M. and Friel, N. (2015). *The School Improvement Partnership Programme (2015): Using Collaboration and Enquiry to Tackle Educational Inequity*. Report to Scottish Education, August 2015.

Congregation for Catholic Education (2002) *Consecrated Persons and their Mission in Schools: Reflections and Guidelines*. www.vatican.va/roman_curia/congregations/cca theduc/documents/rc_con_ccatheduc_doc_20021028_consecrated-persons_en.html.

de Las Casas, B. (1537) *De Unico Vocationis Modo*. Published in English as: *Bartolomé de Las Casas: The Only Way*. Edited by Helen Rand Parish. Translated by Francis Patrick Sullivan, S.J. Mahwah, NJ: Paulist Press, 1992.

Fitzmyer, J.A. (1998). *The Acts of the Apostles*. New York: Doubleday.

Grace, G. (2000). Catholic Schools and the Common Good: What This Means in Educational Practice. In Grace, G. (2016) *Faith, Mission and Challenge in Catholic Education: The Selected Works of Gerald Grace*. pp. 55–64. London: Routledge.

Grace, G. (2001). The State and Catholic schooling in England and Wales: politics, ideology and mission integrity. *Oxford Review of Education 27* (4) pp. 489–500.

Grace, G. (2002). *Catholic Schools: Mission, Markets and Morality*. Oxford: Routledge Falmer.

Grace, G. (2003). 'First and foremost the Church offers its educational service to the poor': class, inequality and Catholic schooling in contemporary contexts. *International Studies in Sociology of Education 13* (1) pp. 35–53.

Grace, G. (2009). On the International Study of Catholic Education. Why We Need More Systematic Scholarship and Research. In Grace, G. (2016) *Faith, Mission and Challenge in Catholic Education: The Selected Works of Gerald Grace*. pp. 114–124. London: Routledge.

Grace, G. (2013). Catholic social teaching should permeate the Catholic secondary school curriculum: an agenda for reform. *International Studies in Catholic Education 5* (1) pp. 99–109.

Grace, G. and O'Keefe, J. (2007). (Eds.) *International Handbook of Catholic Education: Challenges for School Systems in the 21st Century*. Dordrecht: Springer.

Gheeraert-Graffeuille, C. and Vaughan, G. (2020). *Anti-Catholicism in Britain and Ireland, 1600–2000: Practices, Representations and Ideas*. London: Palgrave Macmillan.

Groody, D. G. (2011). *Gustavo Gutiérrez: Spiritual Writings*. New York: Orbis Books.

Gutiérrez, G. (1971). *A Theology of Liberation*. London: SCM Press.

Gutiérrez, G. (1983). *We Drink from Our Own Wells*. London: SCM Press Ltd.

Gutiérrez, G. (1989). *On Job God-Talk and the Suffering of the Innocent*. New York: Orbis.

Gutiérrez, G. (1991). *The God of Life*. Translated by Matthew J.O'Connell. Maryknoll, NY: Orbis Books.

Gutiérrez, G. (1992). *La Casas: In Search of the Poor of Jesus Christ*. Translated by Robert Barr. New York: Orbis Books.

Gutiérrez, G. (1996). Where Will the Poor Sleep? In Gutiérrez, G. and Muller, G.L. (Eds.) (2015) *On the Side of the Poor. The Theology of Liberation*. pp. 83–133. Maryknoll, NY: Orbis Books.

Gutiérrez, G. (2009). The option for the poor arises from Faith in Christ. *Theological Studies* 70 pp. 317–326.

Gutiérrez, G. (2012). *A Hermeneutic of Hope*. The Center for Latin American Studies, Vanderbilt University – Occasional Paper No. 13.

Guitierrez, G. (2015). *On the Side of the Poor: The Theology of Liberation*. Maryknoll, New York: Orbis Books.

Harrill, J.A. (2011). Divine Judgment against Ananias and Sapphira (Act: 5:1–11): a stock scene of perjury and death. *Journal of Biblical Literature* 130 (2) pp. 351–369.

Houtart, F. (1989). Theoretical and institutional bases of the opposition to Liberation Theology. In Ellis, M.H. and Maduro, O. (Eds.) *The Future of Liberation Theology: Essays in Honour of Gustavo Gutiérrez*. pp. 261–271. New York: Orbis Books.

Karris, R.J. and Flood, D. (2007). Peter Olivi on the early Christian community (Acts 2:42–47 and 4:32–35): the Christian way with temporalities. *Franciscan Studies* 65 pp. 251–280.

Klaiber, J. (2013). Fe y Alegría in Peru: solidarity and service in Catholic education. *International Studies in Catholic Education* 5 (2) pp. 144–160.

Madero, C. (2018). New thinking about Catholic education from Latin America: what the bishops said at Medellin (1968), Puebla (1979), Santo Domingo (1992), Aparecida (2007). *International Studies in Catholic Education* 10 (1) pp. 30–43.

McGovern, A.F. (1989) Dependency Theory, Marxist Analysis and Liberation Theology. In Ellis, M.H. and Maduro, O. (Eds.) *The Future of Liberation Theology. Essays in Honour of Gustavo Gutiérrez*. pp. 272–286. New York: Orbis Books.

McKinney, S.J. (2018a). The roots of the preferential option for the poor in Catholic schools in Luke's Gospel. *International Studies in Catholic Education* 10 (2) pp. 220–232.

McKinney, S.J. (2018b). The Preferential Option for the Poor and Catholic Schools. In Whittle, S. (Ed.) *Researching Catholic Education: Contemporary Perspectives*. pp. 95–112. Singapore: Springer.

McKinney, S.J. (2018c) Affirming the Place of Scripture in the Catholic School. In Whittle, S. (Ed.) *Religious Education in Catholic Schools*. pp. 173–192. Oxford: Peter Lang.

McKinney, S.J. (2020). Covid-19: food insecurity, digital exclusion and Catholic schools. *Journal of Religious Education*. Open Access at: https://link.springer.com/article/10.1007/s40839-020-00112-8.

McKinney, S.J. (2021) Covid-19, Child Poverty, Catholic Schools and the Insights of Gustavo Gutiérrez. In Whittle, S. (Ed.) *Irish and British Reflections on Catholic Education*. Singapore: Springer.

McKinney, S.J. and Hall, S. (2016), Nurture groups – Inclusion of the most vulnerable children and young people in Catholic schools. *The Pastoral Review* 12 (4) pp. 28–33.

McKinney, S.J., Hall, S. and Lowden, K. (2020). Poverty and Education in Scotland. In Thompson, I. and Ivinson, G. (Eds.) *Poverty in Education Across the UK: A Comparative Analysis of Policy and Place*. pp. 65–88. Bristol: Policy Press.

McKinney, S.J., McAdam, J., Britton, A., Crichton, H. and Arizpe, E. (2015). Managing the Learning of New Arrival Children in Mainstream Schooling. In Christopher, E. (Ed.) *International Management and Intercultural Communication: A Collection of Case Studies*, Volume 2. pp. 114–131. London: Palgrave Macmillan.

McKinney, S.J. and McCluskey, R. (2019) (Eds.) *A History of Catholic Schooling and Education in Scotland: New Perspectives*. London: Palgrave Macmillan.

Müller, G.L. (2015). Liberation Theology in Context. In Gutiérrez, G. and Muller, G.L. (Eds.) *On the Side of the Poor. The Theology of Liberation*. pp. 54–82. Maryknoll, NY: Orbis Books.

Nolan, A. (1989). Theology in a Prophetic Mode. In Ellis, M.H. and Maduro, O. (Eds.) *The Future of Liberation Theology: Essays in Honour of Gustavo Gutiérrez*. pp. 433–440. New York: Orbis Books.

O'Loughlin, T. (2014). Sharing food and breaking boundaries: reading of Acts 10–11: 18 as a key to Luke's ecumenical agenda in Acts. *Transformation: An International Journal of Holistic Mission Studies* 32 (1) pp. 27–37.

Pao, D.W. (2011). Waiters or preachers: Acts 6:1–7 and the Lukan table fellowship motif. *Journal of Biblical Literature* 130 (1) pp. 127–144.

Pontifical Council for Justice and Peace (2004). *Compendium of the Social Doctrine of the Church*. www.vatican.va/roman_curia/pontifical_councils/justpeace/documents/rc_pc_justpeace_doc_20060526_compendio-dott-soc_en.html#Creatures%20in%20the%20image%20of%20God.

Pope Benedict XVI (2009). *Caritas in Veritate*. www.vatican.va/content/benedict-xvi/en/encyclicals/documents/hf_ben-xvi_enc_20090629_caritas-in-veritate.html.

Pope John Paul II (1984). *Homily delivered at Holy Mass at Edmonton Airport Canada*, 17 September.https://w2.vatican.va/content/john-paul-ii/en/homilies/1984/documents/hf_jp-ii_hom_19840917_messa-edmonton.html.

Pope Paul VI (1965). *Gravissimum Educationis (Declaration on Christian Education)*. www.vatican.va/archive/hist_councils/ii_vatican_council/documents/vat-ii_decl_19651028_gravissimum-educationis_en.html.

Tannehill, R.C. (2012). Acts of the Apostles and ethics. *Interpretation: A Journal of Bible and Theology* 66 (3) pp. 270–282.

Taylor, R. (2018). The relief of Belgian refugees in the archdiocese of Glasgow during the First World War: 'A Crusade of Christianity'. *The Innes Review* 69 (2) pp. 147–164.

Tenbus, E.G. (2010). *English Catholics and the Education of the Poor*. Abingdon: Routledge.

The CTS New Catholic Bible (2007). London: Catholic Truth Society.

Sacred Congregation for Catholic Education (1977). *The Catholic School*. www.vatican.va/roman_curia/congregations/ccatheduc/documents/rc_con_ccatheduc_doc_19770319_catholic-school_en.html.

Torevell, D. (2013). Liberation, Catholic education and the nature of theology: an essay to assist Catholic teachers with problems in this field. *International Studies in Catholic Education* 5 (2) pp. 218–232.

Wodon, Q. (2020). How well do Catholic and other faith-based schools serve the poor? A study with special reference to Africa: Part II: learning. *International Studies in Catholic Education* 12 (1) pp. 3–20.

Chapter 17

Proving and improving

Gerald Grace's model for evaluation of
Catholic schools – a practitioner
perspective from Ireland

Marie Griffin

Introduction: The current Irish context

In Ireland, because of the historical position of the Catholic Church, the majority of schools at both primary and second levels were established and run by Religious Congregations and the local bishops. Article 42 of the Irish Constitution emphasises the right of parents to educate their children according to their conscience and goes on to state that 'parents shall be free to provide this education in their homes or in private schools or in schools recognised or established by the State' (McDonagh, 2019, p. 9). While primary schools are still approximately 89% in Catholic patronage, Catholic second-level schools now just account for just under half of all schools. In the year 2018–2019, the number of primary schools under Catholic patronage fell slightly (0.4%) while there was an increase of nearly 5% in the number of multi-denominational primary schools. There was growth at all levels in the second-level schools because of a population bulge but greater growth in the number of pupils in multi-denominational schools (4%) than in Catholic schools (1%) (DES, 2020).

It has been the policy of the Department of Education and Skills over the past ten years to introduce more diversity into the education system to reflect a changing demographic in a growing population and more people identifying as being of no faith in censuses (in 2016, 10% identified as having 'no religion' compared to 6% in 2011. 78% of people identified as Catholic compared to 84% in 2011[2]). The Minister for Education noted in 2019 that the changes were part of the implementation underway 'to provide for greater diversity and choice in the Irish education system' (DES, 2019). As Grace (2002) points out, this choice for parents is not between ideology and ideology-free schools. 'Secularism has its own ideological assumptions about the human person, the ideal society, the ideal system of schooling and the meaning of human existence' (p. 14). O'Sullivan (2006) notes that the State's role under the *mercantile paradigm* for education involves 'managing both the demands of the various interest groups in the marketplace of education and the educational process itself' (p. 120). Over the past decade, interest groups seeking nonfaith schools have made increased demands on the Department of Education and this has driven the agenda for change as much as

DOI: 10.4324/9781003171553-20

the changing demographic itself.[3] The demands of interest groups and the response of both the State and the Catholic Church constitutes the only public debate on the nature and values of education since the Forum on Patronage and Pluralism in the primary sector (2012).[4] A key proposal of the Forum was to divest the ownership of religious schools in 28 areas to multi-denominational patrons.

Catholic bishops recognise the need for more diversity in the Irish primary school system and a small number of schools have so far been divested to the State. The Church's co-operation is not just for pragmatic reasons; it also advocated for freedom from coercion as well as freedom for religious belief, practice and proclamation. Furthermore, it is not only Irish society that is changing; the Church has changed as well (Conway, 2017). However, local parents do not want change because they are, by and large, very happy with their children's education in the local Catholic school. In one area of Dublin, where the Archdiocese sought to divest one of many Catholic schools in a parish, parents warned of another 'Brexit type disaster' if the Catholic patronage was changed:

> In the case of St Oliver Plunkett's School in Malahide, the parents' association warned that the loss of the school's religious ethos could lead to the cancellation of nativity plays and carol services, and would impact on the "spirit, culture and even the name of the school".
>
> (*Irish Times*, 5 April 2019)

School evaluation in Ireland

While a large percentage of schools are under the patronage of the Catholic Church, these schools, like all schools in the Republic of Ireland, are regulated by the State through the Department of Education and Skills (DES). Every school has its own ethos or 'characteristic spirit' as outlined in the Education Act (1998), 'determined by the cultural, educational, moral, religious, social, linguistic and spiritual values and traditions which inform and are characteristic of the objectives and conduct of the school' (section 2 (b)). The Board of Management has a responsibility to ensure that the ethos is maintained. Catholic schools, while reflecting their local communities, are challenged to give expression to their characteristic spirit through the lens of Catholic faith and to allow the Catholic faith to inform the values and traditions that are lived out and nurtured on a daily basis in the school.

The DES strictly regulates the curriculum of schools on advice from the National Council for Curriculum and Assessment and through the inspectorate's evaluation and inspection processes. Grace (2015) terms the measures of secular performance and compliance with education laws and regulations *Performative Secular Evaluation (PSEV)*. It is 'the evaluation of an institution'. Whole-school inspections were only introduced into second-level schools and formalised in a process for all schools in Ireland in 2004. Like almost all inspectorates, Irish school inspectors fulfil an accountability function, inspecting and reporting on the work of schools and the effectiveness of school leaders, evaluating the 'institution' but they have no remit in evaluating the effectiveness of the school ethos. There may be some reference to ethos in the published evaluation report but in terms of inclusion and student care only:

> The school is very inclusive in keeping with the ethos of the Sisters of Mercy.... Care for students is of a very high standard.
>
> (*Scoil Bhríde*, Tuam)

> Support for students with Special Educational Needs (SEN) is good. The school has a very inclusive ethos.
>
> (St Joseph's, Rush)

There is no reference to school ethos in the Chief Inspector's most recent report (2018).

Mission Catholic Evaluation

The concept of evaluation specific to Catholic schools has long been accepted as a practice in the UK where, under legislation, the governors of faith schools must obtain a separate inspection of 'denominational Religious Education and collective worship'[5] This inspection must be carried out by an inspector appointed by the bishop under the Education Act (2005) (www.legislation.gov. uk/ukpga/2005/18/section/5, accessed 8 December 2020). While this practice is well established in UK schools, it is an unknown concept in Ireland. Canon Law assigns the role of the oversight of religious education to the local bishop (Code of Canon Law #801–806). Irish bishops appoint Diocesan Advisors to visit schools on their behalf but recent research has highlighted a lack of clarity in relation to their role generally and also in relation to any evaluative function (McCormack, 2021).

In that sense, Professor Grace was prophetic in 2015 in urging self-evaluation of what he terms *Mission Catholic Evaluation (MCEV)* in Irish schools. His address raised the question of why Catholic schools need to examine their Catholic identity in practice and so prevent what Grace terms *mission drift*; 'the generally unintended drift from mission commitments over time, as a result of complex factors including social and political pressures and weak school leadership' (2015, CEIST conference address). However, the importance of the evaluation of the catholicity of schools is assuming greater importance, not least because of the changing population demographic. Professor Grace notes that the:

> ...prime focus of MCEV is concerned with a larger perspective related to issues such as the vitality of Catholicity and spirituality in the school, its mission integrity, its distinctive mode of leadership, the extent to which

Catholic Religious and Social Teaching is part of its educational programme and how its overall culture and ethos facilitates a process of integral formation for its students and not just a process of training. It is an evaluation of a distinctive mission.

(2015, CEIST conference address)

In 2002, Grace said that 'one of the prime purposes of the Catholic school and perhaps its fundamental rationale is to keep alive and to renew the culture of the sacred in a profane and secular world' (p. 5).

In his address to CEIST schools, drawing on the research of Potterton and Northmore in South Africa (2014),[6] Gerald Grace promoted the idea of colleague-implemented school evaluation, using colleagues such as recently retired Catholic teachers and principals as external examiners. This self-evaluation would have to operate the same standards of impartiality and objectivity used by the State inspectorate. Grace acknowledged, however, that these colleague professionals would possess the added advantage of a good understanding of what constitutes a Catholic education mission. This type of evaluation, he proposed, was far more desirable and effective than State-mandated school inspection alone. Catholic schools could then publish a combination of PSEV and MCEV as a measure of their effectiveness as Catholic schools. While there are obviously resource implications, financially challenged schools could seek funding from Trusts or diocesan sources. What is necessary is a model of these evaluations that give some real and practical indication of the schools' catholicity.

Grace recognised the need for such a model in his address to CEIST and even suggested a schema as one possible template for the process. He refers to this as the *Vitality and Spirituality in the School* (VSC). To determine the standard for the evaluation, Grace draws on the publication from the Congregation for Catholic Education (1977), *The Catholic School*, and notes that the first priority criterion in any evaluation exercise is contained in the two paragraphs, 'Christ is the foundation of the whole educational enterprise in a Catholic school' (par. 34), and 'Mindful of the fact that man has been redeemed by Christ, the Catholic schools aims at forming in the Christian those particular virtues which will enable him to live a new life in Christ' (par. 36).

In the Irish context, the Catholic Schools Partnership[7] in Ireland has articulated the following similar vision for Catholic schools:

Catholic schools in Ireland are a living expression of a long and varied tradition of education inspired by the life of Christ as lived in the Church. Such schools emphasise the dignity of the human person as a child of God called to work with other persons in creating an inclusive community in service of the common good; where knowledge is sought and respected while faith is nurtured and challenged.

(2015, p. 11)

As well as the VSC, Grace posits the *Vocation and Formation criterion* (VFC). Education in a Catholic school is not a *training* for life but is part of a larger process of formation: a holistic tradition that looks to nourish young people in all aspects of their lives. Education, under this criterion, is not just a means to a 'good job', important as that is, but to a development of a vocation of service to others. In other words, Catholic schools should work on the formula that the development of talent and commitment to the common good is both good citizenship and good for people.

The question then is how these aims are to be recognised and assessed in a Catholic school. Grace proposes, under the VSC , certain basic elements such as a prescribed time for RE, the services of a Chaplain in secondary schools and the presence of the local clergy at primary level, regular celebration of the sacraments and the preparation of students for the same. A sacred space in the schools such as a prayer room is important as are the opportunities for retreats for students and staff. The teachings of Jesus Christ would also permeate other aspects of the curriculum as the occasion arises, and not just in RE. Grace gives no indication how the VFC might be *measured* in the Catholic school but does reference Catholic social teaching and the vibrancy of such teaching and activity might be such a measure.

Grace's model presents a very possible option for Irish Catholic schools. CEIST and other Trust bodies visit their schools annually and report on the provision of RE, school retreats, sacred spaces etc. While the bishops appoint Diocesan Advisors to visit schools and support RE teachers, these Diocesan Advisors have no clear role in evaluating the catholicity of the schools (McCormack, 2021). If these different groups, or the colleague professionals, were to use a common template, such as that proposed by Grace to be then reported by the school and to a central Catholic agency, the nature of catholicity in Irish schools could be charted.

Rather than promote Grace's model in CEIST schools in 2015, CEIST disseminated an approach that was developed by the central body, the Catholic Schools Partnership (CSP). In 2016, after a national consultation process, CSP initiated a process for second-level schools: *Understanding and Living the Ethos in a Catholic Voluntary Secondary School.* [8] This process was carried out entirely within the school community so that it would be characterised by honesty and open dialogue. It also sought to eschew the bureaucracy and mechanism of more formal processes. It was to be a shared reflection by trustees, staff, students, parents, members of the Board of Management and the broader school community about the nature of the school ethos. The emphasis was on the founding intention of the school and an exploration of how this founding intention was finding contemporary expression in the school mission. The process was intended to be 'life-giving and supportive' and was described as a series of conversations. An outline of activity for three years was given where the school selected targets for attention in the context of living out its founding intention. While the CSP process was very valuable, and was developed following a pilot programme, very few schools engaged with the whole programme for a number of reasons. New curriculum initiatives were introduced by the Department of Education at that time and there was some consequent industrial action. It was a clear example of PSEV taking precedence over MCEV. There was also no accountability to any Church organisation, nor to CEIST, for failure to engage in the process.

Also in 2016, following a national consultation process, the Catholic Education Services Committee[9] (CESC) established a working group to develop a strategic plan to bring greater cohesion between Catholic patronage/trusteeship and management at second level in the Republic of Ireland. This plan was put into effect in November 2020 and presages a new robustness of the Catholic-sector response to education matters. The Catholic Education Partnership is the new company charged with oversight and coordination of patronage and management of second-level schools. Through new governance arrangements, there is now greater cohesion that would allow for a more robust response in terms of determining the catholicity of schools.

Another lesson from the earlier CSP process was that support needs to be provided to schools for assistance but also to ensure that it takes place at all. This support and impetus could well be Grace's *colleague professionals* in association with the Trust bodies and the Diocesan Advisors. Support from outside, coordinated at diocesan level also demonstrates in a tangible way that this process has capital and credibility. When this support was given in a pilot programme at primary level, engagement was much higher and more effective.[10] Training would be integral, and clarity would also be necessary on the measures or instruments to be used and the outcome of the evaluations. The central focus of MCEV, according to Grace, would be *mission integrity*, or assessment of how the school is living out its characteristic spirit. The challenges in avoiding *mission drift* are social and political pressures and weak school leadership.

While school leaders are evaluated in their leadership and management of the institution, there is no evaluation of their leadership of the mission. Grace (2015) outlines how school leaders have been transformed into some form of Directors of educational corporations in a manner that is alien to the leadership of Catholic tradition and practice. He notes that research surrounding the concept of servant leadership and the presence of spiritual capital are what make effective faith leaders. Grace (2002) defines spiritual capital as 'resources of faith and values derived from commitment to a religious tradition and possessed by persons who do not act simply as professionals but as professionals and witnesses' (p. 236). He adds these Catholic leaders have 'the animating spiritual capital of Catholic schooling'. They also have a commitment to Catholic social teaching.

Primary teachers in Catholic schools in Ireland were traditionally trained in Catholic teacher training colleges but these colleges are themselves more diverse now and many trainee teachers are 'unchurched'. The Church is chiefly dependent on teachers to carry out the mission of the Catholic Church to meet the challenges of a modern and secular culture as enunciated in *Gravissimum Educationis* (1965). At primary and second level, there is little training available for leaders in faith schools.[11] Such training is not a prerequisite for appointment to leadership in a Catholic school and no specific training is required on appointment. Some questions on commitment to ethos are asked at interview but there is ad hoc ethos support following appointment. The *Alliance for Catholic Education* (ACE) programme from Notre Dame University (USA) is currently working with some school leaders at primary level in Ireland and has also run ethos courses for CEIST teachers and principals but these programmes are not part of an integral faith nourishment programme at national level. A mission renewal for teachers and leaders in Catholic schools will be another challenge for the new Catholic structures in Ireland.

The value of Mission Catholic Evaluation (MCEV) for Catholic schools?

If a Catholic school is to stay true to its characteristic spirit as outlined in the Irish Education Act (1998) and to outline its mission (as required under Charities regulation),[12] then it must have some measure of its effectiveness. There are also other considerations for Irish schools that necessitate their being able to define themselves in a tangible and robust fashion for parents and the wider public but also for the school community itself. With the change in the application process for patronage of new schools, prospective patrons must now outline the nature and ethos of their school to local parents who then declare a choice to DES. The process presents challenges to prospective Catholic patrons who are unaccustomed to 'selling their wares'. To date, most patronage applications have been won by multi-denominational patrons (www.education.ie/en/Press-Events/Press-Releases/2020-press-releases/PR20-11-12-1.html, accessed 5 December 2020).

Because of the hegemony of the Catholic school structures at primary level mainly, the 2018 Education (Admissions to Schools) Act now prohibits Catholic schools from giving preference to pupils from Catholic families. The so-called *baptism barrier* (www.irishtimes.com/opinion/we-need-secular-primary-schools-to-reflect-changes-in-religious-practice-1.2147029, accessed 10 December 2020) highlighted in a small number of oversubscribed schools was a local response to oversubscription. The problem has not been resolved by the legislative change, however, as the schools remain oversubscribed. These changes have taken place with little evidence of exclusive practices in Catholic schools. A single ten-year-old statistic from a 2007 DES audit of enrolment practices which claimed that selection criteria applied to 20% of children seeking enrolment was cited as one of the reasons for initiating the change (Clegg 2019).

This same report found that Catholic schools had more than their proportional share of children from minority, new Irish, special needs and disadvantaged backgrounds (DES, 2007). These schools are fulfilling their mission for the poor and the marginalised and giving contemporary expression to their founding intention but there was no centralised Catholic data or entity to defend the Church schools' position. While DES can report on the number of schools and pupils, Catholic schools themselves have no general data on categories of students and admissions, still less on the value of initiatives and practices. In such circumstances, it is almost impossible to respond to popular criticism or inform public opinion. Consistent and standardised data on school mission self-evaluation, using Grace's model, would be a powerful tool in defending Catholic schools in the public space.

Catholic school research in Ireland

Gerald Grace devoted much of his later career to disseminating research on Catholic schooling through the journal he edited, *International Studies in Catholic Education* (ISCE). In 2002, Grace anticipated that Ireland would become a major source of research studies in the areas of foundation, preferential option for the poor and school effectiveness. It is not apparent that this is the case. Certainly, there have been only ten articles from Irish writers since Grace established ISCE in 2009. Perhaps because of the dominant position of Catholic schools in Irish society, there has never been a need for research on the nature or effects of Catholic schools *per se* as most schools, were, in fact Catholic and any research therefore related to them. This has left a lacuna in terms of data about Catholic schools. Catholic colleges in Ireland, as in the UK, have historically focused on teacher training (like the UK in the past) rather than research, but this is now changing. There are two welcome developments. First, the foundation of the *Mater Dei Centre for Catholic Education* within the Institute of Education in Dublin City University is a welcome development in terms of research on Catholic schooling. Second, the *Irish Institute for Catholic Studies* in Mary Immaculate College, Limerick is a cross-faculty, interdisciplinary, research-oriented and community engaged network of scholars involved in the study of Catholicism and its contribution to culture and society in Ireland and beyond.

Conclusion

In 2015, Gerald Grace proposed a model of mission self-evaluation for CEIST schools in Ireland. The model was prophetic if slightly premature. A similar model addressing the need for a focus on catholicity was presented to Irish schools in 2016 by CSP, which was disseminated to all Catholic second-level schools. This latter model wasn't particularly successful because the performative agenda took precedence, there was no support offered to schools and there was no sense of accountability to Church authorities. The need for the evaluation was also perhaps not as apparent as now.

Today there are growing challenges for Catholic schools from the changing demographic and the State agenda. There is a paramount need for the Catholic sector to speak with a unified voice and to have the data with which to defend Catholic schools. The central voice is now being coordinated by the Catholic Education Partnership and there is an acknowledgement that nourishment of ethos in schools will need support. In the years since his address to CEIST, the time is more opportune for Grace's model of self-evaluation in Catholic schools to be used. We have the way, and now the will is greater.

Notes

1 CEIST is a lay Catholic trust organisation set up in 2007 by five Religious Congregations to assume patronage (and ownership) of their second-level schools into the future. CEIST has 107 non-fee-paying second-level schools across Ireland. There are nearly 60,000 second-level pupils in CEIST schools, about 16% of the national total.
2 www.cso.ie/en/releasesandpublications/ep/p-cp8iter/p8iter/p8rrc/
3 For example, see the Equate education campaign. www.digitalcharitylab.org/2016/02/equate-a-new-irish-campaign-for-education-equality/, accessed 12 December 2020.
4 The Forum on Patronage and Pluralism in the Primary sector arose from the 2011 Programme for Government and constituted a time-limited forum to 'allow all stakeholders, including parents, to engage in an open debate on change of patronage in communities where it is appropriate and necessary'. Four hundred and thirty-four submissions were received and a Forum Report (2012), with recommendations, was published.
5 John Viner: 'When inspection is not by Ofsted'. https://blog.optimus-education.com/when-inspection-not-ofsted, accessed December 5 2020.
6 Potterton and Northmore (2014). *Improving Schools through Evaluation: The Experience of Catholic Schools in South Africa*.
7 The Catholic Schools Partnership (CSP) is an association established by the Irish Bishops' Conference and the Conference of Religious of Ireland. It was formally launched in 2010. It aims, *inter alia*, to:

   • Foster coherence in Catholic education at national level
   • Provide a unified voice for Catholic education in the public forum and with educational bodies and the Government.
   • Support Catholic educators in the core activities of learning and teaching in order to foster high-quality lifelong learning and faith development for all learners.

8 An explanatory booklet and DVD was distributed, through the patron, to every Catholic voluntary secondary school in the country.
9 The *Catholic Education Services Committee* (CESC) is composed of bishops, members of the *Association of Missionaries* and the *Religious of Ireland*, a nominee of the third-level Catholic colleges and two nominees of the Catholic Education Trust companies that are public juridic persons.
10 The Catholic Schools Partnership appointed a Research Assistant to engage with schools in the local Diocese to spearhead the ethos initiative at primary level. The first iteration of this approach took place in the Diocese of Kilmore but has since been replicated in Elphin, Wexford and parts of Dublin. The Diocesan Education Offices were also involved in supporting the initiative.

11 Masters and postgraduate programmes for leaders in Catholic schools are provided by Mary Immaculate College and the Marino Institute. Some of the Catholic Trust bodies also provide less formal training for such leadership.

12 All schools are registered charities and must submit an annual account of their activities to the Charities Regulatory Authority, www.charitiesregulator.ie/en/information-for-charities/annual-reporting

References

Catholic Schools Partnership (CSP). (2015). *Catholic Primary Schools in a Changing Ireland Sharing Good Practice on Inclusion of All Pupils*. Maynooth: Catholic Schools Partnership.

Catholic Schools Partnership (CSP). (2016). *Understanding and Living the Ethos in a Catholic Voluntary Secondary School: A Process Centred on Conversations*. Dublin: Veritas.

Clegg, M. C. (2019). Policy and Partnership, *Studies*, 108 (429), pp. 30–31.

Conway, E. (2017). Why Faith Schools Matter and the Challenge of Divestment, *The Furrow*, 68 (6), pp. 350–361.

Department of Education and Skills (DES). (2007). *Inclusion of Students with Special Educational Needs: Post-Primary Guidelines*. www.education.ie/en/Publications/Inspection-Reports-Publications/Evaluation-Reports-Guidelines/insp_inclusion_students_sp_ed_needs_pp_guidelines_pdf.pdf, accessed 13 May 2021.

Department of Education and Skills (DES). (2018). *Chief Inspector's Report: January 2013–July 2016*. Dublin: Inspectorate.

Department of Education and Skills (DES). (2019). www.education.ie/en/Press-Events/Press-Releases/2019-press-releases/PR19-12-23.html, accessed 10 December 2020.

Department of Education and Skills (DES). (2020). www.education.ie/en/Publications/Statistics/Statistical-Reports/statistical-bulletin-2020-overview-of-education-1999-2019.pdf, accessed 12 December 2020.

Forum on Patronage and Pluralism in the Primary Sector. (2012). *Report of the Forum's Advisory Group*. www.education.ie/en/Press-Events/Events/Patronage-and-Pluralism-in-the-Primary-Sector/The-Forum-on-Patronage-and-Pluralism-in-the-Primary-Sector-Report-of-the-Forums-Advisory-Group.pdf, accessed 13 May 2021.

Grace, G. (2002). *Catholic Schools: Mission, Markets and Morality*. London: RoutledgeFalmer.

Grace, G. (2015). *Catholic Schools Self Evaluation: Five International Challenges*. Address to CEIST Conference, Athlone, 24 September 2015.

Gravissimum Educationis, in Abbott, W. (Ed.) (1966). *The Documents of Vatican II*. New York: Herder and Herder.

McDonagh, F. (2019). What Constitutes a Catholic School in 2019? A Legal Perspective, *Studies*, 108 (429), pp. 8–19.

McCormack, C. (2021). *Using Visible or Invisible Maps? A Case Study of the Role of the Diocesan Advisor*. Unpublished PhD thesis, Dublin City University.

O'Sullivan, D. (2006). *Cultural Politics and Irish Education since the 1950s: Policy, Paradigms and Power*. Dublin: Institute of Public Administration.

Potterton, M. and Northmore, C. (2014). Improving Schools Through Evaluation: The Experience of Catholic Schools in South Africa, *International Studies in Catholic Education*, 6 (2), pp. 178–190.

Chapter 18

Mentoring for Catholic school leadership

Formation of 'Servant Leaders' in the schools of the Sisters of St Paul of Chartres in Thailand

Kaetkaew Punnachet, Boonraksa Sritrakul and Atchara Supavai

Introduction

This chapter aims to discuss the idea of the importance of 'mentoring' to form 'Servant Leaders' in Thai Catholic schools by focusing on transmitting a distinctive value system and ethos. It should be noted at the beginning of this chapter that it is a synthesis of three doctoral research theses supervised by Professor Gerald Grace. All three developed the research ideas from the writings of Gerald Grace (Grace, 1995, 2002). This chapter is divided into five major parts. The first part briefly explores concepts of Catholic schools based on Grace's research and writings (1995, 2002). The second part gives a brief introduction to the background of this chapter. The third part examines the important concept of mentoring the values of Catholic Servant Leadership. The fourth part provides a case study, focusing on mentoring in Catholic formation programmes in Sisters of Saint Paul of Chartres schools in Thailand. It will be concluded that the mentoring scheme described in this chapter, designed to form future leaders in the charism of the Congregation, is one that other schools could emulate.

Grace's concepts of Catholic schools and Catholic school leadership

For Grace (1995, 2000, 2002), Catholic schools are culturally and morally distinctive as educational institutions. Consequently, it is necessary to investigate other 'educational characteristics' such as passion, love, humility, etc. From his research it can be concluded that the Catholic school system has its own unique attributes, different from those of other state schools. Above all, at their best, they are focused on the life and teachings of Jesus Christ according to Catholic tradition.

Catholic school leaders should be distinctive, i.e.: being professionals and 'being witnesses'. Grace (2002) strongly proposed that there should be two

DOI: 10.4324/9781003171553-21

major dimensions of Catholic school leadership: 'professional in leading' and 'professional as witness'.

Sritrakul (2013) elaborated the term 'The professional in leading', which could be perceived as the leader who exercises 'secular' leadership style without any attention to religious values. 'Professional as witness' (Grace, 2002, and Duncan, 1990, in Sritrakul, 2011) implied that the character of a principal and the need to articulate Catholic identities and to create a Catholic educational environment as part of the Christian culture of a school were essential elements.

The concept of the 'professional' as 'witness' is most powerful for Catholic educators. Above all else, the Gospel must be proclaimed by witnesses.[1] The most influential resource is Christ, who practises what He preaches (Sritrakul, 2011). Also, Grace strongly argues that any study of school leadership must start with an understanding of the historical and cultural context (Grace, 1995) in which leadership is developed.

Background of this chapter

It was the work of Grace (1995) about how Catholic school leaders should consider the cultural and organisational context that inspired Punnachet's work (2006) on the idea of *Catholic Servant Leadership* in Catholic schools in Thailand. The research was conducted in eight large schools of the Sisters of Saint Paul of Chartres, which have between 2,000 and 5,000 students. Data were collected by shadowing, through personal interviews and also through the distribution of questionnaires. Her research confirms Grace (1995) and Day et al. (2007), who argue for the need for a distinction between educational leadership and corporate leadership and especially for Catholic school leadership and its values.

Moreover, Supavai (2010) conducted research based on Grace (1995) and Punnachet (2006) on moral and spiritual values. Her research also confirmed that it is necessary to understand the unique values of Catholic school leadership (Grace, 1995, 2000, and 2002). The research found that charity, simplicity, regularity and work as vocation are the four major values that inform SPC leadership styles. Moreover, the research revealed that moral and spiritual values clearly influenced the principals' behaviours.

Furthermore, Sritrakul (2013) based on Supavai (2010) and Punnachet (2006) focused her research on 'systematic leadership succession planning' in the schools of the Sisters of St Paul of Chartres (SPC) Religious Congregation in Thailand. She concluded and provided systematic recommendations on future leadership programmes, which need to include: (a) a systematic programme of mentoring (in theory and practice), (b) an emphasis upon the importance of 'mission integrity' and of the concepts of 'servant leadership' and (c) the development of 'discernment capacity'[2] in those preparing for leadership. It also demonstrated that Catholic values and the values of the culture of Thailand have to be carefully appreciated.

Sisters of Saint Paul of Chartres: Research site and context

As all three studies were conducted in Sisters of Saint Paul of Chartres schools, it will be useful to provide some information about this Religious Congregation in order to have a more in-depth understanding of the context of this study.

Saint Paul of Chartres schools are run by the Sisters of the Congregation of Saint Paul of Chartres, which was founded in 1696 in a small village in France, called Levesville la Chenard, to teach children and to care for the sick: at the time, this care was provided in the patients' homes.

The Congregation is a religious institute of pontifical right dedicated to the apostolate in the Catholic Church. Its members dedicate themselves to education and to the care of the sick and the underprivileged. Thus, they try to be available for all forms of activities within these fields. The mission to spread this work abroad is within the purpose of 'going to those places where they are wanted' (Book of Life: 1988, p. 12). Their primary work was to educate young girls and to visit and care for the poor and sick. With their commitment and hard work, their work expanded.

The charisms of the Sisters of Saint Paul of Chartres are teaching and nursing. They work in 34 countries, in six continents. There are more than 4,400 Sisters worldwide in missions in 34 countries such as Thailand, Hong Kong, Japan, Australia, the Philippines, Madagascar and Central Africa. Sisters of Saint Paul of Chartres have been working in Thailand for more than 120 years. At present, there are 33 schools in 20 provinces under their responsibility around Thailand. There are 3,313 teachers and 67,953 students in these schools (Punnachet and Supavai, 2007).

All three studies in Catholic schools in Thailand have been influenced by the work of Grace (1995, 2002), who argued:

> It is necessary therefore for educational leaders to demonstrate some understanding of moral complexity and some capacity for making explicit the relationships between values and proposed actions in educational institutions.
>
> (Grace, 1995, p. 63)

Supavai (2010) raises another challenging issue about 'faith and values formation' in contemporary culture, since there are fewer members of Religious Orders to work in the schools. This means that students do not see as many visible 'professionals as witnesses' as they did in the past. At their best, Religious Sisters and Brothers in schools are 'the faith made manifest'.

In short, this section provides a broad picture of the background of this chapter. We would like to use Grace's statement to conclude this section.

> The Catholic school system internationally has benefited from the presence of significant spiritual capital among its school leaders... is that spiritual

capital of leadership being reconstituted in new ways, or is it being depleted? If the latter is the case, then the mission integrity of Catholic schooling in the future could become much more problematic.

(Grace, 2002, p. 447)

Mentoring: Transmitting values of Catholic servant leadership

The above does raise the question of how to form Catholic servant leaders in Catholic schools since Catholic schools need a unique leadership. Sritrakul (2013) stressed that today leadership theory has been adopted from business and corporate models which are rooted in fields such as industrial psychology, management literature, political science and social science. The humanities, which include philosophy and ethical dimensions, seem to have been neglected in many leadership theories (Crow and Grogan, 2003, p. 362). The neglect of the humanities in the development of leadership theory is affirmed by Grace (1995), Hodgkinson (1991) and Greenfield (1993), who argued that educational administration is not only a science, but is based predominantly on philosophy and values. This problem seems to be more serious for education, especially when the leaders are in a Catholic environment (Punnachet, 2006).

Grace (1995) reminds us that when borrowing concepts from corporate leadership to use in an educational context, the dangers of losing the sense of 'educational leadership' need to be kept in mind. Grace argued that the adoption of the culture of corporate leadership could critically undermine the work of educational leaders. He further argued that when neglecting the values context of educational settings, educational leaders could merely become 'chief executives, market analysts and public relations specialists' (Grace, 1995, p, 5). This was a potential danger, especially in large secondary schools.

Applying this to the context of religious-run Catholic schools in Thailand, Punnachet (2006) argued that Jesus must be the centre of leadership practice. The 'Spirit to serve' is considered as a crucial factor in the leadership of Catholic schools.

However, Punnachet (2006) suggested that leadership programmes must be transformed from 'training' to 'educating'. This corresponds with Southworth (1995), who pointed out that leadership 'training' has been overwhelmed by management courses preoccupied with technical matters (p. 204). He further argued that management courses often ignore ethical issues and personal values and beliefs.

Supavai (2010) raised an important issue. She said that it is necessary to understand the unique values of Catholic school leadership, as many researchers such as Grace (1995, 2000, and 2002; Bryk et al., 1993) have demonstrated in their studies. In her research on value systems, she found that charity and fidelity are very distinctive, as shown in the interviews. 'Simplicity' seems to be the neglected value. The researcher urged that 'fidelity' should be considered more by SPC members, as it will provide a more distinctive characteristic to SPC schools.

As far as the definition of this value (i.e. fidelity) is concerned, it means to be loyal to the rules of the Congregation and loyal to the teachings of Christ and the Church. It is the most important value for the members themselves. Additionally, 'simplicity' is also an important value, as the Congregation started in a simple way, as a service to the poor. This aspect of mission integrity has weakened over time. The Sisters are now less in the service of the poor than they were at the beginning of the mission.[3]

However, her research found a tendency of the principals to become preoccupied with management issues to the detriment of values-led educational leadership and a reduced impact of the values of the principal on the whole school culture, arising partly from the increasing size of the schools. Grace raised a major question to consider, which focused on Catholic values and market values. He clearly argued that:

> ...the critical question for Catholic school leaders in new circumstances is 'can a balance be found between Catholic values and market values, or will market forces begin to compromise the integrity of the special mission of Catholic schooling? Can Gospel values survive in the face of a more direct relationship with the market place?'
>
> (Grace, 1995, p. 84)

It is important to consider how values are the motivating factors for behaviour, and that values underpin effective leadership and lead to effective schools (Supavai, 2010).

Sritrakul (2013) maintained that mentoring seems to be the most suitable method for forming Catholic educational leaders. To her, mentoring occurs between two persons or two groups. The first is the mentor and the second is sometimes called the protégé or mentee. The purpose of mentoring is to assist mentees in the early years of their work. Basically, mentoring is about assisting change by providing support. Through communication with a mentor, mentees can explain their thoughts and obtain feedback in order to transform their behaviour. There are also some crucial elements whose influence on mentoring must be considered: the qualities, skills and virtues of mentors need to be examined.

Sritrakul explained how Plamondon (2007, p. 6) concludes that 'The concept of a good mentor as founded in essential qualities can be extended to an integrated conceptual model for competence to mentor'. In his model, 'a good mentor demonstrates a balance of virtues, abilities and competencies essential for achieving and maintaining competence to mentor'.

Virtues need to be stressed here. Plamondon (2007, p. 8) explained that:

> Mentor virtues of integrity, caring and prudence are described as the foundation to competence. Integrity reflects the ability to establish and maintain trust in a mentoring relationship, drawing from the presence of

honesty and mutuality. Caring as a virtue means that the mentor demonstrates respect and empathy to others—both within and outside of the mentoring relationship. Prudence indicates the intentionality and appropriateness of the mentor as demonstrated through decision making.

Mentoring: The way to form value systems for Catholic educational leaders

Although mentoring has been used since the Sisters of St. Paul began work in Thailand, through the spirit and values of the Congregation, they have been increasing their schools' effectiveness. It should be noted here that the technique of mentoring is always employed in religious life, as Sisters live their lives fraternally. This is a life which, at its best, 'calls for sympathetic sharing of joys and sorrows, cares and difficulties, work and apostolate, with understanding and tact'.[4] The most important concern is that mentoring serves as an internal promotion. This is the process of choosing internal candidates for principalship. Thus, the most suitable process is more likely to involve pre-service development and mentoring. However, in Thailand there remains an urgent need to frame more systematic preparation for future principals in order to have 'Catholic Values' in the leadership.

Real implementation of mentoring in 2014–2017

It should be noted that after Sritrakul (2013) proposed her thesis to the Congregation Committee, her 'Experimental Project for Mentoring Programme' (Sritrakul, 2013) has been approved and brought to real implementation. The Congregation approved the mentoring project in order the provide help or enable mentors to continue to work with the candidates, especially in their early years in the role. As there is not much time to accumulate experiences, the mentoring technique seems to be a useful way to 'grow leaders over time'.

The experimental team did the following:

1   Choose three mentors from experienced principals and between three and six mentees from aspirants who are willing to participate in the programme.
2   Explained the duties and responsibilities for mentors in helping their mentees.[5] For the best outcome, mentors should act to the best of their ability within plain sight of their mentees and both parties should engage in a compassionate and mutual search for wisdom (Bell, 1996).[6]
3   Each principal formed a team (which will be called a mentor team) at their schools, by selecting experienced teachers to act as mentors for mentees who will be assigned to develop their experiences in a variety of roles that future principals should be familiar with. The reason why principals should form a team is because 'the fact that a principal is experienced and successful is no guarantee that he or she will be a good mentor.'[7] Moreover,

teachers are the ones who are still working in this area and know it better than anyone else. As Leithwood *et al.* [8] argue:

A great many factors in a leader's environment shape his or her actual practices – educational policies, on-the-job leadership opportunities, mentoring experiences and professional development initiatives, for example. But the actual effects of all these external experiences on leaders' practices are mediated by their inner lives – their thoughts, feelings, educational histories, professional identities, values and dispositions. According to this account, attributions of leadership emerge from two distinctly different mechanisms – resemblance to individual leader prototypes (recognition-based attributions) and direct experiences with the potential leader (inference-based attributions).

(2006, p. 68)

In this context, members of the mentor team are skilled religious principals and skilled teachers in school who will provide technical assistance and collect information from participants to help them develop as leaders.

Pair the mentor and mentee by letting the mentee choose her mentor. This served to improve mentees' self-confidence, as they are younger, and will help to ensure that the programme will succeed by making appropriate matches (Cordeiro and Smith-Sloan, 1995).[9]

Prepared topics for mentees to learn from the mentor team and the mentor. Mentees should observe and work with mentor teams under the topics given. Every two months, they should report what they have learned, any problems they have encountered, any questions that have arisen and any suggestions that they wish to make. They will also receive feedback from the team on areas of strength and weakness.

Areas in which mentees had been prepared are as follows:

Table 18.1 An outline of the areas in which mentees had been prepared

	Area	Objective and result	Formator	Cycle
1	Ethnography	Candidates learnt about the culture of the school, which is essential knowledge for a school leader.	Principal Principal Mentor team	1 1
		First and foremost, they learnt about the characteristics of Catholic schools and their Catholic identities. The area of study is based on the view that an effective principal must know about the culture of the place in which she will work and the local society's requirements (from the local authority and the traditions of each area).		1

(Continued)

Table 18.1 (Cont.)

	Area	Objective and result	Formator	Cycle
2	Leadership and management	Mentoring programmes had administrative support, adequate funding and clear leadership (Exworthy and Halford, 1999). Thus, candidates examined how leadership is practised, its moral and ethical aspects, and the interaction between leading and being led.[10]	Principal Principal	1 1
3	Morals and ethics for how students form conscience for faithful citizenship	They knew about the school regulations and should have the ability to be flexible according to their conscience.	Principal	2
4	Evaluation, assessment and organisational learning	They learnt about the SPC Educational Board and state assessment and accountability programmes.	Mentor team	2
5	Staff development	They learnt to understand the characteristic of staff's work in order to understand the content of teachers' tasks. This is to avoid staff overload.	Mentor team	3
6	Curriculum, teaching, lesson planning and evaluation	They know about the curriculum, teachers' lesson planning and students' evaluation.	Mentor team	3
7	Ecumenical education	As they work in a strong Buddhist country, they should respect the culture of other religions, including Islam.	Principal	4
8	Principal's responsibility	They understood duty of choosing students to study, especially the poor and marginalized.	Principal	4
9	Identity of Catholic schools, and mission integrity	They knew the identity[11] of the Catholic school as rooted in Gospel values. They should know and promote the importance of 'mission integrity', the service to the poor; the spirit of servant leadership, to reduce the gap of the power distance dimension of Thai culture and Catholic culture. Promote the passion for and commitment to 'New Evangelisation'. Presenting the faith in new ways, for modern youth.	Experienced Principals	At the end of each school term.
10	'Discernment': applying spiritual reflections to decision-making	They are aware of the importance of how to discern in their decision-making. There should be time to participate in seminars on discernment development, and prayer sessions on policy issues.	Principals and Authority from SPC Board	At the end of each school term.

Conclusion

We believe that all Religious Congregations with their missions in education will benefit from adopting a mentoring process similar to this. For all Catholic schools which are diocesan foundations, we believe that mentoring processes for future leadership, by 'growing your own leaders', should be developed. In-school programmes in Catholic schools can form Catholic religious and lay aspirants in spiritual values as well as professional competencies and organisational skills. The great Catholic model, based on the example of Jesus Christ himself, of 'Servant Leadership' can serve as an ideal to be attempted (although difficult to attain) when contemporary secular models seem to favour models of Executive and Corporate leadership in education.

We offer, from Thailand, one example of how this can be done. This chapter is provided for the glory of God, for the good of the Church and for the service of all Catholic educators across the world.

Notes

1 Pope Paul VI, *Evangelii Nuntiandi* (1976).
2 Discernment needs time and prayer. A retreat or a period of time for principals to revisit their own behaviour could provide more insightful understanding of their own self-awareness and their self-improvement. Perhaps a programme of personal and group retreats with a focus on leadership could be introduced for the Sister-principals. The Sisters could suspend their work for days or weeks to reflect on their leadership roles and relationship with God and on the mission of Catholic education. Personal retreats would need to be done before and after these group retreats, to give each principal the opportunity to reflect on her behaviour. The Sisters would therefore have the opportunity to share their experiences and how they deal with situations openly. They could consequently find ways to practise more Catholic-based educational leadership (Punnachet, 2006).
3 The Congregation is working in many cities and with the hill tribe people, providing quality education to them. In some schools, the Sisters provide all free education for the poor and underprivileged students. Please see Punnachet and Supavai (2007).
4 Book of Life, no. 39.
5 High-quality formation for mentors also prepares them to provide and receive feedback that encourages self-reflection, is not judgemental, does not simply provide a new principal with 'war stories' or 'right answers', and aims at moving new principals from dependence to independence (Wallace and Gravells, 2007).
6 Bell (1996).
7 Wallace and Gravells (2007).
8 Leithwood et al. (2006).
9 Cordeiro and Smith-Sloan (1995).
10 Huber (2004, p. 284).
11 Burke (2000, p. 225, based on Stryker, 1980) argues that in identity theory 'self-categorization is equally relevant to the formation of one's identity, in which categorisation depends upon a named and classified world'. The mentees should be aware of these to understand and fulfil Catholic identity as part of their mission integrity, i.e. to live the mission and not only write it in school mission statements.

References

Bell, C.R. (1996). *Managers as Mentors: Building Partnerships for Learning*. San Francisco: Berrett-Koehler Publishers, Inc.

Byrk, A., Lee, V. and Holland, P. (1993). *Catholic Schools and the Common Good*, Cambridge, MA: Harvard University Press.

Burke, J. P. (2000). Identity theory and social identity theory, *Social Psychology Quarterly*, 63: 3, pp. 224–237.

Cordeiro, P.A. and Smith-Sloan, E. (1995). *Apprenticeships for Administrative Interns: Learning to Talk Like a Principal*. Paper Presented at the Annual Meeting of the American Educational Research Association. San Francisco, 18–22 April 1995.

Crow, G.M. and Grogan, M. (2003). Mentoring in educational leadership for organizational transformation. In Clutterbuck, D.A., Kochan, F. K., Lunsford, L., Dominguez, N. and Haddock-Millar, J. (Eds.), *The Sage Handbook of Mentoring*. New York: SAGE Publications Ltd., pp. 436–450.

Day, C., Sammons, P., Harris, A., Hopkins, D., Leithwood, K., Gu, Q., Penlington, C., Mehta, P. and Kington, A. (2007). *The Impact of School Leadership on Pupil Outcomes*, DfES Interim Report (Year 1). London: Department for Children, Schools and Families.

Exworthy, M. and Halford, S. (2000). Professionals and new managerialism in the public sector. *Social Science & Medicine*, 51. doi:10.1016/S0277-9536

Grace, G. (1995). *School Leadership: Beyond Educational Management*. London: Falmer Press.

Grace, G. (2000). Research and the challenges of contemporary school leadership: The contribution of critical scholarship. *British Journal of Educational Studies*, 48: 3, pp. 231–247.

Grace, G. (2002). Mission integrity. In Leithwood, K. and Hallinger, P. (Eds.), *Second International Handbook of Educational Leadership and Administration*, Part 1 Chapter 13. Dordrecht, Netherlands: Kluwer Academic Press, pp. 427–449.

Grace, G. (2002). *Catholic Schools: Mission, Markets and Morality*, London and New York: Routledge Falmer.

Greenfield, T.B. (1993). The man who comes back through the door in the wall: Discovering truth, discovering self, discovering organizations. In Greenfield, T. and Ribbing, P. (Eds.), *Greenfield on Educational Administration: Towards a Humane Science*. London: Routledge, pp. 92–119.

Greenfield, W. (1995). Toward a theory of school administration: The centrality of leadership. *Educational Administration Quarterly*, 31: 1, pp. 61–85.

Hodgkinson, C. (1991). *Educational Leadership: The Moral Art*. Albany, NY: State University of New York Press.

Huber, S. (2004). School leadership and leadership development: Adjusting leadership theories and development programs to values and the core purpose of school. *Journal of Educational Administration*, 42, pp. 669–684.

Leithwood, K., Day, C., Sammons, P., Harris, A., and Hopkins, D. (2006). *Seven Strong Claims about Successful School Leadership*. Nottingham: NCSL Publications.

Plamondon, K. and CCGHR. (2007). Capacity Building Task Group: available online at: www.inclentrust.org/uploadedbyfck/file/compile%20resourse/new-resourse-dr_-vishal/Mentoring_Module2_e.pdf.

Punnachet, K. (2006). *Catholic Servant Leadership in Sisters of Saint Paul of Chartres Schools in Thailand*. Unpublished PhD Thesis, Institute of Education, University of London.

Punnachet, K. and Supavai, A. (2007). Challenges for the schools of the Sisters of Saint Paul of Chartres in Thailand. In G. Grace and J. O'Keefe (Eds.), *International Handbook of Catholic Education: Challenges for School Systems in the 21st Century*. Heidelberg: Springer, pp. 737–748.

Southworth, G. (1995). *Looking into Primary Headship: A Research Based Interpretation*. London: Routledge.

Sritrakul, B. (2013). *The Preparation for Succession Planning for Future SPC Principals in Thailand*. Unpublished Doctor of Education Thesis, Educational Leadership, School of Education, University of Nottingham.

Stryker, S. (1980). *Symbolic Interactionism: A Social Structural Version*. Menlo Park: Benjamin Cummings.

Supavai, A. (2010). *SPC Principals' Perceptions of and Practices in Relation to Spiritual and Moral Values in SPC Catholic Schools in Thailand: The Challenge of Change*. Doctor of Education Thesis, Educational Leadership, School of Education, University of Nottingham.

Wallace, S. and Gravells, J. (2007). *Mentoring*, 2nd ed. Exeter: Learning Matters.

Chapter 19

Teaching Catholic Religious Education and Islamic Studies in a monopoly Catholic small state

Mary Darmanin

Introduction

Professor Gerald Grace has helpfully provoked important debates regarding faith-based education and schooling (Grace, 2003), as well as outlining research agendas for Catholic education in particular, and religious cultures more generally (Grace, 2004, 2009, 2020). Other contributors to this volume will take up themes from Grace's vast repertoire of insights. Here, I wish to honour Gerald's 'provocations' by looking at the sustainability of Catholic Religious Education as well as Islamic Studies curricula in denominational schools in Malta. Gerald is deeply concerned about the future of religious cultures in a world of 'secular marginalisation' (Grace, 2003, p. 149). He wishes to see research about 'challenges to the faith, moral and social formation of youth and adults' (Grace & Valenti, 2009, p. 2). One such challenge lies in asking how far the Religious Education (RE) curriculum invites young learners to engage with faith from a life-centred approach, without jeopardising a sound knowledge base. For a number of years now, Grace (2004, p. 51) has also encouraged research that incorporates accounts of 'the educational institutions and cultures of Islam'; sociologists of education are called upon to 'deepen their understanding of the cultures of Islam' (Grace, 2020, p. 867).

This chapter takes up Grace's (2003, 2004, 2009, 2020) appeals by examining how the Catholic RE and the Islamic Studies curriculum are seen by teachers to engage young learners such that Catholic RE and/or Islamic Studies curricula and pedagogies fruitfully contribute to sustaining religious cultures.

This chapter reports on data generated from an EU-funded project [REMC][1] on the place of religion in educational systems across Europe, specifically on the religious education of primary school children in Malta, the EU's smallest member state. Malta is a confessional state, where the Roman Catholic Church has held a monopoly over RE for centuries (Zammit Mangion, 1992). Having had small, non-Catholic populations in the past, membership of the European Union in 2004, and the recent immigration from North Africa are presenting a more religiously plural group of pupils in school than the monoculture has prepared for (Eurydice, 2004). There has, to date, never been any RE alternative

DOI: 10.4324/9781003171553-22

to the Roman Catholic doctrinal, knowledge-centred, and outcomes-based curriculum. Malta has no history of a 'world religions' or multi/intercultural-type interpretive RE (Jackson, 2004), nor of a more hermeneutical or interpretive-based Christian one (Dillen, 2007a). In the early 1990s, some curricular reform was undertaken, which led to an 'upgrading' of textbooks, which, as Vella (1992) notes, paid more attention to children's cognitive development than to experiential learning. Some elements of a life-centred approach were also introduced. As the field research reported here demonstrates, many teachers and children felt that this was not a sufficient balance to the rigidities of the doctrinal knowledge-centred outcomes-based approach (Buchanan and Engebretson, 2009). Although centrally prescribed, confessional RE has, over time, been implemented differently across the State, government-dependent Church, and independent school sectors. Teachers' translations of the policy directives as they interacted with the RE curriculum demonstrate how the centrally prescribed syllabi were experienced as limiting; it raises questions regarding the purpose and future of Catholic RE. In contrast, teachers of Islamic Studies were more content with the Islamic Studies curriculum, finding it consonant with their preferred pedagogic modes, as well as their faith and values.

The Maltese RE settlement

The Maltese RE settlement neither protects the human rights of minority-religion pupils through an intercultural RE (Mawhinney, 2007), nor does it operate a system of 'voluntary apartheid' (Halstead, 2005) where minority-faith schools are State funded.[2] In 2008, when fieldwork was undertaken, its denominational State and Church schools did not aspire to be relevant to a more plural society (MacMullen, 2004). Pedagogically, there was no contrast of arguments between diverse faiths, nor were pupils introduced to other faiths or ethical systems as themselves of value (Vermeer, 2010). At the organisational level, it was only the Muslim school which employed non-Muslim (Christian) teachers, whilst the government-dependent Church schools were the most closed, restricting both appointment of teachers and admission of pupils to those of the one faith. There was and is no awareness within the Catholic RE policy community of the cultural-normative integration that even denominational schools may provide (Vermeer, 2010). Notwithstanding, there is some space for ethical autonomy (MacMullen, 2004), cultural attachment (Halstead, 1995) and the development of some hermeneutical (Dillen, 2007a and 2007b) or interpretive skills, these stop considerably short of the critical 'edification' that Vermeer (2010, p. 112), following Jackson (2002), espouses. In contrasting the RE experience of the more curriculum-conforming State school teachers and pupils with those of the innovative life-centred Church schools, and the rather 'fluid' method of the independent school, it is possible to see what different approaches bring to children's RE. The Islamic Studies of the Muslim independent school, which blends a knowledge-centred outcomes-based approach with a hermeneutic spiritual approach, provides a further contrast. It reminds us what Muslim pupils in State schools miss, when their only option is to opt out from Catholic RE, or into Ethics Education (provided since 2012 and slowly being rolled out in all schools), which, despite their supposed constitutional right to a religion, leaves them without a religious education; a problem not addressed by education planners at all.

Given the constitutional entrenchment of Roman Catholicism as the religion of Malta, the mandatory provision of (only) Roman Catholic RE in all State schools, and of agreements with the Holy See and the Episcopal Conference on religious instruction, the RE settlement in Malta can be described as one of monopoly Catholicism, currently becoming more secular with the 2013 introduction of an Ethics Education programme as an opt out of Catholic RE. Within this settlement, the Constitution protects freedom of conscience and of worship through clauses permitting the 'opt out' of Catholic RE. In 1991, 0.08% children opted out of confessional RE in State schools (Vella, 1992), rising to 0.02% in 2009.[3] With the gradual phasing in of the Ethics Education programme, 8.2% of primary and 12.9% of secondary State school children have opted of Catholic RE (hereafter RE). In the independent school sector, 54.8% opt out of Catholic RE (Debono, 2019).

Religious Education and Islamic Studies curricula

In the State school sector, the Maltese Episcopal Conference 'establishes the teaching methods, programmes and texts for students, whilst responsibility for implementing the curriculum policy rests with the State Directorate of Quality and Standards in Education (DQSE)' (Secretariat for Catechesis, 2008, p. 22). The Episcopal Conference also regulates teacher appointments in Religious Education and Religious Counselling. The settlements reached between the State and the Holy See and the Episcopal Conference bind all schools with Catholic pupils to a prescribed RE programme. Government-dependent Church schools and independent schools have more curricular freedom than do State schools. One Church school, had, in the year of study, introduced an innovative 'pilot' curriculum 'powered by Christ'; it was awaiting approval from the Secretariat for Catechesis for this. An Islamic Studies education is available in two independent Muslim schools. Halsall and Roebben (2008, p. 20) categorise Malta's approach to Religious Education as a 'denominational RE system for all' within a 'uniform solution with strong state intervention'; this in contrast to the 'pluriform or mixed solution with weak state intervention' of a number of other EU member states. Despite the uniformity, this study demonstrates that schools in different sectors have some autonomy in transposing curricular directives.

As recently as 2010, in the State sector, RE was one of five examinable subjects in Year 5 of primary school, which allocated children to different streams. At 11+ it allocated them to different secondary schools in a selective system. Since a 'reform' of the selective system in 2010, RE no longer contributes to the allocation of pupils to different schools. However, along with other subjects, until a few years ago, 'benchmark tests' in RE allocated pupils to sets (tracks) within State secondary schools.

In June 2008, the Secretariat for Catechesis, Archdiocese of Malta (Secretariat for Catechesis, 2008, p. 24) published a working document on RE in Malta, courageously noting a number of challenges, amongst which are the datedness of the syllabi and texts in circulation (over twenty years old), emphasising an 'imbalance' in favour of the cognitive domain, rather than the affective. A number of concerns regarding the curriculum for the primary school were raised: that the curriculum neglected spiritual education; the language of the set texts was no longer comprehensible; the material was 'scant'; and that the present generation was 'less acquainted with religious stories' such that they may have been unable to engage with those presented in the syllabi and set textbooks. Additionally, an overlap between RE in schools and Catechesis in the parish was seen to pose further challenges. The religious education of children of minority or no faith in Maltese schools was nowhere addressed in this document, where an assimilationist perspective is assumed. A number of new curriculum initiatives were underway. Though the final report (Secretariat for Catechesis, 2008) was concluded after consultation with stakeholders, the planning for the new initiatives suffered from not incorporating the viewpoints of children, their parents and their teachers.

As a statement of curricular objectives rather than a syllabus, the National Minimum Curriculum (Ministry of Education, 1999) paid lip service to multiculturalism (Borg and Mayo, 2001) at the same time as it entrenched Roman Catholicism as *the* religion worth teaching and learning, arguing that, through it, other values could be accessed: 'knowledge of Religion is in itself essential for the moral and spiritual development of a society around values that lie at the heart of social conviviality and understanding' (Ministry of Education, 1999, p. 48 *passim*). The knowledge/information that students were expected to acquire through the curricular experience include learning about 'their rights and responsibilities in relation to the Creator (for those who believe[4]), to others, themselves, the community, the country, the natural environment and animals' (Ministry of Education, 1999, p. 48).

In terms of skills, it was expected that students would develop the ability to 'search for the religious dimension in the realities and experiences of life; find time to discover and grow spiritually; develop means through which they become conscious of the power of the Spirit especially in times of great difficulty; participate actively and meaningfully in religious celebrations' (Ministry of Education, 1999, p. 53). Amongst attitudes, desired outcomes included to 'trust in and [have] contact with God', to have 'appreciation of Jesus Christ as the Way, the Truth and the Life' and 'courage through the power of the Spirit'. Students should also have 'respect for others who profess a different religion or choose not to profess any' (Ministry of Education, 1999, p. 54).

Detailed prescriptive syllabi were and are issued by the Department of Curriculum Management, now within the Directorate for Quality and Standards in Education (DQSE). They are posted on the Department's website. Level descriptors were developed, but as the Working Document (Secretariat for Catechesis, 2008, p. 24) argues, both the syllabi and the level descriptors 'are not written in comprehensible education language'. All the documents were in the Maltese language, which is the language of instruction for this subject in State schools. Most of the textbooks, teachers' guides and work-books were also in Maltese, though some English language material was available; they are used in those Church and Independent schools where English is the language of instruction.

In the Muslim independent school (MIS), the curriculum is planned by the Imam, together with the Islamic Education/Arabic teachers, who follow standard universal Islamic Studies (hereafter IS). A Libyan textbook has been adopted for Islamic Studies whilst a French one is used for Arabic. In Libya, children enter primary school at age 6 whilst in Malta entry is at age 5. The problem of cognitive difficulty is aggravated because the pupils are not Arabic first-language speakers. The teachers of IS would have liked to be more involved in curriculum planning. The course was designed over seven sessions a week, of which five are usually Islamic Studies and two Arabic language, but with considerable overlap. *Sura* are discussed for meaning, but then memorised and recited.

Methodology

Primary data was collected on the relative roles of school and home in the religious socialisation of primary school children, age 9–11, some of which is reported here, but see Smyth *et al.* (2013) for a fuller account. This chapter is based on in-depth interviews with seven Catholic RE and two IS teachers in five schools in the State, government-dependent Church and Independent sectors in Malta. Observation of lessons and other school-based activities was also carried out.[5] Ethics approval from the University of Malta's Research Ethics Committee was obtained. Recruitment of all participants was on an 'opt-in' basis.

Teachers' accounts of teaching Catholic RE and Islamic Studies

Teachers from the different education system sectors expressed quite distinct attitudes to the curriculum in use in their respective schools. State school teachers were most constrained by the national curriculum and by the demands of a syllabus closely geared to the end-of-cycle 11+ examinations. Interestingly, the case-study Church school had rejected this curriculum, in favour of its own curriculum, despite the official curriculum being the one developed and approved by the Episcopal Conference. The teachers of Catholic RE in an independent school were nearly ignorant of the official RE syllabus; they followed an English language textbook, which, however, left them with less support for teaching RE than they wished. The teachers of Islamic Studies in the Muslim faith school did not articulate any difficulties with the format of the Islamic Studies curriculum, nor with its pedagogic mode, suggesting there is coherence in this curriculum.

State school teachers

Patri Said and Vassalli State schools both followed the centrally prescribed curriculum and textbooks the most closely of all the five schools studied. However, there were some differences between the two schools. In both schools, the regular primary school class teacher is also the RE teacher; each teacher was unhappy about this. RE was one of the examinable subjects at 11+ at the time. Many children from both schools failed this RE exam and this lowered their overall performance. At Vassalli, one teacher argued for a life-centred approach; ironically, he had, at the same time, published a 'crammer' preparing the Year 6 pupils for the 11+. The other teacher approved of the structure and discipline imposed by the text, which as his comment illustrates, did combine elements of both knowledge and life-centred approaches to RE.

> Mr John: If I could, I would change the Religion syllabus. And I would get rid of the examination too. I wouldn't examine at all. Because Religion is not something you teach for faith. It is good to learn things, but religion is something you need to live. And it is this that we should be teaching. To live it. Now if I teach the children, say, the prayer blessings. They can say it [sic] by heart [recite it from memory]. They can recite the Creed. But then what is religion, to live the religion [here used as substitute for 'faith']? If one is going to kick someone without feeling bad, without understanding "I am going to hurt that [other] child" it is useless to know the Creed by heart. So I would make him do something concrete, to help [others]. That's what I think Religion [RE] should be.

A more favourable comment comes from Mr Mark, who found that even with the present curriculum, there is scope for combining a knowledge-based with a life-centred approach.

> Mr Mark: I don't think it is bad, I don't think it is bad. Because you have the first... I like the way you first have a story. Let's say, I covered San Martin this week. It opened on San Martin, then what San Martin did and you develop a lesson about San Martin. And then on how what San Martin did we can do in our own life. And practical things – to have mercy, how to help, to forgive. These things.

However, for other State school teachers, the curriculum appears to be weak even on values and ethics. The Patri Said school teachers found that it was cognitively challenging and a less than relevant approach for their pupils.

MD: How do you feel about the syllabus? Are you happy with it?
MS ATTARD: No. No, not really. As I was saying, I think there's too much content in it. And the book doesn't talk at all – or a little, it only talks a little – about values, which children should be encouraged to practice, ethics which could help them further on in their lives... you have to do all that. *It depends on the teacher*. If the teacher wants to follow the book only, there's nothing prohibiting her, you know, you can just go through the book and it's enough for the exams.

Asked whether she supplements this textbook with other material or discussion on ethics and values, Ms Attard points out that for her, they were 'the most important' part of RE. Disconcertingly, the knowledge and outcome-based curriculum with its examination orientation was too similar to theology [for adults].

Ms Attard: Yes, I do something about ethics and values because I think that's the most important part of Religious Education. It's like theology, what they are presented with is theology. Even the exams are very difficult, they are very tricky. Very tricky.

Ms Tanti, also of Patri Said, talks about the difficulty she had with her lower-achieving Year 6 class and the level of abstraction of the 'cognitive' elements of the curriculum. More than this, the outcome-based curriculum led to two unintended negative consequences. The first was that pupils 'hated' RE; the second, that they forget or 'deleted' it as soon as they sat their examination.

Ms Tanti: They [the textbooks] are good for the exams. Because the children are [geared] for the exams. As soon as they sit the exams they 'delete'. They wipe out everything from their memory. That is the shame, because religion is to be lived. What we do with our lives. It should be something more. Even the resources we are given. For example, they could give us, what can I say? They could give us, for example, recorded stories, drama, and we can discuss them. These are the things that children will remember. But doing this is useless. Because the problem is this. No matter what you do, you are always restricted by the syllabus. I have a half hour [a day]. I have to teach what is required for the examination, because if I don't keep up, I will fall behind.

All four State school teachers felt that the syllabus was too vast and left little time for discussion of more ethical issues.

In a Catholic Church school

An even more critical account of the RE curriculum was articulated by the RE teacher of St Anne's Church School, which had over the last year[6] introduced its own syllabus and curricular materials. Whilst broadly working within the parameters of the national RE curriculum, the far more life-centred approach served as an example of what gains and losses could be expected from a move in this direction. As a trained teacher and member of St Anne's Religious Order, Sister Angela was better prepared theologically than lay teachers of Catholic RE.

> Sr. Angela: The books are out of date, in my opinion. And something that is out of date you do not give to children. And this is then part of the curriculum. And when you begin to see we are updating, in every subject, what about Religion? Plus there are topics that for Year 5 are not that applicable to children.

According to Sr. Angela, it was not only that stories such as of the deaths of Ezekiel and Adam that 'don't make sense' to children, but the curriculum structure which partitioned topics over the primary school years was also without pedagogical principle.

> Sr. Angela: And even how it is divided, that in one year you do Jesus, in another you do the Church, in another year you do... I prefer... This is what I think and what we have tried to do. I prefer it that every year you do a little of everything, do you understand? And you continue to build up. In one year you cannot do everything. But, as you go along, if you start from Year 1, you build up, and we are doing a bit on the Sacraments. [We do] what counts most in this particular year, and you build across the years. Ultimately it is going to make more sense to the children, and they feel part of it.

The enthusiastic Sr. Angela describes the school's curriculum plan and its objectives. From Year 3, children work on the following themes: the Old Testament, the New Testament; the Catholic Church; Morality and Prayer. The pedagogy blends the doctrinal and traditional with the experiential and interpretive. It is interactive, involving modern technology, outdoor activity, games, songs and others. Tellingly, traditional elements, such as learning prayers by rote, fall under the topic 'Catholic Church'.

> Sr. Angela: What we did was we divided into five sections. We took *Old Testament, New Testament*, and then you have *Catholic Church* – because you have certain things that they have to learn. And then again, how to present these? And here is where *Prayer* comes in. The *Sacraments* – there

is *Morality*, where values enter, I mean that is an area itself. Then we have *Prayer*. We are going to try, we are. *Prayer* not as in rote learning because that is under *Catholic Church*. During *Prayer* they are to be living the experience of prayer. Sometimes we will be going out, on a nature walk, and we will meet Jesus... this all used to be missing [from previous curriculum].

There is a close examination of the key religious text; one that was designed with the activities typical of this approach integrated into the body of the text. Sr. Angela describes how she uses group work to model the values of teamwork and to connect topics across themes, which link up to other religious activities carried out at the school level. This involves close collaboration with the class teachers and with the school administration.

> Sr. Angela: Group work yes, also. For example, I don't know. If they are going to make a chart on what we did, if we did '*The first community*', the first Christian community, *Celebrating the Church's birthday, Pentecost*. Then to understand that there was the first community, and how we [Christians] continued to grow. So they had [an introduction] into what the first elements were, how those who were Christian were distinguished from those who were not.

As with the interpretive approach, the children were repeatedly invited to connect the learning to their lives. Activities to support this linking were iterative and community building; they stretched over weeks, over classes, to the whole school.

> Sr. Angela: And we extracted the most important elements, that they share everything. *They lived one heart and one soul*. So they [the pupils] had to, in a group, sort of, break up into groups and discuss what they understand by this. How can we today do something practical? Yes. That if in a particular week they are working on Morality, then all the year groups are too and then the whole junior school can have assemblies and other activities related to this. 'Team effort'![7]

In an Islamic faith school

At MIS, the teachers have to teach Islamic Studies through the medium of Arabic, which is, for a number of the pupils, a second or third language. Ms Bushra carried around with her a large teddy-bear who 'only understands Arabic' to encourage children to communicate in Arabic. Another teacher, Ms Jamila, outlines how the curriculum is spread over the primary school years.

Ms Jamila[8]: We get it [the syllabus] ready planned, it will be divided according to how we should work over the year, and that. Because even in Islam, when we enter a place [x'imkien] we say 'Salaam ghalikom'. It means the religion has Arabic as well. The Arabic [language] lesson, now in Year 1 and Year 2, the first lesson of Arabic, I teach them how to say 'Salaam ghalikom'. When they meet their friends and that, they have to say it.

A major objective is the inculcation of Islamic values and the Islamic way of life.

Ms Jamila: I teach values by talking to them and by praying here. And then we do not have the Qu'ran to teach, not only the Qu'ran. Because in our faith, we have prayer, we have history, Islamic history. I mean about six subjects in Islamic Education. They are not all Islam. And we explain the Qu'ran. How to apply what they have learnt in their lives.

Ms Jamila describes her method, how she moves from the transmitted tradition of the Qu'ran to the textbook, to discussion and finally to a more life-centred approach, asking the children to take on the faith as their own.

Ms Jamila: Today we had a lesson in faith. How to believe. What it means to have really strong faith. You have to believe this and this and that and that. I have the book and I have the stories. We have the words of the Prophet Mohammed. I use these in the lesson to help the children learn. We've already completed this lesson, but there are sections that I need to read to the children. This time instead of reading myself [they will]. It means we have arrived at the last lesson. And then there are questions that they have to work on.

Within this curriculum, there are opportunities for some experiential learning but this too is circumscribed by the limits of the doctrinal approach.

Ms Jamila: We don't use it [group work] much here. But I often take them down to the Mosque where we have prayer and we have the lesson there. And I tend to their questions. I respect whoever wants to raise a question. I explain. Whoever wants to understand something, I explain to him or her. It's like a 'free lesson', talk, just talk. Not a lesson where we have studied this and this and that. Let us go to the holy place. Show all our respect and speak about religion in a proper way. I take them once or twice a year, not often. For them to have free talking, I mean. And we often have cassettes and they listen to them.

Reviewing a lesson I had just observed, Ms Jamila talks about how she introduced the Holy Books, the prophets (including Jesus) and the Prophet Mohammed as the messenger 'rasul', the last Prophet. She had spent time asking children how they could be good Muslims, which led to a discussion on care of the world *Alla* [9] created. The children wanted to know more about the world, but she thought they were leading her too far into 'Geography'. She had drawn mountains and rivers on the board. She then goes on to emphasise that God had created everyone, irrespective of 'colour', such that at the end of the world 'we will be accepted into heaven not on the basis of colour'[10] but on the merits of the life that has been lived. From their response, the children appeared to be actively engaged in examining this teaching through their own interpretation of what 'care for the world created by *Alla*' should look like. Ms Jamila was more than content with the way her pupils responded.

Conclusion

In this chapter the internal limitations of a denominational RE have been explored through looking at how teachers make sense of both more knowledge-centred as well as life-centred approaches. In the case of the centrally authorised knowledge-centred and outcomes-based approach of Catholic RE most evident in Maltese State schools, teachers feel severely limited in what can be achieved, and desire to engage in more spiritual or interpretive work.

Catholic RE teachers' accounts of their pedagogy indicate that for most teachers, a life-centred approach is essential for engaging children's interest in the more doctrinal or knowledge-based curriculum. Strategies to deal with the doctrinal element include storytelling, where children are transported to a state of wonderment through the narrative. Many of these stories about the prophets or the saints allow children to place themselves in a chain of memory (Hervieu-Léger, 2006). Pedagogical strategies also include using media such as DVD films, as well as other visual material.

In both the more knowledge-centred and life-centred approaches, what teachers and pupils do with the curriculum, translates the formal curriculum into something other than what curriculum planners intended. Teachers supplement the formal curriculum such that they indicate a desire to combine both knowledge and life-centred approaches in one coherent programme. St Anne's Church School worked intensively on a new approach. This curriculum was coherent with its objectives, which was to adopt a more interpretive life-centred approach that was, however, firmly anchored in a knowledge base. With more consistency with the ethos of the school, both the teacher and the pupils were ready to invest more into the project of RE. A Muslim faith school with a knowledge-centred approach also integrates a more hermeneutical element such that the children become eloquent 'messengers' or witnesses to the faith values themselves. In the revision of the Catholic RE curriculum that was taking place at the time, neither a 'world religions' intercultural, nor an interpretive 'edification' RE (Vermeer, 2010) was on the agenda. Since then, there have been revisions to the Catholic RE official curriculum (not discussed here); however, this chapter shows that how a RE curriculum is planned, what is taught and how it is taught should be problematised. It appears that teachers of both Catholic RE and Islamic Studies wish to combine interpretive and life-centred elements with knowledge-based foundations of their respective curricula.

Notes

1 This FP-7 study was co-funded by the European Commission and the University of Malta. *Religious education in a multicultural society: School and home in comparative context.* [REMC] Topic SSH- 2007–3.3.1 Cultural interactions and multi-culturalisms in European societies. With partners from Ireland, Scotland, Germany, Belgium and Malta.
2 Though the one Islamic Faith school studied did receive some State funding.
3 Parliamentary Question 11995 of 2009.
4 This comment appears exactly here as it is in the original document, indicating that the document itself was written without due consideration to the rights of citizens and others in the pluri-cultural society Malta was fast becoming.
5 Fieldwork commenced in September 2008 and ended in April 2009.
6 From 2007.
7 This was the inspirational theme the school had chosen to work on that term.
8 Schools have been given a pseudonym that reflects the names the schools have. The Muslim faith school is one of only two in Malta. It was agreed that the school would be 'attributable' since a pseudonym would not provide confidentiality. However, with the exception of the school principal, whose interview is attributable, all teachers, parents and children have been given pseudonyms. 'Ms Jamila' is a pseudonym. Transliteration from the Maltese (or Arabic) into English is the author's own.
9 As pronounced in Maltese.
10 In the original Maltese 'il-kulur taghna'.

References

Borg, C. & P. Mayo, (2001). 'Social difference, cultural arbitrary and identity: an analysis of a National Curriculum document in a non-secular environment', *International Studies in Sociology of Education*, 11:1, pp. 63–84.

Buchanan, M. J. & K. Engebretson, (2009). 'The significance of theory in the implementation of curriculum change in religious education', *British Journal of Religious Education*, 31:2, pp. 141–152.

Debono, J., (2019). 'Growth in pupils choosing ethics over religious studies', in *MaltaToday*www.maltatoday.com.mt/news/national/92553/growth_in_pupils_choosing_ethics_over_religious_studies#.X3GoC2gzbIU, 31 January 2019.

Dillen, A., (2007a). 'Theologizing with children: a new paradigm for Catholic religious education in Belgium', in G. R. Grace & J. O'Keefe (eds), *International Handbook of Catholic Education: Challenges for School Systems in the 21st Century*, Part One. Dordrecht, Springer, pp. 347–365.

Dillen, A., (2007b). 'Religious participation of children as active subjects: towards a hermeneutical-communicative model of religious education in families with young children', *International Journal of Children's Spirituality*, 12:1, pp. 37–49.

Eurydice, (2004). *Integrating Immigrant Children into Schools in Europe: Malta: National Description*, www.eurydice.org/Documents/Mig/en/frameset_immigrant.htm l, last accessed February 2021.

Grace, G., (2003). 'Educational studies and faith-based schooling: moving from prejudice to evidence-based argument', *British Journal of Educational Studies*, 51:2, pp. 149–167.

Grace, G., (2004). 'Making connections for future directions: taking religion seriously in the sociology of education', *International Studies in Sociology of Education*, 14:1, pp. 47–56.

Grace, G., (2009). 'On the international study of Catholic education: why we need more systematic scholarship and research', *International Studies in Catholic Education*, 1:1, pp. 6–14.

Grace, G., (2020). 'Taking religions seriously in the sociology of education: going beyond the secular paradigm', *British Journal of Sociology of Education*, 41:6, pp. 859–869.

Grace, G. & R. Valenti, (2009). 'International Studies in Catholic Education (ISCE): preface and mission statement for the first issue', *International Studies in Catholic Education*, 1:1, pp. 1–4.

Halsall, A. & B. Roebben, (2008). *Religious Education in a Multicultural Society. Literature Review: International and Comparative Perspectives*, Working Draft. www.esri.ie/research/research_areas/education/Remc/working_papers/REMC_Literature_review.pdf, last accessed 8 November 2016.

Halstead, J. M., (1995). 'Should schools reinforce children's religious identities?', *Religious Education*, 90:3/4, pp. 360–376.

Hervieu-Léger, D., (2006). *Religion as Chain of Memory*. Cambridge: Polity Press.

Jackson, R., (2002). *Religious Education: An Interpretive Approach*, London: Hodder and Stoughton.

Jackson, R., (2004). 'Intercultural education and recent European pedagogies of religious education', *Intercultural Education*, 15:1, pp. 3–14.

MacMullen, I., (2004). 'Education for autonomy: the role for religious elementary schools', *Journal of Philosophy of Education*, 38:4, pp. 601–615.

Mawhinney, A., (2007). 'Freedom of religion in the Irish primary school system: a failure to protect human rights?', *Legal Studies*, 27:3, pp. 379–403.

Ministry of Education, (1999). *Creating the Future Together: National Minimum Curriculum*, Floriana: Ministry of Education. https://education.gov.mt/en/resources/Documents/Policy%20Documents/national%20minnimun%20curriculum_english.pdf.

Secretariat for Catechesis, (2008). *Religious Education in Malta: Reflections of the Catholic Community*, unpublished mimeo, Secretariat for Catechesis, Archdiocese of Malta, pp. 1–42. http://gozodiocese.org/wp-content/uploads/2008/06/religious_education_in_malta.pdf.

Smyth, E., Lyons, M., & M. Darmody, (eds), (2013). *Religious Education in a Multicultural Europe*. Basingstoke: Palgrave Macmillan.

Vella, J., (1992). *Compulsory Religious Education in the Primary School: A Conflict between Teachers' Rights/Professional Ethics and the Demands of a Mono-cultural Society?*, unpublished B. Ed (Hons) dissertation, University of Malta.

Vermeer, P., (2010). Religious education and socialisation, *Religious Education*, 105:1, pp. 103–116.

Zammit Mangion, J., (1992). *Education in Malta*. Valletta: Studia Editions.

Chapter 20

A personal response by a doctoral student to the work of Grace

How it provides an agenda for future research and policy development in Catholic education in the Philippines

Joanna Marie S. Oliva

Introduction

In the all the published books, conferences and even personal conversations with Prof. Gerald Grace, he always emphasises the important role that Catholic education is playing in the development and formation of society. He considers it as a fundamental principle that Catholic schools are in the service of the common good, not only of Catholic communities but also of the wider society. He sees that at its best, every educator in a Catholic school should have a vocation not only to educate academically but also to see their role as a mission to form the school's students into good Christians and good citizens with moral commitment and social responsibility, seeing themselves as citizens of the world and not only of one nation.

Grace remarked that one of the prime purposes of Catholic education is 'to keep alive and to renew the culture of the sacred in a profane and secular world' (Grace 2002, p. 5). It aims to educate not only to provide quality education of a secular standard but to truly enlighten the world with the beauty of sacred culture and what it is to be truly human.[1] Since Catholic schools are not only educating Catholic students, Grace stresses that educating for the common good is an irreplaceable source of service for the poor and disadvantaged members of society. He also sees it as a spiritual contribution in the building up of the Kingdom of God in this life and for eternity (2000, p. 2). As a Catholic doctoral student and educator from the Philippines, I have seen and experienced the benefits of acquiring a good Catholic education. It has allowed me to advance in my knowledge and career, and it laid out a bright future for me and my future family, but Catholic education has a greater mission than that.

A brief context of the Philippines

The Philippines is a predominantly Catholic nation with an estimated 83 million baptised Catholics (Philippines Statistics Authority [PSA] 2019), which is

DOI: 10.4324/9781003171553-23

why it is not surprising to see the great cultural and societal influence of the faith that is evident in various social issues. Concrete examples of this are found in a recent study, which indicated that many Filipinos have strong views that are in line with the Catholic Church teachings. Two-thirds (67%) of the respondents said that getting a divorce is morally unacceptable – three times the share of Americans who say this (22%). To date, the Philippines is one of the last two remaining sovereign jurisdictions that still does not legally accept divorce; the other jurisdiction is, of course, the Vatican (*The Economist* 2020). Filipinos strongly against abortion, saying that it is immoral (93%); no country among the 40 surveyed is more universally opposed to abortion on moral grounds (The Pew Research Centre 2015). At the other end of the spectrum, despite the deeply rooted Catholic values as a nation, corruption is perceived to have become worse in the Philippine government, according to the *Corruption Perceptions Index (CPI)* survey for 2019 conducted by Transparency International; it ranked 113th of 180 countries studied on their perceived political integrity (CNN Philippines 2020).[2]

The Catholic Church hierarchy in the Philippines is still respected and honoured by many. However, every time there is an important and pressing issue in the society, and the Catholic hierarchy through its bishops and cardinals pronounces a view on it, many free thinkers invoke the principle of separation of Church and State. While the principle has its proper application, in a developing country like the Philippines with a predominantly and historically Catholic culture, it is much more important to foster cooperation between these two elements of the society than to simply hold them apart. Instead of speaking only about separation of Church and State, the Philippines can cultivate a healthy and responsible partnership between the Catholic Church and the Philippine government; after all, both are serving the same people. Part of that cooperation, of course, would also require pursuing and insisting on respect for the rule of law and upholding the rights and dignity of all people of other faiths, such as the sizeable population of Muslims and a growing number of other Christian denominations in the Philippines.[3] It is also important that the Catholic Church stands as a prime mover for the promotion of the common good and protector of the basic human rights of those most vulnerable and disadvantaged members of society, especially the poor.[4]

There are around 1,500 Catholic schools and universities (Catholic Education Association of the Philippines [CEAP] 2019) spread across the country. These Catholic educational institutions provide classrooms, facilities and quality education around the country, not only in major cities but also in remote towns and the peripheries while relying mainly on their own resources and efforts. For a developing country like the Philippines, it is not surprising that quality education is almost always associated with Catholic educational institutions. Many of these Catholic education providers have been recognised as top-performing schools or universities, both nationally and even internationally. They are known to be providers of quality education, initiating advanced studies and research contributing to the advancement of the Philippine society. Many of the current and past leaders of the Philippines, both Catholics and peoples of other faiths, benefitted from a Catholic education. Furthermore, some Catholic educational institutions are dedicated to 'out of school youths', to the handicapped, to cultural minorities, and those in the periphery (Catholic Bishops Conference of the Philippines [CBCP] 2012). The Catholic Church, through its educational institutions, has a great opportunity to influence the character and social vision of its students. The Catholic educational institutions can consciously form and prepare their students for the future to be morally upright, instilling integrity and Christian accountability in order for them to become true Christian servant leaders and staunch promoters of the common good.

Part I: Promotion of the common good in Catholic education

For the Christian perspective of the common good, it is necessary to go back to the original identity of 'humanity' as the only creature created in the *imago dei* (Genesis 1:27). The goodness and dignity of each individual is defined as an image of God and has the capacity to achieve a multitude of things because man and woman[5] also possesses the likeness of God. That is the primary identity of every individual.

A good Christian community therefore starts to form and thrives when it recognises its own identity as the *imago dei* and sees the identity of others in the same way and they all work together for a common purpose. For this reason, a Christian community should be, by definition, against all forms of prejudice, especially racism. The ministry of Jesus Christ was always inclusive and emphasised the importance of unity, regardless of the differences in race, beliefs, social status, culture and background. His mission was for the poor, outcast and marginalised, grounded in unity (see John 17:20–21). Jesus Christ prayed for unity not only of the community of his disciples but also of the whole world, and likened it to unity with the Father in the Holy Spirit as elaborated in the whole Gospel of John.

This unity in the community of disciples is evident in the way of life of the early Christian communities. Their resources and possessions are not only for their own benefit but for the common good of the whole community, as summed up in the observation in Acts 2:44–45: 'All who shared the faith owned everything in common. They sold their goods and possessions and distributed the proceeds among themselves according to what each one needed'.[6]

This community life and Christian teaching of sharing resources, genuine care for others and care for the poor is part of the Christian tradition. One of the earliest written references to the concept of the common good in the Christian tradition is found in the Christian literature in the *Epistles of Barnabas* written between 70 and 132 AD: 'Do not live entirely isolated, having retreated into yourselves, as if you were already justified, but gather instead to seek the common good together' (Staniforth 1968, p. 162, Chapter 4, verse 10 of the Epistle of Barnabas). For the Catholic Church, the common good is the concern for the life of all. It calls for the exercise of prudence from each and every member of the community, most especially for those who are in authority and in a privileged position.

Catholic education for the common good

It can be argued that a distinctive position of the Catholic education is that it is built on the common good. The Catholic Church is involved in education for the service of the good of society. It presupposes that every person possesses a basic dignity that comes from God and is therefore worthy of respect and thus deserves a good education. However, in the context of the Philippines this is a challenging mandate because all Catholic educational institutions are privately owned.[7] It is a challenge because the poor and disadvantaged in material, social, academic or spiritual terms must be the Catholic educational institutions' primary concern.[8]

Grace (2016) points out that in order to serve the common good, Catholic educational work is a way of building up the kingdom of God. In order to realise this mission, it requires cooperation and partnership among every member of the school community and a willingness to collaborate with the government and its educational authorities. The challenge of achieving this in the Philippines is notable, because many of the Catholic schools in the Philippines and around the world are admitting a majority of students from wealthier families. Schools may have done this because of various reasons; it may be because of local laws, economic conditions or their need to be financially self-supporting. However, it is important that all Catholic educational institutions are consciously not turning attention exclusively or predominantly to those from the wealthier social classes. The exclusivity could initiate elitism and as *The Catholic School* document (1977) puts it: 'could lead to contributing towards maintaining their privileged position, and thereby continue to favour a society which is unjust' (par. 58).

The role of Catholic school leaders in promoting the common good

In bringing about the common good in Catholic education, it is the leaders of Catholic schools who have a very important role to play. They are challenged to see their role as educators not only as a profession but as a vocation. Recognising their work as a vocation allows school leaders to be witnesses and Christ-like in their dealings with children (Lydon 2011). Catholic school leaders are called to become credible witnesses of Christ in how they live their life and how they exercise their faith by serving others. They are to accompany the students in the stages of their personal growth but more importantly in their moral upbringing in preparation for their future profession as a service to society and for the common good. One helpful way of characterising this is through the metaphor of *servant leadership* (Lydon 2018). The goal of Catholic school leaders is to educate through exercising a kind of leadership that promotes a culture of service (Oliva 2019). *Servant leadership* [9] includes taking care of the welfare of the most vulnerable, outcast and weakest of the school community; it thus ought to be highly inclusive. This is a key way of serving the common good.

Catholic school leaders have a duty to ensure that education for the common good is happening in the school community. Leadership should be seen not as a *right* but a responsibility. Leaders administer to the needs of the school community by being of service and providing help. In order to promote the common good, they should constantly consider the welfare of everyone and maintain the integrity of their mission in the daily functions of the whole educational system. They are called to constantly discern what is effective and what is good; what works and what makes sense; and more importantly to do things right and to do the right thing (Sergiovanni 2001).

Part 2: Leadership challenges in promoting the common good

The idea of the common good rests on a Christian optimism about human beings and how it can unite humanity towards a common purpose. It has the potential to change the way education is done and how it influences political and social life. Leaders are provoked to reflect upon the quality of the existing society and the kind of society that is ideal (Bradstock 2015, p. 16). The promotion of the common good does not deny that social conflict will happen and challenges will arise, but it assumes that since humanity is built for community, everyone will be willing to treat each other with good will and to collaborate in pursuing the common good, if understood correctly.

Secular perspective versus Christian perspective of the common good

Leading Catholic schools to achieve the common good is actually a challenging task. It is relatively easy to latch onto one aspect of the common good and fail to appreciate that achieving it is more like a journey – one which leaders keep on needing to be formed. A rigid vision of the common good can be used to silence those who disagree, especially if they are the weaker and more vulnerable group. In Catholic education, school leaders are caught in the difficult tension between an absolute notion of the 'common good' that demands a non-negotiable practice and the common good that is seemingly impossible to define. Leaders who attempt to specify the common good can fall short of being truly common or truly good (Rowlands 2015).

Because of this tension, it is important for Catholic school leaders to interpret and teach the common good in relation to other moral commitments and principles, such as equality, stewardship, human dignity, respect for life and solidarity. The common good also has the commitment to prioritise the well-being of the most vulnerable members of the society, which in Catholic social teaching is referred to as *a preferential option for the poor*. [10] The social teaching of the Catholic Church emphasises continually that those who are more fortunate should renounce some of their rights so as to place their goods more generously at the service of others and placing those with the least, the last and the lost at the forefront. This has been an important theme in the teachings of Pope Francis.

Keeping the balance between equality and freedom

Catholic school leaders face the challenge of keeping in balance both equality and freedom. Promotion of the common good respects the freedom and basic rights of every individual. However, it is important to be conscious that in a community composed of many and unique individuals, each one will have divergent ideas as solutions and different definitions of what is good. A risk of emphasising freedom and equality is that it could give rise to individualism in which one claims his or her own rights without wishing to be answerable for the common good. Catholic school leaders are then challenged to educate the balance of teaching equality, freedom and human rights to the students. It is legitimate for every individual to defend their own rights and the rights of their fellow citizens against the abuse of those in authority, while keeping within the limits and in consideration of the welfare of the common good drawn by the natural law and the Gospels.

Rapid growth of globalisation and secularisation

Part of the mission of Catholic school leaders is to act as counter-cultural witnesses, through being educators that strengthen the spiritual and moral upbringing of the students. Hopefully, they will challenge and change the spiritual and moral culture of the society in the future. In this way, Catholic education can serve the common good of the wider society. This is easier said than done given the dominance of globalisation, capitalism, materialism and secularisation. The idea of the common good and the reality of the materialistic and individualistic culture of the society appear to utterly incompatible. It makes the mission of Catholic school leaders in promoting the common good a difficult one.

Hopes for Catholic education in the Philippines

The mission of Catholic educational institutions in promoting the common good in the Philippines cannot be underestimated. Catholic education is contributing much in educating and in this way promoting the common good in the Philippine society. It has a long history of educating the young not just academically but also in the faith. Its graduates are the current leaders of our nation, and this should be seen as a sign of hope.

However, the reality is more complex. According the Catholic Bishops' Conference of the Philippines (2012: Online), out of its more than 1,300 schools, there are more than 900 small, struggling mission schools spread over different parts of the Philippines, whose teachers work with missionary spirit. Many of these schools rely on their meagre resources as they strive to provide quality education to the marginalised in far-flung areas. It would be helpful if the government could provide some funding for those schools serving the most disadvantaged communities. It is undeniable that there is a healthy competition among educational institutions in terms of academic standards, which includes the Catholic educational institutions. Catholic schools are called to render service to the Church by ensuring that it is present in education and schooling for the benefit of human society. Despite the competition, it is necessary for Catholic schools to also see each other as allies and not rivals in terms of promoting the common good and maintaining the Catholic distinctiveness in the educational mission.

Priorities for the future: Collaboration and sharing of best practices

There is a huge challenge and opportunity to create more collaborative programmes and projects assisting mission schools by involving the Dioceses, Episcopal Commission on Catechesis and Catholic Education, and the Catholic Education Association of the Philippines (CEAP) in encouraging more financially stable Catholic educational institutions, wealthier Catholic school graduates and those who are in leadership positions to consciously contribute and be at the service of these mission schools who directly serve the poor and disadvantaged.

Highlight the role of parents in the educational mission of Catholic education

In the light of the great lockdown of 2020, many students found themselves forced to continue their education from home and to study remotely. Many parents struggled trying to support their children. It is important that Catholic educational institutions maintain a comprehensive effort to involve parents in the formation of their children. Highlighting their role as primary educators of their children may include pastoral and Christian formation programmes for parents and support groups in order to assist them in forming their children in the faith and reminding them that their family life would be the best witness in living out their Christian vocation and promoting the common good in society.

Creating a culture of 'forming the formators'

Continuous formation of formators in Catholic educational institutions will keep Catholic school leaders and Catholic education stakeholders grounded in their Christian commitment and morals. Having the culture of forming formators would allow Catholic school leaders to have regular access to pastoral training and Christian formation programmes. These programmes for all Catholic school leaders can help ensure the understanding and maintenance of the Catholic distinctiveness and educational mission of the Catholic educational institutions in promoting the common good. Formation programmes are distinct from continuing professional development programmes.

Conduct more systematic scholarship and research on Catholic education

Although Philippine Catholic educational institutions are already playing a satisfactory role in fulfilling the educational mission of the Catholic Church and there are many servant leaders, there is a need for more research. There is a need in the Philippines to emulate what Grace achieved in the UK in relation to Catholic education scholarship. Specifically, there is a strong need for more Catholic researchers and scholars to study the integrity and effectiveness of Catholic educational mission in the Philippines and globally. Empirical study would provide evidence on the contribution of Catholic education to society and will encourage a more efficient collaboration with different sectors, especially the government. There are encouraging signs that this is research is developing in the Philippines. In the journal, *International Studies in Catholic Education*, edited by Gerald Grace until 2021, scholars and researchers from the Philippines have contributed important articles, in particular Angelina Gutierrez (2009), Rito Baring (2010), Merceditas Ang SPC (2011), Angelina Gutiérrez (2012) and Johnny Go (2018). Their academic writings and research have raised many issues which now need further investigation. The stage is set for the field of Catholic Education Studies to grow further in the Philippines and for policy to be influenced by this research.

Notes

1 Grace has been influenced by the writing of Emile Durkheim on the sacred and profane cultures of everyday life. See Durkheim (1912).
2 For a discussion of this contradictory situation, see Gutierrez (2012).
3 The Philippine Statistics Authority reported in October 2015 that the next largest religious affiliation in the country was Islam, comprising 6% of the total population and 10.8% were other Christian denominations.
4 There are many examples of the Church in the Philippines serving the poor and marginalised, some of which include orphanages and shelters accommodating and protecting abused, abandoned, neglected and orphaned street children such as Tuloy sa Don Bosco in Paranaque City, Balay Canossa Orphanage in Cagayan De Oro, Our Lady of Victory Training Center in Davao and Rumaha Center in Quezon City.
5 Modern critics of Catholicism believe that a great opportunity was missed by the Second Vatican Council to substitute for 'men' for a more inclusive phrase such as 'all people'.
6 It is interesting to recall that when Marxists in the 19th century introduced the slogan 'From each according to his ability and for each according to his need' as indicative of communism they ignored the fact that this was the practice of early Christians.

7 Catholic private schools in the Philippines have a commitment of providing free education and financial assistance to a commensurate percentage of the paying student population. Many also have *mission schools*, dedicated to serving out-of-school youths, the handicapped and those in the periphery.

8 There has been a long tradition of Catholic education in the Philippines, and this has shown a commitment to the poor. See Catholic Bishops Conference of the Philippines (2012) *Pastoral Letter on 400 years of Catholic Education in the Philippines*.

9 For information on servant leadership, see Punnachet (2009), in *International Studies in Catholic Education*.

10 For a fuller discussion of this, see Grace (2013).

References

Ang, M. SPC (2011). The Education Ministry of the Sisters of St Paul of Chartres in the Philippines: Past Achievements and Present Challenges, in *International Studies in Catholic Education* 3: 2, pp. 145–157.

Baring, R. (2010). A New Approach to Catechesis Involving Students in the Philippines, in *International Studies in Catholic Education* 2: 2, pp. 176–192.

Bradstock, A. (2015). The Unexamined Society: Public Reasoning, Social Justice and the Common Good, in Sagovsky, N. and McGrail, P. (ed.) (2015). *Together for the Common Good*, London: SCM Press.

Catholic Bishops Conference of the Philippines [CBCP] (2012). *Pastoral letter on 400 years of Catholic Education in the Philippines* (www.cbcpnews.com/cbcpnews/?p=324), last accessed February 2021.

Catholic Education Association of the Philippines (2019) *About CEAP* (www.ceap.org.ph/who-we-are/about-ceap).

CNN Philippines (2020). *Corruption in the Philippines worsens in 2019 global index* (https://cnnphilippines.com/news/2020/1/23/Philippines-corruption-worsens.html?fbclid=IwAR3oEreKQjj7onru3FviBhIE3MFkNcsgBkTZHHeeelOnXtGTefQ9pFz0mAI).

Congregation for Catholic Education (1977). *The Catholic School*, Vatican City: Libreria Editrice Vaticana.

Durkheim, E. (1912). *The Elementary Forms of Religious Life*. See new edition by Carol Cosman, *Oxford World Classics*, 2008.

Go, J. C. (2012). Teaching as Goal-less and Reflective Design: A Conversation with Herbert A. Simon and Donald Schön, in *Teachers and Teaching* 18: 5, pp. 513–524.

Grace, G. (2000). *Catholic Schools and the Common Good: What This Means in Educational Practice*, CIE Conference, Johannesburg, 21 September 2000, London: University of London, CRDCE.

Grace, G. (2002). *Catholic Schools: Mission, Markets and Morality*, London: Routledge.

Grace, G. (2013). Catholic Social Teaching Should Permeate the Catholic Secondary School Curriculum: An Agenda for Reform, in *International Studies in Catholic Education* 5: 1, pp. 99–109.

Grace, G. (2016). *Faith, Mission and Challenge in Catholic Education*. New York/London: Routledge.

Gutiérrez, A. (2012). The Preferential Option for the Poor in Catholic Education in the Philippines: A Report on Progress and Problems, in *International Studies in Catholic Education* 1: 2, pp. 135–151.

Gutiérrez, A. (2012). Does a Catholic Education have Lasting Effects on Adult Life? Reflections of Alumn from Catholic Colleges and Universities in the Philippines, in *International Studies in Catholic Education* 4: 1, pp. 16–34.

Lydon, J. (2011). *The Contemporary Catholic Teacher: A Reappraisal of the Concept of Teaching as a Vocation in the Catholic Christian Context*, Saarbrucken: Lambert Academic Publishing.

Lydon, J. (2018). Initial and On-going Formation of Catholic School Teachers and Leaders – A Perspective from the UK, in Lydon, J. (ed.). *Contemporary Perspective on Catholic Education*, Leominster: Gracewing.

Oliva, J. M. (2019). Situational Leadership in Catholic Schools, in *The Pastoral Review* 15:3.

Philippines Statistics Authority (2019). *Census of Population and Housing* (https://psa.gov.ph/population-and-housing/node/120080), accessed October 2020.

Punnachet, T. (2009). Catholic Servant Leadership: Going Beyond the Secular Paradigm, in *International Studies in Catholic Education* 1: 2, pp. 117–134.

Rowlands, A. (2015). The Language of the Common Good, in Sagovsky, N. and McGrail, P. (ed.). *Together for the Common Good: Towards a National Conversation*, London: SCM Press.

Sergiovanni, T. (2001). *Leadership: What's In It For Schools?*Oxon: RoutledgeFalmer.

Staniforth, M. (Tran.) (1968). *Early Christian Writings*. London: Penguin Books.

The Economist (2020). *Why the Philippines is the only country where divorce is illegal –Except the Vatican, of course* (www.economist.com/asia/2020/02/13/why-the-philippines-is-the-only-country-where-divorce-is-illegal), accessed October 2020.

The Pew Research Centre (2015). *5 facts about Catholicism in the Philippines* (www.pewresearch.org/fact-tank/2015/01/09/5-facts-about-catholicism-in-the-philippines/), accessed October, 2020.

Conclusion

Sean Whittle

Shaping the field of Catholic Education Studies

By way of concluding observations, it is important to make explicit what has been repeatedly hinted at throughout the various chapters in this book. Namely, the way in which the shape or focus of research in Catholic education has been given a discernible direction by Gerald Grace. There are a number of themes in this firm steer in the direction of research that deserve to be pointed out. The first is the importance of empirical study in relation to Catholic education. Grace's seminal 2002 work demonstrated the importance of carefully conducted fieldwork when researching Catholic education. It is sustained empirical research which Catholic education needs, rather than pious platitudes or uncritical descriptions. Grace has used his position of executive editor of the journal *International Studies in Catholic Education* (ISCE) to repeatedly publish research which is empirically robust. In bringing this sort of work to the attention of the readers of ISCE, he is providing an ongoing model of what effective research in Catholic education needs to be like. These are models which the newer generations of researchers in *Catholic Education Studies* are able to both emulate and build upon in their own research.

A second theme must be the significance that Grace attaches to the 1977 guidance document issued by the *Congregation for Catholic Education* in Rome, known as *The Catholic School*. Referring to this document has over the past two decades become almost a mantra for Gerald Grace. He has repeatedly described the 1977 document as the 'foundation charter' or universal *mission statement* for all Catholic schools. To be more precise, it is not the whole of this lengthy guidance document but rather paragraph 58 which is so central according to Grace. Within this paragraph, there is a particularly inspiring sentence that declares 'first and foremost the Church offers its educational service to the poor or those who are deprived of family help and affection or those who are far from the faith'. There is an alignment between Catholic education and what we have come to know as the *option for the poor*. Grace has used both his public presentations and role as editor of ISCE to repeatedly draw attention to this sentence from the 1977 document, arguing that it represents a

DOI: 10.4324/9781003171553-24

commitment in Catholic education to those who are poor. Permeating throughout every volume of ISCE are articles which highlight social justice, or Catholic social teaching, or liberation theology, or an analysis of Catholic education in less economically developed parts of the world. This consistent editorial emphasis can be traced directly back to the importance Grace attaches to the vision embodied in this sentence in paragraph 58, and the way it demonstrates the importance of social justice and inclusion in relation to Catholic education.

Another noticeable editorial emphasis that has sought to shape Catholic Education Studies has been Grace's care to ensure the voices of female researchers are properly recognised. Wherever possible, he has tried to ensure the beginnings of gender balance in all the editions of the journal. In addition, Grace does not shy away from what some might consider to be controversial issues, such as the ordination of women as Catholic priests. In commissioning an article on this issue, he wanted, as editor, to provide teachers and students in Catholic schools and universities with the opportunity to consider arguments in favour of the ordination of women, as well as those against. He wanted ISCE to be a critical and probing arena of academic scholarship. An important part of this is the willingness and openness to be self-critical on the part of those who advocate for Catholic education. For Grace, it is a priority to avoid relying on apologetics and the defensiveness that wants to protect Catholic education against any and all critical voices, especially internal ones. What Grace wanted to bring about – and has achieved through ISCE – is a forum for genuine academic and well-researched dialogue about Catholic education, including any weaknesses alongside its strengths. In 2016, at the invitation of the European-based *International Catholic Journal of Education* (EDUCA), Online, he wrote on the importance of Catholic education and principles of openness.

Giving honour where it is due

Gerald Grace deserves to be praised for his achievements in relation to Catholic education. He is responsible for much new thinking, new research and new scholarship in what is now a firmly established field of international study. Much of this is not just down to his ability as an accomplished academic with a sixty-year career. Rather, it is the wider aspects of who he is as a person which have been the crucial factor in fulfilling his mission.

His Catholic Christian faith (which recognises the importance of 'works' as well as faith) chimes perfectly with his academic convictions in relation to the sociology of education. Grace has become someone who has learnt over life how to combine compassionate socialism with academic integrity and a living faith. He has given generously of his time, in what was supposed to be years of retirement, to respond to what has been his mission in relation to Catholic education. If it were not for those intangible qualities in Grace's personality, far less would have been achieved for Catholic education. It is Gerald Grace's charm, kindness, joy of life and above all, commitment, which has allowed him to work so well with others, and nearly always bring out the best in them.

However, in many respects none of what Gerald Grace has achieved since 1997 would have been possible had it not been for his pre-retirement career. Gerald Grace entered the field of Catholic Education Studies as an accomplished and firmly established scholar within the Sociology and History of Education. Thus, when he approached those, such as Professor Peter Mortimore to ask for a base for the *Centre for Research and Development in Catholic Education* (CRDCE) in 1997 or the executives at Routledge in 2009 to argue for a brand-new journal, he did so as a highly respected academic and colleague. Alongside his time and ability, Gerald Grace put his considerable academic reputation at the service of Catholic Education Studies.[1] In many respects, the contributions to this volume are an apt testimony to both his achievements and the qualities of Gerald's character. All the contributors felt deeply honoured and pleased to be able to contribute to this book.

Note

1 Professor Grace has always insisted, in various dialogues about the growth of Catholic Education Studies, that it was the creative work of Professor Anthony Bryk in the USA that brought a paradigm change to the whole field in 1993. 'Anthony Bryk is the true Founder of the modern field of Catholic Education Studies' (Grace).

References

Bryk, A. et al. (1993). *Catholic Schools and the Common Good*. Cambridge, MA: Harvard University Press.

Congregation for Catholic Education. (1977). *The Catholic School*. London: Catholic Truth Society.

Grace, G. (2002). *Catholic Schools: Mission, Markets and Morality*. London: Routledge.

Grace, G. (2016). Catholic Education Principles of Openness, *International Journal of Catholic Education (EDUCA)*, Online, Vol 2, pp. 61–84.

Index

Note: page references in *italics* indicate figures; **bold** indicates tables.